Vision and Violence

Vision and Violence

Arthur P. Mendel

Preface by Richard Landes,
Director of the Center for Millennial Studies

Ann Arbor

THE UNIVERSITY OF MICHIGAN PRESS

2002   2001   2000   1999   4   3   2   1

A CIP catalog record for this book is available from the British Library.

The manuscript for this volume reached the University of Michigan Press only
after the untimely death of its author. The combined efforts of Arthur P.
Mendel's family and friends, and especially of Jonathan Mogul, were most
helpful in identifying the sources of the numerous quotations in the book. But
some could not be identified and we apologize for not giving due recognition
of sources and copyright holders for those quotations.

ISBN 0-472-08636-7

Preface to the Ann Arbor Paperbacks Edition

I once asked a colleague whose specialty was modern German history, what he thought of the thesis that the Nazis were a millennial movement? "Impossible," he replied. "Nazism is secular and millennialism is religious." One could not better summarize the difference between a millennial scholar—one who defines millennial as a belief in a radically transformed future for all mankind—and those historians trained in the dominant professional historiography of the twentieth century. To the millennial historian, the secular is merely another clothing that millennialism has taken (with startling vigor since ca. 1500 C.E.), and Nazism is as much an NRM (new religious movement) as a new political one. To the millennial scholar, Hitler is one of the most powerful and paranoid messiah figures that history has ever produced; and the German response to him (e.g., the Nuremberg Rallies), a classic, if tragic, case of violent millennial enthusiasm.

To the conventional historian, such catchphrases as the "tausend-jähriger Reich" (millennial kingdom) and the "dritte Reich" (third empire) might have millennial content, but it was of minor significance to both those in the propaganda ministry who used it and those Germans who heard it. To them modern revolutionary movements, right and left, are precisely *not* millennial and share little in common with millennialism. The content of Nazi ideology was madness and irrationality rather than millennial passion. To the millennial scholar, the parallels are striking, the lessons to be learned about the dynamics of both millennial peace and violence, creativity and destructiveness, multiple. For them, all the most potent (if not enduring) forms of political transformation in the modern period—Democracy, Scientific Utopianism, Nationalism, Communism, Zionism, Nazism, Environmentalism—are forms of millennial thinking, partly secular, partly still profoundly religious.

If that is an uncomfortable list that leaves you tempted to say: "Then everything is millennial, and the word has no meaning," I suggest two things. First, think again. To label something "millennial" means that it shares a whole range of peculiar traits and, more significantly, dynamics in common with other millennial movements and beliefs. And at times when significant numbers of people believe that the time of transformation has come, these dynamics become powerful and move rapidly. Understanding these dynamics may, if the identification is correct, offer a wide range of important insights, not only into our past but into various contemporary manifestations of the phenomenon—those we already know are millennial and those we do not yet recognize as such. Not everything may be millennial—far from it—but far more than is dreamed of in our secular social paradigms.

Second, read this book. It is the product of a peculiarly potent historiographical trajectory. The author began his work studying a modern, secular movement of major significance (Russian Revolution) and, examining the thinking of a nineteenth century secular revolutionary (Mikhael Bakunin). He discovered Bakunin's religious millennial roots (*Michael Bakunin: The Roots of Apocalypse* [New York: Praeger, 1981]), and from there went on to explore the millennial origins of so many dynamics that mark the character of modernity. Thus, better than most millennial historians (who tend to have their training in earlier periods (Antiquity, Middle Ages), Mendel can trace the path from "Apocalypse and God" to the secular versions of millennial ideologies, the "new" products of the modern world—Apocalypse and Reason, History, Nature. Secular revolution, often violently antireligious, represents not an abandonment of millennialism but a change of clothing that jettisons the embarrassing commitment to a God who never kept the promises that the prophets attributed to Him. It hardly meant a tapering off in the frequency, intensity, and longevity with which such waves of apocalyptic millennial expectation expressed themselves in Western society. On the contrary, the more secular a millennial movement, the more proactive. God having been dropped from the equation, agency shifted almost entirely to "Man." Few scholars understand this dynamic as well as does Arthur Mendel.

Most monotheists believe that the God is both good and just. That of course creates the huge dilemma: why is there evil? Or more particularly, why do the evil flourish and the good suffer so? This painful observation about the nature of moral reality, what philosophers call the problem of theodicy of "the justice of God," plagues any culture that wants to motivate people to behave well, but it poses special problems for monotheists. One of the most powerful solutions to the problem is to conceive of God as giving humans life in order to test them morally and, at some point, passing judgment on their performance. For many such believers, the matter is settled at death, with a suitable punishment, in some scenarios by going to heaven or hell, in others by reincarnating higher up or lower down the hierarchy of human life.

Those who believe in eschatology, however, anticipate something far grander than an individual, case-by-case basis. They believe that God will resolve the problem of evil by rewarding the good and punishing the evil in one dramatic cosmic moment at the very end of time (eschaton means end, final event), at the Last Judgment. At this apocalyptic moment (apocalypse means revelation), the good, the meek, the downtrodden at last have their collective triumph, while all those crimes whose perpetrators were able to hide them by bribery and violence, will lie exposed for all to see. The Lord's Day, then, is double-edged: a Day of Wrath to the sinful and a Day of Joy to the righteous. And it is above all a public day, a public settling of scores. To eschatologists, heaven and hell, even one where the good get to watch the evil suffer, is not enough; the solution to theodicy must be open, collective, total. The "new song" of redemption, of joy, must be sung together.

Anyone hoping to analyze the impact of eschatology on society must consider the following three issues: the location of the final events, the scenario of events themselves, and the timing.

Location: If Judgment takes place on some spiritual plane and outside of time, rather than within history and here on earth, then the eschatological beliefs will have relatively little direct impact on society. If anything, they would probably promote conservative attitudes, since such a moment depends almost entirely on the supernatural actions to God. At best one can prepare for the advent of such a moment by calling for repentance and strict moral behavior. Such believers will rarely attempt to change this physical world except perhaps in an effort to wipe out sin. Constructive social change, however, is useless: the servile and the oppressed should not rebel (Corinthians 7:17–24), they should meekly endure their yoke and await their eschatological reward. If, however, the eschatological reward occurs on earth, in history, in a just society and a just life for those deemed worthy what is variously known as millenarianism, chiliasm, or millennialism, the beliefs carry revolutionary social implications. For millennialists, the present world is permeated by evil whose purging will occur here on earth, and whose institutions will be replaced by those of the messianic realm, the thousand-year kingdom.

Scenario: To some (the pessimists) the world and humans are so permeated by evil that terrible catastrophes must come to annihilate the evil at the dawn of the new world. Extremists of this school foresee immense violence and human destruction, they tend to view things dualistically, seeing everyone as part of the forces of "good" or "evil" with no middle ground. This kind of thinking gravitates toward tales of cosmic conspiracies that culminate in cosmic, and cosmically destructive, wars. To others (the optimists), humanity has already suffered the worst, and the eschatological catastrophes are meant to shake us from our complacency, leading to a collective "change of heart," to mass movements of benevolence and a voluntary embrace of God's justice. Extremists here promise a world of real peace, where the aristocracy beats its swords into plowshares and become commoners, and nations no longer lift up sword against nation, nor study war any more (Micah 4:1–4; Isaiah 2:2–4).

Timing: If the "Day of the Lord" is distant, the eschatological belief lies dormant, posing no direct challenge to the status quo. To the contrary, it can, like the nonphysical scenario, have a conservative effect, convincing people to suffer current conditions for yet some time, especially when joined to a passive, antimillennial theodicy (like Purgatory, Heaven, and Hell for individual souls). Indeed, one might view this set of beliefs as forms of that "opiate of the masses" that Marx identified as the function of religion. When, however, people are filled with an apocalyptic sense of imminence and urgency, and such beliefs spread to large numbers of people—something they are programmed to do— they can cause mass movements, much as Marx wished his teachings might provoke (the "Internationale" is an apocalyptic millennial hymn). Nothing can motivate more powerfully than apocalyptic beliefs. People who believe the rules are about to change dramatically stop playing by the old rules; and their new behavior is public, defiant. With any fear of future consequences, that great inhibitor of our secret desires, gone, people abandon "normal" behavior. They answer the question, "if not now, when?" with "if not now, never; this is our last chance to act."

Perhaps the least well understood aspect of millennial expectations is that they are not merely fearful—both in the sense that believers fear the coming of the Day, or that the nonbelievers need fear the believers. We who do not share the apocalyptic timetable, or even the millennial expectation, have reason to fear the fearful apocalyptic believers—they believe we hate and want to destroy them, and their violence is, in their minds, purely self-protective when it is not world saving. Hitler and Stalin were both megalomic paranoids who rode to power on the millennial tiger and preferred utter destruction to the admission or failure of the relinquishing of power. Indeed, totalitarianism is the desperate effort of a millennial movement that has taken power to *force* the creation of the perfect world, the perfection that, inexplicably, has not come as expected with their victory. At its worse, millennialism is a negative-sum game in which even the "winners" lose. However "mad" and mistaken and self-destructive its adherents might be, such millennial concerns certainly deserve our attention.

But we need also pay attention to the other millennial believers, the optimists who look forward to a great and peaceful transformation. If fear-driven millennialism, with its paranoid conspiracies and its dreams of cleansing violence—what Arthur Mendel calls apocalyptic gnosticism—is a negative-sum game, then optimistic millennialism, what he calls tautological progressivist, strives for the positive-sum. When the nations beat their swords into plowshares and spears into pruning hooks, this is because, at long last, they have put aside the paranoid imperative—rule or be ruled—and accepted the notion that a world without violent dominion is a world where everyone (except the dominators) benefits. While millennialism can be the most violent and destructive force in history, it can also be one of the most constructive and socially creative. In a sense, the positive millennial moment is a kind of collective experience of public and mutual commitment, an affirmation of the social contract. Societies (*Gesellschäfte*) without the ability to experience such moments would reasonably be considered unstable, especially ones in periods of rapid, technology-induced, social change. It is precisely in the exploration of such dynamics as these, that Arthur Mendel has set sail. And the rich cargo that he has brought home from his explorations is well worth our attention.

There are few religious beliefs about which one can safely say: "they were wrong." And yet, no matter how politically correct we might aspire to be, we can safely say that every person in history (now dead) who believed that the apocalyptic finale of history would occur in his or her day, was wrong. No matter how we want to read history, we can all agree that God has not yet come to judge the living and the dead, nor yet punished the evil, nor rewarded the good with either eternal life in heaven or the millennial kingdom of peace, fellowship, and abundance here on earth. Those who entered this apocalyptic vortex, where all would change "in the twinkling of an eye," those who did not, that prophesied year, plant crops or make stores for a winter that would not come—they were wrong. As one of the pioneers of millennial studies, Leon Festinger, pointed out decades ago (*When Prophecy Fails* [New York: Harper and Row, 1959]), this produces a severe case of "cognitive dissonance." How does one deal with the failure of so cherished and deeply held a conviction? How does one live in a world where one is so obviously "wrong." How does one interact with a world one had assumed one would soon no longer need to deal with? Something must give.

To the outsider, what gives *should* be the whole millennial madness. Once the prophecy is falsified, the nonsense should cease. But the cognitive dissonance of such a conclusion is unbearable to true apocalyptic believers. They have experienced too much truth—powerful, salvific, life-giving—in their millennial community to abandon it. The power of the apocalyptic community to transform its members with a sense of intimacy, purpose, and meaning, makes it particularly resilient to prophetic failure. Something must give, but it will not be the millennial worldview, with its semiotic and vocational arousal. Apocalyptic millennialists are nothing if not passionate, their message vastly more encompassing than the apocalyptic error in which they find themselves caught.

One answer to these questions, then, is "No." No, one cannot live with this enduring world, so penetrated with evil that it failed to listen and repent. At one extreme of this spectrum lies suicide. At another extreme, lies mass murder. They combine in suicide massacres. Here, as Mendel analyzes in this book, lies the world created by the answer: God, through his prophecy, has assembled his troops of which I am one; now the time has come for the final, annihilating battle in which I must fight with the forces of good. At a more politically passive and disciplined extreme, believers want to be martyred and will try and provoke an attack on them. On the one side, the future martyr engages the apocalyptic "other," trying to provoke that one to attack the believers, shouting out publicly the most politically sensitive aspects of millennial morals, denouncing a corrupt leadership (proselytizing/prophesying in an apocalyptic time). At their best, the results produce a glorious martyrdom at the hands of a brutal and uncomprehending power elite; at their worst, frustrated and enraged, they produce suicidal killing sprees. Much of this is toxic stuff and leads to the kinds of violence that few understand as clearly as Mendel.

Another is to say, "Yes." Yes I can live with this world of enduring evil, but I will stay loyal to my true millennial commitments, I will continue to live my life with my beliefs intact. But of course something has happened, and at the simplest level, the failure of prophecy involves changing the timing, redating, so that the same apocalyptic tension that had sustained the earlier beliefs can endure. A caller to a French radio talk show admitted that the space station Mir had not fallen on Paris at the time of the last total solar eclipse of the millennium (8–11–99) as the perfumer Paco Rabannes, with the help of Nostradamus, had predicted. But that did not mean that Paco (and Nostradamus) were wrong about the event, just the timing. Apparently, the thought of Paris being destroyed by a rogue space station appealed far more to this person, than the intellectual inconsistency.

Such simple redating, however, is rarely enough, especially in the case of an apocalyptic community. There are other, more profound responses to the cognitive dissonance felt by a postapocalyptic believer who chooses to return to the world and to "normal time." These responses also range widely. On one side we find a splitting of the apocalyptic and the normal selves, positing, as do the gnostics, a radical division between the world of salvation and this material world of evil. On another, we find a reintegration that tries, in a disciplined embrace of the world, to save what was best and most noble about the millennial vision, while distancing oneself from the initiating apocalyptic belief. Sometimes this involves only a slight distancing, a small adjustment in the apocalyptic timetable, in which case, the reignited apocalyptic enthusiasm often goes into missionizing. In other cases, the apocalyptic drops back a whole register, to be replaced by forms of behavior that are more enduring, more generational.

Normally, at this point, an historiographical breakdown occurs. The conventional millennial historian ceases to pay attention to a movement that is no longer apocalyptic, hence no longer shares the outrageous and marginal characteristics that mark groups who are moved to extreme behavior by a sense of imminence. At the same time, the "normal" historian picks up the story but with little understanding of the millennial genealogy and postapocalyptic trajectory of the phenomenon in question. But this is just where both millennial and "normal" scholars should show the greatest interest. How does vision lead, not to violence, but to peace? Characteristically, Mendel explores these alternative dynamics, arguing, among other things that they characterized the Rabbinic response to the apocalyptic catastrophe of the destruction of the Temple in 70 C.E. Such an analysis of postapocalyptic behavior permits the millennial scholar to perceive parallels over time. These rabbinic communities constituted what Brian Stock, looking at Christian culture in Western Europe in the aftermath of 1000, has called "textual communities," that is to say, groups of manual laborers who structured their common life around an egalitarian law-text that binds its members, literate and illiterate, together.

Stock called the textual communities of the eleventh century "laboratories of social change," and one can argue plausibly that they provided much of the extraordinary social creativity of the "High Middle Ages" with its unceasing production of new communities in law, new religious movements and "houses," universities, communes, rural settlements. The most successful of these postapocalyptic textual communities are highly disciplined and hard working—real egalitarianism means manual labor for all. Often they find a way to restructure their egalitarian ethos, their social flexibility—they are, ipso facto voluntary communities—into an enduring (indeed thriving) social unit. (Max Weber described the process as a shift from charisma to routinization/rationalization.) They become valuable members of the larger society, contributing notably, often generously, to its prosperity and growth.

Mendel explores with unerring penetration the ethos of these postapocalyptic, world embracing, experiments. At their best, they follow the paths of millennial peace, which Mendel calls "tautological" because they cleave to the difficult understanding that, in apocalyptic conditions especially, violence leads to violence, peace, to peace. Here, embedded in the apocalyptic dynamic, lies the terrible paradox of millennialism—why it is one of the most constructive and destructive forces in the social universe. This insight came to him on a kibbutz where he beheld one of the most egalitarian social experiments in the history of millennial communism, in its latter stages of routinization. Here he found, in the writings of the kibbutz ideologues, the path to the "middle ground" with which he concludes the book. And in the humanity, the modesty, the commitment to acknowledge the other, that such tautological millennial paths teach, we find the earliest and most enduring experiments of civil society, of open society.

For all its spectacular manifestations and revealing dynamics, millennial studies has not attracted much attention among historians and normative social scientists. The field really only dates back to the postwar period, when the anthropologists reported on the Cargo Cults of Melanesia, and the historian Norman Cohn sought the origins of the two most devastating millennial movements of his day—Communism and Nazism—in a millennial impulse most medieval historians had generally ignored. For most historians millennialism could not be consequential: it was both wrong and short-lived. What role can so ephemeral and incorrect a belief play in the long-term and consequential history of humankind? Millennialism has thus been the province of historians who specialize in the marginal, the curious, the strange and bizarre. Millennial prophets, also known in medieval historiography as "eccentrics," are grouped with various madmen, mountebanks, and mesmerizers, the stuff of fascinating if irrelevant narratives. History, especially in our modern age, is the victory of those with reason, those who deal with empirical realities rather than with the phantasms of the unhinged human imagination.

With such an approach, the standard historical narrative on this topic had been relatively simple. Millennialism had been grafted onto Christianity by "judaizers" (the Book of Revelation is really a Jewish text); it showed early popularity but, as prophecy failed, fell away, especially once the Roman empire had converted and millennial beliefs became unwelcome throughout the church. Augustine put an end to millennial beliefs in the Latin church by arguing that the millennium of peace and justice was already in progress, explaining the continuation of war and injustice by arguing that the millennium existed only in the "celestial city," while we must endure in a "terrestrial city" where its perfection remains invisible. After Augustine, no one in the West believed in millennialism until Joachim of Fiore (end of the twelfth century). Even after this eight-hundred-year silence had been broken, however, millennialism remained a marginal phenomenon until the Reformation. Still, however visible in the sixteenth century and beyond, even to our own day, millennialism remains a marginal phenomenon about which most scholars and most laymen are relatively ignorant.

Over the last two generations of work, millennial studies has reworked much of this picture.

- Millennialism is not marginal, it is a widespread belief system shared by many people, especially in the monotheistic cultures, but also quite notable in Buddhism and Taoism. It is, however, most often a quiescent phenomenon, only episodically bursting forth in the characteristic dynamics of an apocalyptic episode.
- Analyzing how postapocalyptic behavior influences not only the most egregious (and violent) cases of denial, but also the more constructive dynamics of postapocalyptic reentry.
- Christianity did not add millennialism to its repertoire after the death of Jesus; it was the essential idiom of Jewish apocalyptic thinking, especially popular preaching. Christianity emerges out of the Judaism of the first century C.E. Palestine, during one of the most sustained periods of apocalyptic excitation in the history of the phenomenon.
- The imperial church did not wipe out millennial beliefs in Christendom, especially in the West, they merely drove them underground. The image of Rome as Whore of Babylon continued to circulate orally in Christian circles after Rome became Christian.
- Throughout the supposed period of silence (400–1200), this underground tradition repeatedly, but episodically, burst forth. Moments of catastrophes, signs, and wonders created ideal conditions for prophets and messiah figures—men and women—to draw large and enthusiastic crowds of believers.
- The most common clerical response to these outbreaks was to argue a very-distant date for the messianic millennium, that is, the end of the current millennium. This technique is responsible for giving the year 1000 an overwhelmingly apocalyptic tone that, in France in particular, generated immensely powerful and creative social forces.
- Joachim did not put an end to Augustine's ban on millennialism; he put an end to Augustine's ban on written millennialism. His work, approved by the pope, was the first time that a vision that looked forward to a *coming* millennium reappeared in Christian theological texts.
- Joachim opened the floodgates of an elite millennialism to match the popular one, continually exciting and disturbing relations

between elites and commoners throughout the following centuries, inducing both a wide range of religious creativity and a corresponding inquisitorial hostility to these new forms.

The "great divide" of 1500, between medieval and modern, appears, in the millennial context, as a shift from religious to secular millennial projects and movements. Millennial phenomena survive all forms of secularization (Renaissance, Enlightenment, Atheism) not only undiminished but intensified—millennialism, apocalyptic episodes, anti-Judaism.

Millennial movements play a far greater role in the dynamics of modernity than most historians have imagined. On the one hand, millennialism constitutes the single most powerful antimodern abreaction; on the other, the very same movement can, in the postapocalyptic period, become a major agent of modernizing.

This leaves the historian a great range of issues to consider and explore, and given the richness of the terrain, one can justifiably ask, why have they not done so earlier? Partly it was just the rhythm of research agenda driven by paradigms of "objectivity" and secular behaviors. But partly also, the lack of attention to millennial phenomena comes from the methodological problems posed by millennial studies. Few phenomena leave so little trace in the documentation. This is true for a number of reasons.

Most apocalyptic prophets do not write, since writing is the ultimate medium for disconfirmation. If they do write, they couch their prophecies in a language at once rich and opaque, so that the text can not only survive disconfirmation but trigger further outbreaks of apocalyptic fervor. In either case, it does not tell the historian "how" it was read.

Most elites dislike apocalyptic behavior and the egalitarian millennial ethos that underlies it, the more authoritarian and imperial, the less they will like it. They will almost always oppose apocalyptic behavior and occasionally go after the millennial ideology that survives disappointment. Whereas we do not have an abundance of millennial texts, we do have repeated orders to burn seized millennial texts.

Most of the narratives of apocalyptic movements are written by "historians" who know how the tale came out. If an apocalyptic movement works like a Doppler effect—waxing sharply at the approach, waning quickly after passage—then our narratives are the equivalent of turning on the tape recorder after the waning has started. These narratives, written in the "retrospective perfect," cannot inform us reliably on the period of the apocalyptic fever.

Some narratives are written by the successful former apocalyptic believers, one of whose apologetic purposes is to discard and disown the mistaken belief that first brought them together.

The archivists, especially in periods where there is important clerical control of the documentation, tend to dislike apocalyptic texts and do not preserve them.

All these varied dynamics conjoin to muffle the sounds of the apocalyptic believers in our texts. For most of the history of modern professional historiography (i.e., since the late nineteenth century and the growth of the positivist paradigm with its immensely valuable research project of editing and analyzing texts), historians have tended to respond to this muffled voice by wishing it good riddance. This impulse lies behind the insistence among medieval historians that the year 1000 was "a year like any other." Very little explicit evidence, and absence of evidence indicates indifference. The apocalyptic year 1000 is a legend whose "neck we must strangle" (Jean Delumeau). To such a historian, the small traces of millennial belief and activity that appear in the documentation are so much flotsam and jetsam of a ship Augustine had sunk centuries earlier. These are surely waters through which he can sail the ship of historiographical analysis without any attention to them.

The millennial historian, however, reads the texts more carefully and tries to restore the voices of millennial visionaries and their enthused audiences and then follow them through their many guises of postapocalyptic readjustment. For such historians, the brief mentions of such phenomena represents the tip of an oral iceberg that has forced its way into the hostile and crude medium of writing (much as a nuclear scientist must read the presence of subatomic particles by the visible traces they leave behind). Such a task necessitates conjecturing about discussions that went on orally, not in writing. It means compensating for the skew of the sources. It means asking what carried more weight at the time, the apocalyptic discourse we can only imagine, or the sober, anti-apocalyptic discourse that our texts preserve for us. Just because Augustine was *right* about the sack of Rome in 410 *not* being the end of the world, does that mean that contemporaries listened to him as closely as we, the literate community that came after him, have? Just because no narrator of Charlemagne's coronation mentioned, in the famously laconic texts that survive, that it occurred on the first day of the year 6000 from the creation of the world, does that mean that no one discussed this, that no millennial meaning accompanied this world-shaping event?

All these matters are for the historians of the next century to answer. The task of establishing the groundwork for such investigations has been done by a generation of millennial scholars tilling a neglected vineyard. The turn of the millennium has obviously brought out a range of apocalyptic and millennial attitudes that few of our social analysts saw coming and has thus given millennial studies the attention it deserves. And in all the great works that populate the field, and proliferate at the close of the millennium, Arthur Mendel's *Vision and Violence* will hold a place of enduring value, not only because it is a brilliant work of analytic synthesis, but because it is passionate, because it courageously asks difficult questions and passes clear judgments.

The judgments can become uncomfortable. Christians who easily accept that Revelation is really a Jewish text whose presence in the Christian canon is an embarrassment, and who, at the same time, cannot understand why "fellow" Christians love this book nor why they can thrill to the call of apocalyptic antisemitism, need to read this book. They need to read and to meditate on it, for it contains uncomfortable insights about their own apocalyptic genealogy that they have systematically avoided thinking about. Of course these very problems millennial studies raise—prophetic issues of justice and integrity—make it problematic. Modern historiography avoids value judgments and certainly steers clear of using them in comparing religious responses. Millennial scholars cannot avoid such matters without rendering themselves irrelevant.

The joke is told about the drunk under the lamppost looking for his key. A Good Samaritan offers to help and, after searching carefully, inquires if, indeed, the seeker lost his keys here. "Oh no," he replied, "I lost them in the bushes. But this is where the light is." In a similar fashion, conventional historians have largely refused to leave the light of their positivist attachment to what they have explicit evidence for, their texts. The exegetical techniques necessary for searching the bushes annoy them, the messy world of value judgments and passions that so animate the prophets and their audiences so offend them that they do not hear their echoes in the writings of a Karl Marx, whether or not they like those writings. Perhaps this millennial cusp of 2000 will, like some great full moon, sufficiently illuminate the bushes that historians and social scientists will step out of their lamplight and off of their cobblestones and venture into the bushes. If that is the case, they can ask for no better guide than these historical meditations of Arthur Mendel.

Boston, August, 1999

Richard Landes
Department of History, Boston University
Director, Center for Millennial Studies at Boston University

Contents

Introduction

Until now, the world could afford the fantasy of Apocalypse. Throughout the nearly two thousand years since Hellenistic Judaism and its Christian offspring introduced it into our culture, the apocalyptic fusion of bliss and horror was usually confined to innocuous religious imagination. Even when the vision inspired real events, they affected only limited periods and populations. At no time need one have taken seriously the prophecy of universal devastation. No longer is that so. Tens of thousands of nuclear warheads controlled by leaders still strongly influenced by two of the most powerful apocalyptic movements in history—Christianity and Bolshevism—make that prophecy disturbingly realistic, especially given the current worldwide revival of fundamentalism.

Why has the Apocalypse persisted century after century, changing nothing but its mask—from God to Reason, History, and Nature? The major portion of this book surveys the history of that vision from its emergence out of the ruins of the ancient Hebrew and Greek civilizations, through its late medieval religious revival, down to its successive secular expressions in the French, Russian, and German (Nazi) revolutions. Following that survey, we confront the Counterculture as a millennial movement. The closing focus is on the recent growth of fundamentalism in the three major religions of our civilization, Christianity, Judaism, and Islam.

Those who have not surrendered to therapeutic denial know that the danger of that apocalyptic heritage and its present fundamentalist expression is very real, and know also that it is likely to increase as we near the turn of the century. As the year 2000 approaches, we will probably experience further explosions of irrationalism of the kind that welcomed the present century (and devastated the first half of it) as well as the still more profound and prolonged upheavals that engulfed the West at the time of the first millennial passage. If one recalls the consequences of earlier alliances between such waves of irrationalism and modern weapons and organizational technology (the Third Reich for example), and then adds the force and effectiveness of the more recent advances in those technologies, one might well conclude that the apocalyptic prophecy has History—at least our history—on its side. That, however, is not the conclusion this study draws; our culture is richly and powerfully endowed by an opposing worldview that repeatedly has calmed apocalyptic seizures in the past and is already demonstrating strength enough to do so again in our own time.

1

Apocalypse and God: Ancient Theory

We are so accustomed to rapid social change and dynamic discontent that we forget how recent and rare they are in human history. Through most of time, life went on unchanged, generation after generation, and social discontent was largely unknown. To be discontent with what "is" assumes the sense of an "ought to be," the will to alter reality accordingly, and the belief that we can do so. Even in our era of relentless progress, few of us are seriously distressed because we cannot be in two places at one time, see into the future, or take off like Superman. That's the way things are. Most people, during most of the past, accepted most things that way. In much of the world, where traditional societies survive, they still do.

To sustain that stable reconciliation with reality, those responsible for the communal mind composed and instilled appropriate scenarios that, among their other services, explained suffering away before it could undermine the essential acceptance. Since good and evil were opposing poles in permanent equilibrium, the Taoist said, efforts to replace evil with good were futile, senseless, and, ultimately, harmful. What else but misfortune could one expect in this material world of pain (*dukka*) and its "wheel of suffering," the Buddhist agreed. For the Hindu, a struggle against suffering and the conditions causing it was not only vain but blasphemous as well, since distress experienced in this lifetime was the karmic consequence of behavior during earlier incarnations. Closer to home, faith in divine retribution has similarly justified suffering for countless Christians and Jews and constrained feelings, thoughts, and actions against it.

In all these cases, the thrust and outcome are the same—acceptance. Whatever is, simply is. Why be discontent with what is unalterable or, at least, unalterably beyond our control? How could one oppose evil or end suffering if they are a part of the Taoist good/evil balance (yin-yang), Hindu karma or illusion *(maya)*, Buddhist wheel of suffering, or if they are caused by the ineluctable will of Fate, the malevolent caprice of one of the Greeks' Olympian gods, or the triumph of Persia's demonic Ahriman? More than that: should one even try to oppose karmic suffering, divine retribution, or the will of the gods?

While such attitudes, together with their underlying cosmologies, are still present in our culture, they have long since been supplanted as dominant ideologies by our theories of progress. If, in traditional societies, the present is structured and motivated by the past, for us the present is a mirror of the future and, paradoxically, driven by it. Few themes have been more frequently worked and reworked, and it is not my intention here to compose yet another version. I am concerned, first of all, with the origins of that progressive, optimistic vision, our belief both in the desirability of social change and in our power to achieve it. What are the roots of our vision of the "good society" and our commitment to its realization? But there is a second theme still more central for this study. How is that good society to be achieved? Can it be established swiftly, at once, or must it evolve gradually? Who will carry out the transformation? One leader? An elite? A particular nation, people, class, or race? All of us? Above all, and my principal focus, how much violence will be necessary or permissible? And against whom? The answers to such questions cannot be found in "objective" reality. They must be sought in our heritage of ideas, in the particular ways we perceive and interpret reality, in our theories, philosophies, and religions.

We begin with the source of the vision that commits us to the world, to change, and to the attainment of the good society. For the most part, it is a gift to us from the ancient Hebrews and their Bible, on which so much of our culture is founded. Biblical man and woman are committed to this world, come what may, because their God not only created it, but called it good, "very good." They know both that "the earth is the Lord's and all that is in it" (Psalms 24:1) and that, as God's image, they are obligated to have dominion over it. On guard against attempts to spiritualize material reality out of existence, Hebrew sages through the centuries have repeatedly emphasized the divinity of the world and the necessity of our continuing attachment to it and to our tasks within it. Not only does the Hebrew Bible begin with the assertion that God created the heaven *and* the earth, but it even omits the refrain "and it was good" after recounting the creation of the heaven on the first day, adding it only after the creation of the earth on the third. Making the point still more insistently, the authors of the second Genesis account put the earth first, before heaven, in the list of creations.

Strengthening the message from another perspective, while the Bible announces the divine creation of earth as well as heaven, it emphasizes their distinct and permanent separation. An eternal "firmament" divides the waters above from those below: "The heavens are the heavens of God, but He has given the earth to the children of man" (Psalms 115:16). Heaven was "not fit for earthlings," the sages taught.[1] Kept at a great distance, they said, the sun maintained life and growth, but if brought too near, it could only destroy.[2] "The secret things belong unto the Lord our God; but the things that are revealed belong unto us and our children for ever, that we may do all the words of his law" (Deuteronomy 29:29). "Seek not what is too wonderful for thee. And search not out that which is hid from thee. Meditate upon that which thou must grasp. And be not occupied with that which is hid. Have naught to do with that which is beyond thee. For more hath been shown to thee than thou canst understand."[3]

The earth and the earth alone was the home and destiny of mankind. Down to the Hellenistic book of Daniel, the Hebrew Bible says little, if anything, explicitly about resurrection, immortality, or eternal bliss and damnation. It is a story of mankind's finite life on earth, from which he came and to which he will return. "You are dust, and to dust shall you return" (Genesis 3:19). To dust, not to heaven. Nor, except for several ambiguous remarks, is anything said about the fate of the souls of the departed. They just depart, remembered for the good and bad they did while alive and leaving to their heirs the challenge to do better. Made from nature, confined within nature, and returned to nature—such are the limits of the drama in which all humans must make their free moral choices, decide between the good and evil within themselves, and thereby either advance or undo the continuing work of creation. The flaming sword that keeps man from Eden's tree of life and its miracle of immortality never leaves its post.

One of the Bible's most dramatic and ingenious declarations of humanity's commitment to the world and its mastery is contained in that "expulsion" episode. If men and women were created in the image and likeness of God and if those words refer, as commentators usually assume they do, to human reason, moral free choice, and creativity, then humanity must, first of all, get out of Eden. In "paradise," Adam is intellectually and morally, as well as physically, as naked as an infant. Everything for him is still instinctual. He has neither knowledge nor conscience. Everything is provided for him. When confronted by God, he runs away, hides, and blames others, both Eve and God, for bringing her to him. He has no obligations, hardly says a word, and is ignorant even of his mortality. Indeed, with everything given him and everything good, what need was there for a conscience to distinguish between good and evil (or reason and knowledge) to master reality, much less make things better? In short, Paradise is infancy and Adam an infant who barely, if at all, had risen beyond the soul (*nefesh*) he shared with other animals, and who gave no evidence of possessing that higher soul (*neshama*) that revealed the divine image on which he was formed or divine spirit (*ruakh* 'breath') that gave him life. Being forced to leave the infantile paradise thus symbolizes a momentous ascent toward maturity, toward self-awareness, knowledge, conscience, and responsibility. Is it any wonder that, instead of killing them for their "disobedience," God clothed Adam and Eve or that the Bible honored the woman after her "disobedience" by having her named Eve (Chava), meaning Life? She was indeed, as the sages write, the mother of life, not only literally with respect to her children, but also symbolically with respect to the human enterprise by "tempting" Adam out of infancy.

To assume that God wanted Adam to remain in Eden is to believe that God wanted him to remain the weak and witless creature he was in the garden, that God did not want the creature that was to be his image to acquire knowledge and conscience, that God was dismayed at the thought that Adam's "eyes will be opened" (Genesis 3:5). The key symbols of the narrative—the unlabored fruit so tempting to sight and taste, and the "punishment" of having to work for the fruit of one's labor—announce the lessons: growth beyond an infant's immediate and total gratification (always the miraculous core of the millennial fantasy); the necessity of laboring against obstacles to achieve one's aims; the accompanying necessity of Law and its constraints to curb the rush of infantile desires; and the value of reason to overcome those obstacles and conscience to see the wisdom of those constraints.

Out of Eden, Adam and Eve began the adventure that still absorbs us—to attain dominion over the world by the constant refinement of reason and to advance toward the good society through the practice of moral freedom. It is only in this endless enterprise, in which reason, freedom, and conscience are both means and ends, that humanity both is and becomes the image of God. Genesis begins with the second letter of the Hebrew alphabet, ב (bet), the sages note, rather than the first, א (aleph), because the first symbolizes the possibility of movement in all directions, including down, up, and backwards, while the second encourages movement in only one direction—forward (in the right-to-left Hebrew reading).[4] When Moses asked God by what name he wanted to be called when Moses spoke for him to the Egyptians in defense of the enslaved Hebrews, God chose a name that is sometimes translated "I will be what I will be." God himself, in other words, awaits the completion that only his created image, man, can achieve. Similarly, when the heaven and earth were "finished" by that seventh day, they were so only in the sense of being prepared for their tasks, as the word "finished" suggests in Hebrew, based as it is on a root meaning tool or instrument. Correspondingly, the passage also speaks of heaven and earth and all their "hosts," selecting a word that implies a dedicated and determined company ready to meet its obligations.[5] And if God rested on the seventh day, it was from the "work which God created to make" (Genesis 2:3), a strange wording which has meaning only in the sense that it was now the turn of God's "work," his creatures, to continue to "make," to carry on the work of creation to the world's completion. While the weekly Sabbath is experienced as a foretaste of the Great Sabbath when the work of the world is done, it is no less considered a day of communion with God to gather renewed strength and inspiration for the coming week's work of world repair and completion.

That "repair of the world"—primarily a moral repair—was the task that Judaism gave the world and one of its principal contributions to it. The Biblical sages highlight the moral purpose of that world "repair" in the phrase "knowledge of good and evil." For them, knowledge of good and evil is knowledge as such. Both knowledge and the thought behind it have meaning and value mainly in association with ethical purpose. In this worldview, thought and understanding are not, essentially, for contemplation and wonder, but for mastering and changing reality for the better. While humanity is instructed to subdue the world and to hold dominion over it by the power of reason, both the reason and the dominion are to be used in the service of the good. It was fine that Tuval-Cain invented "cutting instruments of brass and iron," but it was criminal for Lamech to use that knowledge to murder. It was right and good for mankind to learn how to make bricks and mortar in the absence of natural stone, but it was wrong to use that knowledge to build a Tower of Babel in order to "make a name" for the builders and, worse, as legend interprets the story, to be more concerned about the safety of the bricks than about the safety of the laborers.[6] Consciousness and conscience, ideas and ideals, engage and assume each other in this tradition. If man is *Homo sapiens*, it is mainly because, in this Biblical understanding, he is also ethical man, who knows and acts toward moral purpose.

What is perhaps most remarkable about the Biblical message of moral commitment and action is the fact that it provides virtually all of the basic blueprint for the good society. Little of substance was added thereafter. If the "expulsion" from an infantile Paradise gave humanity the reason and freedom needed to fashion the world, the Biblical-Prophetic program told humanity that God wanted it fashioned in the form of peace and justice. "Seek justice, correct oppression, defend the fatherless; plead for the widow" (Isaiah 1:16–17). From Amos, the first of the great Prophets, to the most recent appeals for social justice in our own time, the call has been much the same. What could later social critics add to Amos's attack on those "who sell the righteous for silver and the needy for a pair of shoes, pant after the dust of the earth on the head of the poor and turn aside the way of the humble"; those who "oppress the poor, crush the needy. . . . [T]rample upon the poor and take exactions of wheat . . ."? What more could be added to the Judaic Biblical message which "has shown you, O man, what is good; for what does God require of you but to do justice, and to love merry, and to walk humbly with your God?" (Amos 2:6–7, 4:1, 5:11–12; Micah 6:8).

For the first time in human history a people worshiped its God and sought to win his favor not primarily through sacrifice and ritual but through ethical behavior; not by magical gestures, but by social justice. There were, indeed, sacrifices and other rites as there were among all the religions of the time. But even before the destruction of the first temple and the exile to Babylon eliminated sacrifice by removing the people from its sacred temple site, the emphasis was already more on ethical human relations than on rituals.

> Even though you offer Me your burnt offerings and cereal offerings, I will not accept them, and the peace offerings of your fatted beasts I will not look upon. Take away from Me the noise of your songs; to the melody of your harps I will not listen. But let justice roll down like waters, and righteousness like an ever-flowing stream. (Amos 5:22–24)

> "Wherefore have we fasted, and Thou seest not? Wherefore have we afflicted our soul, and Thou takest no knowledge?" Is this the fast that I have chosen? Is it to bow down his head as a bulrush, and to spread sackcloth and ashes under him? Will thou call this a fast and an acceptable day to the Lord? Is not this the fast that I have chosen: To loosen the fetters of wickedness, to undo the bands of the yoke, and to let the oppressed go free. And that ye break every yoke? Is it not to deal thy bread to the hungry and that thou bring the poor that are cast out of thy house. When thou seest the naked that thou cover him, And that thou hide not thyself from thine own flesh? Then shall thy light break forth as the morning, And thy healing shall spring forth speedily; and thy righteousness shall go before thee, the glory of the Lord shall be thy reward. Then shalt thou call, and the Lord will answer; thou shalt cry, and He will say: "Here I am." (Isaiah 58:3–9)

Given the era and its values, even more notable than this appeal to social justice within the nation was the Prophetic appeal for peace between nations, the vision of a time when "they shall beat their swords to plowshares, and their spears into pruning hooks"; when "nation shall not lift up sword against nation, neither shall they learn war any more"; when "the wolf shall dwell with the lamb, and the leopard shall lie down with the kid, and the calf and the lion and the fatling together. . . ." In place of the early and conventional God of war that sanctioned violence during the period of national formation and expansion, we find a God who "makes war cease to the end of the earth, . . . breaks the bow, and shatters the spear, . . . burns the chariots with fire!" Rather than the familiar tribal God who assures military victory, justifies territorial conquest, and legitimizes hatred and annihilation of other peoples (the war god shared by all primitive religions), we have an unprecedented God who feels great concern and compassion for the enemies of his "chosen people." When Jonah urged God to destroy Nineveh, the Assyrian capital, God replied: "You pity the plant, for which you did not labor, nor did you make it grow, which came into being in a night, and perished in a night. Should I not pity Nineveh, the great city, in which there are more than a hundred and twenty thousand persons . . . ?" "Blessed be Egypt, my people, and Assyria, the work of my hands," he proclaims on another occasion, not satisfied simply with blessing "Israel, my heritage." When, the sages wrote, the angels wanted to sing for joy at the destruction of the Egyptians in the Red Sea, God was furious: "My creatures are perishing, and you are ready to sing!"[7] "My son, as for me," David told Solomon, summarizing this essential aspect of the heritage, "it was in my mind to build a house unto the name of the Lord my God. But the word of the Lord came unto Me saying, Thou hast shed blood abundantly, and has made great wars: thou shalt not build a house unto My name, because thou hast shed much blood upon the earth in My sight" (1 Chronicles 22:7). And again, "But God said unto me: Thou shalt not build a house for My name, because thou hast been a man of war, and hast shed blood" (1 Chronicles 28:3). So lofty and universal was this moral of compassion that God himself was subject to its demands, as Abraham reminded him when God was about to wipe out Sodom in punishment for its sins: "Perhaps there are fifty righteous within the city. . . . That be far from Thee to do after this manner, to slay the righteous with the wicked. . . . Shall not the Judge of all the earth do justly?" (Genesis 18:24–25).

Next to these two momentous religious innovations (worshiping God through social justice and creating a God of peace who loves his people's enemies) and to the fact that they became the principal source and inspiration for social and international reform programs ever since, the most remarkable feature of this Biblical vision is its relative moderation. We are not told to spurn or abandon our material goods but to help the poor and otherwise unfortunate and not exploit them. We are not urged to be celibate, only to avoid adultery. While we must not murder, we can forcefully defend ourselves. The

Biblical code of ethics, stringent enough, is made for human beings as they are in this world as it is, for those who are "lower than angels" (Psalms 8:6). It is characteristic of the message and intent of the Bible that it makes no attempt to conceal human flaws, least of all those of the people's heroes and leaders, Moses and David included. The underlying assumption and conviction, the basic theme and plot of the drama, rest on the belief that mankind, made in God's image, can, over time, sufficiently control the "evil inclinations" in human nature to establish the good society of peace, freedom, justice, and material well-being, with every man his vine and fig tree. ("Sin rests at the door. Its desire is toward you, yet you can conquer it," as God told Cain [Genesis 4:7].) What was beyond humanity's present capacities was left out of the vision. In essence, the Biblical aim and message involve an elementary tautology: humanity will attain the good society as soon as, and no sooner than, humanity itself becomes good through the trials and errors of its own free moral choice.

To preserve that tautological project and the free moral choice it required, progress toward the ideal had to be left to humanity itself: divine intervention had to be severely and skillfully restrained. We see an example of this compromise between human freedom and divine intervention in the story of Exodus. While the narrative has God redeeming the Jews from Egyptian bondage, he is also shown working through man, and a most hesitant, reluctant, all-too-human man at that, one who needs constant persuading and encouraging. Far more important, however, was the immediate consequence of the "redemption": the Hebrews were not redeemed into an infantile paradise, a new heaven and new earth, but into forty oppressive years in the desert, where they had to wander until the generation of slaves had been replaced by a generation of free men and women capable of meeting the responsibilities of creative freedom. (And the first recorded, characteristic Jewish quip, made at that time of desert trials—"Weren't there enough graves in Egypt?" [Exodus 14:11]—shows that they were already well on their way toward developing the necessary attitudes for that long, hard road ahead.) Also, how did God respond when the prolonged hardships had driven the people to the low point of golden-calf desperation? Here, surely, was the place and time for some miraculous intervention and salvation. Instead, God chose just that moment to impose on his chosen people still more weighty responsibilities, his rigorous commandments. Finally, the man who leads the people out of bondage and through their desert hardships dies at the edge of the promised land, leaving to the people themselves the task of building their new life and nation in freedom.

But precisely because it is up to flawed and limited humans themselves to realize the good society, they must believe, in the very core of their beings, that human nature and human effort can, in time, do the job, achieve the repair of the world. Psychologists speak of "basic trust." With it, one remains optimistic even when things go bad; without it, one is pessimistic even if everything is fine. For individuals, the ground of that "basic trust" is the content and quality of childhood. It is the same for a people. For the Jewish people, a rich and solid foundation of "basic trust" is rooted in their national childhood, the Biblical era and its belief in a parental God who loves both the world he created and his image, humanity; who wants mankind to achieve its ideals in this world; and who, therefore, created a world favoring that achievement.

This concept of God as a loving parent, unique in the ancient world, is an integral part of the Biblical message and, consequently, a founding assumption in our western worldview.

> For I am a father to Israel,
> And Ephraim is my first-born.
>
> (Jeremiah 31:9)

> It was I Who taught Ephraim to walk,
> I took them up in My arms;
> But they did not know that I healed them.
> I led them with cords of compassion,
> With the bands of love;
> I became to them as One Who eases the yoke on their jaws
> I bent down to them and fed them gently.
>
> (Hosea 11:3–4)

> Is Ephraim a darling son unto Me:
> Is he a child that is dandled?
> For as often as I speak of him,
> I do earnestly remember him still;

Therefore My heart yearneth for him,
I will surely have compassion upon him, saith the Lord
(Jeremiah 31:20)

But Zion said: "The Lord hath forsaken me,
And the Lord hath forgotten me."
Can a woman forget her suckling child.
That she should have no compassion on the son of her womb?
Yea, these may forget,
Yet will not I forget thee.
(Isaiah 49:14–15)

It is as disobedient children that God judges his people for their
sins: "children have I reared and brought up, But they have rebelled
against Me" (Isaiah 1:2). "For my people are foolish, they know me
not; They are stupid children, they have no understanding" (Jeremiah 4:22). And while God feels that he must punish them so that
the good in them prevails over the evil, how reluctant he is to do so
and how he hesitates! "How can I pardon you? Your children have
forsaken Me. . . . They judge not with justice the cause of the fatherless. . . . They do not defend the rights of the needy. Shall I not punish them for these things? . . . With his mouth each speaks peaceably
to his neighbor, but in his heart he plans an ambush for him. Shall I
not punish them for these things?" "Behold, I will refine them and
test them, *for what else can I do* because of My dear people?" (Jeremiah
5:7–9 and 28–29, 9:7–8, 9:6). At times, God refuses to carry out the
punishment.

How shall I give you up, O Ephraim! How shall I surrender you,
O Israel! How can I make you like Admah! How can I treat you
like Zeboiim! My heart is turned within Me, My compassion
grows like a flame. I will not execute My fierce anger, I will not
again destroy Ephraim; For I am God and not man, Thy Holy
One in your midst, And I will not come to destroy. (Hosea 11:8–
9)

In a very little while My indignation will come to an end . . .
Come, My people, enter your chambers,
And Shut your doors behind you;

> Hide yourselves for a little while
> Until the indignation is past.
>
> (Isaiah 10:25, 26:20)

When parental duty does take over and God punishes his children, he identifies so much with them that he, too, suffers the pain.

> Thus says the Lord: . . .
> O My dear people, gird on sackcloth,
> And roll in ashes;
> Make mourning as for an only son,
> Most bitter lamentation,
> For suddenly the destroyer will come upon *us*.
>
> (Jeremiah 6:22 and 26)

> Thus says the Lord of hosts:
> Consider, and call for the mourning women to come;
> Let them make haste and raise a wailing over *us*.
>
> (Jeremiah 9:17–18)

Finally, as a necessary assumption behind the "basic trust" in the world, the parental God must assure his children Israel that, in the end, all will be well, not in some compensatory afterlife in another world, but right here in this world. From the first of the major Prophets, Amos, through the apocalyptic works of Hellenistic Jews, this remained a constant motif.

> Behold, the days come, saith the Lord,
> That the plowman shall overtake the reaper,
> And the treader of grapes him that soweth seed;
> And the mountains shall drop sweet wine,
> And all the hills shall melt.
> And I will turn the captivity of My people Israel,
> And they shall build the waste cities, and inhabit them;
> And they shall plant vineyards, and drink the wine thereof;
> They shall also make gardens, and eat the fruit of them.
> And I will plant them upon their land,
> And they shall no more be plucked up
> Out of their land which I have given them,

Saith the Lord thy God.

(Amos 9:13–15)

Thus saith the Lord:
Refrain thy voice from weeping,
And thine eyes from tears;
For thy work shall be rewarded, saith the Lord;
And they shall come back from the land of the enemy.
And there is hope for thy future, saith the Lord;
And thy children shall return to their own border.

(Jeremiah 31:16–17)

For as I have sworn that the waters of Noah
Should no more go over the earth,
So have I sworn that I would not be wroth with thee,
Nor rebuke thee.
For the mountains may depart,
And the hills be removed;
But My kindness shall not depart from thee,
Neither shall My covenant of peace be removed,
Saith the Lord that had compassion on thee.

(Isaiah 54:9–10)

The relevance of the world-destroying flood, recalled in that last quotation, to the "basic trust" in the world is obvious and decisive. How could there be basic trust in a world whose Creator threatened such total annihilation as punishment for moral errors? How could a loving parent be so ruthless? It was, therefore, essential for the survival of the reformist vision, the belief in a gradual repair of the world, that God had a change of heart after the flood.

I will not again curse the ground any more for man's sake; for the imagination of man's heart is evil from his youth; neither will I again smite any more every thing living, as I have done. (Genesis 8:21)

The immense significance of this promise is not only the promise itself but the reason given for it, God's acceptance of the fact that "the imagination of man's heart is evil from his youth." It may be recalled that the flood was unleashed in the first place because "the Lord saw that the wickedness of man was great in the earth, and that every imagination of the thoughts of his heart was only evil continually" (Genesis 6:5). By vowing never again to destroy the world as punishment for moral error, God was, in effect, reaffirming the basic plot of the Biblical drama and message. Of course, man was capable of great evil: he was formed from the earth and was flesh as well as divine spirit. Overcoming that evil by the strength of the goodness that was also a part of this human image of God was humanity's task. Moreover, God, himself, as the commentators emphasize, was the creator of evil as well as good. "I form the light, and create darkness; I make peace, and create evil: I am the Lord, that doeth all these things" (Isaiah 45:17). In fact, since God created all things from nothing, ex nihilo, he created the "darkness on the surface of the deep" before he created the light, and the Bible again hints at this priority in time, so the sages suggest, when it puts darkness first in the refrain, "and there was evening and there was morning." Even after the light was called forth, God intentionally permitted part of the darkness to remain rather than have light displace it completely. Darkness and light would reign together, intermingling: "the darkest night may contain elements of day and the brightest day may contain elements of night. . . . Even the apparent 'darkness' of the deeds of the wicked may contain sufficient merit in the eyes of God to be considered day."[8] Were it not for that continuing "darkness," humanity would not have the good-and-evil capacities that define it; there would be no moral freedom, and the entire enterprise of world repair toward the good society would be meaningless.

The flood's apocalyptic annihilation is, thus, fundamentally inconsistent with the overall Biblical intent and design. Moreover, what purpose did it serve? The "darkness," the "evil inclination" goes right on: the generations after the flood are no better than those before it. So inconsistent as well as useless was it that the Bible's authors even portray God as uncertain and unhappy about the whole dismal affair. Recalling that comparable creation accounts composed by other societies in that part of the ancient world also contain flood stories, often strikingly similar to the Biblical version (even down to small details), one could argue that the Bible was following a conventional formula (one that, perhaps, reflected actual flood disasters). Unlike those who wrote these other accounts, however, the Hebrew scribes wanted to use the disaster to make a moral point, punishment for sin; but they went too far. In any case, they seem to have realized how inconsistent such "apocalyptic" punishment was with the larger Biblical vision and so had God promise never again. In the end, therefore, we are left with something similar to the story of the sacrifice of Isaac: a series of events is narrated not in order to provide an example of what should be done, but as a judgment against doing it and an announcement that the Hebrew people were breaking with regional conventions—human sacrifice in one case, apocalyptic world destructions in the other.

Throughout their history, Jewish sages have interpreted their initial, Biblical vision of God as a fusion of protection and punishment. While careful (usually) to avoid any threat to monotheism, the sages distinguished between "Elohim," God as justice and law, and "YHVA," God as compassion and mercy. The first is also conventionally associated, as in the opening chapters of Genesis, with the creation and functioning of inanimate nature; the second generally enters the scene when human beings are involved. If, the sages write, there were only a God of compassion and mercy, "sins would abound"; but were there only a God of strict law (constant and uniform law as in nature), then the world—the human world, at least—could not endure.[9] The trouble with Paradise was that there was only a God of mercy, doing everything for Adam as though he were a helpless infant. As a result, that is what Adam was. But with the opposite extreme (as in the case of world-destructive, apocalyptic floods), life becomes so unbearable that its victims abandon hope and trust in the world. To suggest the proper balance, the sages picture God preparing to infuse his divine spirit into the world as though he were a king preparing to pour water into empty glass vessels: "If I pour hot water into them, they will burst; if I pour cold, they will contract and snap. So he mixed hot and cold water and poured it into them and they therefore remained unbroken."[10]

Such, in essence, is the Hebrew Bible's gradualist project and its assumptions. Made in the image of God, man has freedom, reason, and conscience to undertake the repair and completion of the world. The specific aims of that project, which have remained as viable and inspiring today as they were the first day they were announced, were precisely stated and restated in the successive Biblical encounters between God and Israel and in the pronouncements of the Prophets.

To complete the work of creation meant to heal the world's wounds and repair its flaws, bringing peace where there is war, justice where there is injustice, freedom where there is repression, welfare where there is material deprivation, joy where there is pain. Given man's inherently dual nature and manifold limitations, it was assumed that the realization of those ideals necessarily lay far in the future and could only be achieved slowly. Yet, given as well the fact that the world was created by a loving parent who cared boundlessly for the well-being of his children, it was also taken for granted that the ideals could and would be fulfilled, that God's world smiled on the dreams of his children.

But the smiles and long-run optimism did not preclude suffering along the way. The tautology, by which the good society would be reached only when the people comprising it became good, worked in reverse as well: bad times resulted when people acted badly. Humanity's punishing ills were self-inflicted. That punishment, however, would never again be an annihilating punishment of a sinful mankind in order to clear the way for a new and better breed: it was the parental means through which the wayward children suffered the consequences of their errors, mended their ways, and thereby moved a little nearer to that distant good society.

History was the arena for those moral challenges and lessons. Occasionally humanity met the trials successfully and moved toward the goal. Usually they failed. History was neither structured nor (until the Book of Daniel) determined. It was simply a place, a broad space of time, within which morally free men and women confronted the good and evil in themselves and themselves determined, by the outcome of those encounters, whether humanity advanced toward or regressed still farther away from the good society.

There was, thus, no role for apocalyptic-revolutionary violence in this vision. Violent social transmutation, of the kind that characterized late medieval religious millennial upheavals and modern secular ideological revolutions, is the strategy of those who are committed to a swift and total realization of the ideal and who are not constrained by doubts about their maximalist ends and means. The Biblical vision starts with the premises that the goal is too distant; the way too slow and uneven; and both the travelers and their guides too limited and uncertain for violent theory and practice. Moreover, why, in any case, should the people of the Book predict the violent emergence of a new world when they had, as their model, the extraordinarily *nonviolent* creation of this one? Inspired perhaps by the apocalyptic scenario of a new world arising from the ruins of the old, literary and artistic creation fantasies are filled with all sorts of violence—shattering explosions, vast upheavals of land and sea, raging storms, crashing bolts of lightning, and so on. Yet, what could be more gentle and peaceful than the original story in Genesis? God just "hovers" over the formless deep, as a mother bird hovers over her nest (the same verb, "hovers" *[merakefet]*, is used in both phrases) and then does no more than say, "let there be. . . ." No thunderbolts or volcanic eruptions, nothing but a few words.

That is one side of the Hebrew Bible's guidance for social change, the gradualist side. But there is another. Notwithstanding the nonviolent initial Creation, the vow never again to destroy the world in punishment for evil, and the various ways this view of man and world promote a patient and pragmatic repair of society, the Bible also takes the first steps in the transformation of that nonviolent vision into the catastrophically violent, apocalyptic vision, both religious and secular-revolutionary.

The first ingredient in the blend that was to produce the Apocalypse was divine blessing for violence against enemy nations and their alien gods, a common enough experience throughout religious and political history. It was at God's command that Joshua brought down the walls of Jericho and destroyed "utterly all that was in the city, both man and woman, young and old, and ox, and sheep, and ass, with the edge of the sword" (Joshua 6:21). "So Joshua smote the whole country of the hills, and of the south, and of the vale, and of the springs, and all their kinds: he left none remaining, but utterly destroyed all that breathed, as the Lord God of Israel commanded" (Joshua 10:40).

At every step of the way in the Israelite wars with Canaanites and Philistines, priests and prophets not only blessed the campaigns but inspired and even initiated them in the name of Yahweh, as Samuel did when he told Saul of God's orders to "smite Amalek, and utterly destroy all that they have, and spare them not, but slay both man and woman, infant and suckling, ox and sheep, camel and ass" (1 Samuel 15:3). And when Saul spared some livestock as well as the defeated King, Agag, it was the prophet Samuel himself who, after roundly denouncing Saul for disobeying divine instructions, "hewed Agag in pieces" (1 Samuel 15:33).

While attributing military victory to the power of one's God is as familiar as religion itself, the same cannot be said for the way the ancient Israelites responded to military defeat and other disasters, a response that was to make a still more important contribution to the later Apocalypse. The usual reaction of the ancient world to natural, tribal, and personal disasters was to blame them on some evil force— Ahriman or Tiamat, the endless conflicts and intrigues of Olympian immortals, an error in reading signs and omens, a flaw or omission in the performance of a ritual, an ineluctable turn in a predetermined cosmic cycle, or just Fate, the stars. The peculiar monotheism of the Jews precluded all such explanations. Since there was only one God who was all-powerful, he must have wanted the disaster to occur. And since he was also all-good and could not be guilty of an evil or unjust act, the fault must lie with the people themselves. Disasters were justified punishment for sin. This second pattern of divine violence (violence against the Hebrews themselves as divine punishment, in contrast to divinely sanctioned violence against alien nations) was particularly associated with the crushing defeats suffered at the hands of Assyrians in the seventh century B.C.E. and Babylonians in the sixth century. Apparently, the priests and prophets first used these defeats as evidence of God's wrath against the people for not fulfilling the cultic and moral commandments that the priests defined. They then went on to predict still worse disasters to come, and in terms that were already fearfully apocalyptic enough to have stoked the fury of countless fire-and-brimstone sermons ever after.

> Ah, Assyria, the rod of My anger,
> The staff of My Fury!
> Against a godless nation I send him,
> Against the people of My wrath I command him,
> To take spoil and seize plunder,
> To tread them down like the mire of the streets.
>
> (Isaiah 10:5–6)

> Behold, the name of the Lord comes from far,
> Burning with His anger, and in thick rising smoke;

His lips are full of indignation,
And His tongue is like a devouring fire;
His breath is like an overflowing stream
That reaches up to the neck;
To sift the nations with the sieve of destruction . . .

(Isaiah 30:27–28)

As the tongue of fire devours the stubble,
As the dry grass sinks down in the flame,
So their root will be rottenness,
And their blossom go up like dust . . .
For all this His anger is not turned away
And His hand is stretched out still . . .
So the Lord cut off from Israel head and tail,
Palm branch and reed in one day . . .
The Lord . . . has no compassion on their fatherless and widows;
For everyone is godless and an evildoer,
And every mouth speaks folly . . .
Through the wrath of the Lord of hosts
The land is burned.
And the people are like fuel for the fire;
No man spares his brother.

(Isaiah 5:24–25, 10–14, 17, 19)[11]

Volcanic as all this violence is, it is not yet apocalyptic. The Prophets' violent rhetoric does not predict God's imminent and total destruction of the sinners and their sinful world, to be followed by the miraculous appearance of a purified and perfect Kingdom of God. The Prophets are warning the Hebrews of the terrible consequences of their sins in the hope and expectation that they will cease doing evil and, thereby, begin *themselves* to establish a world of peace and justice. They do not come to announce the end of the world, time, and history, but rather to promote repair of the world *in* time and history. To recall an earlier argument, these are still parental punishments and threats of punishment for disobedient children, to persuade them to behave as they should. Nor do references to the coming "Day of the Lord" and similar phrases contest this interpretation. However such remarks were to be interpreted later, there is no reason to consider them in their own time as anything more than these threats of horrendous suffering to frighten the people into moral reformation: they are not yet apocalyptic predictions of the end of the world.

The priests and prophets, however, were taking great risks in using past and prospective disasters to strengthen their campaigns for moral reform. If the national and natural disasters as well as other "punishments" continued to occur, as they inevitably would, no matter what the people might do to reform, then the people might lose heart and cease to believe that change was in their power. The Babylonian destruction and exile had just that effect, and the result was another step in the direction of the Apocalypse: the Prophets (Jeremiah, Ezekiel, Isaiah II) seem to give up hope that the people can reform themselves sufficiently to avoid these dreadful punishments. The leopard cannot change its spots. God himself must save his people by, in effect, creating a new humanity purged of evil.

> For the palace shall be forsaken;
> The city with its stir shall be deserted;
> The mound and the tower shall be for dens for ever,
> A joy of wild asses, a pasture of flocks;
> *Until the spirit be poured upon us from on high.*
>
> (Isaiah 32:14–15)

But this is the covenant that I will make with the house of Israel after those days, saith the Lord, I will put My law in their inward parts, and in their heart will I write it; and I will be their God, and they shall be My people; and they shall teach no more every man his neighbour, and every man his brother, saying: "Know the Lord"; for they shall all know Me, from the least of them unto the greatest of them, saith the Lord; for I will forgive their iniquity, and their sin will I remember no more. (Jeremiah 31:31–34)

A new heart also will I give you, and a new spirit will I put within you; and I will take away the stony heart out of your flesh, and I will give you a heart of flesh. And I will put My spirit within you, and cause you to walk in my statues, and ye shall keep Mine ordinances, and do them. And ye shall dwell in the land that I gave to your fathers; and ye shall be My people, and I will be your God. (Ezekiel 36:26–28)

I, even I, am He that blotteth out thy transgressions for
Mine own sake; And thy sins I will not remember.

(Isaiah 14:22)

It was now mainly up to God to change the leopard's spots,
provide the new and pure heart, *"cause* you to walk in my statues,"
and no longer up to the sinful people themselves: "Return to me; for
I have saved you," not return and I will save you. But once redemption and salvation were up to God rather than to flawed and limited
humanity, there was no limit to what one could expect or predict by
way of radical, miraculous transmutation. It could come at any moment, whenever God chose to descend into time and history, and
could attain any degree of individual and social perfection God desired. Correspondingly, there was a significant change in the focus
of divine punishment, also pointing toward the later Apocalypse,
religious and secular-revolutionary. As in the period when the
prophets had blamed national disasters on the sins of the people, the
threat of violence was again directed against the sinners, but with a
difference. Suffering as punishment was no longer the fate of *all* the
Hebrews. There was now a saved and pure "remnant."

A remnant will return, the remnant of Jacob, to the mighty God.
For though your people Israel be as the sand of the sea, only a
remnant of them will return. (Isaiah 10:21–22)

Henceforth, the phrase "Day of the Lord" could be used to mean
what it would later mean in the Apocalypse, a time—perhaps today—when God chose to destroy the sinners and reward the saved
remnant as compensation for their unjust suffering. With this, we are
already well on our way to one of the distinguishing features of
religious and secular apocalyptic movements: the radical division between the sinners and the saved, with the saved assigned the duty
to execute the judgment of God (or Reason, History, and Nature)
against the sinners. In Isaiah 25:8 we find, for the first time, a clear
expression of the ultimate miracle, "He will swallow up death forever"—the most compelling of all indications that we are already
dealing with transmutation by divine power rather than with the
earlier Biblical vision of personal and social transformation through
free human moral choice and action.

The last series of changes, this time going all the way to the Apocalypse, occurred hundreds of years later. But to grasp the nature and significance of that final stage in the transition from the gradualist vision to the apocalyptic, we must make a brief detour into the simultaneous evolution of a neighboring culture, that of the Greeks during the Hellenistic era. It was the merger between that development and the emerging Hebrew apocalyptic vision that ultimately produced the Apocalypse.

For all their many differences, the main focus of Greek and Hebrew concern was the same—this world. Although they lived and judged this life differently (one focusing on the future through the prism of ethics, the other on the present through the values of intellect, excellence, beauty, and heroic nobility),[12] neither had much time for or interest in any other world. Or so it was, at least, during the period when both cultures were flourishing and optimistic. That period ended. For both cultures, optimism gave way to prolonged crises and uncertainty.

The defeat in 404 B.C.E. of the Athenian fleet during the Peloponnesian War, the subsequent loss of foreign possessions, and the replacement of the democratic polis by oligarchical rule were but the beginning of a steady decline of Athenian culture and society. The rapid and extensive expansion of imperial power under Philip II of Macedonia added still more disruptive influences, especially through fostering mass population movements and culture fusion. Throughout the Near and Middle East, long and deeply established local civic interests gave way, on the one hand, to narrow private, individual concerns and, on the other hand, to all-encompassing, universalistic worldviews, in part reflecting the displacement of local politics by those of the new Hellenistic Empires. This world was no longer so pleasant a home, and the search began for another.

Among the plethora of competing mystery cults and religions, some derived from early Greek Dionysian and Orphic rituals and some reflecting the newer, "oriental" influences, one of the most appealing was the philosophy of Plato, mainly in its later, neo-Platonist rendering. For intellectuals who found such cults as the Dionysian and Orphic too irrational, violent, and indecent, Plato provided the perfect solution. Drawing his inspiration from the Orphic separation of spirit from matter and its refinement of Dionysian frenzy, Plato carried the refinement further, completely purged and sublimated Dionysian emotions, and produced, in the end, an ideally respectable exit from the world that has marvelously well served intellectuals ever since. Not that there was anything new about this divorce of spirit from body and the accompanying spiritual ascent. From time immemorial, shamans had been leaving their bodies and ascending to the home of the gods in order to implore favors for the tribe or, perhaps, roam the spirit world to find and return the wandering souls of the sick. For Plato and the later neo-Platonists, mystics, and philosophical idealists, however, the aim of this ascent was distinctly personal rather than social, immortality for themselves after death or solipsistic tranquility before, rather than one or another benefit for others.

First, they separated mundane physical reality with all its defects, contradictions, interminable changes, and ubiquitous corruptions from the transcendent world of divine spirit, mind, Reason, Idea, Ideal, Plenum, Pleroma, Light, Logos, Nous, and the variety of other names for the realm of pure, timeless, immaterial, unchanging perfection. Then they hypostatized that perfect realm into the only authentic "Reality." The result was a blissful liberation from the pain-filled material world and a refuge in an inner and higher realm of absolute Truth, Beauty, and Goodness. In its earthly existence, Plato wrote, the soul was like "the sea-god Glaucus, whose original form can hardly be discerned, because parts of his body have been broken off or crushed and altogether marred by the waves, and the clinging overgrowth of weed and rock and shell has made him more like some monster than his natural self." Distant from its original home and cruelly distorted out of its pristine form, the soul, still enraptured by "the memory of holy things," was "like a bird fluttering and looking upward, careless of the world below." Our souls forever yearned to "fly away from earth to heaven as quickly as we can," to return to the spiritual realm where we had once enjoyed all that was "innocent and simple and calm and happy," where we were "pure ourselves and not yet enshrined in that living tomb which we carry about, now that we are imprisoned in the body, like an oyster in his shell." Happily, the yearning was not in vain, for the lost soul could indeed go home again, by leading a life of pure Reason, spurning the "folly of the body," ending the futile search for "what men call happiness by making earth here the soul's food," and nurturing a "love of wisdom," the form and substance of authentic Reality.[13]

> . . . unwilling to leave the Soul in her degradation with Matter, God endowed her with an intelligence and the faculty of perceiving, precious gifts which were intended to recall to her her high origin in the spiritual world, . . . to restore to her the knowledge of herself, to indicate to her that she was a stranger down here. . . . Since the Soul received this instruction through perception and intelligence, since she recovered the knowledge of herself, she desires the spiritual world, as a man transported to a foreign land sighs for his distant hearth. She is convinced that in order to return to her original condition she must disengage herself from worldly bonds, from sensual desires, from all material things.[14]

For both Greeks and Jews of earlier centuries, human life and mind had been firmly joined to the ordinary, everyday, material, and social world of the here and now. To be the image of God meant, to Biblical Jews, to possess the reason and creative capacities needed to master nature and to live justly with others as their God had repeatedly commanded. For Plato and his successors through the centuries, to be made in the image of God meant to possess in the soul and rational mind—the two were, for them, synonymous—a vehicle for *leaving* the temporal, material world. As interpreted by Platonists, Gnostics, and mystics, the Delphic Oracle "know thyself" meant to know that one's true self, one's soul/mind was kin to God, a microcosm of the divine macrocosm, and that by turning inward, liberating oneself from the tyranny of the flesh and rationally contemplating the perfection of the True, the Beautiful, and the Good, one would return to one's authentic self, merge with God, escape the mortality of the body and the endless suffering of physical and social corruption, and, thus, free oneself from Fate and Death.

Although Plato, along with the Stoics, had somewhat bridged the gap between the two worlds of spirit and matter by postulating a soul for the world and by granting the material world at least the honor of being a flawed reflection of the ideal world, it took just a small step to complete the break. That step was taken by the Gnostics. While the gnostic scenarios are often intricately complex, the problem they set out to solve is simple and direct. If, as in the Platonists, the earlier Dionysian, Orphic, and Pythagorian cults, and the later cults of Mithra and Isis, the material and the spiritual realms were radically separated, and if, as everyone involved in such movements took for granted, the human spirit suffered so much because it was trapped in this evil and alien material world, then the only question that mattered was how to get back to the soul's true spiritual home. The Gnostics knew the way back. Or, put more accurately, Gnostic knowledge (*gnosis* 'knowledge') was itself the way back. In all its many variations, that knowledge involved, essentially, an awareness that one's authentic home was in the spirit world, where one's soul was born; that, in one way or another (and this is where the stories diverge), the divine soul got caught in the material cage; and that this knowledge of "who we were, and what we have become: where we were . . . whither we are hastening, from what we are being released"[15] would inspire in the initiate the desire to separate himself from the material world, turn inward to contemplate the eternal divine soul reflected in all human souls, and, thereby, return home both now and, after death, forever. Finally, there was the all-important question of how one came by that precious knowledge, the truth that would make men free. Here, too, most gnostic tales share a common theme: a messenger is sent from above, a Prince by his father the King, to bring the liberating knowledge/gnosis and lead the trapped souls back home.

There are many volumes that survey and analyze the variations on this basic gnostic pattern, but in all of them this is, indeed, the basic drama. There are always two worlds, God's world of the spirit, in which the human soul was born and to which it properly belongs and yearns to return, and the earthly, material world created and/or ruled by another power that is either sui generis, coexistent with the true God, or created by the true God but a rebel against him. The human soul, whether through its own fault (a narcissistic love of its own image that it sees reflected in lower, material nature or a desire for power comparable to that of the lower, chthonic demiurge) or through the clever schemes and manipulations of the lower power and his demonic "Archons," becomes trapped in the material prison. After all sorts of intrigues and adventurous convolutions comparable to the most imaginative modern science fiction, the messenger sent by the true God, the divine Father, succeeds in freeing the hapless souls by teaching them who they really are, how they got caught, and how—by purity and detachment—they can go home again.

Looking down from that highest summit and perpetual light, and having with secret desire contemplated the appetency of the body and its "life," so-called on earth, the soul by the very weight of this its earthly thought gradually sinks down into the nether world. . . . In each sphere [that it passes] it is clothed with an ethereal envelopment, so that by these it is in stages reconciled to the company of this earthen garment. And thus it comes through as many deaths as it passes spheres to what here on earth is called "life."

Who has thrown me into the suffering of the worlds, who has transported me to the evil darkness. So long I endured and dwelt in the world, so long I dwelt among the works of my hands. . . . How long have I endured already and been dwelling in the world!

Having once strayed into the labyrinth of evils,
The wretched [Soul] finds no way out . . .
She seeks to escape from the bitter chaos,
And knows not how she shall get through.

From the day when I came to love the Life,
from the day when my heart came to love the Truth,
I no longer have trust in anything in the world.
In father and mother
I have no trust in the world.

In brothers and sisters
I have no trust in the world . . .
In what is made and created
I have no trust in the world.
In the whole world and its works
I have no trust in the world.
After my soul alone I go searching about,
which to me is worth generations and worlds.
I went and found my soul—
what are to me all the worlds? . . .
I went and found Truth
as she stands at the outer rim of the worlds.[16]

While much of this, as we will see, was to become part of the apocalyptic despair and withdrawal, there are several aspects of Hellenistic Gnosticism that are especially important in comparing it with the apocalyptic vision: its attitude toward the body and sexuality, its predictions concerning the future of the physical world, and the place of violence in its expectations. For the Gnostics, the world of flesh and other matter reeks of darkness, pain, falsity, corruption, and all other evils. Whatever attached the soul to that world was vile and evidence of the soul's degeneration. Only one human passion was right and pure—the yearning to detach oneself from that corruption, withdraw inward into the inner soul itself, and thereby begin the return homeward to the realm of the spirit, the soul's original, ultimate, and only authentic home.

> Grief and woe I suffer in the body-garment into which they transported and cast me. How often must I put it off, how often put it on. . . .

> They brought living water and poured it into the turbid water, they brought shining light and cast it into the dense darkness. . . . They brought the living fire and cast it into the devouring fire. They brought the soul, the pure Mana, and cast it into the worthless body.

> Thou has taken the treasure of life and cast it onto the worthless earth. Thou has taken the word of Life and cast it into the word of mortality.[17]

Sexuality was doubly evil. Not only was it a characteristically vile function of the body, totally divorced from the spiritual realm, but, through childbirth, it created more of the despised body traps to snare lost souls and further fragment the Spirit, making its ultimate reintegration all the more difficult and distant. So hopelessly corrupt was this earthly world of body and flesh that it was clearly the creation and possession not of God but the Devil. The only sensible solution for human souls, therefore, was to leave it: the body and the rest of the physical world could not be redeemed or purified. Purity and perfection were attributes of spirit, not matter. Consequently, there is no plan for the destruction of the existing material world in the hope of creating a pure earth. Violence was irrelevant. The world was not to be destroyed: it was simply to be abandoned by the departing souls, homeward bound.

The neo-Platonist, gnostic withdrawal from the present world and yearning for an alternative, spiritual realm of purity and perfection was to play a decisive part in the apocalyptic vision of a "new heaven and new earth." But the gnostic and apocalyptic worldviews differed fundamentally on the central issue—violence, the destruction of this sinful temporal world in the belief that another, ideal world would replace it. The reasons for that difference are the key to an understanding of the final apocalyptic vision. As part of the Hellenistic world, Jewish communities were also offered the neo-Platonist/Gnostic solution of spiritually leaving a hopelessly flawed and painful world. No doubt the appeal was powerfully attractive. They, too, had been subject to prolonged Hellenistic disruptions and turmoil. In addition, they had suffered their own special deprivations and humiliations as a result of submission to successive foreign dominations, from the Persians (who had replaced the Babylonian rulers), through Alexander III and his Seleucid and Ptolemaic successor states, to the Roman viceroys and legions. With that domination went the usual economic exactions and, far more intolerable to them, religious oppression, at times determined efforts to wipe out Judaism altogether. A brief period of independence following the second-century B.C.E. Maccabean rebellion had only further exacerbated the troubles by soon collapsing into bitter and violent factional rivalries, ending in renewed submission to a foreign power, this time Rome.

Thus, Hellenistic Jews, too, had reason enough to want to escape this sorry world. But how could they? Their entire religion was based on the belief that a good, loving, parental God had created this world and had called it "very good." Since the Greeks had all along assumed that the world was the work of a cabal of gods who were immoral, unpredictable, and basically indifferent to humanity and that it was helplessly subject to impersonal Fate, it was relatively easy for them to believe that the world belonged to demonic "Archons." The Jews, however, had to find another answer, one that permitted them to remain loyal to a divinely created, earthly world. If life for Hellenistic Jews had become intolerably harsh, but they were prohibited by their defining faith to follow the Greeks out of it into a spiritual realm of bliss, purity, and perfection, then there was only one solution: change, *at once,* the existing natural, physical, temporal world into the good society of peace, justice, and material abundance that had long been their ideal.

With that, all the earlier transitions toward the Apocalypse fell into place. Since God had replaced humanity as the instrument for world transformation and could effect the miracle swiftly, completely, and at any time, there was no reason why he could not do it now. And what better time for a loving parent to rescue his children than when their suffering was at its worst? As for the existing evil society and its sinful oppressors, they would be justly punished in the catastrophic destruction needed to sweep away the old and make room for the new, the kind of violence that God had often previously used to punish both the enemies of the Israelites and the backsliding Israelites themselves. Neo-Platonists and Gnostics could achieve their aims immediately by simply abandoning the world and society. Destruction was superfluous. Those committed to the world and society who similarly wanted to realize their ideals at once could only do so by violent transmutation.

The result was an outpouring of apocalyptic themes in the popular Jewish literature of the time, particularly in the so-called Apocrypha and Pseudepigrapha works (*The Book of Enoch, The Assumption of Moses, Twelve Patriarchs, Jubilees,* etc.). Considered together, these works present all the essentials of the apocalyptic pattern: total rejection of the present world; absolute faith in the imminence of an ideal, divine kingdom of the saved; certainty that a divinely sent Messiah will bring this salvation; and—the key feature generally missing in neo-Platonist and Gnostic works—emphasis on the terrible violence that will accomplish the miraculous transmutation.

> In these days downcast in countenance shall the kings of the
> earth have become,
> And the strong who possess the land because of the works of
> their hands,
> For on the day of their anguish and affliction they shall not (be
> able to) save themselves.
> And I will give them over into the hands of Mine elect:
> As straw in the fire so shall they burn before the face of the holy:
> As lead in the water shall they sink before the face of the righteous,
> And no trace of them shall any more be found.

In those days they shall be led off to the abyss of fire: (and) to the torment and the prison in which they shall be confined for ever. And whosoever shall be condemned and destroyed will from thenceforth be bound together with them to the end of all generations. And destroy all the spirits of the reprobate and the children of the Watchers, because they have wronged mankind. Destroy all wrong from the face of the earth and let every evil work come to an end: and let the plant of righteousness and truth appear: and it shall prove a blessing; the works of righteousness and truth shall be planted in truth and joy for evermore.

And then shall all the righteous escape,
And shall live till they beget thousands of children,
And all the days of their youth and their old age
Shall they complete in peace.[18]

The Apocalypse reached its final form in the most influential of all Hellenistic Jewish apocalyptic works—the Christian Gospels, together with their accompanying texts, particularly Paul's writings and John's Revelations. The Judeo-Christian Gospels differed from other Jewish apocalyptic works of the time, however, in two basic ways. First, they told the story of a Messiah who had already come rather than one whose arrival, while imminent, still lay in the future. Second, they moved Jewish apocalyptic thought and expectation much closer to Gnosticism. Most Jewish apocalyptic expectations remained far more attached to the natural, physical, temporal world. Although they look forward to heaven and (since Daniel) resurrection, they seem far more attentive to the preceding Messianic Kingdom on earth, where the saved remnant, as we learn from the Book of Enoch, will live in "light and joy and peace . . . and their lives shall be increased in peace and the years of their joy shall be multiplied in eternal gladness and peace, all the days of their life."[19]

And then shall the whole earth be tilled in righteousness, and shall all be planted with trees and be full of blessing. And all desirable trees shall be planted on it, and they shall plant vines on it: and the vine which they plant thereon shall yield wine in abundance, and as for all the seed which is sown thereon each measure [of it] shall bear a thousand, and each measure of olives shall yield ten presses of oil. And cleanse thou the earth from all oppression, and from all unrighteousness and from all sin, and from all godlessness: and all the uncleanness that is wrought upon the earth destroy from off the earth. And all the children of men shall become righteous and all nations shall offer adoration and shall praise Me, and all shall worship Me. And the earth shall be cleansed from all defilement, and from all sin, and from all punishment, and from all torment, and I will never again send [them] upon it from generation to generation and forever.[20]

What some of these apocalyptic prophets seem to have in mind is an idealized earthly theocracy, of the kind that the sages of the time believed John Hycarnus, the Hasmonean King, had anticipated. In *Aristedes*, we even find a socially conscious messianic monarch restraining the flow of population from the countryside into the towns and setting fair wages.

Compared to these texts, the Gospels far more clearly reflect otherworldly gnostic sentiments and ideas. Jesus is the familiar gnostic messenger, "not of this world," who is sent by his divine Father, the "son" sent by the heavenly King, to save lost souls corrupted by the material world and "raise up" the souls, return them to their divine home. "You are from below, I am from above, you are of this world, I am not of this world. . . . I came from the Father and have come into the world again, I am leaving the world and going to the Father." As for the sinful world, there is even the implication that its "ruler," "the prince of this world," is not God, an essential gnostic judgment.[21]

No less gnostic, and in this respect especially different from other Jewish apocalyptic texts, is the Gospels' carefree disregard for material needs and radical opposition to sexuality. Whereas the other Jewish apocalyptic works anticipate a material abundance for the saved in a redeemed earth, the Gospels tell us, "[D]o not be anxious about your life, what you shall eat or what you shall drink, nor about your body, what you shall put on. . . . Look at the birds of the air: they neither sow nor reap . . ." (Matthew 6:25–28). The spirit would be the life of the new Adam, not the body and its corruptions: "Do not labor for the food which perishes, but for the food which endures to eternal life. . . . I am the living bread which came down from heaven; if any one eats of this bread, he will live forever" (John 6:27 and 51). And if the bread of the spirit could supplant that of the body, the passion of the spirit could surely replace that of the flesh: "The sons of this age marry and are given in marriage; but those who are accounted worthy to obtain that world and the resurrection from the dead, neither marry, nor are given in marriage." Whatever the later compromises, the Gospels preferred "eunuchs who have made themselves eunuchs for the sake of the kingdom of heaven": "if your right eye causes you to sin, pluck it out and throw it away."

The contrast between the Gospels' gnostic focus on heaven and the spirit and the other Jewish apocalyptic texts' continuing attachment to matter and earth is assumed in Dante's commentary on some lines in Psalm 114: "When Israel went out of Egypt, the house of Jacob from a people of strange language; Judah was his sanctuary, and Israel his dominion." Following conventional medieval hermeneutics, the poet sees four levels of meaning in those lines.

> If we look to the letter only, what is conveyed to us is the deliverance of the children of Israel out of Egypt in the time of Moses; if we look to the allegory of it, what is signified is our redemption accomplished through Christ; if we consider the moral sense, what is signified is the conversion of the soul from her present grief and wretchedness to a state of grace; and if we consider the anagogical sense, what is signified is the passing of the sanctified soul from the bondage of earthly corruption to the freedom of everlasting glory.[22]

For traditional Judaism, apocalyptic as well as Biblical, the first level—freedom here on earth—is enough. Christians and Jews both celebrate the festival of rebirth-redemption in the spring of the year. The Easter redemption recalls the resurrection of Jesus and the promise of redemption for all true believers *from* earth, time, and death. Passover, too, signifies redemption—from slavery to freedom here *on* earth. The first offers solace in the hope of a better existence in *another* world. The second strengthens a determination to achieve a better life in *this* world. The transformation from the Judaic liberation to the Christian salvation is dramatically enacted at the last "passover" supper and in the new meaning of redemption that the Gospels give it.

Still, to recall again Dante's commentary, neither the Gospels nor early Christianity were concerned only with "the passing of the sanctified soul from the bondage of earthly corruption to the freedom of everlasting glory." That would be completely gnostic and too radically inconsistent with the Jewish roots of the new credo. In the theological and political conflicts fought in the first years of the Church, therefore, the Marcionites, Valentinians, and other gnostically oriented Christians were defeated by Irenaeus, Clement, Ignatius, Augustine, and others who insisted on Jesus' corporeality and, consequently, on his real suffering on the cross and who believed in the resurrections of the body as well as the soul. What the Gospels and their heritage wanted was a "new heaven *and* a new earth," both a liberation of the soul from the sinful material world back to the heavenly Father and the redemption of the fallen world. Revelation's vision of a thousand-year millennial kingdom on a redeemed earth before judgment and heavenly immortality may have been an attempt to accommodate both desires. But the dilemma and the tension remained. To resolve that dilemma, Christians would have to achieve, in and through matter (the Judaic heritage), the purity and perfection that the Gnostics sought by a radical rejection of matter. The ideal was a unity of matter and spirit: the Incarnation—pure, uncontaminated, virgin flesh.

It is here that we see the essential difference between the traditional Judaic vision, including the apocalyptic, and that of its Christian offspring. The Judaic vision accepts the body and its needs and satisfactions. We are to marry, be fruitful and multiply, and look forward to material abundance in the new earthly kingdom, while preserving the family through marital fidelity, maintaining peace, judging fairly, and helping those less fortunate. In the Gospel vision, we are told that heaven prefers "eunuchs," that we must not concern ourselves with material things, that we must not merely help the unfortunate but, in effect, live as they do, turning the other cheek if we are assaulted and responding to theft by giving more to the thief. Commenting on these ethics of the Gospels, one Christian theologian wrote:

> From every worldly point of view, this sermon is hopelessly utopian, visionary, and unrealistic, for it is indifferent to the demands of man's life in history.... In truth, it rests upon a

dissolution of man as a historical being, as a creature who is bound to the world.[23]

But what happens to these "hopelessly utopian, visionary, and unrealistic" demands if there is no "dissolution of man as a historical being"? The traditional Judaic ideals, even in their apocalyptic form, are far less extreme than those set forth in the Gospels. One may welcome, praise, and cherish that more demanding code. But what are the personal and political consequences of this maximalist, radical program of absolute purity and perfection? How is that gnostic purity, spiritualized body, Incarnation to be achieved? Part of the answer is apparent in two thousand years of varying degrees of Christian self-punishment. If the ideal of purity is embodied in the Incarnation, the means to its realization is symbolized in the Crucifixion, intense suffering for purity and salvation, the way down as the way up, the birth of the spiritual self through an assault on the physical self, martyrdom as victory. In the Gospel story, Incarnation precedes Crucifixion. In the living experience that it inspired, the relationship is reversed.

Basically, these concepts and attitudes represented a further stage in the ideological and psychological evolution that began in the ancient Hebrews' response to successive disasters. When, to recall the earlier argument, divine retribution shifted from other nations and their alien gods to the wayward Hebrews, the priests and prophets could only blame the sinful people themselves for their just suffering. In the logic that ensued, the suffering that was to have been a punishing lesson to inspire moral reform became, itself, a redemptive experience: through suffering, one paid the price for sin and thereby regained—redeemed—one's former innocence and divine blessing. Suffering, thus, became a good in itself, a process of constant purification and investment in Salvation.

Had all this involved only individuals it would not be relevant to the Apocalypse and its impact on our culture. But it did not. An essential feature of the Judaic tradition was its focus on the people, nation, society, and world as a whole. The people, not only the individual, suffered punishment and was saved. Consequently, the Christian dialectic leading through suffering to salvation, Crucifixion to Incarnation, came to be seen as the fate of society and the world, as well as that of the individual. The world, too, could be purified and its divine essence redeemed only through the pain of apocalyptic punishment. The sinful world must and would again suffer the cataclysmic devastation that God had promised, after the flood, never to unleash again. Nothing other than this violent miracle could magically purify flesh, transmute matter into spirit, achieve on earth the "hopelessly utopian, visionary, and unrealistic" ideals of gnostic purity and perfection.

In both the Judaic apocalyptic works from Daniel on and their Judeo-Christian Gospel offspring, this dialectic of despair was ideally suited to desperate times. With suffering everywhere and seemingly unavoidable, what could be more appealing than a worldview that turned that suffering into an assurance of salvation? And since the harsher the suffering the sooner the salvation, the worse became the better. This even reached the point of ennobling the sins that brought on the suffering, since without them there would have been no divine salvation. Since Adam's sin "has brought more benefit to us than harm," St. Ambrose (fourth century) argued, "sin is more fruitful than innocence." "Unless Adam had sinned," Pope Gregory the Great concurred a century later, "it would not have behooved our Redeemer to take on our flesh," and notwithstanding all that mankind had suffered as a result of the Fall, "who of the elect would not willingly endure still worse evils, rather than not have so great a Redeemer?" By the seventh century, and perhaps as early as the fifth, this fusion of sin and salvation had won a prominent place in the Easter Eve service of the Roman liturgy, in the words that bless the paschal candles: "O certe necessarium Adae peccatum, quod Christi morte deletum est! O felix culpa, quae talem ac tantum meruit habere redemptorem." The sin, the Fall, was not only "a happy fault," but a "surely necessary" one as well.

> O Goodness infinite, Goodness immense,
> That all this good of evil shall produce,
> And evil turn to good—more wonderful
> Than that which by creation first brought forth
> Light out of darkness! Full of doubt I stand,
> Whether I should repent me now of sin
> By me done or occasioned, or rejoice
> Much more that much more good thereof shall spring—
> To God more glory, more goodwill to men

From God—and over wrath grace shall abound.

(John Milton, 1667)[24]

Both the Hebrew Bible and the Christian Gospels have long been sources of solace and hope. They have inspired the finest sentiments and tempered the worst. Yet, both books have another side with quite different implications and effects. We have seen something of that other side of the Hebrew Bible and its contributions to apocalyptic violence. The contribution of the Gospels and their associated texts is no less, and perhaps more—first, because it was through Christianity that the Apocalypse became a part of our culture and, second, because of the gnostic radicalism within the Christian message, the maximalist ideals of a purity and perfection far more extreme than even the Jewish apocalyptic writers proclaimed. The more radical the goals, or, to recall Altizer's description, the more "hopelessly utopian, visionary, and unrealistic," the more purifying suffering it would take to realize them.

> The radical nature of the ethical demand of Jesus leaves no room for a positive attitude toward civic, political, and cultural responsibilities. And this is precisely because it is given in indifference to all these things. Guignebert succinctly states this truth: "The true inwardness of the gospel ethics can only be understood in the light of its essential relation to the Kingdom, whose coming will, in essence, liquidate humanity." . . . Its "dawning" presence has already liberated the believers from their enslavement to the world; its imminent consummation will issue in the absolute destruction of the world. . . . [Faith] is dedicated to the destruction of everything that man has become as a historical being within the world. . . . It is only by annihilating or reversing the reality of the world that religious man can realize his goal of union with the sacred.[25]

Since, as this study argues, the initial religious model of apocalyptic transmutation became the pattern and inspiration for the later secular-revolutionary versions, the consequences of that gnostic extremism should be self-evident. The purer the Incarnation, the more severe the Crucifixion, as violently enforced by the authoritarian "remnant" left in the wake of the successive apocalyptic upheavals.

The potential for such violence inherent in the original vision is most apparent in Revelation. Virtually the whole of that text is an account of the violence, devastation, suffering, and death necessary to purge the world and clear the way for the pure and perfect Kingdom. Wave after wave of horrendous suffering cascade down on the sinful world as the seals of secret scrolls are broken, trumpets sounded, bowls of divine wrath overturned, and the forces of the Apocalypse given "power over a fourth of the earth, to kill with sword and famine, by pestilence and wild beasts," then "to kill a third of mankind," as "men gnawed their tongues in agony" (Revelation 6:8, 9:15, 16:10). Nor is that enough: after the sinners have suffered their just punishments and the faithful remnant have received their just rewards in the Messiah's thousand-year "millennium," Satan is unleashed and the Gog-Magog Armageddon begun. Once again the masses of sinners who "swarmed over the breadth of the land, encircling the camp of God's people" (Revelation 20:9) must be annihilated, this time by fire sent down from heaven to consume them. Still, the well of suffering and vengeance is not empty: there is yet the Final Judgment.

> But as for the cowardly, the faithless, the polluted, as for murderers, fornicators, sorcerers, idolaters, and all liars, their lot shall be in the lake that burns with fire and brimstone, which is the second death. (Revelation 21:8)

It is all the will of God. An angel, not a demon, blows the trumpet to summon the "four angels . . . to kill a third of mankind." The "Lamb" himself is alone deemed pure and, thus, worthy enough to break the seals, begin the torment, and, at the End, lead the saintly hosts into the final battle, the "great supper of God."

> He is clad in a robe dipped in blood, and the name by which he is called is The Word of God. And the armies of heaven, arrayed in fine linen, white and pure, followed him on white horses. From his mouth issues a sharp sword with which to smite the nations, and he will rule them with a rod of iron; he will tread the wine press of the fury of the wrath of God the Almighty. On his robe and on his thigh he has a name inscribed, King of kings and Lord of lords.

Then I saw an angel standing in the sun, and with a loud voice he called to all the birds that fly in midheaven, "Come, gather for the great supper of God, to eat the flesh of kings, and flesh of captains, the flesh of mighty men, the flesh of horses and their riders, and the flesh of all men, both free and slave, both small and great." And I saw the beast and the kings of the earth with their armies gathered to make war against him who sits upon the horse and against his army. And the beast was captured, and with it the false prophet who in its presence had worked the signs by which he deceived those who had received the mark of the beast and those who worshiped its image. These two were thrown alive into the lake of fire that burns with brimstone. And the rest were slain by the sword of him who sits upon the horse, the sword that issues from his mouth; and all the birds were gorged with their flesh. (Revelation 19:13–21)

It is often assumed that such violence is found only in Revelation and that it contrasts radically with the Synoptic Gospels' message of tenderness, love, and forgiveness. Yet, while the tenderness, love, and forgiveness are indeed there and have inspired centuries of compassionate deeds, they are not the only message in the Gospels.

Do not think that I have come to bring peace on earth; I have not come to bring peace, but a sword. For I have come to set a man against his father, and a daughter against her mother, and a daughter-in-law against her mother-in-law; and man's foes will be those of his own household. . . . (Matthew 10:34–36)

So it will be at the close of the age. The angels will come out and separate the evil from the righteous, and throw them into the furnace of fire; there men will weep and gnash their teeth. (Matthew 13:49–50)

And when you hear of wars and rumors of wars, do not be alarmed; this must take place, but the end is not yet. For nation will rise against nation, and kingdom against kingdom; there will be earthquakes in various places, there will be famines; this is but the beginning of the sufferings. (Mark 13:7–8)

And brother will deliver up brother to death, and the father his child, and children will rise against parents and have them put to death. . . . (Mark 13:12)

"Even now the axe is laid to the root of the trees," John the Baptist warns the Pharisaic "brood of vipers"; "every tree therefore that does not bear good fruit is cut down and thrown into the fire." The Holy Spirit "will clear his threshing floor and gather his wheat into the granary, but the chaff he will burn with unquenchable fire" (Matthew 3:7, 10, 12). It would be difficult to surpass the violence and pain in that image of burning eternally, which seems to have been the favorite punishment for the "sinners," to judge by the number of times we find references to sinners "weeping and gnashing their teeth" in the flaming torment (see Matthew 8:12, 24:51, 25:30; Luke 13:28). "I came to cast fire upon the earth; and would that it were already kindled" (Luke 12:49); "If a man does not abide in me, he is cast forth as a branch and withers; and the branches are gathered, thrown into the fire and burned" (John 15:6). In addition to burning the chaff, the barren trees, and the withered branches, we find salt that has lost its taste "trodden under foot by men" (Matthew 5:13) and the destruction of tenants who have misused their rented vineyards (Mark 12:9).

The anger expressed against the money changers, in other words, seems more than a momentary lapse. "But as for these enemies of mine, who did not want me to reign over them, bring them here and slay them before me" (Luke 19:27); "whoever blasphemes against the Holy Spirit never has forgiveness, but is guilty of an eternal sin" (Mark 3:29); "the blood of all the prophets, shed from the foundations of the world, may be required of this generation" (Luke 11:50); "I tell you, it shall be more tolerable on that day for Sodom than for that town," which had rejected Jesus' disciples (Luke 10:12); "Woe to that man by whom the Son of man is betrayed! It would have been better for that man if he had not been born" (Mark 14:21).

Behind such rage against the world and the fervent desire to see it suffer and die lies radical alienation. As the world "hates me because I [Jesus] testify of it that its works are evil" (John 7:7), so must it hate all who follow Jesus: "Blessed are you when men hate you, and when they exclude you and revile you, and cast out your name as evil, on account of the Son of man!" (Luke 6:22). "If the world hates you, know that it has hated me before it hated you" (John 15:18–19). And the hated disciples must reciprocate, following Jesus in his root and branch rejection of the world. "If anyone comes to me and does not hate his own father and mother and wife and children and brothers and sisters, yes, and even his own life, he cannot be my disciple . . ." (Luke 14:26). "Truly, I say to you, there is no man who has left house or wife or brothers or parents or children, for the sake of the Kingdom of God, who will not receive manifold more in this time, and, in the age to come, eternal life" (Luke 18:29–30). When one would-be disciple decided to follow Jesus but asked, "Lord, let me first go and bury my father," Jesus answered, drawing the logical conclusion from those foregoing remarks about family ties, "Follow me, and leave the dead to bury their own dead" (Matthew 8:21–22). In sum, "he who hates his life in this world will keep it for eternal life" (John 12:25).

Denunciation of the existing world and its sinners as too corrupt for repair and their condemnation to total destruction is the first principle of apocalyptic theory and practice. The second is an absolute certainty that this just retribution and accompanying world transmutation are imminent.

"Repent, for the kingdom of heaven is at hand" (Matthew 3:2, 4:17, 10:7), "for truly, I say to you, you will not have gone through all the towns of Israel, before the Son of man comes" (Matthew 10:23); "Truly, I say to you, there are some standing here who will not taste death before they see the Son of man coming in his kingdom" (Mark 9:1); "Truly, I say to you all this will come upon this generation" (Matthew 23:36); "The time is fulfilled and the kingdom of God is at hand" (Mark 1:15). "Truly, I say to you this generation will not pass away till all these things take place" (Matthew 24:34–35); "Let your loins be girded and your lamps burning, and be like men who are waiting for their master to come home from the marriage feast, so that they may open to him at once when he comes and knocks" (Luke 12:35–36); "Do you not say, 'There are yet four months, then comes the harvest'? I tell you, lift up your eyes, and see how the fields are already white for harvest" (John 4:35); "Now is the judgment of this world, now shall the ruler of this world be cast out." (John 12:31)

With the old world annihilated, all things would be made new again. Rebirth, a new creation, ex nihilo, and this time the right way. The last would be first. The meek would inherit all. As for the rich, "woe to you that are rich, for you have received your consolation. Woe to you that are full now, for you shall hunger. Woe to you that laugh now, for you shall mourn and weep" (Luke 6:20–21, 24–25) and "be thrown into the outer darkness; there men will weep and gnash their teeth" (Matthew 8:12). But the new creation would go far beyond mere social transformation—all the way back to Eden.

Where was the force to make it all happen, when everything seemed so hopeless and all the good people so powerless? What or who could bring about the catastrophic upheavals that would lead the suffering faithful into their new heaven and new earth, make the last first, return them to innocent bliss, and plunge the faithless rich and mighty into pits of eternal fire? Only absolute certainty of deliverance for the pure and vengeance against those who had flourished in sin could inspire the ecstatic martyrdom and justify the sanctimonious cruelty that are the hallmarks of all apocalyptic upheavals. In later periods, the "laws" of Reason, History, and Nature would work that magic. Now, in the Apocalypse's first performance, it was divine miracle. It is to demonstrate this magical potency that miracles occupy center stage in the Gospel drama—the miraculous healings, the walk on water, the proliferating loaves and fish, the revival of the dead, the parables comparing the coming of the Kingdom to new birth from buried and decayed seeds, and, the ultimate proof toward which the drama as a whole irresistibly advances, the resurrection of Jesus himself. God and his Son can and will miraculously make all things new, novum ex nihilo, transmute torment and death into joy and eternal life.

The Apocalypse was now complete and ready to begin its long and violent career in our history. For, whether explicitly religious, as were the medieval and early modern messianic movements, or implicitly so, as were their secular revolutionary successors, all apocalyptic movements thereafter mirrored the original model. For all of them, the existing society is beyond repair, too corrupt for reforms and doomed to complete annihilation; for all of them, the coming Kingdom, the "new heaven and new earth," is beyond compare or criticism, purged of the sins of the old aeon; and for all of them, the transition between the two realms is beyond compassion, cataclysmically violent and unforgiving toward those condemned to "mourn and weep," "weep and gnash their teeth." Similarly, they all agree that those hoping to be saved and to enter the Kingdom must heed the message of the Savior Leader and his small band of disciples (the apostles, vanguard, cadre, party), since only the Leader and his disciples know the Truth and the Way, as revealed to them by the supreme power—God, Reason, History, or Nature, depending on the period. For none of them, moreover, are the Leader and his Truth in any way blemished by the catastrophic violence, since the "birth pangs" of the new order are not his choice, but, rather, the implacable decree of those same omnipotent forces—God, Reason, History, or Nature. As for the enemies in each case, they have not only been the reactionary Establishment, the Sadducees and Roman officials of the successive eras, but also the Pharisees, the moderate opposition, those compromising "hypocrites," whose lack of millennial zeal threatens to blur the line separating the pure and blessed new from the foul and accursed old and thereby forestall the catastrophe that will lead the faithful to paradise and their enemies to torment and death. Finally, the outcome has always been the exact opposite of that promised—not millennial liberation but authoritarian domination.

NOTES

1. *Bereshis: Genesis*, commentary anthologized from Talmudic, Midrashic, and Rabbinic sources, trans. Rabbi Meir Zlotowitz (New York: Mesorah Publications, 1977), 49.

2. Ibid., 59.

3. *Ben Sira* 3:21–23.

4. *Bereshis: Genesis*, 31.

5. Ibid., 80.

6. Nehama Leibowitz, *Studies in Bereshis (Genesis)*, trans. Aryeh Newman (Jerusalem: Alpha Press, 1981), 102–3.

7. Isaiah 2:4, 11:6–9, 19:25; Psalms, 46:9; Jonah 4:10–11; *Pentateuch*, Exodus, ed. J. H. Hertz (London: Soncino Press, 1962), 270.

8. *Bereshis: Genesis*, 35–45.

9. Ibid., 32, 88.

10. Ibid., 87–88.

11. See also, Jeremiah 47:10; Joel 14:7; Zephania 1:18; Malachi 3:19; Amos 5:18; Ezekiel 6:2–3.

12. "It was, we might say, a distinguishing characteristic of the Greek religion that it did not concern itself with the conscience at all" (G. Lowes Dickinson, *The Greek View of Life* [Ann Arbor: University of Michigan Press, 1958], 16; see also 27, 32–33, 66).

13. Ibid., 62–64; Hans Jonas, *The Gnostic Religion* (Boston: Beacon Press, 1963), 159; Thomas J. J. Altizer, *Oriental Mysticism and Biblical Eschatology* (Philadelphia: Westminster Press, 1961), 40.

14. El Chatibli of the Harranites, in Jonas, *Gnostic Religion*, 162 n. 15.

15. Elaine Pagels, *The Gnostic Gospels* (New York: Random House, 1979), xix.

16. Jonas, *Gnostic Religion*, 52, 56, 90–91, 158, 160.

17. Ibid., 56, 58–59.

18. Robert Henry Charles, ed., *The Apocrypha and Pseudepigrapha of the Old Testament* (Oxford: Clarendon Press, 1913), 2:194, 217, 569.

19. Ibid., 2:190.

20. Ibid., 2:195.

21. John 6:38, 8:23, 12:31, 16:28, 17:16, 18:36.

22. George Santayana, *Three Philosophical Poets* (Cambridge, Mass.: Harvard University Press, 1910), 105.

23. Altizer, *Oriental Mysticism*, 187.

24. For this and the foregoing quotations, see Arthur O. Lovejoy, "Milton and the Paradox of the Fortunate Fall," *Essays in the History of Ideas* (New York: George Braziller, 1955). Professor Lovejoy traces this theme, with appropriate quotations, during the thousand years of Christian history leading up to Milton's remarks.

25. Altizer, *Oriental Mysticism*, 95, 111–12, 160–61, 162.

2

Apocalypse and God: Medieval Practice

The Apocalypse is a self-fulfilling prophecy. It promotes the suffering it predicts. Those who believed Jesus was the Messiah suffered persecution, martyrdom, and, no doubt, crushing disappointment when their savior did not return. The sinful world went on as before, and the believers had to live in it. Nor was the suffering limited to believing Christians. Hellenistic Jewry included many who had rejected Jesus as a divine messiah but who shared the apocalyptic fervor and, as "zealots," were convinced that if they began the uneven struggle against the Roman forces, God would complete it for them, destroy the idol worshippers, and establish the Kingdom of God on the ruins of the pagan empire. The results included a series of brutal defeats, the destruction of the Second Temple, and the expulsion of the Jewish people and near eradication of their culture from the Land of Israel.

Since the apocalyptic promise of immediate and total transmutation of the world had failed to materialize, Christians turned for solace and hope to the other side of their Gnostic-Judaic heritage and adopted the characteristically Gnostic posture of being "in" but not "of" this fallen world of flesh and sin, trapped in an alien realm until either death freed their souls or Jesus returned to establish the millennial Kingdom. It was as Gnostics that Christian hermits flocked to the desert by the thousands to await the End as anchorites in isolation, silence, prayer, and contemplation, proving their merit by spiritual feats of heroic deprivation. Since everything material, particularly the body and all that served the needs of the flesh, belonged not to God but to the demonic "ruler of this world," the heroes of the faith were those who were most repelled by such needs. Total chastity of body and mind, minimal food and sleep, the most severe physical hardships—such were the signs of the genuine spiritual athlete. So the Byzantine Emperor sought advice from Simeon Stylites, revered for his thirty years on a pillar; Saint Anthony was embarrassed to be seen eating; and Methodius Symposium considered virginity true martyrdom and the surest way back to paradise.[1]

It was still as Jews rather than Gnostics, however, that Christians officially rejected Docetism, the belief that Jesus was pure spirit and only appeared to have a body and to suffer physically. It was as Jews that they insisted on physical as well as spiritual resurrection and that they continued to sanctify marriage and children, notwithstanding the Gospels' Gnostic preference for "eunuchs." When Paul warned against the lures of the flesh and preached that one no longer need follow the traditional Jewish Law, that faith, not works, would assure salvation, he was reflecting the gnostic spirit (with faith replacing gnosis/knowledge). But the very nature of his missionary and organizational efforts expressed a quite different attitude and aim, that of establishing a church for this world—a world that was supposedly near its end ("the appointed time has grown very short. . . . For the form of this world is passing away" [1 Corinthians 7:29–31]). We find a similar ambivalence in the core apocalyptic Christian text, Revelation; whereas the work itself is entirely devoted to a description of the apocalyptic catastrophe that will soon destroy the old world and initiate the new, it begins with a series of letters sent by John to other officials of the nascent church to reprimand their deviations from organizational orthodoxy, an issue that should not have been so crucial if the End were at hand.

Among the most stunning examples of the persistent gnostic alienation inherent in early Christendom are those found in Augustine's works. For a time a convinced neo-Platonist, Augustine later turned fiercely against such views, particularly as expressed by the Gnostics. Nevertheless, much of what he wrote was filled with neo-Platonist and Gnostic renunciations and denunciations of the material world of flesh and corruption as vehement as those that Simon Magus, Marcion, Valentinus, and other Gnostics and Manicheans had published.

> . . . a darksome pool . . . [of] heartaches, troubles, griefs, and fears; such insane joys in discord, strife, and wars; such wrath and plots of enemies, deceivers, sycophants; such fraud and theft and robbery; such perfidy and pride, envy and ambition, homicide and murder, cruelty and savagery, lawlessness and

lust; all the shameless passions of the impure—fornication and adultery, incest and unnatural sins, rape and countless other uncleanlinesses too nasty to be mentioned; the sins of religion—sacrilege and heresy, blasphemy and perjury; the iniquities against our neighbors—calumnies and cheating, lies and false witness, violence to persons and property; the injustices of the courts and the innumerable other miseries and maladies that fill the world, yet escape attention. . . . Who can be free from fear or grief in a world of mourning and bereavement, of losses and legal penalties, of liars and deceivers, of the false imputations, violences and other wickednesses of our neighbors . . . of the tragedies of being robbed or reduced to slavery, of bonds and prison walls, of banishment and torture, of limbs cut off and eyes torn out, of bodies made to minister to an oppressor's lusts, and of all other no less dreadful possibilities. . . . And think of the dread we have of the countless accidents of nature, of the extremes of heat and cold, of winds and rains and floods, of thunder, lightning and winter storms, of earthquakes, landslides . . . of poisoned fruits and waters, of pestilential air . . . of the bites of wild animals.[2]

Yet, to balance this despair of anything good in the material world, there are equally forceful expressions, among early Christian leaders, of the kind of materialistic optimism that characterized the Jewish apocalyptic pronouncements. For example, Iranaeus, a second century Bishop of Lyons and major critic of Gnosticism, made the following statement.

The days will come in which vines shall grow, each having ten thousand branches and in each branch ten thousand twigs, and in each twig ten thousand shoots, and in each one of the shoots ten thousand clusters, and on every one of the clusters ten thousand grapes, and every grape when pressed will give five and twenty measures of wine. And when any one of the saints shall lay hold of a cluster, another shall cry out "I am a better cluster, take me; bless the Lord through me." In like manner [the Lord declared] that a grain of wheat would produce ten thousand ears, and that every ear should have ten thousand grains, and every grain would yield ten pounds of clear, pure fine flour.[3]

Lactantius, in his *Divine Institutes*, said: "The earth will open its fruit-fulness, and bring forth most abundant fruits of its own accord; the rocky mountains shall drop with honey; streams of wine shall run down, and rivers flow with the milk."[4]

This essentially Judaic expectation of an earthly material paradise was no match, however, for gnostic pessimism and spiritual purism, especially given the continuing delay of the Second Coming. In time, an Augustinian resignation, along with the neo-Platonist and gnostic alienation that fed it, prevailed throughout Christendom. Original and continuing sin condemned humanity to this vale of pain, and the best the good Christian could do was to suffer it patiently, draw comfort and guidance from the sacramental life provided by Christ's temporal vicar, the Mother Church, and await the promised bliss in the next world. Disappointed in their hope that faith in Jesus would carry them now out of this sordid and painful world and into a divine kingdom of eternal bliss, Christians turned that faith itself into a Kingdom of God within and the Church into an island of grace, the home of the saved remnant in a world of *Two Cities*.

> In regard to mankind I have made a division . . . those who live according to man . . . those who live according to God. And . . . in a deeper sense, we may speak of two cities or two human socie-ties, the destiny of the one being an eternal kingdom under God, while the doom of the other is eternal punishment along with the Devil.[5]

To live in the City of God meant to live the sacramental Christian life and thereby prepare oneself for the life to come. As for the social, economic, and political world outside—that was as God decreed it to be and, in any case, adequate for living according to God and his temporal Church.

> [T]he peace of mortal man and God is the well-ordered obedi-ence of living in faith under the eternal law; the peace of men is well-ordered concord; the peace of the home is the well-ordered concord of its residents, in giving commands and in obeying them; the peace of the city consists in the well-ordered concord of the citizens, both commanding and obeying. . . .[6]

When life ended, this resigned acceptance would be more than amply rewarded; for in heaven, "we shall rest and see, see and love, love and praise. This is the end without end. For what other end do we propose to our lives than to attain to the kingdom of which there is no end?"[7]

Paradoxically, the gnostic alienation and detachment that determined the mood and outlook of medieval Christianity accompanied a constant expansion of the Church's temporal power and wealth. As the heir to the Roman Empire, the Church emerged as the ruler of a massive, dedicated, and rigorously disciplined organization unrivaled by any secular power. And having acquired such immense temporal power, if only by default, the Church was understandably critical of apocalyptic sentiments that could disturb the smooth operation of its organization or question the legitimacy, power, or wealth of its directors.

For the Jews, the paradox was the opposite. The apocalyptic era and its aftermath had left them powerless and oppressed. The world could hardly be less congenial for them. Yet the lesson they learned from the disaster was the wisdom of the pre-Hellenistic ideals that had committed Jews hopefully and patiently to this world. If Christians grew more and more powerful in a world they despised, the Jews returned to, and rededicated themselves to, a world that despised them. Tradition marks the beginning of this return and renewal with a decision by one Rabbi Yohanan ben Zakkai to leave besieged Jerusalem on the eve of its destruction, move to Yavne near the coast, and establish a school there. With the destruction of the Second Temple, Yavne was to develop rapidly into a principal center of Jewish learning and the site of the codification of the Law. Just at the time when other Jews, overwhelmed by this final blow (the destruction of the Temple), were beginning to write the Gospel story of a Messiah who had come to reward the pure with Paradise and avenge their unjust suffering with eternal damnation for their tormentors, the Jews of Yavne began to lay the foundations for the Talmud, the "teaching," that was to guide the people toward the good society in this world.

"God revealed this world, not the world to come," as Yohanan ben Zakkai put it, and it was with the same focus on this world that he forbade his students to discuss mystical writings (such as "Work of Creation," and "Work of the Chariot") that were generally associated with apocalyptic visions and expectations. The destruction of the Temple did not mean the end of the world: "My son, be not grieved," Rabbi Yohanan said to Rabbi Joshua, consoling him after the destruction. "We have a means of atonement that is equal [to Temple sacrifices], namely the practice of benevolence, as it is said 'For I desire lovingkindness and not sacrifice.'" In sum, "all his life Rabban Yohanan ben Zakkai occupied himself with making enactments, with laying foundations for the national institutions, and with inculcating Torah and precepts and ideals that would improve the life of the individual and the community," improve, that is, the life lived here on earth and in time.[8]

As one would expect, given the authorship and general circumstances surrounding the composition of the Talmud, much of this "teaching" deals with religious concerns—regulating services and rituals, specifying tithes, providing instructions for holy days (especially the Sabbath), and so forth. But no less attention is given to ordinary civil and criminal law involving the daily life of the community—questions of marriage, contracts, divorce, property rights, damage compensations, land transfers, employee rights, trial procedures and punishments, a vast amount of ethical guidance, and advice on such prosaic concerns as diet, medical treatment, and the like. The guide is written for people as they are, limited human beings, with inclinations toward evil as well as toward good. Taken as a whole, it is a vastly ambitious attempt to provide ordinary humanity with specific examples for living in peace and justice while engaging in the countless human interactions that comprise actual social existence. It is, thus, a guide for the "repair of the world," for the continuing work of creating the good society. In the vision of medieval Jewish mystics, the divine "sparks," "trapped" in the material world, are to be redeemed, not by removing them (gnostically) from that world and returning them to their spiritual home, but by using the sparks present in each and every segment of physical and social reality to inspire and direct the "repair" of that reality, transform it gradually toward the fulfillment of the Prophetic ideals. The sage Hillel once said that the core of Judaism was the belief that one must not do to another what one would not want done to oneself and that all the rest was commentary: the Talmud and the many related works that followed together represent that commentary—one long, arduous effort to find ways to turn glowing ideals into specific guidance for human beings as they are, living in this world as it is.

And that old world would be around for a long time. Talmudic sages saw no messiah on the horizon. Had there been messianic expectations, there would have been no need to spend a century codifying the laws and further centuries on commentaries advising the community how to apply them. Usually, in fact, the rabbis are vigorously explicit in their rejection of messianism. They had learned their costly lesson and were determined to spare their people any repetitions.

> If you are planting a tree and someone comes and says, "the Messiah is coming!" go on planting. . . . Grass will grow in your cheeks and the son of David will still not have come. . . . Whoever gives his mind to four things, it is better for him if he had not come into the world—what is above, what is beneath, what was beforetime, and what will be hereafter. . . . You will certainly not want to hasten more than the Creator. . . . All the predestined dates have passed, and the matter depends only on repentence and good deeds. . . . Blasted be the bones of those who calculate the end. . . . He who announces the messianic time based on calculation forfeits his own share in the future. . . . Israel will have no Messiah, for he has already been vouchsafed to them in the days of Hezekiah.[9]

Repeatedly through the centuries, the rabbis taught the community "not to press the End." Be wary, they warned, of the mystical fantasies that often blossomed from fervent piety: "As Moses and Aaron discovered quite early, the closer one is to *kedusha* ['holiness'], the greater the danger of the disciples who follow you introducing 'strange fire' . . . that the Lord had not commanded." The Torah was given in the first place, according to one of the sages, not to enflame passions, but to calm them: "Why was the Torah given to Israel? Because they are fierce. . . . The Torah was given to them so that by occupying themselves with it their fierceness would be lessened and their hearts softened."[10]

One way of opposing apocalyptic messianism was to demystify it, to return it, in effect, to the original temporal and political meaning it had in the Hebrew Bible. "There is no difference between this world and the days of the Messiah except bondage to foreign powers," except, that is, the return of the Jews to their homeland after their long "exile."[11] Maimonides said this in a similar manner.

> The Messiah will arise and restore the kingdom of David to its former might. He will rebuild the sanctuary and gather the dispersed of Israel. Do not think that the Messiah needs to perform signs and miracles, bring about a new state of things in the world, revive the dead, and the like. It is not so. . . . Let no one think that in the days of the Messiah anything of the natural course of the world will cease or that any innovation will be introduced into creation. Rather, the world will continue in its accustomed course.[12]

Perhaps the most telling evidence for this antipathy toward apocalyptic messianism is the absence of any explicit reference in the Talmud to the Jewish apocalyptic writings that comprised so much of Jewish literature in the pre-Talmudic Hellenistic era, even though the Talmudic sages clearly show their familiarity with those works.[13]

But the rabbis' battle against apocalyptic messianism did not go unchallenged. The urge toward millennial extremism remained strong, especially as the hope for more moderate, political redemption went unrealized. Consequently, notwithstanding the severe warnings against messianic claims and calculations, there are also, in the Talmud, examples of apocalyptic messianism clearly reminiscent of the suppressed Hellenistic apocalyptic prophecies.

> After four thousand two hundred and ninety-one years after the creation of the world, the world will be orphaned. [Of the subsequent years] some will be marked by wars of the sea monsters, some by the wars of Gog and Magog, and the remainder will constitute the Days of the Messiah, and the Holy One, blessed be He, will renew His world only after seven thousand years.[14]

> In the last days false prophets and corruptors will multiply and sheep will be turned into wolves, love into hatred; lawlessness will prevail, causing men to hate, persecute, and deliver up each other; and Satan, the "world-deceiver," will in the guise of the

Son of God perform miracles, and as ruler of the earth commit unheard of crimes.[15]

In the footsteps of the Messiah presumption will increase and respect disappear. The empire will turn to heresy and there will be no moral reproof. The house of assembly will become a brothel, Galilee will be laid waste, and the people of the frontiers will wander from city to city and none will pity them. The wisdom of the scribes will become odious and those who shun sin will be despised; truth will nowhere be found. Boys will shame old men and old men will show deference to boys. "The son reviles the father, the daughter rises up against the mother . . . a man's enemies are the men of his own house" [Micah 7:6]. The face of the generation is like the face of a dog [i.e., brazenness will reign]. On whom shall we then rely? On our Father in heaven.[16]

In distinguishing between the messianism that occasionally reappears in the Talmud and the predominant Talmudic opposition to it, one characteristic should be kept in mind. Even in messianic prophecy, the focus remains temporal: the Kingdom to be established on earth was to begin with a clearly political event that formed the core of Jewish messianism in general—the return to the Jewish homeland, the Land of Israel. From the Biblical Exodus to modern Zionism, Jewish messianism has preserved this emphatic "realism," in the sense of a temporal, as against a supernatural, aim. The goal of repossessing this specific geographic territory promised by God to Abraham and his heirs further strengthened the attachment to the world already reflected in the Biblical ideal of achieving a future good society on earth through human moral progress. If the Zionist leader, Herzl, was shocked that some of his followers should regard him as their "messiah," it was because he had forgotten that, for Jews, the messiah was, from the beginning, someone proclaiming and leading precisely the kind of political "redemption" that he had organized. Even Persian King Cyrus had been called a messiah for permitting the Jews to return to Jerusalem after their Babylonian exile.

This experience of national "exile" thus helped keep "redemption" down to earth, literally. It reaffirmed everything that Jews had said and felt for centuries about the first Exodus from slavery to freedom. That central Biblical story and its constant echoes in Talmudic studies, daily prayers, and seasonal celebrations, and the hardships borne in "diaspora" combined to guarantee the continuing force of that memory and of the yearning for another redemption back to the land promised to Abraham, Isaac, Jacob, and their descendants. Had that memory not been so insistently present and its example so emphatically relevant to those undergoing this third exile (after Egypt and Babylon), and had there not been this concrete, earthly "Zion" as a focus for the "redemption," it is likely that the prolonged suffering of medieval Jews would have made them completely "otherworldly."

Even as it was, they absorbed many Christian "gnostic" attitudes, especially with respect to devaluing temporal life as merely a preparatory path into the next world. As a result, the doctrinal differences between Christians and Jews narrowed. Both had their laws—sacraments or commandments—sanctified by the same God and administered by revered clerics. Both awaited the Messiah's first or second coming. And while the Jews now also gave much more attention to the next world and included in their liturgy references to a "revival of the dead," Christians, condemned to remain in this fallen world, had little choice but to learn to live with it.

Fundamental differences remained, however, and were dramatically demonstrated at the close of that era, when social routine and stability were once again undermined by radical changes and apocalyptic reactions to them. The collapse of familiar routines, the challenge of new ways of living and thinking associated with the emerging Renaissance culture, the loss of emotional supports provided by the traditional village communities and extended families formed through generations—all of this, coming so soon after an unprecedented natural disaster, the Black Death that wiped out a third of the population, sent desperate people again, as earlier chaos and suffering had sent Hellenistic victims, in search of millennial salvation.

Could all that disruption and its concomitant distress mean anything other than the long expected final outburst of demonic evil before the End? The conclusive testimony that these were, indeed, the Last Days was the fact that the traditional sanctuary, the rock to which Jesus had told the people to cling while awaiting his return, the Mother Church herself, had been corrupted by its earthly treasures of power and wealth, seduced by the demonic "ruler of this world." "The corrupt manners of the whole Popish clergie crie out that there is none other chief Antichrist to come than he that is come alreadie in the Roman Bishope." Rather than provide the world a solution to its problems, the Church itself seemed to many the core of the problem. The "Antichrist" Pope, the "whore of Babylon," along with "the mitered bishops of his beastlie kingdom and their great bellied monks and priests" found themselves facing much the same opposition that the Sadducee Jewish Establishment had confronted during the first onslaught of Jewish-Christian apocalyptic zeal.[17] And the response to what was perceived to be a sinfully rich, powerful, legalistic, distant, and impersonal Church was essentially the same as well. Within the Church, and increasingly outside of it, a passion for purity and piety swept the communities of the faithful—arduous pilgrimages, rigorous asceticism, a fascination with the power of relics, new cults of saints, a well-nigh universal veneration for the Virgin Mary, a flurry of construction of great cathedrals as acts of communal devotion. The monasteries, especially, were subject to enthusiastic purification movements enforcing fulfillment of the old vows, adding new and more stringent deprivations, and, in general, changing the monasteries from the wealthy centers of largely secular interests (law, medicine, and philosophy) some of them had become, back to communities of poverty, simplicity, obedience, and rigorous physical labor.

The Church was able to direct most of this renewed devotion into channels that served rather than undermined its authority. But two expressions of the fervent piety were more difficult to contain—a burgeoning mysticism and a revived Apocalypse. Since the mystics claimed direct access to God by way of their own souls and private spiritual exercises, they had less need, if any, for the Church's intervention. As for the renewed Apocalypse, since a principal function of the Church had been to fill the gap left by the delay in Jesus' Second Coming, the apocalyptic prophets who proclaimed that the delay was over were at the same time announcing the end of the Church's tenure. In effect, the two together represented a return to the dual source of Christianity: the mystics revived the Platonic-Gnostic assumption that the divine soul in each human reflected the one divine, transcendent spirit and that each soul, if guided by right knowledge (*gnosis*) and practice, could return to God even in life; while the new apocalyptic prophets expressed again the faith in an immediate and miraculous transmutation of the world that had initially given rise to the first Jewish-Christian apocalyptic sects.

Of the two, the mystics were the less dangerous to the Church, for they were concerned mainly with their own personal salvation and were never very numerous. The apocalyptic prophets, on the contrary, appealed to whole communities and were extraordinarily successful in those appeals. This distinction between the mystic and the apocalyptic prophet should not be overstated, however, since the two were closely related: the ideas of the mystics, as we will see, generated some of the most extreme excesses of the apocalyptic communities. In fact, the two were then, as they had been at the outset of the Christian era and would be again and again in later centuries, contrasting poles of the same radical alienation. No longer able to bear reality, the suffering soul responded with either the "all" of total, apocalyptic destruction and transmutation of the world or the "nothing" of total gnostic-mystical withdrawal and detachment from the world. The same revolutionary "all" and solipsistic "nothing" have guided disenchanted critics of our culture and society ever since, some shifting from one pole to the other, from a passive, detached contemplation of the ideal within oneself to an apocalyptic-revolutionary struggle to realize the ideal in the world outside. In both cases, what had to be avoided at all costs was the flawed reality in the middle.

Also, although the mystics' gentle and lofty thoughts and sentiments seem so distant from apocalyptic rage, the conviction that one is thoroughly infused with ultimate Truth easily leads to the equally strong conviction that everything one does, however violent, mirrors the will of that Truth. Moreover, while hardly universal, the psychological association linking asexual "purity" and sanctimonious cruelty is by now among the most familiar relationships in intellectual and political history. The message and mood of mystics such as the thirteenth-century Meister Eckhart and those of the later romantics and philosophical "idealists," therefore, may be as central to this argument as are the explicitly violent theory and practice of the apocalyptic revolutionaries, religious and secular.

The first step in this voyage inward and upward—and then, for some, violently outward—is withdrawal from conventional social reality. Meister Eckhart speaks for all who take this step when, echoing the Gnostics and anticipating the later romantics and philosophical "idealists," he prescribes the prerequisites for this detachment.

> I have earnestly and with all diligence sought the best and the highest virtue whereby man may come most like the original image as he was in God when there was yet no distinction between God and himself before God produced creatures. And having dived into the basis of things to the best of my ability I find that it is not other than absolute detachment from everything that is created. It was in this sense that our Lord said to Martha: "One thing is needed," which is to say: He who would be untouched and pure needs just one thing, detachment.

> Perfect detachment is without regard, without either lowliness or loftiness to creatures; it is minded to be master of itself, loving none and hating none, having neither likeness nor unlikeness, neither this nor that, to any creature; the only thing it desires to be is to be one and the same. For to be either this or that is to want something. He who is this or that is somebody; but detachment wants altogether nothing. It leaves all things unmolested.

Once detached and free, "the soul turns back upon itself and finds itself," and at the same time "is able to see God face to face in his own self." Eckhart drew more audacious conclusions than even the neo-Platonists and Gnostics had drawn from this assumption of affinity between the soul and God: he made the two identical. "The eye wherein I see God is the same eye wherein God sees me: my eye and God's eye are one eye, one vision, one knowing, one love." "I say, God must be very I, I very God, so consummately one that this he and this I are one is. . . ." The basic theme in Eckhart is what it had been for the Gnostics: withdrawal from the world and return of the soul to its true divine home, "wherein he may once more become like the original image as he was in God when there was yet no distinction between God and himself before God produced creatures." Eckhart made the deeper personal need involved in this inward withdrawal and merger with God remarkably apparent.

> Back in the womb from which I came, I had no God and merely was, myself. I did not will or desire anything, for I was pure

being, a knower of myself by divine truth. The I wanted myself and nothing else. And what I wanted was, and what I was I wanted, and thus I existed untrammeled by God or anything else. But when I parted from my free will and received my created being then I had a God. For before there were creatures, God was not God, but rather he was what he was. When creatures came to be and took on creaturely being, then God was no longer God as he is in himself, but God as he is with creatures.[18]

The soul thus touched, or, as Eckhart put it, "kissed" by God, could at once intuit the deepest hidden truths of Scripture: one need no longer trouble oneself with lesser interpretations—literary, allegorical, and moral—but leap at once to the anagogic, the mystical understanding that inspired prophecy and revealed the divine kingdom.

About the time that Eckhart was preaching in Saxony, a book called *Little Flowers* appeared in Italy with a similar message. The volume was a hagiography of St. Francis of Assisi, who had lived a generation earlier. It, too, combined the boundless joy of mystical inner union with God and an equally euphoric adoration of the outer world of nature, the world of the Gospel's lilies and birds, uncontaminated by human sin. By detaching oneself totally from society and its material hopes and desires, by giving up all worldly goods and trusting entirely to God for one's basic needs (as did the rest of nature), by abandoning even the monastic roof over one's head to wander freely in nature preaching the Gospel, one could return to the innocence of Eden. While St. Francis's insistent anti-intellectualism and penchant for suffering and martyrdom differentiated him from Eckhart, the two shared the same general vision and influence: bliss now, a realized eschatology in life through mystical union, directly in and through the soul and/or indirectly through merger with God's world of nature.

For St. Theresa of Avila as well, the mystical route to salvation was a spiritual inward and upward voyage, through successive "mansions" into an "interior castle" where one could leave one's body and see, hear, and merge with God. Whatever the special characteristics of one or another mystic, they all shared an apophantic theology, a theology of intuition and feeling rather than knowledge and doctrine. The title of the fourteenth-century mystical classic,

Cloud of Unknowing, tells the essential story. Only if one first forgot what one knew in life and from that "Cloud of Forgetting" ascended to the "Cloud of Unknowing" could one hope for the grace of revelation and bliss.

The Church, understandably, found much of this most disconcerting and dangerous, even though Eckhart was an exemplary Dominican and chief administrator of the order in Saxony, St. Francis a loyal and respectful son of the Church, and St. Theresa a brilliant Carmelite organizer. But, while all three were themselves unquestionably obedient to the hierarchy, their message opened the way for radical disobedience or worse. If one could fully and directly commune with God, intuitively understand the hidden meanings of the Scriptures, and attain grace, bliss, and even eternal salvation in this life all by oneself, what need was there for the Church? Similarly, however popular and inspiring St. Francis's pantheistic nature hymns became for later romantics, they were a clear threat to the Church, and for the same reason: if one could find God everywhere in nature, why bother with ecclesiastic intermediaries?

Still, however threatening these implications were for the Church, the actual danger was limited as long as the mystics kept their revelations to themselves or to a small following and remained as loyal to the establishment as were the Dominican Eckhart, Francis and his Franciscans, and the Carmelite Theresa. When, after Eckhart's death, a Papal Bull was issued against him and his views, it was because those views had been adopted by movements, that, unlike earlier monastic revivals, not only openly rebelled against Rome, but had come to see the Papacy itself as the leader of a demonic world that would soon be annihilated in the apocalyptic upheaval. Rather than take the Gnostic and neo-Platonist path to salvation through inner withdrawal and union, as Eckhart and St. Theresa had done, these later true believers once again, as had the first Jewish-Christians, put their hope and faith for redemption in immediate world transmutation.

And this time, they did more than wait and pray. If the first, the Hellenistic Jewish-Christian, Apocalypse had established the theory, the apocalyptic movements that accompanied and responded to the demise of the medieval world translated that theory into violent practice. Of all the expressions of confusion, fear, and fervor that characterized the tumultuous transition from the medieval to the modern world, these apocalyptic outbreaks are the most relevant to our theme—first, because they embodied and revived the assumptions and expectations of the initial Judeo-Christian Apocalypse; and, second, because these late medieval fundamentalist revival movements paradoxically modernized the Apocalypse to fit the later secular-revolutionary era, both by their extreme violence and by their emphasis on Biblical and Gospel social and economic ideals.

The fact that these apocalyptic movements—and the first modern social-revolutionary explosions—were guided by the earlier religious model is obvious from the claims made by and about the would-be messiahs. They all proclaimed themselves divine incarnations who had come bearing God's truth; they all announced the beginning of the millennium; and they all proved their divine origins by their talent for miracles and their capacity for suffering. Eudo de Stella, Tanchelm of Antwerp, Peter the Hermit from Amiens, Fulk of Neuilly, the mendicant hermit crowned Count of Flanders, Jacob the Master of Hungary, Domenico Savi of Ascoli, the flagellant messiah Konrad Schmid, Loy Pruystnick of Antwerp, the mystic Heinrich Suso, Nicholas of Basel, the brothers Janko and Livin of Wirsberg, Hans Bohm and other leaders of the Bohemian Taborites, the peasant messiah Joss Fritz and his Bundschuh movement, Thomas Muntzer, the leaders of the Anabaptist New Jerusalem of Munster, and on and on—all claimed to be the long-awaited Savior, sent by God to save his children from the demons of this sinful world and lead them into the divine Kingdom, latter-day gnostic messengers sent by the heavenly Father to retrieve divine souls from the demiurgic Archons.

The mystics had laid the groundwork by dismantling the barriers that Augustine, among others, had raised against the belief that one could attain to God, merge one's soul with his, and lose one's person totally in God even in this life. The messianic true believer simply took the next step: by becoming one with and in God, he would be God, the second Incarnation for this Second Coming.[19]

> The perfect man is God. . . . The perfect man is more than a created being. . . . He has attained that most Intimate union which Christ had with the Father. . . . He is God and man. . . . Rejoice with me, I have become God! . . . I am made eternal in my eternal blessedness. Christ has made me his equal and I can never lose that condition. . . . When a man has truly reached the great and

high knowledge he is no longer bound to observe any law or command, for he has become one with God. . . . This soul has no will but the will of God, who makes it will what it ought to will. . . . It is the same with me as with Christ in every way and without any exception. Just like him, I am eternal life and wisdom, born of the Father in my divine nature; just like him, too, I am born in time and after the way of human beings; and so I am one with him, God and man. All that God has given him he has given me, too, and to the same extent. (Brethren of the Free Spirits, *Schwester Katrei*, Marguerite Porete, Jan van Ruusbroec.)

One can readily imagine the likely consequences should those holding such views become socially and politically active, leave their celibate monastic cells and Platonic-gnostic-mystic inner sanctuaries, and go out into the world to destroy the demonic forces and institutions in order to build the promised Kingdom of God on the ruins. It was the second time that neo-Platonist/gnostic purity and perfection merged with the Judaic (Hellenistic) apocalyptic vision. For a thousand years, the Church had blocked the disruptive consequences of the first merger by reserving union with God for the afterlife and the "new heaven and new earth" for the distant Second Coming. The results of the merger were as disastrous in the late medieval centuries as they were to be repeatedly in modern times, and for the same reasons: (1) the leaders claimed a monopoly on absolute truth—from God in the late medieval apocalyptic upheavals, from Reason, History, and Nature in the modern era; (2) they set as their goal the establishment on earth of a pure and perfect millennial society, with blueprints decreed by God, (Reason, History, or Nature); and (3) they adopted brutally violent means in their crusades to purify the evil world and justified the violence by appealing to God's will (or to Reason, History, or Nature). Since the mystics had shown how the true believer could become one with God (or privy to the "objective" laws of Reason, History, or Nature), whatever that true believer considered necessary, however costly in destruction and suffering, was what God (Reason, History, or Nature) considered necessary. If one massacred whole communities, one did so not because of one's own finite and fallible mind, will, or need, but because of God's infinite will and purpose. One of the earliest groups to demonstrate these implications of the *unio mystica,* the mystical union with God, was the fourteenth-century Brethren of Free Spirits.

> Where does your insight lead to? Into untrammelled freedom. Tell me, what do you call untrammelled freedom? When a man lives according to all his caprices without distinguishing between God and himself, and without looking before or after. . . . (Suso of Cologne)

> The truly free man is king and lord of all creatures. All things belong to him, and he has the right to use whatever pleases him. If anyone tries to prevent him, the free man may kill him and take his goods. (Johann Hartmann)

> It would be better that the whole world should be destroyed and perish utterly than that a "free man" should refrain from one act to which his nature moves him. (Brethren of the Free Spirits)

Besides drawing their claims to divine truth and messianic leadership from the first Judeo-Christian Apocalypse, these late medieval apocalyptic saviors derived their assurance of victory from its dialectics of suffering. For them, too, victory was guaranteed not because they were so strong, but because they were so weak: they suffered so gravely that God would surely descend to help them destroy their evil enemies. Both personal and social salvation followed this dialectical route from suffering to bliss. Just as austere asceticism and final martyrdom purged the individual of sin and assured him personal salvation, so must a particular town or region or the entire world suffer to purge itself of its corruptions. And just as one was, therefore, justified in punishing oneself through self-flagellation in order to be personally pure and saved, so must one be prepared to make others "weep and gnash their teeth" in order to purify and save them and thereby establish the Kingdom.

> Accursed be the man who withholds his sword from shedding the blood of the enemies of Christ. Every believer must wash his hands in that blood . . . every priest may lawfully pursue, wound and kill sinners. . . . The just . . . will now rejoice seeing vengeance, and washing their hands in the blood of the sin-

ner. . . . Whoever strikes a wicked man for his evil doing, for instance for blasphemy—if he beats him to death he shall be called a servant of God; for everyone is duty bound to punish wickedness. (John Capek, Peter Chelcicky, *Book of a Hundred Chapters*)

To the Taborites of Bohemia, the establishment of a regional community of saints by such methods was only the beginning, since they considered themselves "the army sent through all the world to carry the plagues of vengeance and to inflict revenge upon the nations and their cities and towns, and judgment upon every people that shall resist them. Thereafter 'kings shall serve them, and any nation that will not serve them shall be destroyed.'" As Thomas Muntzer put it, "Harvest time is here, so God himself has hired me for this harvest. I have sharpened my scythe"; or, as he said at greater length elsewhere:

The sword is necessary to exterminate them. And so that it shall be done honestly and properly, our dear fathers, the princes must do it, who confess Christ with us. But if they don't do it, the sword shall be taken from them. . . . If they resist, let them be slaughtered without mercy. . . . At the harvest time one must pluck the weeds out of God's vineyard. . . . But the angels who are sharpening their sickles for that work are no other than the earnest servants of God. . . . For the ungodly have no right to live, save what the Elect choose to allow them.

Take no notice of the lamentations of the godless! They will beg you in such a friendly way, and whine and cry like children. Don't be moved to pity. . . . Stir people up in villages and towns, and most of all the miners and other good fellows who will be good at the job. We must sleep no more! . . . Get this letter to the miners!

At them, at them, while the fire is hot! Don't let your sword get cold! Don't let it go lame! Hammer, cling, clang on Nimrod's anvil! Throw their tower to the ground! So long as they are alive you will never shake off the fear of men. One can't speak to you about God so long as they are reigning over you. At them, at them, while you have daylight! God goes ahead of you, so follow, follow!

In a sermon attributed to John Ball, we find this violence similarly associated with its Gospel justification.

> He that soweth the good seed is the Son of Man; the field is the world; the good seed are the children of the kingdom; but the tares are the children of the wicked ones; the enemy that sowed them is the devil; the harvest is the end of the world; and the reapers are the angels. . . . As, therefore, the tares are gathered and burned in the fire; so shall it be in the end of this world. The Son of Man shall send forth his angels, and they shall gather out of his kingdom all things that offend, and them which do iniquity; and shall cast them into a furnace of fire; there shall be wailing and gnashing of teeth. Then shall the righteous shine forth as the sun in the kingdom of their Father. Who has ears to hear, let him hear.

In the original Apocalypse, all that was still only words and vision. The war of Gog-Magog, Armageddon, and the vengeance they promised were all in the future. Then, in the centuries that followed, the Church wanted peace and stability, partly because, as I suggested earlier, its very existence and role depended not on the fulfillment of the promised Kingdom, but on its continued delay. All that had now changed. Another era of apocalyptic violence had begun, this time in practice as well as theory, and it was to continue, in one form or another, religious or secular, until our time. In this first phase of active apocalyptic violence, the Church was alternately among the victims and among the perpetrators. When Jerusalem was taken in the Crusades and both Jews and Moslems punished for their sins, "the horses waded in blood up to their knees, up to their bridles. It was a just and wonderful judgment of God that the same place should receive the blood of those whose blasphemies it had so long carried up to God." Some Jews fled for refuge into the main synagogue and were burned alive there, others were seized and held for ransom. But the Crusaders did not have to wait until they reached the Holy Land before purifying the world. In town after town as they moved across Europe eastward, they offered Jews the choice of conversion or death. In just two months of 1096, somewhere between four and eight thousand were killed.

> We have set out to march a long way to fight the enemies of God in the East; and, behold, before our very eyes are his worst foes, the Jews. They must be dealt with first. . . . You are the descendents of those who killed and hanged our God. Moreover, [God] himself said: "The day will yet dawn when my children will come and avenge my blood." We are his children and it is our task to carry out his vengeance upon you. . . . Those who will not accept baptism are no Christians or people of Holy Scripture, so they are to be killed, then they will be baptised in their own blood. (From the "prophet" Rudolph's People's Crusade)

> The emperor has taken Saragossa. A thousand Franks are sent to search thoroughly the town, the mosques, and synagogues. With iron hammers and axes they smash the images and all the idols; henceforth there will be no place there for spells or sorceries. The King believes in God, he desires to serve him. His bishops bless the water and the heathen are brought to the baptistry. If any one of them resists Charlemagne, the King has him hanged or burnt to death or slain with the sword. *(Chanson de Roland)*

As the original apocalyptic vision justified the violence of the chiliasts, so did it sanction their revolutionary social ends. In both means and ends, in other words, the apocalyptic theory at the beginning of the Christian medieval era and the apocalyptic practice at its close helped set the stage for the secular-revolutionary millennialism that was to follow. From the "messianism of the poor" that accompanied the first two Crusades (1096 and 1146), through the fourteenth-century social violence of the Tafurs (vagabonds), Free Spirits, Pastoureaux, and English Peasants' Revolt, to the millennial movements of the Bohemian Taborites, Thomas Muntzer's Allstedt millennium, and the Anabaptists' New Jerusalem of Munster, we clearly see the modernization of the Apocalypse into an earthly utopia, based on communal ownership and achieved through violent class struggle. Armageddon is still to be fought between Satan's evil minions and the Lord's holy remnant, but the evil forces are now, even more explicitly than in the Gospels, the rich and the "great," and the saved, the poor and the "little." A few declarations from some of these upheavals should be enough to illustrate the main points—first, that these apocalyptic movements have already become social-revolutionary movements; and, second, that they are still bound up enough in the message and model of the initial apocalypse to represent a bridge joining that original vision to the later secular revolutions.

Give, give, give, give up your houses, horses, goods, lands, give up, account nothing your own, have all things in common. (Free Spirits)

The Lord shall reign, and the Kingdom shall be handed over to the people of the earth. . . . All lords, nobles, and knights shall be cut down and exterminated in the forest like outlaws . . . the Sons of God shall tread on the necks of kings and all realms under heaven shall be given unto them. . . . As Mine and Thine do not exist at Tabor, but all possession is communal so all people must always hold everything in common, and nobody must possess anything of his own; whoever owns private property commits a mortal sin. (Taborites)

And if we are all descended from one father and one mother, Adam and Eve, how can the lords say or prove that they are more lords than we are—save that they make us dig and till the ground so that they can squander what we produce? They are clad in velvet and satin, set off with squirrel fur, while we are dressed in poor cloth. They have wines and spices and fine bread, and we have only rye and spoilt flour and straw, and only water to drink. They have beautiful residences and manors, while we have the trouble and the work, always in the fields under rain and snow. But it is from us and our labour that everything comes with which they maintain their pomp. (John Ball)

Look, the seed-grounds of usury and theft and robbery are our lords and princes; they take all creatures as their property: the fish in the water, the birds in the air, the plants on the ground have all got to be theirs. . . . They publish God's commandments amongst the poor and say, "God has commanded, thou shalt not steal. . . ." They oppress all people, and shear and shave the poor ploughman and everything that lives—yet if [the ploughman] commits the slightest offence, he must hang. (Thomas Muntzer)

"All things were to be in common," in the words of Jan Bockelson, a leader of the Anabaptists' New Jerusalem at Munster. Money was prohibited within the community. To further curtail privacy and foster communalism, communal dining halls were arranged and laws were decreed against locking home doors, night or day. At the same time, the political side of the millennial kingdom, which our own century has come to know so well, gradually took its grim shape. Not only was any criticism or attempt to leave town punishable by death, but the same punishment was ordered for any infraction of the rigorous moral code. Adultery, theft, avarice, slander, lying, and even quarreling all became capital offenses. They took the Gospels seriously: "whoever says, 'You fool!' shall be liable to the hell of fire. You, therefore, must be perfect as your heavenly Father is perfect" (Matthew 5:22, 48).

In the event that this was not enough to change the leopards' spots, special detachments of guards were formed to do battle with Satan's sinners and, once and for all, assure purity and perfection. "God often acts in this way," Bockelson explained, "and whoever resists the will of God calls down God's wrath upon himself. Now I am given power over all nations of the earth, and the right to use the sword to the confusion of the wicked and in defence of the righteous. So let none in this town stain himself with crime or resist the will of God, or else he shall without delay be put to death by the sword." And Munster was to be only the beginning: from it, the true believers were to march out as the Lord's punishing sword to purify the world. "The glory of all the Saints is to wreak vengeance. . . . Revenge without mercy must be taken on all who are not marked with the Sign," that is, who are not Anabaptists.

Had this Munster terror been a unique event, there would be little need to trace the formation and evolution of the Apocalypse. But, as we now realize, it was only a rehearsal for what was to come. The importance of Munster, the Taborites, the Free Spirits, and the other early movements attempting to establish a pure and perfect society by violence and oppression, is, to restate the main point here, their pivotal role linking the initial Judeo-Christian millennial vision and violence with later, and current, revolutionary totalitarianism.

If Christians reacted to the late medieval time of troubles with renewed apocalyptic fervor, there was even more reason to expect Jews to do so; for not only did Jews experience the same general dislocations and distress that Christians suffered, but, in addition, they had to endure those special deprivations and assaults that were the lot of the Jews in medieval Christendom. And, indeed, there was, at the time, a marked increase in Jewish mysticism and at least one tumultuous messianic movement, albeit at a somewhat later period. There were, however, basic and revealing differences that distinguish the Jewish mysticism and messianism from their Christian counterparts. If one compares, for example, the Jewish mysticism of the Cabala with the Christian mysticism reviewed previously, one is struck by the relatively concrete, this-worldliness of the Cabalists. Rather than enrich heaven at the expense of earth, the Cabalists subtly recruit the former in the service of the latter. The focus of their messianism, first of all, was the same "redemption" back to the Land of Israel that, as we saw above, was the enduring hope of Talmudic sages and world Jewry as a whole through that era. More important, however, is the special depth and meaning that the mystics gave to that "redemption" of the Jews from "exile" to the Land of Israel. While the core of their redemption scenario is distinctly gnostic, the Jewish mystics drew conclusions that are exactly opposite of those drawn by the gnostics and their Christian mystic successors, conclusions that strengthened attachment and commitment to this world rather than foster detachment and withdrawal from it. Lonely and in search of a subject to love, so the Cabalists' story goes, God willed the world into being. In order to provide a place for it, God himself had to withdraw, or contract, into himself. Intending, apparently, to create a purely spiritual "other" in his image, he then emanated a pattern of ten spiritual attributes, called Sephirot (wisdom, understanding, beauty, etc.), in the general shape of man, the so-called Adam Kadmon. But when God then tried to infuse the form with his own divine spirit, a terrible tragedy occurred that was to determine the character and direction of everything that happened in the world thereafter: while the higher attributes were able to contain the grandeur of the divine light, the lower were not. They shattered, and the fragments then congealed to form matter, together with its many flaws and limitations, the source of evil. However, there remained within that material world, in all its manifestations, "sparks" of the divine light from the failed infusion.

What happens then radically distinguishes the Cabalists' story from those of the Gnostics and Christian mystics. For Gnostics and Christian mystics, the divine light within the material realm is trapped (a trapped soul, when the matter is human flesh), and, to recall the earlier account, "redemption" meant the liberation of the spark-soul from the despised, demonic material world and its return to God's spiritual realm. For Jewish mystics, on the contrary, the divine sparks within matter has a vital and sacred purpose: rather than be "redeemed" out of matter and back to heaven, they were to serve as the ideals within matter that inspire, motivate, and guide the redemption of the material world, the reform and "repair" of the world (*tikun ha'olam*). By heeding the divine voice (the "spark") both within himself and in the revealed Law, man would redeem first himself and then the world, repairing thereby the damage done at the time of creation and completing the work as God had originally intended it. Man was God's partner in the continuing work of creation.

Both as humans created in God's image and as God's chosen people, Jews were destined, in the mystics' vision, to play a central role in this "repair of the world," first by achieving their own spiritual redemption through returning to God and to a truly religious life (*tshuvah*, 'return/repentence') and, then, by helping to redeem the rest of the world. But even that first stage of Jewish spiritual self-redemption could not be achieved as long as the Jews lived in "exile," under the domination of others and distant from the sacred land that God had promised them. If the "redemption of the sparks" and, thus, the "repair of the world" needed the work of the Jews, the Jews could only fulfill that destiny after they themselves had achieved spiritual redemption, and that, in turn, could only occur after their return to the land of Abraham, Isaac, and Jacob.

The Jewish mystics' redemption *of* matter rather than *from* matter and their concretely territorial, "Zionist" salvation are two expressions of the earthiness of Jewish medieval mysticism. But they are not the most important evidence. For that we turn to an aspect of Jewish mysticism that best reflects this earthiness and, thereby, most sharply distinguishes Jewish and Christian mysticism, or, more generally, Judaism and Christianity: attitudes toward sexuality. It is because of the relationship between sexual repression and aggression—"purity" and apocalyptic violence in the present context—that attention is given here to this theme.[20]

Reflecting and perpetuating essentially gnostic feelings and thoughts about the flesh, Gospel Christianity "prefers eunuchs," looks forward to that heavenly time when men and women "neither marry nor are given in marriage, but are like angels in heaven," and, in general, demonstrates the fear and suspicion of the flesh that have guided much of Christian doctrine and practice ever since. Monastic and convent celibacy of thought as well as action became, therefore, the ideal. Christian mystics, aspiring to a still more complete and intimate union with God, were, accordingly, the most zealous in this purifying repression.

Fundamentally different attitudes toward sexuality are reflected in Judaism (Biblical, Talmudic, and mystic), with correspondingly different implications in terms of the relationship between repression and aggression. The first of the 613 commandments that Jews have traditionally derived from the Bible is to "be fruitful and multiply." A man must leave his childhood home and parents and "cleave to his wife." He "who does not have a wife lives without joy, without blessing, and without goodness." "Where there is no such union of male and female, men are not worthy of beholding the Divine Presence."[21] Seeking an image to express the joy felt in anticipation of his people's promised redemption, the prophet Jeremiah chooses "the voice of the bridegroom and the voice of the bride." The encounter at Sinai is described as the moment of God's betrothal to Israel and God's covenant "between Me and Israel" as an expression of marital intimacy. Similarly, Isaiah: "as the bridegroom rejoices over the bride, so shall thy God rejoice over thee"; Jeremiah: "I remember the devotion of your youth, your love as a bride, how you followed me in the wilderness. . . ." Hosea makes successive comparisons between his own relations with the woman he loves and God's relationship with Israel: "You will call me 'my husband,' . . . and I will betroth you to me forever; I will betroth you to me in righteousness and in justice, in love and in mercy. I will betroth you to me in faithfulness, and you shall know the Lord." The first marriage, between Eve and Adam, is so honored that "God served as Adam's best man."[22]

The word *holy (kadosh)* also means betroth. Even the study of the Torah is to be suspended so that a scholar may "get up and cheer and hail the bride," should a bridal procession pass his way.[23]

In discussing the obligations of the groom, the Talmud prescribes the number of times he should satisfy his wife's sexual desire (which is the usual way the Talmud and later commentaries state the relationship): "for men who have no occupation, every day; for laborers, twice a week; for donkey-drivers, once a week; for camel-drivers, once every thirty days," since the latter two work away from home a week or month at a time. Should a man wish to change his occupation from donkey-driver to camel-driver, which paid better, he must first consider his wife's wishes, for "a woman prefers less money with enjoyment to more money with abstinence." At times, the details are remarkably graphic: "A man may not treat his wife the way the Persians do, who perform their marital duties with their clothes on. . . . A husband who says, 'I will not perform my marital duty unless she wears her clothes and I wear mine,' must give his wife a divorce and pay her ketubah money." (In Maimonides, *Code,* similarly, we read: "A man may not withhold from his wife her conjugal rights. If he transgresses and does so withhold in order to torment her, he has violated a negative commandment of the Torah. . . . If he has become ill or enfeebled so that he is unable to have sexual intercourse, he may wait six months . . . perchance he will recover. After that, he must either obtain her consent or divorce her and pay her her ketubah.")[24]

A particularly striking indication of the Judaic affirmation of sexual relations, especially when one recalls the relationship in Christianity between celibacy and sanctity, is the association made between the Sabbath, the most holy day in the Jewish calendar, and sexuality. The joy of Sabbath is likened to the joy of marriage. At times, God is the groom and the Sabbath the bride, brought into the world on the seventh day as the bride is led into the prepared bridal chamber. At other times, the groom is the Sabbath, and the people of Israel the bride; or, Israel is the groom welcoming in the Sabbath bride. In yet another variant, God is the groom and the bride is both Israel and the Sabbath: "Grant us that we may be like Thy bride, and that Thy bride may find tranquility in Thee, as it is said in Ruth Rabbat: a woman finds nowhere tranquility except in her husband." Marital imagery fills the Sabbath service. The celebration opens on Sabbath eve with the song, "welcome to the bride." The use of wine for sanctifying the celebration is explained by reference to the similar use of wine in blessing a wedding, since the Sabbath is "the bride that enters the wedding canopy." It is with two bunches of myrtle, Aphrodite's symbol of love, that the celebrant goes out to greet the Sabbath bride— "Come O Bride, Come O Bride"—and with myrtle as well that he enjoys the final moments of the Sabbath, taking pleasure in its fragrance as part of the closing service that ends the Sabbath.[25]

The difference in attitudes toward sexual relations is most apparent, however, when we compare Christian and Jewish mystics. Absolute chastity, a total avoidance of sexual or sensual acts or thoughts, has always been the minimal first step for aspiring Christian mystics. In startling contrast, the main exponents of Jewish mysticism, the Cabalists, place sexuality near the very center of their worldview. One finds, for instance, a full-blown gnostic myth of the soul adapted to fit a radically ungnostic sexual interpretation. According to this adaptation, sexual intercourse reunites souls that were joined in heaven, before being sent down to inhabit the bodies of men and women, and thereby restores the original androgynous union of male and female in a single being. Both Gnostics and Cabalists locate the origin of souls in heaven, and both imagine these original souls as androgynous, uniting male and female as pure spirit reconciles all opposites. However, for Gnostics, the descent of these souls into the world of flesh was a tragic fall, and restoration back to spiritual oneness could be achieved only through liberation from the world of flesh and sin, beginning with everything sexual. For the Cabalists, on the contrary, physical sexual union was precisely the way for the embodied souls to regain their original unity.

> These souls descend pellmell below, male and female souls together. When the time for marriage comes, the souls must find each other again, each male soul must find the female soul which was his mate before the descent to earth.
>
> And when they are united they appear absolutely as one body. From that we deduce that a man alone is considered as a half body. All is peace when they are united, all truly appears to be one body. And, in truth, it is so. Here also, when the male is united to the female, both constitute one single body, and all

worlds rejoice, for all receive the blessing of this perfect body. . . . That is why whosoever is neither male nor female [who is not married] is called a "half body"; a blessing cannot be bestowed on a thing which is faulty or imperfect.

Note that the Holy One, blessed be his name, does not make his abode where the male and female are not united; he showers his blessings only there where the male and female are united. That is why the Scriptures say: "He blessed them and called their name Adam." Thus the Scriptures do not say, "He blessed him and called his name Adam," because God only blesses when the male and female are united. The male alone does not deserve even the name of man, as long as he is not united to the female; that is why the Scriptures say: "And he gave them the name of man."[26]

Drawing the logical conclusions from their essential dualism, the Gnostics spurned children, since they regarded them as just more body traps for souls and further dispersions of the spirit. The Cabalists, on the contrary, cherished and celebrated children for just that reason: their embodiment of divine souls represented a further descent and participation of the divine spirit in the material world.

It is written: "And the Lord God blessed them and said: Be fruitful and multiply," etc. This is the commandment to be assiduous in this world in the procreation and begetting of children to spread the glory of the sacred name in all directions by producing spirits and souls for the glorification of the Holy One, blessed be his name, above and below. Whosoever is not assiduous in keeping the commandment to procreate diminishes the Shape of his Master and prevents him from descending here below. The lack of new souls descending here below prevents the Shekhina [Divine Presence] from coming down to this earth, since it is the souls who constitute the glory of the King in this world, for thus it is written: "The multitude of the people is the glory of the king and the small number of the subjects is the shame of the prince." The King is drawn to this world by the number of souls; and if the number of souls in this world is lessened, the Shape of the King is diminished. The man who abstains from procreating is as guilty as if he shed the blood of his neighbor; for he prevents a reproduction of the heavenly Shape since man is made in the image of God. It is for this reason that it is right that man should be assiduous in keeping the commandment to procreate, so that the glory of God may be spread in all directions.[27]

Sexual intercourse between husband and wife not only united one soul to another, restored thereby the heavenly androgynous unity, and, through childbirth, further involved the divine spirit in the material world; it also, and more significantly for the Cabalists, fostered the union of God and his feminine hypostasis, the Shekhina or Matrona. That divine reunion, in turn, sent a flood of blessings down into the material world, hastening the arrival of the messianic age. Since tradition already celebrated the Sabbath as a wedding, the Cabalists considered Sabbath eve an especially appropriate time to promote this cosmic union of God and his Shekhina.

> On the eve of the Sabbath, when the Matrona lies with the King, they form but one body. . . . When the Matrona is united to the King, all the worlds are blessed and every universe is full of joy . . . for it is the night of Friday that the Matrona is united to the King and takes her delight in him. . . . The sages who understand the mystery of the union of the King and the Matrona on the night of Friday keep their conjugal relations for the night of Friday.[28]

While the richly sensual *Song of Songs*, which was read by a husband to his wife on Sabbath eve, may seem bizarrely out of place among sacred works to some, it is, thus, entirely appropriate in this tradition. Nor need one argue whether it should be taken literally as a passionate male-female love poem or symbolically as an expression of the Israel's love of God. For the Cabalist it is both, since, as they repeatedly emphasized, the sexual love of husband and wife, the reunion of God and his Shekhina, and the communion of God and Israel were all simultaneously and intimately joined.

No less relevant to our theme than the joy and honor that Jewish mystics bring to sexuality is the role they assign to humanity in this cosmic-temporal sexual scenario. While the millennial blessings come down from above "as the seed that the male imparts to the female," those blessings and the divine reunion that occasions them are dependent on man, "who knows how to bring about this union."[29] "Note that each day a heavenly voice cries unto men: This union depends on you alone."[30] What happens above (and its effect on the world) is determined by what happens below.

> Smoke which rises from here below lights the lamps above, so that all the lights shine in the sky; and thus it is that all the worlds are blessed. As it rises, the smoke from here below delights the sacred shapes above, who are set over this world. . . . Thus the sacred beings on high feel a desire to unite with the sacred beings above them, and so on, until the King is united to the Matrona; and it is thus that, through desire below, the waters here below gush forth first of all to receive the waters from above; for the seed above does not gush forth without a previous desire below. . . . "And there went up a mist from the earth and watered the whole face of the ground." That is the desire felt by the female for the male: mists rise first of all from the earth to the heavens; and after forming clouds, the heavens water the earth.[31]

It is through woman, therefore, that man, in conjugal union with her, encourages the higher union of God and his Shekhina, thereby increasing the flow of blessings downward—as the mists from below must first rise for the rain to fall and nourish the earth, so that it, too, may be fruitful and multiply. As it is woman who opens for man the way to the Shekhina ("the mystery of the Shekhina envelops all women; and that is why the Shekhina abides only with him who is united to woman"), so is it also the Shekhina or Matrona, God's feminine hypostasis and temporal "presence," who opens man's way to God.

> The Holy One, blessed be his name, through his great love for the "Community of Israel," entrusted all his power to the Matrona. The King said: "There are sixty queens, and eighty women of the second rank, and countless maidens; but one alone is my dove, and my well beloved, she stands alone, etc. My whole house is in her hands. . . . From this day on, whosoever has need of me may speak with me only through the Matrona, for thus it

is written: Let not Aaron go into the Sanctuary except through Her." Thus, the Matrona is the perfect mediator with the King, and all powers are in her hands, and this is what makes the glory of the Matrona.[32]

In effect, the Shekhina is, for these Jewish mystics, what Jesus is for Christians—both divine manifestation and the intermediary between God and man. The difference, however, in the way man approached and won divine favor from these intermediaries was fundamental. For the Christian mystic, the way through Jesus the son to God the father was an individual, isolated route that first of all required the abandonment of sexual relations. For the Jewish mystic, the way through the Shekhina to God was precisely by way of sexual relations. We see this, again, in the Cabala's advice to men who have been away from home and their wives and who, thanks to the guidance of the Shekhina, had returned safely.

> When the man comes to his dwelling he must ask his wife to grant him her favour, seeing that it is she who has obtained for him union with the Spouse above. When man comes back to his wife, he must ask her to grant him her favour for two reasons: first of all, because the pleasure of conjugal relations on returning from a journey is a good deed, and all pleasure resulting from a good deed is shared by the Shekhina. . . . Does man therefore sin if he abstains from conjugal relations? Yes, truly, he commits a sin because he undervalues the worth of the Spouse on high, who abides with him only by reason of his union with his wife.

A forthrightly sexual cosmology dramatically distinguishes Jewish mystics of the time from their Christian counterparts, but what about deeds, the Jewish Munsters and Muntzers? One would expect to find them: more closely bound to this world by their concepts and traditions, the Jews should have been even more likely than the Christians to try to establish paradise here rather than wait for heaven. Also, although Talmudic Judaism was, for the most part, vigorously opposed to messianic movements, the Talmud itself does contain a clear if subordinate current of thought fostering such hopes and expectations.[33] One might argue that the absence of power made any Taborite-style enterprise impossible. But the Taborites, Free Spirits, Munster chiliasts, and other Christian visionaries hardly had free reign. They had to batter their way against the fierce and ultimately victorious opposition of both secular and ecclesiastic authorities. Nor had powerlessness daunted earlier Hellenistic Jewish zealots. On the contrary, it was virtually a prerequisite for the zeal: the core of the messianic dialectic is divine intervention on the side of the hopelessly outnumbered "remnant," turning seemingly certain defeat into glorious triumph, bringing to victorious completion the sacred struggle that the besieged believers had faith enough to begin.

Yet only one significant messianic movement captured the hearts of world Jewry during these centuries—the seventeenth-century Sabbatian movement—and it was fundamentally different than the Taborite, Muntzer, and Munster experiences at precisely the central point in this comparison—the extent of violence.

From mid-1665 through 1666 a wave of ecstatic messianism engulfed Jewish communities from Jerusalem westward.[34] Although its eschatology was principally the work of the "prophet" of the movement, Nathan of Gaza, the movement is known by the name of its "messiah," Sabbatai Zevi. On the surface, it shares much with the Christian messianic movements reviewed earlier. There is the same euphoric conviction that redemption is at hand, the same cessation of normal communal life in preparation for the great day, the same visions and testimonies of miracles and strange happenings, the same conflict between believers and skeptics, and the same flood of Biblical quotations to prove the imminence of the miraculous transmutation.

Notwithstanding these similarities, however, the two movements, Christian and Jewish, were radically different in their actions. In the Sabbatian movement, there was little of the mass antinomian extravagance or the violence that characterized the Christian chiliastic outbursts. What makes this especially notable is the fact that both the example of the leader, Sabbatai Zevi, and the theories that explained the movement could easily have justified such antinomianism and violence. "Strange" actions became, indeed, the principal signs by which Sabbatai Zevi demonstrated his messianic calling. In addition, the theologians of the movement drew upon several earlier prophecies that envisioned the introduction of an entirely new Torah at the time of redemption, one that would replace traditional Torah and Talmud constraints and permit everything that those had prohibited.

Yet, even in the case of the leader himself, the antinomian, "strange" acts were completely nonviolent and did not go beyond ritual violations and innovations—mentioning the divine name YHVA in public, eating forbidden foods, altering festival dates and conventional rituals (turning fast days into feast days, for instance), performing new symbolic rituals such as arranging his marriage with the Torah, striking a grave with a rod, rocking a fish in a cradle, and knocking on the Holy Ark. There is little evidence, moreover, that these practices were imitated by those communities that identified themselves as his followers: the "strange" acts seem only to have been taken as signs of Sabbatai Zevi's own messianic identity, not as permission (much less a requirement) for his followers to violate traditions. The only exception to this seems to have been his request that others, too, change certain fast days to feast days, because the fasting commemorated tragedies, whereas the time of joyful redemption had arrived: with the appearance of the Messiah, the Shekhina had already begun her ascent to rejoin God, and celebration, not woeful laments, were in order. (It is perhaps significant that when successors of the Sabbatian movement, the followers of Jacob Frank and the later Donmeh sect of Salonika, did assume for themselves as well the right to practice "strange" antinomian rituals, they were converted from Judaism to Christianity.)

Rather than adopt new beliefs, rituals, or laws, those who accepted Sabbatai Zevi as the Messiah and were convinced that salvation was near (that they would all soon return to their homeland, the Land of Israel) demonstrated their faith by the most rigorous performance of the traditional laws. Accepting themselves as sinners and their sins as the cause for the long delay in the redemption, they concluded that only by praying more fervently and frequently, fasting longer, giving more charity, and in other ways repenting their past sins could they speed the end of their "exile" and their return to "Zion." Unlike the Free Spirits, Taborites, and Munster leaders, who saw themselves as the pure and saved remnant called upon to punish the sinful "others," the Sabbatians considered themselves the sinners who must purify themselves through rigorous fulfillment of the traditional law, thereby raising the divine sparks in their own beings and setting in motion the larger *tikun* ('repair') that would redeem the world.

Sabbatai Zevi, Nathan predicted, would "take dominion from

the Turkish king without war, for by hymns and praises which he will utter, all nations shall submit to his rule." Only in the case of the "German lands" did Nathan in one place predict violence, but he elsewhere omitted even that exception in prophesying that the "Messiah will go forth to the war without hands," that is, without weapons. As Gershom Scholem, the principal scholar of the movement, writes, Sabbatai Zevi was "essentially a passive personality" with an "essentially passive temperament." "He never attempted to influence the course of 'outer' historical events, but passively waited for things to happen." In sum, "Sabbatai was no fighter." Similarly, "there was nothing military about Nathan's fantasies." Even where tradition made explicit provision for a military phase of the Redemption, by predicting the appearance of a militant messiah from the house of Joseph to clear the way for the coming of the messiah of peace from the house of David, Sabbatai Zevi pacified the prophecy by declaring that the warrior Joseph had already come and gone in the person of a former disciple of his who had been killed in the Chmielnicki massacres of 1664 (significantly, a victim, not a victor).[35]

The same reluctance to practice the violence already implicit in the theory is evident in the way the movement interpreted the "holiness of sin," as Gershom Scholem called this belief. According to Sabbatians, the only way to redeem the sparks trapped in the *kelippa*, the broken vessels that formed the world of matter and evil, was to descend into the lower depths of that world. To achieve that descent, however, the savior himself would have to take on the appearance of the evil he was to redeem. While still pure both in intention and in soul, he would nevertheless seem sinful to the world, as Sabbatai Zevi did when he converted to Islam, the last remaining core of evil where the last sparks had yet to be redeemed before the great redemption could be complete. Such a theory could easily have been used for a means-justify-the-ends argument sanctioning violence or any other evil. But that was not at all what Sabbatai Zevi did: here, too, sin and suffering were to be borne only by the savior himself, not by his followers, much less by any outsiders.

Finally, as evidence of this remarkably nonviolent messianism, there was little physical violence between believers and doubters. Sabbatai Zevi explicitly refused to punish sinners, whether gentile or disbelieving Jew; they, too, he said, were the children of God, all divine souls to be saved, not destroyed. No doubt animosities raged between those who believed and those who did not, but it is quite extraordinary to note how few authenticated cases there are of physical abuse, especially when one recalls what happened in Munster and similar millennial communities. Particularly surprising are the actions taken by the established authorities in the Jewish communities as the movement developed and after it had ended. While there are all sorts of threats, little seems to have been done other than excommunicating Sabbatai Zevi and his closest disciples. On the contrary, every effort seems to have been made after things had cooled down to forget what had happened and allow the now-disillusioned believers to return to the community and to their former lives—a radically different fate from that suffered by the apocalyptic zealots in Christian Europe after the Establishment regained power.[36]

The nonviolence and relative passivity of the movement did not, however, spare Sabbatai Zevi and his followers the lasting infamy they were to suffer thereafter in mainstream Judaism. The enormous disruptions, losses, humiliations, strife, and ultimate disillusionment too painfully recalled the disasters that had resulted from the first wave of Jewish messianism over fifteen hundred years earlier. The Jewish people once again were harshly schooled in the dangers of zealous millennialism and returned with renewed dedication to their patient *tikun*.

Throughout the history of our western civilization, the three worldviews that have been the focus of these opening chapters remained the favored responses to evil, at least for those who believed that something could and should be done about it. At one extreme are the Gnostics, neo-Platonists, and religious mystics who consider the world irredeemably evil and want only to leave it, usually by way of an interior passage leading to some spiritual realm of purity and perfection. When those belonging to this tradition did commit themselves to the fallen world, it was to show others how to leave it, by turning their thoughts and hopes inward and upward, in order to ease their suffering. It was seldom to change the conditions causing the suffering. At the other extreme are the apocalyptic maximalists, religious and secular, who insist on having things both ways—staying in the world but making it pure and perfect through some sudden and violently cataclysmic transmutation. In between is the tautological vision of the Biblical and Talmudic sages and those who adopted their message—knowingly or otherwise—and lived by it through the ages. For them, the creation of the world was still going on, and it was up to them, limited though they were, to move it slowly forward toward the good society, first of all by putting their own moral house in order. If nations ceased to make war on each other, there would be peace between nations. If the moral commandments were kept, there would be harmony within each nation. If the strong and the rich helped rather than hurt the weak and the poor and if every man had his vine and fig tree, there would be justice and material well-being for all. The aims are moderate—compared to "new heaven and new earth" millennial goals—because they depend on men and women as they are, rather than on transfigured paragons, "new hearts," or divine miracles. And since they depend on humans as they are, on their own personal and social triumph over their own darker inclinations, the realization of the ideals, relatively moderate though they are, must be distant and slow in fulfillment. But however far off the goal, the vision assumes that it can be reached, for at its core is the faith that men and women, made in the image of God and with the breath of his spirit, are good, morally free, rational, and creative enough to build the good society and that their God has so constructed existence that the task of repairing the world can be accomplished, notwithstanding disheartening impediments and grave setbacks.

In itself, that vision neither has nor needs violence. On the contrary, the ends are necessarily present in the means—that is the essence of the tautology: peace is the way to peace; justice to justice; harmony to harmony. Anger, conflict, violence, and oppression can only breed more of the same, not their opposites. There is nothing here of that fateful dialectic of violence that was later to counterpose ends and means, making destruction the way to creation, conflict and suffering the agencies for peace and bliss. It is neither a dramatic nor an ecstatic vision. And if it is so familiar, even banally so, it is because it became the prevailing worldview of western society through most of its post-Renaissance evolution. Liberalism, humanism, theories of gradual social progress, and most of the other traditions that comprise the ideology of the open society are among its offspring and heirs.

Violence enters when faith in humanity weakens. Ceasing to believe that the good in man could overcome the evil, priests and prophets employed past and predicted disasters as ogres to frighten the people into the moral transformation necessary for realizing the vision. When that failed, when suffering continued as cruelly as ever, indicating to the priests and prophets the tenacity of the sins that divine wrath was justly punishing, these teachers of the people took the next step and surrendered the task of redemption completely to God. Henceforth, God himself would provide the "spirit" from above and the "new heart" to a "holy remnant," saved for his "name's sake." But that, too, proved inadequate: the saved still suffered and the sinners still thrived. For many increasingly desperate Hellenistic Jews who found existence no longer bearable, but whose loyalty to a divinely created temporal world was too strong for them to follow the gnostic route out of it and into some transcendent spiritual realm, only one recourse remained: God himself not only would have to remake his world entirely, but he must do it now, destroying the old world and its sinners and creating a brand new heaven and earth where the unjustly suffering righteous would find reward for their goodness and faith, leaving the sinners to "gnash their teeth" in torment.

With that the era of millennial violence began. Over and over again the initial drama was to be reenacted—a time of troubles and despair inspiring renewed faith in a swift and violent social transmutation that would at once replace the all-bad by the all-good. The remaining chapters will follow the later stages of this history of vision and violence, after the Apocalypse changed its mask from religious to secular. As an introduction and transition to this secular Apocalypse, however, it may be helpful to give some examples of individuals who experienced that transition in their own lives.

A dramatic case is that of one of the world's most notorious "atheists," the nineteenth-century anarchist revolutionary, Michael Bakunin.[37] Immersed in childhood in a devoutly religious milieu, which, he later recalled, had "indissolubly fused" with his life and "penetrated deeply" into his soul, he remained committed to following what he considered the footsteps of Jesus until years after he had begun his revolutionary career. His messianic urge began correspondingly early as well. At twenty-one, he already saw himself guided by the "divine hand that has inscribed in my heart these sacred words, encompassing my whole being: 'He shall not live for himself.'" He was convinced that, as he wrote a friend, "our passage will not be fruitless: we will revive the dead, lift the fallen." Consistent with the personality pattern that generally seems to accompany such remarks, he looked at the world through alienated eyes ever since, at thirteen, he had been condemned to a military school he hated and exposed to adolescent behavior he loathed and feared. Even then, a sharp division cut life and the world in two. On the one side was everything sensual, sexual, animal, material; it was a world of "lies," "filth," and "vulgar license." On the other side was the divine world of purity, mind, God, spirit, soul—everything pure, true, and beautiful. From the beginning of time, he taught his young friends, the two had been locked in permanent struggle, and the main purpose of existence was the triumph of the spirit over the flesh, God over matter.

As Jesus, he said, had triumphed over matter and led others toward this spiritual victory, so he himself was called upon to become a leader in this sacred battle.

Forget, Alexandra, that you are speaking to a young man you know, forget my person and look upon me as the being called upon to save you, to open before you the doors of truth. Pour your heart entirely into mine, do not be held back by false shame. I speak with you in the name of God, who wants to have you among his children. He will speak to you through my lips. My soul at this moment is expansive enough to encompass your whole soul. Tell all, dear friend, I can understand you, I feel all your feelings, and I will return them to you purer; I will return to you that purity which you, so you believe, lost, but which, in fact, is only hidden in the depths of your soul: it will emerge again more lustrous than ever. . . . Dear friends, move more quickly along the path that I will show you, that God will show you through my lips, and you will be happy, your bliss will be immortal, infinite. . . . Oh my God! Have I not yet and forever blessed you for having allowed me to read the hearts of these friends so dear to my heart? Have I not yet blessed you for having predestined me for this splendid mission of leading to you such fine souls, so clearly created for you, although they have temporarily gone astray thinking that they were serving you? . . . I feel God within me. . . . My soul is all love . . . I sense paradise within me. I am a man; I will be God . . . I suffer because I am a man and want to be God. I am tranquil because I know my powers, because I see myself standing on the road that will continually bring me nearer to God. . . . One must purify one's soul in order to become God, for that is man's aim. . . . Thus, man represents the eternal struggle of the animal and the divine. The animal will be destroyed, and man will become God. . . . Love is God. Passion is man. Changing passion to love—this is man's task.

The model of Jesus is frequently in Bakunin's letters, charting out for him the road he must take. He, too, believed that he was "not of this world," that "my fatherland is more splendid," that he was living "directly in Christ and through him in the spiritual World." He insisted that whatever seemed evil was only the "illusion, death, and limitation that were overcome by Christ's revelation." Bakunin believed that just as it was "to establish true friendship, this holy commune, that He had come among the people," so must it be his own purpose and the purpose of his youthful followers "to realize his teaching on earth," to establish "the divine external world, the holy commune, the sacred church. . . ." He congratulated his followers for "being present at my christening into truth, present at the beginning of my eternal life," and for being among the earliest participants in "the commune of the Holy Spirit" that he was establishing with them. "Look at Christ, my friends, who suffered so much, who did not even know the joy of being fully understood by those around him, and yet he was happy, for he was the son of God, for his life was suffused with divinity, filled with self-denial, for he did everything for mankind and found all his satisfaction, his pleasure in the dissolution of his material I and the salvation of all mankind." Following Jesus' lead, Bakunin, too, would be "God's interpreter," confident that "all wills must give way before the one that appears before them as God's interpreter." All his young friends and relatives, therefore, must follow his guidance. Above all, "we must all remake ourselves in order to enter into the new world . . . to purify ourselves in order to prepare the soul for the temple of God."

But purity did not at all mean gentle passivity. In his relations with his young friends, he insisted on submission and obedience; and when envisioning the prospects they all would face in establishing their "commune of the Holy Spirit," he foresaw immense suffering and sacrifice, since they must at all cost avoid compromises with the evil world. There must be no "golden mean." They must realize that the price of victory would be high: "No mercy for those who do not deserve it. . . . Nothing can stand against us. We will remake everything according to our will. . . . Our union was concluded on the ruins, on the utter destruction of this world."

When Bakunin became politically active and took his first step into a revolutionary career, he brought this religious messianism right along with him. In 1842, at the age of twenty-eight, having left Russia completely apolitical less than two years earlier in order to study philosophy in Germany, he published his first revolutionary declaration. Not only did it reflect apocalyptic extremism, but its entire theme and thrust was an apocalyptic rejection of any moderate compromise, any policy other than total social transmutation achieved through violent struggle. It was this article that ended with what was probably Bakunin's most famous statement: "the passion for destruction is a creative passion." And, indeed, that passion is given full reign throughout the article, which summons humanity to a "storm of destruction," "ruthless negation," "the complete annihilation of the present political and social world," "the restless and ruthless annihilation of every positively existing thing."

But, and this is as explicit in the article as is the violence, that destructive passion was, for him, still a holy passion in a holy war. Bakunin still believes he is following in the footsteps of the Gospel Jesus, preaching "a new, vital and life-creating revelation, a new heaven and new earth, a young and magnificent world in which all present discords will resolve themselves into harmonious unity!" His cause is still "a religion," and he and his fellow revolutionaries "precursors of the future religion," who, in their destructive violence, are fulfilling their "holy priestlike office." "Indeed, for us alone, who are called the enemies of the Christian religion, for us alone is reserved, and even made the highest duty even in the most ardent of fights, really to exercise love, this highest commandment of Christ and this only way of true Christianity." Leaving no doubt about the source of the inspiration, he closed the article with a quotation from St. John's letters accompanying Revelation: "I know what you are doing; you are neither cold nor hot. How I wish you were either cold or hot! But because you are lukewarm, neither hot nor cold, I intend to spit you out of my mouth." Bakunin's letters home reflect the same continued religious sentiment and dedication. He spoke lovingly of divine grace, expressed his confidence in immortality after death, and sent one of his friends a cross, promising that he, too, would wear one.

This explicitly religious messianism continued through the 1840s, changing only gradually to a secular revolutionary elitism. Thus, for example, when Bakunin praised the violent vision of the revolutionary Weitling, who also insisted that the revolution destroy everything "in which even the slightest remnant of the old evil is concealed" and that "the break between good and evil must be effected by catastrophic means," Bakunin approvingly adopted those "catastrophic means" for his own "sacred goal of realizing the society of brotherhood and freedom, realizing the Kingdom of God on earth." By the explosive end of that decade in the revolutions of 1848–49, he had gathered all this together into what was to become and remain thereafter the essential Bakuninist credo. Although Jesus and St. John are no longer mentioned, the Apocalypse is obviously still the center and foundation of the message.

> It is necessary now to destroy this old world that is crumbling under the weight of its own injustices. It is necessary to wipe all this off the face of the earth in order to have a clear place for the new world. The new world, brothers, means a real and complete liberation of all individuals as well as all nations—the onset of political and social justice—the kingdom of love, of brotherhood, the boundless kingdom of freedom.

> The hour of decision is upon us. We must openly and courageously make a choice: will we take the side of the ruins of the old world in order to prop it up a moment more, or will we stand on the side of the new world whose dawn is breaking, the new world that belongs to the future generations and to the coming millennia?

> The new spirit with its destructive, disintegrating power has irreversibly invaded mankind and has penetrated society down to its deepest and darkest levels. The revolution will not rest until it has completely destroyed the old, decrepit world and has created from it a new and splendid world.

> The miracle of revolution will arise from the depths of this flaming ocean. . . . In Moscow, out of a sea of blood and fire, the constella-

tion of Revolution will ascend on high in splendor to become the guiding star for the benefit of all liberated humanity. . . . Unleash this popular anarchy in the countryside as well as in the towns and intensify it until it rolls on like a furious avalanche, devouring, destroying everything.

Years later, toward the end of his life, Bakunin caught the essence of his apocalyptic vision by praising his ideological forebearers—Wyclif, Huss, Ziska ("the avenger of the people, whose memory still lives as a promise for the future . . . who, at the head of his Taborites, covered the whole of Bohemia, burning the churches, massacring the priests and sweeping away all the German and imperial vermin") and the Anabaptists of Munster, with their "attempts at a mystical-communist organization."

When, in the first decades of this century, the Apocalypse swept through Russia bringing the violent upheavals that would have enthralled Bakunin, a chorus of latter-day Bakuninists were on hand to sing its praises.

The Second Coming has begun. . . . In explosions, catastrophes, and fires the old world was disintegrating. These "explosions" were already taking place in those who were beginning to prepare themselves for the events of the New Era with which our souls were illuminated, as if with the Sun. . . . We believe that you will reveal Yourself to us, that before us lie neither the mists of October nor the yellow thaws of February. Let them believe that You are still asleep in the icy grave. . . . But no, you will be resurrected. You yourself promised to appear in the rosy light and the soul prayerfully bows before You, and in the dawn, before the crimson icon-lamps, your yearning prayer can be overheard. Manifest thyself! The time has come, the world has grown ripe like the golden fruit exuding sweetness, the world grieves without You. Manifest thyself. (Biely)[38]

The people . . . are becoming weary of themselves, and languish even more than for water—for fire . . . herald of the Great Noon. . . . [We] believe in the end, see the end, want the end . . . at least the beginning of the end. . . . From the early morning and from the heights of the oaks still surrounded by fog—we see that which no one else sees: we are the first to see the Sun of the Great Day already shining. We are the first of all to say to him: Yes, Appear, O Lord! (Merezhkovsky)

Christ is the only possible catastrophe of the world, for in Him the world becomes nothing. But this catastrophe is both creative and transformative. And in the name of this possible and necessary catastrophe, we, the tortured, we, the final ones, we, the perishing, accept Christ. (Zakrashevsky)[39]

The most famous poem celebrating the Russian Revolution, appropriately called "The Twelve," ends, still more appropriately, with Jesus at the head of the "twelve" red guard revolutionaries. Similarly, the man who was to become the first head of the Soviet Ministry of Education, A. V. Lunacharsky, was not at all embarrassed, Bolshevik materialism notwithstanding, to compare "our Party" to the Gospels' "mustard seed" that would "grow with fantastic quickness into a huge tree," or to see the workers as the new crucified Christ.

And on the hill of Golgotha arises a new Messiah; his blood has been spilled and they have nailed him to the cross. They mockingly say to him, "YOU, liberator of the world, liberate yourself from hard labor camps, prisons, and the grave where we have put you for your deeds!" But it is impossible to kill Labor; it is resurrected and continues its preaching, its difficult struggle. It carries once more its cross from Golgotha to Golgotha . . . for in truth the Savior of the World never dies.

The basis of Christianity, in Jerusalem and everywhere else, was comradery and brotherhood arising from the very lowest levels of the population. . . . Christianity in Rome and in Palestine was a movement of the proletariat. . . . To all this mass of the poor, the enslaved, those who live in gloom and degradation, Christianity gave a bright light to hope, joy, and a future. With Christianity arose the sense of a people and a feeling of brotherhood among the unfortunate, the cast off, the despairing. Christian martyrs had more faith than common sense, but their heroism showed the height of enthusiasm that is awakened by the idea of communism.[40]

As the greatest poet of the Revolution, Alexander Blok, put Jesus at the head of the Revolution, so the leading novelist of the Revolution, Maxim Gorky, saw a rebirth of the first Christians in the young Bolsheviks. To "Mother," in the novel of that name, Gorky described the Bolsheviks as follows.

[A]ll their [the revolutionaries'] faces blended into one thin, composed, resolute face with a profound expression in its dark eyes, kind yet stern, like the look of Christ's eye . . . on his way to Emmaus. . . . Without being aware of it, she prayed less; yet at the same time she meditated more and more upon Christ and the people who, without mentioning his name, as though ignorant of him, lived, it seemed to her, according to his will, and, like him, regarded the earth as the kingdom of the poor. . . . And it seemed to her that Christ, himself, whom she had always loved with a perplexed love, with a complicated feeling in which fear was closely bound up with hope, and joyful emotion with melancholy, now came closer to her and was different from what he had been. His position was loftier, and he was . . . more cheerful. Now his eyes smiled on her with assurance, and with a live, inward power, as if he had in reality risen to life for mankind, washed and vivified by the hot blood lavishly shed in his name. Yet those who had lost their blood modestly refrained from mentioning the name of the unfortunate friend of the people.[41]

NOTES

1. See Jeffrey Burton Russell, *A History of Medieval Christianity: Prophecy and Order* (New York: Thomas Crowell, 1968), 23.

2. Augustine *The City of God* 22.22.

3. Iranaeus, quoted in Frank E. Manuel and Fritzie P. Manuel, "Sketch for a Natural History of Paradise," in *Myth, Symbol, and Culture*, ed. Clifford Geertz (New York: Norton, 1971), 103.

4. Ibid.

5. Augustine *The City of God* 14.1.

6. Augustine *The City of God* 19.13.

7. Augustine *The City of God* 22.30.

8. Joshua Bloch, *On the Apocalyptic in Judaism*, Jewish Quarterly Review Monographic Series, no. 2 (Philadelphia: Maurice Jacobs, 1952), 137, 187;

Ephraim E. Urbach, *The Sages: Their Concepts and Beliefs,* trans. Israel Abrahams (Jerusalem: Magnes Press, 1975), 667–68.

9. *Avot of Rabbi Nathan,* chap. 31; *Lam.R.* 2:2, sec. 4; *Hag.* 2:1; *Song of Songs Midrash* 4:34; *Sanhedrin* 97b; *Derek Erez Rabba* 11; *Ben Sira* 3:31–33, quoted in *Hag.* 13a; *Yer Hag* 77c; Hillel, quoted in Urbach, *The Sages,* 681.

10. *Talmud, Betzahn* 25b.

11. Samuel, a third-century Babylonian sage, quoted in Robert M. Seltzer, *Jewish People, Jewish Thought: The Jewish Experience in History* (New York: Macmillan, 1980), 307.

12. *Mishnah Torah,* "Wars and Kings," chaps. 11–12.

13. Bloch, *On the Apocalyptic,* 75ff.

14. Bloch, *On the Apocalyptic,* 95.

15. Urbach, *The Sages,* 676–77, 681.

16. *Mishna Sota* 9.15.

17. Ernest Lee Tuveson, *Millennium and Utopia* (Berkeley: University of California Press, 1949), chap. 2.

18. Excerpts from Meister Eckhart are from D. T. Suzuki, *Mysticism, Christian and Buddhist* (New York: Harper and Row, 1971), 10, 15–16, 54–55, 59, 85, 98–99, 102.

19. This section depends heavily on sources collected in Norman Cohn, *Pursuit of the Millennium* (New York: Oxford University Press, 1971). The quotations are from 70, 75, 121, 155, 174, 175, 177, 179, 182–85, 199, 203, 212–17, 237, 239, 247–48, 272, 274.

20. See *Babylonian Talmud, Yevamot,* 62b; *Zohar, Aharei Mot,* 59a.

21. Ibid., *Berakhot,* 61a.

22. *Avot Rabbi Nathan,* chap. 4; see also Abraham Heschel, *The Sabbath* (New York: Farrar, Straus and Giroux, 1971).

23. *Babylonian Talmud, Ketubbot,* 62b, 48a; *Mishna, Ketubbot,* chap. 5, par. 5.

24. Heschel, *Sabbath,* 53, 54, 61, 124–26, 128.

25. *Zohar, Vaygasch,* 207b, 208a; *Idra zouta,* 296a; *Bereshis,* 55b.

26. *Zohar,* Appendixes, 273a.

27. *Zohar, Beschalah,* 46a.

28. See above.

29. *Zohar, Va-Yaghel,* 200a.

30. *Vayhi* 244a; *Bereshis* 35a.

31. *Zohar, Beschalah,* 51a.

32. *Zohar, Bereshis,* 50a.

33. Maimonides, *Laws Concerning Marriage,* chap. 14, secs. 7–9.

34. My account is based on Gershom Scholem, *Sabbatai Sevi: The Mystical Messiah,* trans. R. J. Zwi Werblowsky (Princeton: Princeton University Press, 1973).

35. Ibid., 225, 272, 273, 287, 380, 608, 664.

36. Ibid., 335–51, 656–57. Gershom Scholem seemed disappointed by the nonviolence of the movement: "Of course, neither Sabbatai nor his followers should be judged by the standards of modern political action, or condemned because their behavior does not live up to our ideas of revolutionary leader-

ship. But even judging by the standard of his own day, there is something depressing about Sabbatai's passivity" (693). Even more remarkable than this comment was Scholem's apparent attempt to make up for the "passivity" by injecting a rhetoric of violence into his descriptions of the events, even though he offered little or no data to substantiate it. See, for example, 242, 390, 395n, 412, 414, 512, 513, 523, 575–76, 676, 862, 863, 877, 879.

37. This survey is drawn from my study of the Russian anarchist, Michael Bakunin; Arthur P. Mendel, *Michael Bakunin: Roots of Apocalypse* (New York: Praeger, 1981).

38. Samuel D. Cioran, "In the Imitation of Christ: A Study of Andrei Biely's *Zapiski chudaka," Canadian Slavic Studies* 4, no. 1 (Spring, 1970): 76, 80.

39. B. G. Rosenthal, *D. S. Merezhkovsky and the Silver Age: The Development of a Revolutionary Mentality* (The Hague: Martinus Nijhoff, 1975), 76–77.

40. Cioran, "Imitation of Christ," 78.

41. David G. Rowley, "Millenarian Bolshevism" (Ph.D. diss., University of Michigan, 1982), 151–52.

3

Apocalypse and Reason

The Apocalypse of Reason began where we left the Apocalypse of Faith in the preceding chapter, with the messianic assaults on the Roman Catholic Church, whose wealth, power, and alleged corruption left no doubt in the minds of the new pure remnant that the End was near. Underlying this new apocalyptic upsurge, as it had the earlier upheavals and would those to come, was the psychological turmoil that generally accompanies rapid, profound, and costly social change. In this case—the period of Renaissance and Reformation—cause and effect are evident enough in that familiar dualism: the Renaissance transformation in virtually all areas of social, economic, political, and cultural life provoked the confusion, fear, anger, and desperate hope that nurtured the apocalyptic expectations of the early Reformation. The emotions that fed the apocalyptic mood of the Reformation, in response to Renaissance disruptions, mirrored those that had first turned fearful Jews into Jewish-Christians in response to comparably prolonged and unnerving Hellenistic dislocations.

There was, however, an obvious difference. The Christian Church had acquired its enormous power through centuries of decline and disintegration of the secular Roman Empire. Apocalyptic Protestantism (and Luther remained, to his death, convinced that the End was at hand) emerged on the eve of the most astounding era of material and intellectual progress the world had yet known. The transformations that these latter-day chiliasts took to be signs of the End were, in fact, hints of an extraordinary new beginning. But the fears of the faithful were entirely justified; what was being reborn was the secular world that Christianity had replaced and fundamentally opposed.

Still, however understandable the reaction, Protestantism could not have survived with an apocalyptic mood and message. Not only did Protestantism have to go through the same adjustments that

Roman Christianity had gone through when it made its peace with a fallen world that insisted on staying alive in defiance of all doomsday prophecies, but the peace to be made was with a young, robust, vigorously creative, and productive secular world. Denied the benefits of stagnation and hopelessness that permitted medieval Christianity to retreat inward and upward, Protestantism had to transform itself into a theology and psychology congenial to the dynamic reality of rapid change and flourishing growth. And it did so with remarkable success, mainly by transforming its immense burden of guilt and self-punishment from an unyielding enemy of material progress into its most devoted and powerful accomplice, the famous "work ethic."

Circumstances favored this transformation of Protestantism into a steadfast ally of those very Renaissance attitudes and innovations that at first had provoked its gloomiest prophecies. Many of those who had felt themselves besieged by the devils of secularism found it increasingly hard to resist the dazzling intellectual and material wonders that secularism kept bestowing on this unworthy world. At the same time, those who had been literally besieged in the brutal religious wars with Rome saw their Protestant cause gather triumph as rich and powerful kings and princes took their side. Even humanistic rationalism grew markedly less threatening as Protestants realized that it could be recruited into the service of sanctity and truth as well as sin and error.

> For God in this last age hath shewed his singular and marveylous good wyll towards mankynd: especially . . . by raysing up some Valla, Agricola, Erasmus, Melancthon, and others, which with great study and payne, have brought all sciences and knowledge of the tongues to their puritie, and delivered unto us a more easie way to the attayning the perfect knowledge of them all; by which, almost all Europe is set free from rude barbarousnes. (Geveren)[1]

The contrast between the opening reference to "this last age" and the rest of the passage highlights the tension inherent in this shift from apocalyptic despair to a secular optimism that was already beginning to prevail and that would define the sentiments of the West for centuries to come. For those like the ambivalent author of that last statement, it was, at best, a difficult transition, as one can see from the way he concluded his remarks.

> But by experience we see these gyftes of long tyme to haue been at the full, and now decrease. For not that aduised judgement, not that sharpenesse of wyt, not that great industrie, and exercise in studyes are now, which have been. (Geveren)[2]

One of the most intriguing aspects of this transition is the apparent reluctance of some theorists to give up their apocalypse, even though they acknowledged and applauded the changes that were occurring everywhere around them. Thomas Burnet, James Burnett (Lord Monboddo), and William Worthington all seemed to welcome the evidence that the world was daily progressing, largely due to "an increase of knowledge." "The wisdom and goodness of God has so ordered matters," Lord Monboddo wrote,

> that civil society has likewise furnished a remedy, in some degree, for these evils; for, as the love of knowledge has, by the means of civil society, and that close intercourse and communication of men which it produces, invented and cultivated arts and science, by which the defect of our intelligence, the cause of all our evils, is . . . in some degree remedied.

Worthington similarly had only praise for a divine plan that arranged for "melioration and improvement in all its parts, and in every capacity." He was confident that "the state of the new heaven and earth will be a restoration of the paradisiacal state, but much improved, exalted, refined, and spiritualized," and was delighted by the fact that

> the redemption of man and nature are carried on together; for the subduing of all kinds of evil, both natural and moral, upon one large and comprehensive plan, for the recovery of the whole creation, from this complicated malady, under which it all groans together.

And Thomas Burnet, finally, felt sure that "when the End of all things approaches, Truth, being revived, may shine with double Lustre, as the Prelude of a future Renovation."

Strangely, however, none of the three were willing to let this belief in progress displace their faith in a final, apocalyptic catastrophe. Worthington predicted that "the latter ages of the world, next preceding its final dissolution by fire, will, in general, be the best and happiest." Lord Monboddo still envisioned a "convulsion of nature," and Thomas Burnet agreed.

> Earthquakes and Subterraneous Eruptions will tear the body and bowels of the Earth; and Thunders and convulsive motions of the air, rend the Skies. The waters of the Sea will boyl and struggle with streams of Sulphur that run into them; which will make them fume, and smoke, and roar, beyond all storms and tempests. And these noises of the Sea will be answered again from the Land by falling Rocks and Mountains.

Nothing, in fact, seemed to do greater honor to God than his precisely calibrated mechanism for bringing about that ineluctable devastation.

> We think him a better Artist that makes a Clock that strikes regularly at every hour from the Springs and Wheels which he puts in the work, than he that hath so made his Clock that he must put his finger to it every hour to make it strike: And if one should contrive a piece of Clock-work so that it should beat all the hours, and make all its motions regularly for such a time, and that time being come, upon a signal given, or a Spring toucht, it should of its own accord fall all to pieces; would not this be look'd upon as a piece of greater Art, than if the workman came at that time prefixt, and with a great Hammer beat it into pieces?[3]

Such apocalyptic expectations were to remain an undercurrent throughout the coming centuries of stunning scientific, economic, social, and cultural progress. But, during most of that long era, they made no more than a distant murmur, hardly audible amid the chorus of hosannas in praise of the burgeoning modern world. At first, the pessimists confronted the assault of progress by acknowledging and then dismissing it. In spite of all the good things brought forth by the minds of such Protestant thinkers as "Valla, Agricola, Erasmus, Melancthon, and others," or the fact that "all Europe is set free from rude barbarousness," the world was none the less in its "last age," to recall an earlier quotation, and it was already apparent that such achievements "now decrease." Unable to deny the dramatic progress occurring all around them but continuing to cherish visions of the End, the doom sayers retreated to the ancient cyclical scenario, trying to preserve their pessimism not only in spite of the progress, but because of it.

> It is to be feared, lest the power, wisedom, sciences, bookes, industrie, workmanships, and knowledges of the world, being come to so great excellencie; doe fall againe, as they have done in times past, and come to decay: by confusion succeeding after this order and perfection; rudenese after ciuilities; ignorance after knowledge; and barbarousness after elegancie. (Le Roy)[4]

> First the arts arise in some places through the practice and the labor of talented men, then they develop, later they flourish for a while at a fixed level, then languish in their old age, and finally begin to die and are buried in a lasting oblivion by the eternal calamity of wars, or because too great abundance (an evil much to be feared in these times, of course) brings satiety to the frivolous, or because God inflicts just punishments upon those who direct useful knowledge to the ruin of men. (Bodin)[5]

After a certain period of flourishing growth, Francis Bacon observed, men "return to the depraved conditions of their nature, and desolation is seen in the fields and cities."[6]

But this cyclical theory was weak on several grounds. First, it flew in the face of the obvious fact that, instead of turning back and down, the course of things seemed to keep advancing forward and upward: the dire predictions of decay, deterioration, and oblivion simply proved false. Second, the cyclical theory was just too pessimistic for the times. The apocalyptic vision at least offered the promise of eternal bliss following abysmal wretchedness; the cyclical theory offered nothing more than a return to the ancient fatalistic pattern of alternating fat and lean periods over which man had no control.

Consequently, a new worldview gradually took shape. The cycle of good and bad eras was tilted upward so that each good was somewhat better than the one before; each bad, not quite so awful. Then, the peaks and troughs diminished, the gap between the extremes narrowed until they disappeared altogether into that straight line upward that was to define and direct the Western mind down to our own century—the straight line of steady progress.

Since it has dominated Western culture throughout our era, one tends to forget how young "the theory of progress" really is. During the millennium of medieval Christianity, the only meaning that "progress" had involved an individual's moral progress here on earth in preparation for the blessed eternal life that would begin after death. Before that, the flow of time and life for the classical world either continued the earlier, Near Eastern cyclical fatalism or assumed a steady decline from some past "golden age." Nor did the Judaic Biblical mind define History as a story of inevitable progress. As we have seen, if God and man met in History, they did so only in the context of successive moral challenges that humanity confronted. Until Daniel, there is no implication at all of an inevitable, "providential," stage-by-stage, steady advance, whether moral or otherwise; there are only the challenges that man sometimes meets and sometimes fails to meet and the *possibility* of mankind gradually realizing the prophetic ideal. Also, when Daniel did introduce his vision of succeeding ages of oppression moving inevitably toward a predetermined redemptive End, his focus was only on the End, not on the eras leading to it. Through Augustine, Daniel's perspective entered the medieval world and mind, which, consequently, also concerned itself with only two ages—a sinful, fallen present that must somehow be endured and the approaching apocalyptic End that brought salvation.

Early signs of the new theory of progress are evident in the works of Giambattista Vico. Although he still accepted the cyclical theory with respect to the rise and fall of each national experience, Vico saw the story of mankind as a whole as one of progress from "small, crude" beginnings to the "enlightened, cultivated, and magnificent times" of his own age.[7] Developing a line of thought Francis Bacon had used in his *Novum Organum*, the optimists argued that the ancient classical world was not humanity's Golden Age, but its inexperienced youth: humanity's wisdom came with maturity, as it did with individuals. Future meant better, and progressively more so.

[T]his world is a school, as well for intellectual, as for moral, advance; and the longer human nature is at school, the better scholar it should be. . . . All these particulars, I say, considered, why should it seem altogether impossible, that heaven's latest editions of the human mind may be the most correct, and fair; that the day may come, when the moderns may proudly look back on the comparative darkness of former ages? (Edward Young). God dispenseth not all his Favours together; but the manifestations of his will grow greater successively. (John Edwards)[8]

It shall so at length come to pass, that Justice, Peace, and Equity shall more universally and fully flourish in the world than ever yet they have done. (Henry More)[9]

There was now even a scriptural finale to this vision, without the accompanying apocalyptic violence.

. . . no Decay attends this Fulness of Time . . . we may be sure that if we spend that Time which God shall vouchsafe to give us in this World, in that Manner as he expects we should, and as he hath enabled us to do if we will, we shall leave as fair Examples of Wisdom, Virtue and Religion to those who shall succeed us, as any have been left to us by those who have gone before us; and our Posterity pursuing the same Method, the last Age will appear at the Day of Judgment less undaunted than any that hath gone before it. (Earl of Clarendon)[10]

A passage from a contemporary interpretation of Daniel, appropriately reread to suit the times, highlights the vast distance between these post-Renaissance optimists and their medieval predecessors. When Daniel foresaw a time when "many shall run to and fro," he was not predicting apocalyptic chaos and panic, according to Jonathan Edwards, but rather a future of economic prosperity and flourishing commerce, a time of "free and peaceable Travelling by Sea and Land, from one Part of the World to the other."[11]

From the middle of the eighteenth century, this sanguine belief in constant progress became synonymous with the life of reason, virtue, and civility. So self-evident was the fact of progress that to lack faith in it meant to lack elemental good sense.

Knowledge, as Lord Bacon observes, being power, the human powers will, in fact, be enlarged; nature, including both its materials, and its laws, will be more at our command; men will make their situation in this world abundantly more easy and comfortable; they will probably prolong their existence in it, and will grow daily more happy, each in himself, and more able (and I believe, more disposed) to communicate happiness to others. Thus, whatever was the beginning of this world, the end will be glorious and paradisiacal, beyond what our imaginations can now conceive. (Priestley)

What a picture of the human race, freed from its chains, removed from the empire of chance as from that of the enemies of its progress, and advancing with a firm and sure step on the pathway of truth, of virtue and of happiness, is presented to the philosopher to console him for the errors, the crimes, and the injustices with which the earth is still soiled and of which he is often the victim! It is in contemplating this vision that he receives the reward of his efforts for the progress of reason, for the defense of liberty. (Condorcet)[12]

The connection between this glowing confidence in man's mastery of his earthly existence and the collapse of the medieval worldview has often been noted. As long as humanity considered its temporal existence merely a prelude for immortal rapture, there was little motivation for much concern about this present world and life. The important issue was salvation, what happened to people when they left the earth, not the harsh fate of life on earth. If the earth was the center of God's universe, it was only because the earth was a way station to test candidates for admission into the eternal Kingdom.

The new reason and science tore that worldview to shreds. Astronomers demoted the earth from the center of God's universe to a trivial cosmic speck. Geologists pushed the age of the speck far back, before the coming of man, who was supposed to have been earth's raison d'être. Physicists demonstrated that the laws governing the sublime heavenly realms of God and his Angels were the same laws that ruled this lowly material earth. Explorers discovered new and radically different societies and thereby turned Christianity into just one of many religions. Bit by bit, progress in knowledge about the material world chiseled away at the foundations of the spiritual world.

As a result, humanity lost both its divinely rooted self-esteem and its promised city of eternal salvation. New grounds for both the esteem and the promised salvation would have to be found. Denied heaven, man turned back to earth. Deprived of the centrality assigned him in the medieval drama of salvation, he would achieve a comparable self-esteem through temporal achievement. Shaken in his hopes for immortality in heaven after death, he would find solace and compensation in living life here on earth as fully as possible, in enjoying a pseudoimmortality by accumulating property and fame, and in imagining humanity's future progress toward an earthly paradise. Most of all, instead of turning to heaven for help in enduring the miseries of earthly existence, he would henceforth devote himself and his labors to the eradication of those miseries. All the rest followed logically—the reorientation from ritual to reason, the rejection of authority and tradition in favor of direct empirical observation, a commitment to rational analysis unconstrained by spiritual loyalties, and the habit of pragmatically testing reality by action in it and on it. Those ideals of rationalism, pragmatism, and instrumentalism, together with the material abundance that was their proof and prize, encompassed all areas of individual and social existence. The result was our modern Western world.

But if progress and the attitudes that drove it forward were carrying the West toward the modern world, they were also announcing its return to the cultures and spirit that medieval Christianity had replaced—those of classical Greece and Rome and that of Biblical Judaism. The point need not be argued with respect to the classical revival, since that is what Renaissance is generally understood to mean. With respect to Biblical Judaism, however, the point is far less obvious. Yet, when we recall that worldview, as outlined in chapter 1, we see that many of its assumptions and aims were the same as those that led humanity out of the "dark ages" into our own era: (1) human purpose and destiny is centered in this world, not in some compensatory afterlife; (2) men and women have the physical, intellectual, and moral capacities needed to master themselves and their world and thereby realize their ideals; and (3) the constraints of objective reality and the limits of human abilities and character permit no more than a gradual achievement of those ends.

The eighteenth-century writer, Ferguson, is solidly within this gradualist tradition when he writes that "the seeds of every form are lodged in human nature; they spring up and ripen with the season," and that, consequently, societies "proceed from one form of government to another by easy transitions." While humanity continues on its way "towards still higher perfection," in Turgot's words, it does so only "slowly." Fusing, as it were, Ferguson's and Turgot's thoughts, Kant, in 1784, defined progress as a "steady and continuous, though slow, development of certain great dispositions in our nature."[13] With such sentiments as these, we have left the apocalyptic vision far behind. This world, this life, and this existing human nature are once again godly and good, in spite of all the shortcomings. Once again, the flaws are there to challenge and evoke human efforts, not to justify apocalyptic devastation; to inspire a commitment to repair imperfect temporal existence, not flight from it.

But the Renaissance and post-Renaissance return to Biblical commitment, work, hope, and their underlying "basic trust" in the world is only a partial return. While the renewed focus on earthly existence and faith in the capacity of human reason and enterprise to master and mold reality are, indeed, Biblical, the *purpose* of that focus was not, and the nature of that difference was to lead Reason into the same apocalyptic disasters that Faith had fostered before it. To see this decisive difference, one need only recall the basic aims of all that marvelous progress in science, technology, exploration, commerce, and organizational and administrative forms. Did they promote the peace, justice, and public well-being that were at the very center of the Biblical vision? War, then as now, was the most powerful of all the motors that drove this "progress" forward. And where was the justice and welfare, assuring every man his vine and fig tree? The spectacular technological and economic growth through these centuries gave the vineyards and orchards as well as most of their produce only to the few, leaving but a pauper's portion, along with the labor, to the many. The Lord, so the Prophets had promised, would provide abundantly, but only in return for the fulfillment of a covenant that rested squarely on social justice. Power and wealth in and for themselves, without peace and social justice, were precisely what the Prophets had denounced.

With few exceptions, and those only in the late eighteenth century, there is little evidence indicating significant benefits for the propertyless laboring multitudes from the amazing "progress" during these post-Renaissance centuries. If anything, their lot may well have been getting "progressively" worse as a result of the land enclosures, the steady rise in prices due to the influx of precious metals, the submission of the once independent craftsmen and artisans to the demands of merchant suppliers and buyers, the destruction of traditional patterns of individual and communal village life, the oppressive conditions of life and work in the primitive factory towns, and the host of other familiar sources of distress that usually accompany rapid economic development. Marx was surely right in both parts of his description of this process: it was enormously successful in accumulating capital, and it showed a brutal disregard for the plight of those who did the physical work. National wealth and popular welfare clearly moved in opposite directions in these centuries of "primitive capitalist accumulation," notwithstanding the golden predictions of the theorists of progress and the alluring program of the Enlightenment, with all their inspiring words about peace, justice, and equality. No doubt the potential power of those words to inspire their realization was enormous. But it has only been in the last century-and-a-half that they have had that effect. As for the preceding four or so centuries, from the fifteenth through the eighteenth, which built the modern world, a strong case could be made for the argument that the multitudes lost more than they gained from the transition. We may recall once more the Tower of Babel, built by a science that had learned how to make brick and mortar in the absence of stone but that cared more for the bricks and the building than for the lives of the builders.

Why did this happen? Why did Renaissance reason and progress prove to be so little concerned about the welfare of "the people"? Much of the blame rests on the fundamental principle of the new worldview—the "rationalism" that initiated the transformation and that has arranged its priorities ever since. Moreover, introducing a pattern that was to be repeated with each succeeding Apocalypse, the "rationalism" that had helped restore calm and sanity after the late medieval apocalyptic revival became itself a source of the next apocalyptic outbreak.

The drama begins with the return to the world. Inundated with Renaissance achievements and viewed from a secular perspective, the world looked good again, good enough, in fact, for God to be brought back to it, after Gnostic and Christian earthly suffering and hopelessness had largely confined God to heaven. But the God that came back was not the *same* God that had left. The God that Kepler, Galileo, and Newton put in power was not the Biblical and medieval God of good and evil, moral meaning and purpose, parental love and punishment. He—or it—was a master mechanic and mathematician. The God of the scientists was the Genesis God Elohim, the impersonal mode of God the creator and organizer of the material universe, not Adonay (YHWA), the parental God of love and compassion.

To prove God's existence, Newton and his fellow rationalists could ignore humanity entirely and focus exclusively on the marvelous order and regularity that reigns throughout the universe and that, consequently, implies a rational creator.

> To make this system, therefore, with all its motions, required a cause which understood, and compared together the quantities of matter in the several bodies of the sun and planets, and the gravitating powers resulting from thence. . . . To compare and adjust all these things together in so great a variety of bodies, argues that cause to be not blind or fortuitous, but very well skilled in mechanics and geometry.[14]

There was no need for the Bible or any other religious text or message, since God did not "less admirably discover himself unto us in Nature's Sacred Dictions."[15]

Obviously, one did not approach this new God the way one did the old. Manifesting himself impersonally through universal order and natural law, the God of Reason was blind and deaf to subjective human emotion, intuition, revelation, tradition, and the other vague and fuzzy epistemologies by which Biblical and medieval communities had hoped to learn something about God's will. There was now only one key that opened the way to universal Truth—mathematics.

> True philosophy expounds nature to us; but she can be understood only by him who has learned the speech and symbols in which she speaks to us. This speech is mathematics, and its symbols are mathematical figures. Philosophy is written in this greatest book, which continually stands open here to the eyes of all, but cannot be understood unless one first learns the lan-

guage and characters in which it is written. This language is mathematics and the characters are triangles, circles and other mathematical figures. (Galileo)

The universal order, symbolized henceforth by the law of gravitation, takes on a clear and positive meaning. This order is accessible to the mind, it is not preestablished mysteriously, it is the most evident of all facts. From this it follows that the sole reality that can be accessible to our means of knowledge, matter, nature, appears to us as a tissue of properties, precisely ordered, and of which the connection can be expressed in terms of mathematics. (Newton)

Experience day by day protested and showed by infinite examples, that good and evil fortunes fail to the lot of pious and impious alike. . . . They therefore laid down as an axiom that God's judgments far transcend human understanding. Such a doctrine might well have sufficed to conceal the truth from the human race for all eternity, if mathematics had not furnished another standard of verity in considering solely the essence and properties of figures without regard to their final causes. . . . There is no need to show at length, that nature has no particular goal in view, and that final causes are mere human figments. (Spinoza)[16]

When Truth moved from the moral world of good and evil to the mathematical measurement of physical regularity, the passions followed. Galileo "shrinks in horror" at the thought of "irregularity in the moving power, whether this be within the body or foreign to it, or from some inequality of the body in revolution," and Copernicus recalled how he "began to grow disgusted that no more consistent scheme of the movements of the mechanism of the universe, set up by that best and most law-abiding Architect of all things, was agreed upon by philosophers. . . ." Kepler, after his calculations of planetary orbits, stated these ideas in a similar manner.

It is not eighteen months since I got the first glimpse of light, three months since the dawn, very few days since the unveiled sun, most admirable to gaze upon, burst upon me. Nothing holds me; I will indulge my sacred fury; I will triumph over mankind by the honest confession that I have stolen the golden vases of the Egyptians to build up a tabernacle for my God far away from the confines of Egypt. If you forgive me, I rejoice; if you are angry, I can bear it; the die is cast, the book is written, to be read either now or by posterity, I care not which; it may well wait a century for a reader as God has waited six thousand years for an observer! (Kepler)[17]

The desires for truth, goodness, and beauty were all satisfied by this mathematical (and, ultimately, Platonic) knowledge-contemplation of the divine universal order.

Our views of Nature, however imperfect, serve to represent to us, in the most sensible manner, that mighty power which prevails throughout, acting with a force and efficacy that appears to suffer no diminution from the greatest distances of space or intervals of time; and that wisdom which we see equally displayed in the exquisite structure and just motions of the greatest and subtlest parts. These, with perfect goodness, by which they are evidently directed, constitute the supreme object of the speculations of a philosopher; who, while he contemplates and admires so excellent a system, cannot but be himself excited and animated to correspond with the general harmony of nature.[18]

Had this new religion of mathematical order been limited to the mathematicians, astronomers, and physicists, there would have been little or no danger. But it was not. The new truths revealed by these mathematicians of astronomy and physics proved to be so persuasive, indeed, incontestable, that the methods and assumptions of the scientists who revealed them seemed equally irrefutable. Consequently, common sense concluded that *all* thought in *all* areas of individual and, especially, social existence must adopt the same methods and assumptions. If those concerned with social problems followed the example of the natural scientists, they would be rewarded with a cornucopia of objective truths comparable to those won by the natural scientists; they would gain the same mastery over society that objectivity had given the natural scientists over nature; and they would have the same power to improve society through the application of those objective truths that the scientists enjoyed in their continuing application of natural laws for the benefit of mankind. In the end, Truth itself came to be defined as that—and only that—which could be mathematically or (a second best) empirically demonstrated.

> If we take in our hand any volume; of divinity or school methaphysics, for instance, let us ask, Does it contain any abstract reasoning concerning quantity or number? No. Does it contain any experimental reasoning concerning matter of fact and existence? No. Commit it then to the flames: for it can contain nothing but sophistry and illusion. (Hume)[19]

So overwhelmed were the scientists, scholars, and other learned members of society with the achievements of what Descartes called "universal mathematics" that they denied the authentic objective existence of anything that could not be mathematically measured. Only matter and motion were really there, Locke and his admirers claimed, while all the other "qualities" we experienced were purely subjective, that is to say irrelevant as far as reason was concerned, and, therefore, morally suspect as well.

Truth was thus kept safely distant from and pure of everything characteristically human, except man's ability to count, weigh, and measure. The medieval approach had been completely opposite. Since the medieval mind made man and his personal feelings and destiny the center and purpose of the universe, it understood nature anthropomorphically, in terms of human needs and experiences. Truth was what humans subjectively sensed—all the color, texture, and tone along with all the purposes that God had created nature to fulfill. What mattered was not the causal or functional "how," but the teleological "why." If one thought about rain, it was not in relationship to evaporation, condensation, and temperature changes, but to God's power and goodness in making the world blossom for the sake of man. The mistletoe existed in order to relieve the tree of chronic distresses and to teach man the evils of parasitism. Similarly,

> the four elements are Earth, Water, Fire, and Air, of the which each hath his proper qualities, that is hot, cold, dry, and moist. . . . Two of these qualities are called Active—heat and

coldness. The others are dry and wetness and are called Passive.... In the liver is the place of voluptuousness and liking of the flesh.... By spleen we are moved to laugh, by the gall we are wroth, by the heart we are wise, by the brain we feel, by the liver we love.... The cause why the dragon desireth the elephant's blood, is coldness of the elephant's blood by the which the dragon desireth to cool himself.[20]

Asked whether or not a tree had feeling (a typically anthropomorphic medieval inquiry), Roger Bacon thought it did not. Why? Because feelings are present in order to sustain the body by attracting it to what is beneficial and repelling it from what is harmful, and since a tree could neither move forward nor back, why would God give it feeling?

Little wonder that medieval science progressed slowly! But if the medieval world suffered from too little scientific objectivity, it is doubtful that it suffered more than the modern, rational world has from too much of it. To remedy the anthropomorphic subjectivism of medieval thought, the rationalists purified their search for objective truth in all areas by driving out all subjective desires, values, interests, feelings, needs, and sensations. Such value categories as "good" and "evil" were particularly excluded since, as Hume observed, the ultimate cause of things "has no more regard to good above evil than to heat above cold." As if revenging itself for the centuries of abuse it had suffered from medieval subjectivism, Spinoza's "reason" now treated the emotions the same way.

Most writers on the emotions and on human conduct seem to be treating rather of matters outside nature than of natural phenomena following nature's general laws.... There should be one and the same method of understanding the nature of all things whatsoever, namely, through nature's universal laws and rules. Thus the passions of hatred, anger, envy, and so on, considered in themselves, follow from this same necessity and efficacy of nature.... I shall consider human actions and desires in exactly the same manner as though I were concerned with lines, planes and solids. (Spinoza)[21]

But this led the consistent *social* scientist of the Enlightenment into a terrible dilemma. There were two aspects of this dilemma, the first involving "Reason," the second, "Nature". With respect to "Reason," what did it have to do with the values, needs, desires, aims, and purposes of the Enlightenment "rationalists"? If "Truth" demanded either mathematical or empirical proof, and if reason could say nothing about good or evil or about anything else that could not be mathematically or empirically demonstrated, then the Enlightenment rationalists could have no "true" ground at all for any of the social ideals that were their ultimate concern. Rationalism and empiricism are marvelously expert in discerning what "is" and in determining the most efficient ways of achieving what one decides "ought to be." But they were and remain totally deaf, dumb, and blind with respect to deciding on the aims, the "ought-to-be," or on the morally acceptable or objectionable ways of reaching them. The price paid by the modern mind for mastering the "means"—the objective knowledge required to know and control reality—was the loss of a solid ground for determining the "ends," the direction and shape of that control that are inevitably irrational and subjective concerns.

Similarly, turning to the second aspect of the dilemma, "Nature" is equally useless and irrelevant for those who want to change existence and realize the "ought-to-be." Nature simply *is*. The laws of nature are what they are, because they tell us about what, in fact, actually prevails. When the astronomers and physicists—the inspiration behind the social rationalists of the Enlightenment—mathematically described the nature of heaven and earth, they were describing processes that had gone on, were going on, and would continue to go on. Yet the whole purpose, meaning, and motivation of Enlightenment theory and, later, revolutionary practice, did not care at all about what existed before and now: their exclusive concern was to change the "is" into what they were persuaded "ought to be." Moreover, not only was nature a hopeless guide for the reforming rationalists because it dealt only with the *is* rather than the *ought;* it was also useless because the "is," the existing actuality, includes everything, good and bad indiscriminately. If these intellectuals were really serious about following "Nature" in their social aims, they would have had to accept the *existing* privileges of the nobles, the despotic crown, the benighted and oppressive Church, and all the other "irrational" institutions that the Enlightenment intended to sweep away. To believe consistently and genuinely in "Nature" and "Natural Law" would mean to believe, with the poet Pope (significantly using Newton as his inspiration), that:

> All discord, harmony not understood,
> All partial evil, universal good:
> All, spite of pride, in erring reason's spite,
> One truth is clear, Whatever is, is right.[22]

But that was just what the Enlightenment refused to accept!

The Enlightenment repeatedly and boldly proclaimed this contradiction and consequent dilemma in their characteristic use of nature (all-inclusive, amoral existence) to validate their ideals. Appropriately echoing the natural scientists, Holbach describes the universe as a "vast assemblage of everything that exists," presenting "only matter and motion . . . nothing but an immense, an uninterrupted succession of causes and effects." Yet it is to this same impersonal "assemblage" that he turns for moral guidance and salvation as though he were praying to Jehovah himself.

> "O thou," cries this Nature to man, "who, following the impulse I have given you, during your whole existence, incessantly tend towards happiness, do not strive to resist my sovereign law. . . . It is in my empire alone that true liberty reigns. Tyranny is unknown to its soil, slavery is forever banished from its votaries; equity unceasingly watches over the rights of all my subjects, maintains them in the possession of their just claims; benevolence, grafted upon humanity, connects them by amicable bonds; truth enlightens them; never can imposture blind them with his obscuring mists. . . . Show us then, O Nature! that which man ought to do. . . . Banish error from our mind; wickedness from our hearts. (Holbach)

Natural law, for Constantin Volney, was

> the *regular and constant order of facts* by which God rules the universe; the order which his wisdom presents to the sense and reason of men, to serve them as an equal and common rule of conduct, and *to guide them*, without distinction of race or sect, *towards perfection and happiness.*[23]

If rebellious Frenchmen at the end of the century proclaimed the "rights of man" in their *Declaration of the Rights of Man and Citizen*, it was because "nature," they said, had made those rights "imprescriptable," just as rebellious Englishmen living in the American colonies had arisen a little earlier in the name of those same "natural" rights: "The aim of every political association is the preservation of the natural and imprescriptible rights of man. . . ."

Those who were first aware of the dilemma that resulted from employing reason and nature to justify ideals were those who were first trapped in it—the Enlightenment philosophers themselves. Notwithstanding the bravado with which Hume dismissed everything that could not be proven mathematically or experimentally, he remained profoundly troubled by the fact that

> Epicurus's old questions are yet unanswered. Is He [God] willing to prevent evil, but not able? Then he is impotent. Is he able, but not willing? Then he is malevolent. Is he both able and willing? Whence then is evil? (Hume)[24]

Moreover, even were it true that objective reality was no more concerned about the distinction between good and evil than it was about the difference between hot and cold, what would happen, some of the Philosophers wondered, if ordinary human beings started to live their lives according to that rationalist truth? It was all well and good for Newton's God to be a first-rate cosmic engineer, to build that marvelously precise machine, and to set it all going, but what about sin and salvation, meaning and purpose? Oppressed by such doubts, Hume himself wrote, in 1737,

> I am at present castrating my work . . . ; that is, endeavouring it shall give as little offence as possible. . . . A man has but a bad grace who delivers a theory, however true, which . . . leads to a practice dangerous and pernicious. Why rake into those corners of nature, which spread a nuisance all around? (Hume)[25]

Diderot felt similarly uneasy about his rationalistic, godless worldview.

> I have not even dared to write the first line: I say to myself, if I do not come out of the attempt victorious, I become the apologist

of wickedness; I will have betrayed the cause of virtue. . . . I do not feel myself equal to this sublime work; I have uselessly consecrated my whole life to it. (Diderot)[26]

John Morely, his own rationalism notwithstanding, was even more dissatisfied with "divinity, Reason, writing on the wall the appalling judgment that there is no God; that the universe is only matter in spontaneous motion."[27]

The rationalists themselves realized full well that they had to find something to replace the Biblical and medieval God of good and evil, human meaning and purpose. They could not merely denounce or ignore God; they must show the theologians, in Diderot's words, that "we are better, and that philosophy makes more good men than sufficient or efficacious grace."[28]

With the traditional Biblical God of good and evil abandoned along with the rest of the institutions and beliefs of the "old regime," and with his replacement by nature, reason, "lines, planes, and solids," and "universal mathematics" that "had no more regard for good above evil than to heat above cold," the Enlightenment rationalists had to find some other grounds for legitimizing their convictions and goals. The problem was to choose from the totality of what "naturally" existed, those institutions, attitudes, and qualities of personal and social life that were considered good and just: to "distinguish between the variety of human nature that which is essential to it," as Rousseau put the problem.[29] They found their first answer, their first selective screen, in the study of history, whose chief purpose it was, to quote Hume, "to discover the constant and universal principles of human nature."[30]

Not surprisingly, what History proved was that "the constant and universal principles" were just those ideals that the Enlightenment favored and fought to realize! The "objective" lessons of History demonstrated that individual and social happiness were promoted by the "rational" institutions they proposed; whereas only suffering resulted from such "irrational" institutions as monarchies, churches, and aristocracies. "Other historians relate facts to inform us of facts," Diderot said in praising Voltaire's historical work. "You relate them to excite in our hearts an intense hatred of lying, ignorance, hypocrisy, superstition, tyranny; and this anger remains even after the memory of the facts has disappeared."[31] Conversely, Condorcet criticized Montesquieu for being "more occupied with finding the reasons for that which is than with seeking that which ought to be,"[32] although the criticism itself was unjustified, since Montesquieu was no less committed to drawing history into the service of moral truth, as the rationalists defined it.

> I have many times begun and many times abandoned this work; I have repeatedly thrown away the sheets already written; . . . I followed my object without forming any design: I was unable to grasp either the rules or the exceptions; I found the truth only to lose it: but *when I discovered my principles, everything I sought came to me.* (Montesquieu)[33]

The same "principles" guided Diderot and Fontanelle, determining the value choices that shaped their view of the past.

> Some may think that a knowledge of history should precede that of morality: I am not of that opinion: it seems to me more useful and expedient to possess *the idea of the just and the unjust* before possessing a knowledge of the actions and the men to whom one ought to apply it. (Diderot)

> History is good for nothing if it be not united with morality. . . . It is certain that one may know all that men ever did and still be ignorant of man himself. (Fontanelle)[34]

In part, the "rationalist" historians were again using history as had the Prophets and Talmudic sages—as a repository of moral lessons by which a present generation could look to the experiences of earlier generations in order to build wisely for future generations. But there was a critical difference between the Biblical attitude toward history and that of the Enlightenment. Biblical history surveyed moral challenges and provided lessons in reviewing the responses to them. But that Biblical, historical account was in no way considered the source for selecting and legitimizing ideals, values, and goals. That came from God through revelation. For the rationalist historians of the Enlightenment, on the contrary, legitimation and foundation for the rationalists' program was precisely what they expected from history, their main reason for turning to it for help.

History, however, could no more provide that legitimation than could Nature, and for the same reason. Just as Nature encompasses good and evil alike and so cannot be a judge between them, so does History include all events and institutions, good and bad, so can hardly provide the measure for choosing between them. It was, moreover, as obvious to historians then as it is now that History is used by all ideologies and parties to "prove" their cases and support their causes.

We are still living with the rationalists' problem, still searching for some solid ground of being and purpose to replace religious faith. Failing to find that ground in Reason, Nature, or History, the rationalists left us two responses. The first response was, in effect, to ignore the whole problem of ends by concentrating exclusively on the sphere of means, turning the "means" into the "ends," devoting personal and social existence to an endless (in both senses of the word) development of instruments, agencies, and techniques. Knowledge as power replaced knowledge of good and evil. The result was the stupendous "progress" that continued from the Renaissance until the present and defines our era—the incessant drive for more, bigger, faster, higher, more productive.

As its ultimate consequence, this instrumentalist "progress" transformed the would-be master into a mirror image of his slave. Lacking the ground for choosing any other "end" but the continual improvement of the "means," man himself became little more than another machine, a well-tooled instrument programmed to build and constantly advance the state of science, technology, and organization. Nor did man simply become the servant of his creation: he remodeled himself into a veritable clone of his machines, an auxiliary piece of productive equipment committed to the incessant expansion of science, technology, industry, and commerce, yet knowing no more than would any other machine what to do with these achievements other than plow them back into still more progress of these same instruments.

This first way out of the dilemma posed by the rationalists' definition of truth involved a most depressing paradox. Humanity had been deposed from the centrality that medieval theology and cosmology had given it in this life and deprived of the heavenly bliss that they had promised for the next. Now, in this Age of Reason, a new empirical and rational humanity struggled to regain its lost dignity by mastering the world as powerful "individuals" and making up for its lost heaven by turning worldly achievements both into monuments for personal immortality and instruments for constructing an earthly paradise sometime in the future. The trouble was that the rationalists' strategy for restoring and strengthening man's wounded ego—their scientific worldview—required not only a further weakening of that ego, but its virtual elimination; for that, in effect, is what was implied in this adoration of scientific "objectivity" and its impersonal, mechanistic agencies.

Unfortunate as that evolution was, however, it was less so than were the consequences of the second solution offered by the rationalists. If the first response to the means-ends dilemma inspired a dehumanizing submission to the means without regard for any other end, the second solution inspired a ruthless commitment to the End without regard to the means. Kepler, Galileo, and Newton made God the mathematical engineer who built the natural order and established its laws. The laws were constant and universal. It was all awesomely marvelous, but it excluded everything human, other than a capacity to measure. Holbach, Helvetius, Condorcet, Robespierre, and the other theorists and practitioners of Enlightenment idealism simply assumed and proclaimed that their personal ideals about life and society belonged entirely to that objective, universal, necessary, and rational order, that their moral and ethical "truths" were as valid as were the laws of astronomy and physics.

If there is one attribute that more than any other characterizes the modern radical intelligentsia, left and right, it is the conviction that the ideas and ideals they espouse are somehow irrefutably objective and necessary—in a word, scientific. The modern roots of this delusion are here, in the period bridging the scientific revolution and the Enlightenment, when the demonstrated discoveries of the first were uncritically converted into the axiomatic assumptions of the second.

The more distant sources lay in the tradition of Platonist "idealism," which persisted through the Middle Ages and reappeared both in Christian contemplation and in the mathematical prism of the astronomers. Through that prism of Platonist "idealism," only what is perfect and permanent is "Real." For Platonists, that meant the transcendent, hidden "Idea" of which actual existence was but a flawed and shadowy appearance. For the astronomers and physicists, who contemplated God in their mathematical universe, it encompassed the objective and constant laws of nature. For the philosophers and revolutionaries of the Enlightenment, that pure and perfect reality included "Reason," the Laws of Nature, and—the main issue here— their own personal social ideas and ideals. Since those ideas and ideals were, for the rationalists, not mere opinion, desire, or narrow self-interest (as were, in their view, all other, opposing ideologies) but objective truth as compelling as the law of gravity, anyone dis-agreeing with them obviously lacked genuine knowledge or basic sense. And since only a few fully understood those absolute truths, that knowledgeable elite must necessarily direct the application of those truths and the education of the rest of society to the point of understanding and cherishing them.

As to the manner and pace of that authoritarian direction, the "ought" must become the "is" at once. Society was a machine that could be stopped, taken apart and set rationally right. It would be as absurd to consider a partial and gradual change from the bad society to the good (the unnatural to the natural) as it would be to apply only part of a mathematical proof, chemical formula, or physical law. The militant rationalist was a social "scientist" in possession of and re-sponsible for objective truths about individual and social behavior, and he "shrunk in horror" when confronted with irrational and un-natural institutions the way Galileo had when he confronted signs of planetary irregularities. Moreover, to recall an earlier argument, the rationalist idealist must make the "ought" the "is" as quickly as possible in order to get solid "scientific" foundations for his ideals: until then, he was caught in the contradiction of justifying his ideals by claiming for them a "natural" objectivity that would be credible only *after* they left the disreputable world of the "ought" and became respected members of the existing "is."

The transmutation would be as totalitarian as it would be authoritarian. Cartesian "universal mathematics" reigned in human affairs no less necessarily than they did in the natural order. That was the whole point of this ideology, as it was the essential implica-tion of Spinoza's instructions to consider human problems as though one were dealing with "lines, planes, and solids," thus extending to human affairs the Platonic perfection and regularity that Plato himself had reserved for the transcendent Idea and Renaissance scientists had confined to nonhuman natural phenomena. Once in power, the rationalist revolutionaries would see to it that all of society corresponded to their model of purity and perfection as precisely as did the planets to their objective laws. With little or no experience in compromising pragmatically with reality or with opposing points of view and accustomed to shaping theories at will to suit their private needs (unresisting paper taking anything), they would have little patience with anything or anyone inconsistent with their theories. If character and biography predisposed the revolutionary rationalist to totalitarian domination, this ideological heritage guided him to it and justified the way he used it.

The result was maximum violence. With the proof of History behind them and the light of Reason and Science guiding the way ahead, the revolutionary intellectuals need stop at nothing to realize their ideals. Indeed, what was there to stop them, to check the violence? Since the rationalists' ideas reflected Reason, Nature, and Law, any discord between those ideas and the existing facts proved only that the facts were wrong, illegitimate, and doomed. Only violence could achieve and preserve power for the elite who alone knew the truth and the way. Only violence could sweep away the irrational old and make way for the rational new, especially since the transmutation must occur swiftly. Only violence could force those too ignorant or perverse to appreciate the rational new order to accept it and be truly free. And since the old God of good and evil had been supplanted by an almighty "universal mathematics" that cared no more about the difference between good and evil than it did about the difference between hot and cold, where, in any case, was the moral authority to say, "thou shalt not . . ."?

From September 1793 through most of July 1794, twelve men on a "Committee of Public Safety" ruled France. They had much in common as they met behind closed doors, usually at night, when the most important business was done. With one exception, they were all of the middle class, and, again with one exception—an actor—they had all become respectable professionals. Eight of the twelve were lawyers. Most were young: eleven were under forty at the time of the Revolution; four were under thirty. All of them were intellectuals, dedicated *philosophes* passionately serving the truths of Reason and Nature and determined to use them to establish, at last and at once, the good society that ignorance, superstition, and custom together with their guardians and beneficiaries—nobles, priests, and kings—

had so long delayed.[35] If they ruled it was because, to quote from the preamble to one of their decrees, they best understood "reason and philosophy, which today enlighten France and will soon govern the world" and because their goal was to substitute "the empire of reason for the tyranny of custom," as the "incorruptible" Robespierre put it. Gifted by Reason with absolute truth and, therefore, power, the leaders honored Reason in return at their "Feast of Reason," worshiped her in their "Temple of Reason" (the former Cathedral de Notre Dame), and set her at the head of their rationalist decalogue ("Reason only shalt thou heed . . .").[36]

Notwithstanding their domination and the ruthless terror, they claimed to rule not by "the iron hand of despotism, but by the reign of justice and reason." In their own eyes, they were doing no more than applying to society the reason that the mathematicians, astronomers, and physicists had been applying for centuries with such stunning and beneficial results for all mankind. "Everything is changed in the physical order; where is there any similar change in the moral and political order" Robespierre asked, then went on to answer, defining his mandate: "The world has been half revolutionized: how can the other half be accomplished? Human reason is still like the globe it inhabits: half lit by the sun, and half shrouded in darkeness."[37]

Unfortunately for ordinary French men and women, whereas the already revolutionized half was lit by the sun of knowledge about a nature that factually existed now, the knowledge that would enlighten the other half, society, was knowledge of an as yet unrealized natural law that would prevail only after the apocalyptic-revolutionary destruction of the existing, unnatural and irrational institutions. "Believe me," St. Just urged, "everything that exists around us must change and come to an end, because everything around us is unjust." Robespierre continued this thought when he stated: "Nature tells us that man was born for liberty; experience shows man enslaved. His rights are written on his heart." "What is our aim? It is the peaceful enjoyment of liberty and equality, and the reign of eternal justice whose laws are engraved, not on stone and marble, but in the heart of every man."[38]

If "everything" had to be changed, then the revolution would have to bring about "an entire regeneration . . . create a new people."[39] Nor were the Twelve thinking merely or even essentially about economic and political changes usually associated with such revolutions. What the "incorruptible" Robespierre and the other "pure men," as he called them, in the committee were after was a fundamental *moral* revolution, a moral rebirth that would purge France of any hint of crime, injustice, vice, corruption, dishonesty, graft, lies, obscene language, indolence, tax fraud, army malingering, carousing, violations of the "maximum" wages or prices, and all other immoralities and impurities, especially those associated with the ubiquitous, all-inclusive crime of "hypocrisy." In sum, "the function of government is to direct the moral and physical forces of the nation,"[40] or, as Robespierre said on another occasion,

> We wish an order of things where all low and cruel passions are enchained by the laws, all beneficent and generous feelings awakened. . . . We wish to substitute in our country morality for egotism, probity for a mere sense of honor, principle for habit, duty for etiquette, the empire of reason for the tyranny of custom, contempt for vice for contempt for misfortune . . . that is to say, all the virtues and miracles of the Republic for all the vices and puerilities of the monarchy. We wish in a word to fulfill the course of nature, to accomplish the destiny of mankind, to make good the promises of philosophy, to absolve Providence from the long reign of tyranny and crime.[41]

When the Twelve carried out their periodic purges, "purifying scrutinies" as they were called, they did so as objective scientists purging "bad humors" from the "body politic." And if the means were so brutal, it was only because the "bad humors" ran so deep. As with any effective assault on a diseased limb—and that was the most accessible and most persuasive analogy—to be cruel was to be kind. Such must be the attitude for the responsible moral leader, who, in St. Just's words, "commands the future; to be feeble will avail him nothing; it is for him to will what is good and to perpetuate it, to make man what he wishes him to be." In other words, "All is permitted to those who act in the Revolutionary direction," according to instructions issued by one of the commissions sent out to crush resistance in the provinces.[42]

Consequently, to quote a line often repeated during these months, "Make terror the order of the day." Convinced of the ultimate goodness as well as truth of their cause, the revolutionaries felt no more need to disguise their deeds or intentions than did their medieval religious predecessors or their Bolshevik and Fascist heirs. For all of them, the "monsters must be unmasked and exterminated," since "however painful an amputation may be when a member is gangrened, it must be sacrificed if we wish to save the body." "Traitors must be unmasked and struck without pity," Robespierre instructed the commissioner sent out to deal with Lyon. Unable to carry out those instructions with appropriate zeal, the commissioner lost his job to someone better suited by his belief that "indulgence is a dangerous weakness."[43] Robespierre himself provided the classic summary for the Terror.

> In times of peace, virtue is the source from which the government of the people takes its power. During the Revolution, the sources of this power are virtue and terror. . . . You put down all the enemies of freedom by means of terror, and you are justified—as founders of the Republic. The government of the Revolution is the despotism of liberty against tyranny. . . . The murderers who rend the flesh of their country at home; the intriguers who seek to purchase the conscience of the representatives of the people; the traitors who sell themselves; the pamphleteers who besmirch us and are preparing for a political counter-revolution by means of a moral counter-revolution—are all these individuals any less dangerous than the tyrants whom they serve? (Robespierre)[44]

As for the "bad humors" and gangrened limbs to be cut away, they included, most obviously, all those identified with the old order, the nobles, clerics, and members of the royal court. But that barely begins the list. Opposition of any kind meant treason, and treason meant death by guillotine. Since France under the Twelve was ruled by the best, the most rational, and the most virtuous of men, anything that went wrong must have been caused by treacherous conspirators—any battles that were lost, any rise in inflation, any shortage of goods, any defective arms or machinery, any sign of discontent or resistance, any bad news that lowered popular or military morale.

Not that it was necessary to be specifically accused of any of these crimes for someone to be a suspect. Anyone belonging to the wrong class was a "suspect," as were those with unfortunate "connections," those whose "conversation or writings" hinted at sympathies for the "enemies of liberty," those who could not demonstrate an adequate "discharge of their civic duties," those who had lost positions in the Convention (the revolutionary assembly to which the Twelve were supposedly subordinate), those in any way related to emigres, those who had "not consistently manifested their attachment to the Revolution," and so on. As that last "crime" suggests, even indifference or merely inadequate support could be fatal: "If there are traitors or even persons lukewarm to the cause of the people we bring the sword that is to strike them."[45] In the words of St. Just, one of the most zealous of the zealots,

> You need no longer deal gently with the enemies of the new order of things, and liberty must at all costs prevail. You have to punish not only traitors, but even the indifferent; you have to punish all those who remain passive within the Republic and do nothing for it. . . . Those who cannot be governed by justice must be governed by iron; tyrants must be oppressed! (St. Just)[46]

In the unlikely event that the vast scope of these definitions of suspects, traitors, and conspirators was not broad enough, the commissioners sent to the provinces to eliminate resistance were given the right to accuse anyone that they themselves considered "suspect."[47]

Since the "reign of justice and reason" was more consistent with trials than with summary executions, "trials" were usually arranged, unless there were simply too many "traitors" to permit any treatment other than rapid, mass disposal. But the patriots had no reason to fear that the trials would stand in the way of revolutionary justice: evidence sufficient to send the traitor off to the guillotine could be "any kind of documents, material or moral, written or spoken, which naturally claim the assent of any just and reasonable mind." To make sure that the point was not missed, that law went on to state that "the standard of judgment is the conscience of jurymen enlightened by patriotism: their aim is the triumph of the Republic and the ruin of its enemies." As for witnesses, the jury could carry on without them if it so desired. And the same option held for defense attorneys, since the "conspirators" did not deserve them anyhow. In all cases of "treason"—and we have seen how broadly that was defined—only the death penalty was permitted.[48]

> Here the desire for legitimate vengeance becomes an imperative need for him who considers the public interest; for the public interest requires that our enemies be visited by terror, that the threats of their conspiracies be broken, that they be punished for their crimes, and that they be made to forfeit the happiness that they want nothing of. . . . We are not speaking here merely of the priests, nobles, relatives of emigres, administrators and other perjured officials on whom the law has already expressly passed sentence; we assume that, in their case, you have already done your duty; your own heads will answer for it. But we speak here, more particularly, of all those who, though not mentioned by name in the decrees, are recommended by them to the watchful eye of the nation; we speak of those hypocrites who have always mouthed, but only mouthed, their respect for the law and the person and yet who, every day, oppressed you and, in the case of the poor, violated the most sacred of laws, those of humanity and nature . . . REPUBLICANS, these are your duties. Let no consideration of age or sex or kinship hold you back.[49]

If further justification were needed, the local Torquemadas could quote Rousseau.

> In order then that the social compact may not be an empty formula, it tacitly includes the undertaking, which alone can give force to the rest, that whoever refuses to obey the general will shall be compelled to do so by the whole body. This means nothing less than that he will be forced to be free. (Rousseau)[50]

In Lyon, Alsace, Nantes, and the vast area of the Vendee, there were too many traitors to permit individual trials. More expeditious methods were devised on the spot. In Nantes, between 1,500 and 2,000 were bound, loaded onto barges and rafts, and drowned when the craft were scuttled in the Loire. In Lyon, batches of prisoners were tied together and mowed down by cannon shot until some 1,800 were thus dispatched. In addition, orders were given—but not executed—for the destruction of the entire town.

3. The city of Lyons shall be destroyed. Every habitation of the rich shall be demolished; there shall remain only the homes of the poor, the houses of patriots who have been led astray or proscribed, the buildings employed in industry and the monuments devoted to humanity and public instruction.

4. The name of Lyons shall be effaced from the list of cities of the Republic. The collection of houses left standing shall henceforth bear the name of Ville-Affranchie—the Liberated City.

"We will make France a graveyard," the Commissioner in charge vowed, "rather than not regenerate it in our own way." In the Vendee, where the peasants opposed the Revolution, a half-million had been killed by the time the terror came to an end.[51]

Strange as it always seems to those outside the millennial mood, the executioners felt pride and joy in their gruesome labors of salvation, purification, and regeneration. "Men speak of sensibility," Collot d'Herbois said, "We too are men with sensibilities. The Jacobins have every virtue. They are compassionate, humane, generous; but they reserve all these feelings for the patriots who are their brothers, which aristocrats will never be." Still more self-assured, his friend, the indestructible Fouché, described to him how "tears of joy stream in my eyes and flood my soul": "We have only one way of celebrating victory. This evening we send two hundred and thirteen rebels under the fire of the lightning bolt." Judge Dorfeuille was similarly overjoyed by the Lyon executions: "May this festival," he wrote to the president of the Convention, "forever impress terror upon the souls of rascals and confidence upon the hearts of republicans . . . I say festival, citizen president; yes, festival is the word. When crime descends to the grave, humanity breathes again, and it is the festival of virtue." Achard, whom Robespierre considered a follower, was positively ecstatic: "What delight you would have tasted if you had seen day before yesterday the national justice upon two hundred and nine scoundrels! What majesty! What imposing tone! It was all edifying. How many villains bit the dust in the arena of Botreaux! What a cement for the Republic!"[52]

Adding a gruesomely sanctimonious note to these terrorists' sentiments and rationalizations, Fouché argued that it was not the justly punished traitors who really suffered, but the tender Jacobins, whose ardent devotion to the Revolution forced them to kill so many.

> Yes, we dare to admit it, we are shedding much impure blood, but for humanity, and for duty. Representatives of the people, we will not betray the people's will. . . . Our mission here is difficult and painful. Only an ardent love of country can console and reward the man who, renouncing all the affections which nature and gentle habits have made dear to his heart, surrendering his own sensibility and his own existence, thinks, acts and lives only in the people and with the people, and shutting his eyes to everything about him, sees nothing but the Republic that will rise in posterity on the graves of conspirators and the broken swords of tyranny.[53]

History, Nature, and Reason joined in chorus not merely to exonerate the executioners but to acclaim them noble heroes, selfless servants of the People. Notwithstanding the fact that most of the victims of the terror were commoners and that the only contact this committee of middle-class intellectuals had with the "people" was by way of sporadic Parisian street demonstrations, the Twelve never doubted that they ruled only for *le peuple*. It was, in fact, this vague abstraction that became the principal source of justification for the violence, more supportive even than History, Nature, and Reason.

> Since the French people has manifested its will, everything opposed to it is outside the sovereign. Whatever is outside the sovereign is an enemy.

> In the Convention have been found pure men who have proved that good institutions are not founded on the subtle spirit of intriguers, but on the wisdom of the people. This Constitution has emerged in eight days from the midst of storms, and becomes the center where the people can rally without giving itself new chains.

> In profiting from the energy of the people, we shall at last exterminate the enemies of the Revolution. . . . It is time, more than time, to fix the destiny of the Revolution; and surely we should

congratulate ourselves, for the very misfortunes of the people arouse its energy and put us in a position to exterminate our enemies.[54]

How the Twelve knew what the "people" wanted or needed (and knew it with the certitude that astronomers, physicists, and mathematicians claimed for their knowledge) remains a mystery, especially since, as Robespierre conceded, "the people in mass cannot govern itself." And elections were out of the question: "when the revolutionary machine is rolling," Billaud-Varenne explained, "you injure the people in entrusting it with the election of public functionaries, for you expose it to the naming of men who will betray it."[55]

The "people" for the Jacobins, in other words, were what the "workers" were to be for the Bolsheviks, the "Volk" were to be for the fascists, and "souls" had been for the Inquisitors—legitimizing abstractions that had as little to do with actuality as the rationalists' "Nature" had to do with existing nature. There is, moreover, an instructive parallel in the way the rationalist saviors handled these two abstractions—the people and nature. What the rationalists claimed to be "natural" was what did not yet exist, but what should exist, because it was "reasonable" (i.e., "natural"). It was the same with the "people," the "will of the people," the "General Will"—all of which referred not to the existing French men and women, but to the future people, the "new man," that the revolutionaries would mold in their new, "natural," "rational" society. The goal, to repeat Robespierre's remark, was to bring about "an entire regeneration and . . . create a new people." The connection between the two abstractions is even closer: the right and reasonable "nature" that the Revolution would establish was none other than the reason and virtue of the new "people," the "eternal laws" that had always been written on the people's hearts, however long and deeply those inscriptions had been buried under layers of irrational and unnatural social corruptions. It was because of those irrational and unnatural social corruptions that the actual people lacked the capacities to know their own best interest, and so had to be led by enlightened intellectuals dedicated to their liberation. And since it was also because of those irrational and unnatural institutions that the transition period between the old world and the new must be so painful, it was unfair to judge the validity or nobility of the revolutionary cause by its violent measures. Let the future judge!

To the shouts of approval already gathered from Nature, Reason, History, and the People, the rationalist revolutionaries thus added a final voice to sanctify their cause—the voice of posterity.

> O posterity, sweet and tender hope of humanity, thou art not a stranger to us; it is for thee that we brave all the blows of tyranny; it is thy happiness which is the price of our painful struggles: often discouraged by the obstacles that surround us, we feel the need of thy consolations; it is to thee that we confide the task of completing our labors, and the destiny of all the unborn generations of men! (Robespierre)[56]

Lamenting the loneliness of the selfless liberator, St. Just took courage in the belief that

> obliged to isolate himself from the world and from himself, man drops his anchor in the future and presses to his heart the posterity which bares no blame for the evils of the present. (St. Just)[57]

Although himself swept into the maw of the Terror, Condorcet, as we saw earlier, remained to the end exhilarated by the vision of the glorious future the Revolution surely would bring to humanity. Explicitly making the point that is implicit throughout this analysis, Diderot realized long before the Revolution that "posterity is for the philosophers what the other world is for the religious."[58] Recalling the final words of an old veteran of the Revolution, his biographer noted that

> at the moment of death, raising to heaven a look of ecstasy, [he] was heard to murmur: "O sun of '93, I shall die at last without having seen thy rays again." This man, like the first Christians, lived in the hope of the millennium.[59]

The apocalyptically religious character of the Terror was evident in much more than this familiar comparison between posterity and heaven, however. It was apparent in almost all aspects of that revolutionary experience, notwithstanding the anticlericism, persecution of religious communities, and eulogies to Nature and Reason. What were the ecstatic visions that Reason and Nature had given the revolutionaries if not "revelations" about ultimate Truth as authoritative as divinely revealed Truth had been? What was Robespierre's "entire regeneration" of a "new people" if not a vision of a "new heaven and new earth?" What was that concealed "heart" of virtue if not the Biblical "new heart" that was miraculously to replace the old heart and thereby create the new Kingdom? What was the brutal revolutionary violence if not the apocalyptic devastation that would wipe away the old so that the new could emerge pure and safe from contamination? And who were those limbs to be amputated and "bad humors" to be purged if not those doomed to "weep and gnash their teeth"? From the point of view of the victims, what difference did it make whether their executions were ordered in the name of God or Reason, Heaven or Posterity?

But there is no need to argue the point from inference and analogy. The leaders themselves seemed eager to sanctify the Revolution by drawing their symbols from the scorned religious heritage whenever possible. They repeatedly referred to revolutionary martyrs, republican temples, revolutionary hymns and sermons, and so on. The following is one such "hymn," chanted in the Temple of Reason (Notre Dame).

> Descend, O Liberty, daughter of Nature; The people, recovering thy immortal power, Upon the stately ruins of old imposture, Raise once again thy altar! Come, conqueror of kings, Europe's example, Come, over false Gods complete thy success! Thou, Saint Liberty, inhabit this temple, Be of our nation the Goddess![60]

There were even, to complete an earlier reference, revolutionary decalogues.

> To the people only shalt thou swear
> Obedience religiously.
> On every king though shalt declare
> Hate and war eternally.
> The laws the people shall ordain
> Thou shalt observe most faithfully.
> Thy liberty though shalt maintain

As long as life in thee shall be.
Equality thou shalt keep dear
By practising it constantly.
From selfish acts thou shalt keep clear,
Done thoughtlessly or purposely.
For offices thou shalt not plead,
To serve in them improperly.
Reason only shalt thou heed
To guide thee in futurity.
Republican thou strict shalt live
That thou mayst die as worthily.[61]

To replace traditional religious holidays, some thirty-six festivals were decreed, celebrating, for example, "The human race," "The French people," "The martyrs of liberty," "The republic," "Patriotism," "Truth," "Justice," "Stoicism," "Infancy," "Old age," "Misfortune," "Agriculture," and "Our ancestors." And these secular revolutionary saints seemed even more insistent on attendance and active participation than the Church had been. "The priests in other days used to say, any parishioner who fails to come to mass three Sundays in a row risks excommunication. Well, let us say, any citizen who fails to come to our civic festivals will be denied employment, denied our friendship and confidence." To provide the proper setting, there were such things as a "patriotic holy water font," a "pilgrimage of the patron of Liberty," a "patriotic sign of the cross," an "altar" to revolutionary and other secular heroes, and repeated reference to the "miracles" accomplished by the "holy Guillotine." To crown it all, Robespierre proclaimed a national faith in a Supreme Being.

The idea of a great Being who watches over oppressed innocence and punishes triumphant crime is essentially the idea of the people. This is the sentiment of Europe and the world; it is the sentiment of the French people. That notion is attached neither to priests nor to superstition nor to ceremonies; it is attached only to the idea of an incomprehensible Power, the terror of wrongdoers, the stay and comfort of virtue. (Robespierre)

It was in the service of this god of Reason, Nature, the People, and Posterity that, as Couthon said, the Revolution had torn away the deceptive "veil" of the established Church. Listening closely to Couthon and his associates, however, it seems rather that the veil torn aside was the one he and his fellow revolutionaries had used to hide the apocalyptic religious essence of their own secular messianism.[62]

Rather than displace religion, the cult of Reason dialectically absorbed it and, thereby, only intensified its apocalyptic violence and authoritarianism (as the following cult of history would absorb and intensify the apocalyptic violence and authoritarianism of both religion and Reason). Even in the brief time the Twelve had to execute their secular apocalypse, they unfolded with crushing clarity the totalitarian implications of their rationalist faith. France was politically centralized as never before. The Twelve tried to organize and regulate the French economy far more thoroughly than even the royal French mercantilists had tried to do in the preceding century. The army was transformed from a collection of professionals and mercenaries into the first modern, national army based on conscription.

> [A]ll Frenchmen are permanently requisitioned for the service of the armies. The young shall go and fight, the married men shall forge weapons and transport food, the women shall make tents and clothes and serve in the hospitals, the old men shall have themselves carried into public places to rouse the courage of the warriors and preach hatred of kings and the unity of the nation.[63]

The reality and the threat of the guillotine, the ubiquitous commissioners sent out to enforce obedience, and the extensive network of local militant organizations to carry on after the commissioners had left combined to create the essential features of any terror—universal suspicion and dread, mutual recrimination for self-protection, summary and arbitrary executions, mock displays of revolutionary enthusiasm, and all the rest of the horror that our era has come to know so well. Nowhere, finally, was this future oppression more clearly anticipated than in the dictators' educational plans. According to Palmer, St. Just, who had boundless faith in the power and virtue of both the "legislator" and his central institutions, viewed the mobilization of the young as especially vital.

Boys over five belong to the state. No parent may interfere with his child's wishes. Boys are to be organized in legions, battalions and companies, taught martial exercises, and assigned to farmers to work in the fields. They are to be brought up in the love of silence, under stern discipline, wearing a uniform of coarse cloth, eating vegetables, and sleeping on mats of straw.[64]

The violence and domination would end "in a very simple way, and without being harassed by factions, when all the people have become equally devoted to their country and its laws."[65] In his novel, *The Possessed*, Dostoevsky has one of the revolutionary leaders say,

I am perplexed by my own data and my conclusion is a direct contradiction of the original idea with which I start. Starting from unlimited freedom, I arrive at unlimited despotism. I will add, however, that there can be no solution of the social problem but mine.

In light of our own more recent experience, which has allowed us to understand more fully the nature and consequences of the Twelve's revolutionary innovations, we would now change "despotism" to "fascism." Those with insight enough had no need to wait for more evidence: the theory and practice of these first secular saviors were enough to teach the essential lessons. For de Tocqueville, the experience as a whole was an example of the "foolish hope that a sudden, radical transformation of a very ancient, highly intricate social system could be effected almost painlessly, under the auspices of reason and by its efficacy alone."[66] Much earlier, even before the Twelve took power, one of the moderates—a Girondist—saw the core and source of the disaster.

The principles, in their metaphysical abstractness and in the form in which they are being constantly analysed in this society—no government can be founded on them; a principle cannot be rigorously applied to political association, for the simple reason that a principle admits of no imperfection; and, whatever you may do, men are imperfect. . . . I would gladly, if you like, applaud the chimera of perfection that they are after. But tell me, in divesting in this way man of what is human in him, are they not most likely to turn him into a ferocious beast?[67]

NOTES

1. Ernest Lee Tuveson, *Millennium and Utopia* (Berkeley: University of California Press, 1949), 46. Professor Tuveson's "Study in the Background of the Idea of Progress," to quote the subtitle, provides a rich mine of fascinating material about the intellectual transition from the late medieval to the modern world. I have based much of my own analysis of the period on this material.

2. Ibid.

3. Ibid., 120, 142–45, 160, 165–66, 189, 190.

4. Ibid., 65.

5. Ibid., 57.

6. Ibid., 66.

7. Sidney Pollard, *The Idea of Progress* (Harmondsworth, England: Penguin, 1971), 37.

8. Tuveson, *Millennium*, 151–52, 135.

9. Ibid., 95.

10. Ibid., 110.

11. Ibid., 137–38.

12. Ibid., 147, 150–51; Pollard, *Idea of Progress,* 67, 80, 92; John Herman Randall, *The Making of the Modern World* (Boston: Houghton Mifflin, 1940), 383–84.

13. Tuveson, *Millennium*, 196; Pollard, *Idea of Progress*, 85, 94.

14. E. A. Burtt, *The Metaphysical Foundations of Modern Physical Science* (Garden City, N.Y.: Doubleday, 1954), 289–90.

15. *Chapters in Western Civilization* (New York: Columbia University Press, 1954), 1:306.

16. Ibid., 306; Randall, *Modern World*, 246, 260.

17. *Chapters in Western Civilization*, 296, 298, 301.

18. Colin Maclaurin, quoted in Carl L. Becker, *The Heavenly City of the Eighteenth-Century Philosophers* (New Haven: Yale University Press, 1966), 62–63.

19. Randall, *Modern World*, 273.

20. Thomas Mendenall, Basil Henning, and A. S. Foord, eds., *Ideas and Institutions in European History, 800–1715* (New York: Henry Holt, 1956), 168–69.

21. Becker, *Heavenly City*, 38; Randall, *Modern World*, 247.

22. Randall, *Modern World*, 275.

23. Randall, *Modern World*, 274, 278–79; Becker, *Heavenly City*, 45.

24. Becker, *Heavenly City*, 68.

25. Ibid., 25.

26. Ibid., 80.

27. Ibid., 76.

28. Ibid., 81.

29. Ibid., 87.

30. Ibid., 71.

31. Ibid., 91–92.

32. Ibid., 101.

33. Ibid., 104; italics added.

34. Ibid.; italics added in quotation from Diderot.

35. This survey of the Jacobin reign of terror is largely based on R. R. Palmer, *Twelve Who Ruled* (New York: Atheneum, 1965).

36. Palmer, *Twelve*, 144, 325, 375.

37. Ibid., 126; J. M. Thompson, *Robespierre and the French Revolution* (New York: Macmillan, 1953), 124.

38. Fred Weinstein and Gerald M. Platt, *The Wish to Be Free* (Berkeley: University of California Press, 1969), 118; Thompson, *Robespierre*, 108, 124.

39. Weinstein and Platt, *Wish to Be Free*, 121.

40. Palmer, *Twelve*, 311.

41. Ibid., 275.

42. Weinstein and Platt, *Wish to Be Free*, 120; Palmer, *Twelve*, 167.

43. Palmer, *Twelve*, 12, 52, 157, 163, 165, 194.

44. Kenneth M. Setton and Henry R. Winkler, eds., *Great Problems in European Civilization* (New York: Prentice-Hall, 1955), 367–68.

45. Albert Mathiez, *The French Revolution*, trans. Catherine Alison Phillips (New York: Russell and Russell, 1962), 370–71; Palmer, *Twelve*, 182.

46. Mathiez, *French Revolution*, 388–89.

47. Palmer, *Twelve*, 146.

48. Thompson, *Robespierre*, 118–19.

49. Rude, *op. cit.*, pp. 211, 214.

50. Setton and Winkler, *Great Problems*, 362.

51. Palmer, *Twelve*, chaps. 3, 7.

52. Ibid., 170–71, 174–75.

53. Ibid., 175.

54. Ibid., 33, 35, 48, 51, 75.

55. Ibid., 33, 126.

56. Becker, *Heavenly City*, 142–43.

57. Weinstein and Platt, *Wish to Be Free*, 118.

58. Becker, *Heavenly City*, 149–50.

59. Ibid., 158–59.

60. Ibid., 157.

61. Palmer, *Twelve*, 325.

62. Becker, *Heavenly City*, 156–58; Crane Brinton, *A Decade of Revolution* (New York: Harper and Brothers, 1934), 157–58; Will Durant and Ariel Durant, *The Age of Napoleon* (New York: Simon and Schuster, 1975), 73–74; Palmer, *Twelve*, 144.

63. Durant and Durant, *Age of Napoleon*, 63.

64. Palmer, *Twelve*, 283.

65. Weinstein and Platt, *Wish to Be Free*, 129.

66. Ibid., 133.

67. J. L. Talmon, *The Origins of Totalitarian Democracy* (New York: Norton, 1970), 20–21.

4

Apocalypse and History

The early nineteenth-century critics of the French Revolution—"conservatives," "romantics," and philosophical "idealists"—drew the expected conclusions from that apocalyptic explosion. The reign of terror and the Napoleonic wars that followed convinced them, first of all, that Reason was hardly the essence of human nature. The eighteenth-century rationalists were uncommonly naive, they argued, in believing that one need only get rid of such "irrational" and "unnatural" institutions as the monarchy, the church, and the nobility for the natural goodness and reason of the "people" to blossom forth and flourish ever after. The Revolution, they concluded, had proven that exactly the reverse was true: kings, priests, and noblemen were needed to keep the lid on the barbarously irrational and irreparably sinful nature of the common people and to guide them through the appropriate rituals of a sane and civil society. Emotion, not reason, was the mainspring of behavior, and without those traditional political, religious, and social-class restraints, the human community would always disintegrate into anarchic and self-destructive chaos.

Moreover, the critics went on, even had those admittedly authoritarian institutions been guilty of all the Enlightenment's accusations, they still could not be swept away at will, discarded and replaced according to some neatly rational design. Society was not a machine that could be stopped, dismantled, and repaired or remade, but a living, organic process, with each constituent organ so inextricably interconnected with the others that to remove even one of them would mean to kill the whole. The human society was also much more akin to a living being than to a dead machine, because it evolved through a long and complex history and, as a result of that organic evolution, possessed a definite and unique organic identity that could no more be exchanged for another identity (however "rational") than one human being could exchange his or her basic character for that of another.

If one sought to understand the nature of humanity and society, therefore, the last place one should turn for guidance would be to the astronomers, physicists, mathematicians, and other scientists who viewed reality as an impersonal, inhuman composite of "lines, planes, and solids" or "primary qualities" of weight and extension to be analyzed objectively. Instead, one should follow the lead and insight of those who could sensitively appreciate the tone and texture, the feel and flow of living human experience, those who sensed reality subjectively and introspectively from within reality itself, through that wonderfully sensitive and precise inner mirror of reality—one's own soul. Poets, philosophers, painters, musicians, religious sages—these should be our teachers, not the mathematicians of dead matter and motion or any other scientists who took as their guide and model an alien and alienating objectivity.

In many respects, this conservative-romantic-idealist litany represented a return to the medieval mind that the rationalists had supplanted. The world once again was experienced subjectively; the emphasis was once more on past revelation rather than on future progress; the emotions regained their precedence over the claims of objective Reason; and the established social fabric was again protected by God and custom.

The arguments were clever, persuasive, and—after some twenty years of revolution, terror, and war—appropriate to the mood of the time. But if they were meant to put an end to apocalyptic devastation, they failed utterly. No sooner had the lessons been learned and the arguments formulated, than these same arguments began to form the main features of the next apocalypse, the Apocalypse of History (as the lessons learned by Renaissance and Enlightenment rationalists from the failed Apocalypse of Faith had provided the foundations for the Apocalypse of Reason). As a result—which this chapter will survey—the violence of Lenin, Stalin, and their followers was to be blessed by the ineluctable "Laws of History" as Revelation had blessed the Inquisitors and Taborites and Reason blessed the Jacobin Twelve.

The Apocalypse of History began in a German resolution of the French rationalists' basic problem—their lack of an objective ground for their values and aims. The French had turned for support, first, to Reason and Nature, then to the lessons of History and, finally, to the gratitude of Posterity, but none of them furnished the required guarantees. German philosophical idealism, especially as formulated by Schelling, Fichte, and Hegel, easily found a solution by going back to Plato: the absolute, objective ground of values was a transcendent realm of eternal, pure, and perfect "Ideas," to which learned philosophers had access through speculative reasoning and intuition. The path to the absolute lay within our own souls and minds, not in the empirical world outside. In Schelling's words:

> In all of us there swells a secret marvelous power of freeing ourselves from the changes of time, of withdrawing to our secret selves away from external things, and of so discovering to ourselves the eternal in us in the form of unchangeability. This presentation of ourselves to ourselves is the most truly personal experience, upon which depends everything that we know of the suprasensual world. This presentation shows us for the first time what real existence is, while all else only appears to be. It differs from every presentation of the sense in its perfect freedom, while all other presentations are bound, being overweighted by the burden of the object.[1]

Only through that interior mirror of the absolute could one become aware of the "True Life," the "One, unchangeable, and eternal," as Fichte put it. All the rest, all that "vain, miserable, and unblessed external world" was only "Apparent Life." Truth, in short, was reached not by observing or measuring external reality, but through and in thought itself, the human mind whose capacity for deductive reasoning made it one with absolute, divine reason: "the eternal can be apprehended only by Thought." Thought "alone is the eye to which God can become visible." The ideal way to genuine knowledge, consequently, was "the concentration of mind, and its indwelling in itself. . . . The actual life of knowledge is, at bottom, the essential Being of the Absolute itself."[2]

Echoing these views in Russia, where the Apocalypse of History was later to come to fruition (and that is the reason for this focus on lesser known Russian thinkers), one leading St. Petersburg idealist argued during this post-Enlightenment era, that "true knowledge consists of ideas, not sense data, since experience and observation deal with the transient and limited forms of things, but do not touch their limitless and eternal essence." In much the same vein, a prominent Moscow colleague wrote that,

> everything perceptible must be known through the Spirit, and since this is only possible if the laws of the knowing Spirit conform to the laws of phenomenal existence, it is clear that the forms of knowledge are in accord with the forms of being and that they may be reciprocally explained.

Similarly, from two students of these St. Petersburg and Moscow teachers, we learn that "rational being . . . reflects the essence itself of the Absolute"; and that "all knowledge will be founded on one science alone, that of a knowledge of the self." Since reason was "merely a reflection of Absolute mind, the essence of universal life," those engrossed intuitively in rational speculation "looked down on the physicists and chemists . . . who rooted about in 'vulgar matter.'"[3]

Superficially, all this sounds like echoes of the Gnostics, neo-Platonists, and Christian mystics, familiar commentaries on transcendent spiritual realms and on the inner voyages into mind and soul that lead the seeker to them. But, as in most other currents of life and thought in the decades after the French Revolution, what occurred was not a simple return to earlier worldviews but a merger between those earlier views and Enlightenment rationalism. In this case, concerning the focus on intuition, introspection, speculation, and other interior enterprises, the philosophers did, indeed, adopt earlier Gnostic and neo-Platonist concepts of mind, but in doing so they by no means limited mind's subject matter to things spiritual. To know the nature of mind and the world within was to know as well the world outside.

> [T]he pure "I" in knowing itself knows the world objective to it. It knows itself and at the same time knows the other as well, and this other is for it the truth, . . . In understanding the laws of the physical as well as those of the mental world, the reasoning consciousness understands its own concepts, but, nevertheless, regards them as something existing outside itself and alien to it . . . it perceives them, but does not understand them, does not

find itself in them . . . the truth man can achieve without having
to depart from himself . . . every man in his own individuality is
universal, and possessing the universal within himself he can
ascend to it without leaving his own individuality, can know the
universal, the true, and realize it by the force of his own free
will.[4]

Abstract as these ideas might seem, they played a vital part in
the theory and practice that generated the apocalypse of history. For
what they implied was the power of intellectuals to decipher the past,
present, and future, distinguish the concealed essential "laws" of
history and society from the superficial "appearances," and in all
other ways fully understand reality without ever leaving their rooms
and libraries. Of course, their intuitions and speculations would have
to be fleshed out by illustrative facts from the real world outside, but
those facts would never be more than selected illustrations for a priori
intuitions: no matter what reality did or did not do, the intellectuals'
intuited truths were invulnerably secure. German "idealism" had
solved the dilemmas of the eighteenth-century rationalists not by
finding that long-sought objective, demonstrable ground for the true
and the good, but by postulating an inner (and transcendent) source
for intuitive truth that could easily do without any objectively verifi-
able support.

George Frederich Hegel, the most illustrious and influential of
the German idealists, is mainly responsible for this merger between
Enlightenment rationalism and the Platonist-Christian tradition and,
especially, for transforming a static Platonic idealism ("unchangeable, eternal") into the dialectical philosophy of history that was later
to legitimize Lenin's apocalypse of history. Plato himself pointed the
way in his dialectical dialogues. According to the logic of those dialogues, the goal (in Plato's case, Truth) is reached through a series
of contradictions: an initial statement provokes an opposing argument that contradicts or negates it; then, the two join into a synthesis,
which in turn becomes the target for the next negation, and so on, all
the way to Truth.

It was this dialectical pattern that Hegel transferred from Plato's
dialogues to the realms of cosmic, universal, and human history. On
the plane of human history, each cultural period was dominated by
a particular religion or set of ideas that determined all aspects of

civilization for that period. But the situation was radically unstable, because the prevailing worldview also promoted an opposing ideology and civilization that challenged it, fought to negate and replace it, just as Plato's ideas challenged each other on the way to Truth. History, thus, necessarily moved by successive conflicts, with successively dominant ideologies determining correspondingly successive civilizations. Behind the whole process, finally, was a drama of cosmic proportions through which the divine spirit, Absolute Reason, evolved toward its ultimate and predetermined destination, Absolute Freedom. At that point, all opposites would be reconciled. Human freedom would be in accord with objective necessity; subject and object would be one. And the Spirit, separated from itself at the time of material creation (the gnostic scenario), would regain its lost unity.

In effect, Hegel withdrew the philosophy of history from the Enlightenment and returned it to the medieval view of providential history. As we saw in chapter 3, the Enlightenment approach to history was similar to that of the ancient Hebrews: human history comprised a collection of situations and challenges that taught lessons through which humanity could, it was hoped, better chart its course into the future. Even the addition, toward the end of the eighteenth century, of the euphoric theory of progress did not basically alter this perspective, since the eighteenth-century belief in progress essentially meant what "basic trust" had meant to the people of the Book—a conviction that the arrangement of the world and the capacities of man together favored the realization of humanity's noblest ideals. What it did not imply, and what was the distinguishing assumption of the nineteenth-century philosophy of history and its twentieth-century revolutionary beneficiaries, was a faith in some objective demiurgic force that determined the direction, stages, and end of human history.

In Hegel's Universal Absolute, his all-powerful, all-knowing, all-inclusive *Weltgeist* ('World Spirit/Mind'), and its prearranged purpose and plan, we have returned to Daniel's preordained historical stages, Augustine's correspondingly deterministic reinterpretation of the Bible, and Joachim of Fiore's prophetic history. When he returned to providential history, however, Hegel by no means ceased worshiping in the "Temple of Reason." If Hegel's providential God of History seems so cold and impersonal, it is because he is still, as well, the rational God of the astronomers, physicists, and mathematicians.

It was this fusion of the medieval providential God and the rationalists' impersonal God of Reason, together with the dialectical theory, that laid the foundations for the Apocalypse of History. The fusion merged the worst of the two worlds described in previous chapters. Jacobin "Reason" was dangerous enough by itself, because of its "objective" indifference to good and evil and its "scientific" treatment of human affairs as though they, indeed, involved no more than "lines, planes, and solids," matter and motion that need only by counted, weighed, or measured. However, because of its absolute, impersonal objectivity, Reason also had nothing to do with aims, purposes, directions, or other ends. As with the rationalists' "Nature," "Reason" was always here and now: it did not go anywhere. It was eternal and eternally the same. One could choose to change the world, but Reason could not tell the reformer what those changes should be nor compel any such transformation, much less contain within itself the dynamics and energies to generate it.

The providential God of medieval Christianity, by contrast, had all sorts of aims and purposes that formed and motivated individual and social existence. The essential meaning of "providence" was its deterministic design according to which human History unfolded, stage by stage, to its assigned apocalyptic and redemptive end. The principal and full realization of that design, however, was predestined to occur not on earth but in heaven. And, still more important as a restraint on the implicit apocalyptic violence, the medieval God had remained a Biblical parental God who, unlike Reason, cared deeply about human beings and about the difference between good and evil.

The dangers inherent in each of the two credos were, thus, at least to some extent checked by other of their basic features. By combining the two, Hegel eliminated those safeguards and produced, in effect, a divine Reason that (1) providentially gathers all human experience into an inevitable historical evolution toward a preordained ideal; (2) secularly locates the ideal on earth; and (3) rationally abstains from all moral judgments about the process and means of that unfolding, remaining no more concerned about the difference between good and evil on the way to the End than between hot and cold, treating all tyranny, oppression, injustice, and other violent evils (considered "necessary" phases of that process) with the detachment of a mathematician dealing with his lines, planes, and solids.

As if this did not provide sanction enough for violence, Hegel added another warrant in his dialectical theory of history. Whatever one might say about the validity of that transformation of Plato's dialectical dialogues into laws of cosmic and human development, there is little doubt that its consequences for modern history have been enormous. What the dialectical theory did was turn the Apocalypse from the one-time climactic catastrophe it had been for both the Christian visionaries and the rationalist Twelve into a scenario of permanent revolution, a continuing series of conflicts needed to keep history moving toward the final Eden of Absolute Freedom. Rather than hold ordinary human compassion and morality in abeyance long enough for Armaggedon or Revolution to destroy the sinners and permit the righteous to reign forever in peace and plenty, compassion and morality henceforth had to be permanently excluded from judgments about human affairs: the wars of Gog-Magog would have to go on and on. Finally, rather than merely foster an indifference to violence, as was the case with the pseudoscience of the Jacobin terrorists, Hegel's historical dialectics encouraged an expectation and even preference for it, since only through "dialectical" contradiction and conflict could progress continue and the ideal be realized.

Whereas the Gnostic-Platonist-Christian mystic response to evil in the world was to *transcend* it, Hegel's solution was to *transfigure* it. The evil, irrational reality was transfigured into a good and rational reality by arguing that *whatever* now existed, however bad it seemed, contained potentially and dialectically within it, as the acorn does the oak, the ultimate ideal toward which the universe had been heading since it began. And since that final goal—Absolute Freedom—was rational and good, so was the entire evolution leading to it and all the phases along the way. If something existed at all, if it was "real" in the sense of being actual, it must play some part in this benevolent progress of Reason, Spirit, Mind, the Absolute. As Hegel put it, "the Real is the Rational."

If one truly understood this hidden unfolding one would realize that all "apparent" evil represented the "cunning of History," through which existence advanced steadily toward its sublime End. "History . . . is no theater of happiness. Periods of happiness are blank pages in it."[5] No amount of oppression, destruction, corruption, suffering, injustice, degradation, or other abominations could disturb the olympian tranquility of those with insight enough to grasp this inner dialectical logic of Being and its destiny.

> [T]he History of the World occupies a higher ground than that morality which is personal in character—the conscience of individuals, their particular will and mode of action. . . . What the absolute aim of Spirit requires and accomplishes, what Providence does, transcends . . . the imputation of good and bad motives.[6]

In formulating his dialectical philosophy of history, Hegel reconciled his early support of the French Revolution and his later conservatism. In 1795, for example, he expressed his revolutionary hopes in a letter to Schelling: "With the dissemination of ideas as to how things ought to be, the indolence of those sedate people who eternally take everything just as it is will disappear." Elsewhere, he similarly called for the end of institutions that "no longer agree with the customs, needs, opinions of mankind." Later, in 1802, after all the turmoil, he saw things quite differently.

> For it is not what exists that makes us vehement and causes us suffering; rather, it is what is *not as it should be*. But if we see that it *is* as it *must* be—i.e., that it is not arbitrary or accidental—then we also see that it *should* be as it is. . . . What is universally valid is also universally effective; *what ought to be*, as a matter of fact, *is*, too; what merely *should* be, and is *not*, has no truth.[7]

By thus modernizing "God's Will" into historical inevitability, Hegel provided our world an all-purpose legitimation of violence that was equally serviceable on the "right" or the "left." For those accepting and defending the status quo, "the Real is the Rational" meant that all that existed, in fact, however oppressive, was rational, necessary, and, in the end, good. For those in opposition, it meant that anything as manifestly "irrational" as inequality, authoritarian rule, censorship, and the like was not "real" and must be replaced— and dialectically, through violent negation. (Once in power, characteristically, the revolutionary "left" adopted the "right" Hegelian defense of the authoritarian status quo.)

Appropriately, considering Hegel's own conservative politics, the "right" came first. As we will see, however, and this is the main reason for reviewing the conservative argument in a study of apocalyptic movements, virtually all the theories that the "right" Hegelians used to justify violence and domination were later to be adopted by the "left" Hegelians. It was easy for them to bring so much along, since so little had to be abandoned in order to reorient Hegel leftward. From the perspective of the new, "left" militants, in fact, the "left" is where Hegel properly belonged.

First of all, the "left" held on dearly to the dialectic—that most powerful engine of sanctified violence. True, Hegel had argued that dialectical conflict had come to an end in the reign of Frederick William III—Hegel's own time—and that, henceforth, the Spirit would unfold under the rational guidance of the rational Prussian State rather than result from the usual blind struggle. For the "left" militants, however, that argument represented nothing more than Hegel's own political self-protection. The dialectic, they argued, would most certainly go on, and more violently than ever. Similarly, the "left" was perfectly willing to accept Hegel's remarkable claim that his own philosophy represented the pinnacle and climax of philosophy, that with it human understanding had attained a complete grasp of Absolute Reason. But, they said, it was entirely wrong to draw a conservative conclusion from that, as Hegel's "right" epigones had done. Quite the contrary—"the task of the philosophy of the spirit," the left Hegelian Moses Hess wrote, "now consists in becoming a philosophy of action."[8] Elaborating the point, Polish Hegelian Count August von Cieszkowski wrote:

Absolute idealism has achieved all that it is possible for philosophy to achieve. . . . Philosophy must therefore now be content primarily with being applied, and just as the poetry of art has been transformed into the prose of thought, so philosophy must descend from the heights of theory into the battlefield of practice. Practical philosophy, or, to put it more accurately, the philosophy of practice—the most concrete action of life and social conditions, the development of truth in concrete activity—is the future lot of philosophy as such.[9]

The Bauer brothers, Edgar and Bruno, were still more specific about the character and impact of this advance from theory to "practice."

> Only extremism can assume and carry through a principle in its purity; only extremism has the power to create. A principle never mediates; it only destroys, and its inner strength is proportionate to its destructive power. . . . In the inmost part of the State a chasm will open which . . . with an earthquake that will shake to ruins our aristocratic framework, will send forth the hordes of oppressed against law-protected egoism. . . .

> Now criticism does not any longer merely send idea against idea, it sends into the field men against men; it finds in the practical force that it wields the proof of its own power.[10]

> The catastrophe will be frightful: it will of necessity be a great one, and I would almost go as far as to say that it will be greater and more monstrous than that which accompanied Christianity's entrance on the world scene.[11]

Thus, when "left" Hegelian Karl Marx made his famous remark that, heretofore, philosophers had only "understood" the world, but that their real obligation was to "change" it, he was voicing the first principle of the entire movement.

As for the rest of the "right" Hegelian heritage, the "left" was more than happy to claim it as their own and to use it against the Establishment as the "right" has used those same theories in its defense. There was the same marvelous End with its resolution of all contradictions, attainment of absolute freedom, and liberation from all alienation; the same possession of intuited higher and deeper truths that confirmed all the theories and sanctioned leadership; the same impersonal and impregnable historicism that defined good and evil only in terms of aiding or hindering inevitable "progress"; and, above all, the same impersonal objectivism that not only easily accommodated any amount of violence, but, because of the dialectical "law," explicitly required it.

How much bolder and more exhilarating it all was than the passive reconciliation of the old guard, "right" Hegelians! As a "right" Hegelian, the leading Russian publicist Belinsky ("Furious Vissarion") had to stifle his rebellious rage and "reconcile" the two sides.

> Unconditional submission to tsarist authority is not only useful and necessary for us, but it is the highest poetry of our lives—our nationality, if by the word nationality is to be understood the act of fusing particular individualities into a general consciousness of the personality and selfhood of the State. . . . [The individual] must renounce his subjective individuality, recognize that it is false and illusory, and put himself in harmony with what is universal and general, recognizing that in the latter alone is truth and reality. [The fault of] the subjective person [is that he] is in eternal struggle with the objective world, and hence with society. . . . Free individual actions, unreconciled with external necessity, deviating from the life of society, produce collisions. . . . Yes, live not as you like, not as you think you should, but as the ruler decrees, and that ruler is—civic society.[12]

Turning to the "left," he could let his passions roar: "Oh, away with that hateful universal, that Moloch, devouring life," Belinsky exclaimed when he awoke from his right Hegelian reveries.

> The destiny of the subject, of the individual, of the person, is more important than the destinies of the whole world and the health of the Chinese emperor (i.e., the Hegelian *Allgemeinheit*) . . . I thank you humbly, George Frederick Hegel; I bow to your philosopher's gown. But with all due respect for your philosophic philistinism, I have the honor to inform you that if it were granted to me to climb to the highest rung of the ladder of development, at that very point I would ask you to account to me for all the sacrifices to the conditions of life and history, all the victims of hazard, of superstition, of the Inquisition, of Philip II, etc., etc. Otherwise I would throw myself down head foremost from the highest rung.

> I curse my odious effort of reconciliation with an odious reality! Long live great Schiller, noble advocate of humanity, bright star of salvation, emancipator of society from the bloody prejudices

of tradition! . . . For me now the *human personality* is above history, above society, above humanity.[13]

The awakening was even more explosive for Belinsky's fellow Hegelian, Bakunin. He, too, had tried passive reconciliation. "None of us should think about how things might be better with us; [we] should instead regard the external world as something given, in which one must find oneself and thereby transform the external into the internal." Adopting almost the same terms of surrender and submission that Belinsky used, Bakunin sharply criticized the rebellious individual who

> wanders about in sick alienation from any kind of natural and spiritual reality, in one or another fantastic, arbitrary, nonexistent world or who arms himself against the real world and imagines that with his illusory strength he can destroy its powerful existence, who imagines that the realization of the finite propositions of his finite judgement and the finite aims of his finite will comprise the entire good of mankind, and who does not realize, poor fellow, that the real world is higher than his wretched and feeble individuality, that sickness and evil are not part of reality, but part of himself, of his own alienation.[14]

But how long could passive acceptance remain the philosophy of someone with Bakunin's temperament?

> Passions, intensified through constraint, rage within me; emotional forces seethe and demand nourishment, but all this remains inactive, limited only to dreams, which themselves cannot fill the emptiness of my heart. . . . Everything in me demands action, movement, but all my activity is completely restricted to working for the future . . . basing my work on reminiscences of the past. . . . I will stand firm against the persecution of implacable fate! The greater the travail, the greater the service, and the better the chance of strengthening one's character! Man is born for eternal struggle against the impediments that he constantly meets on his life's path. . . . You say that one cannot always do what one chooses to do. Nonsense. One can do whatever he has strength enough to want to do. Strength of will, my friend—that is everything.[15]

No wonder he was so open to the influence of the German "left" Hegelians and so swiftly moved from writing articles opposing any kind of rebellion to those calling for "a storm of destruction," "ruthless negation," "the complete annihilation of the present political and social world," "the restless and ruthless annihilation of every positively existing thing."[16] We have already seen something of the article from which those quotations are taken, "On the Reaction in Germany," when it was cited to illustrate the close kinship between modern secular and medieval religious apocalyptic visions. One can see in Bakunin a fascinating merger of all three sources of apocalyptic violence discussed thus far—the violence of apocalyptic Christianity, the violence of Jacobin reason, and the violence of Hegel's dialectical History.

While Bakunin's influence was considerable, it hardly compared to that of the left Hegelian who did more than anyone else to move Hegel's dialectical historicism from right to left—Karl Marx. Because Marxism has long since become a worldwide religion with a host of factional denominations and sects, the difficulty in determining just what Marx "really" meant is probably insurmountable. But it seems safe enough to say that two main schools of interpretations together claim the largest following: (1) the moderate, western European "revisionists"; and (2) the revolutionaries, principally represented by Lenin and his disciples, the apocalyptic branch of the faith.

That division between reformist and apocalyptic Marxism, however, concerns contrasting means, not ends; with respect to the goals, Marxism is unified: its vision is that of the Biblical Prophets—social justice, the good society without (to quote the *Communist Manifesto*) "conquest, enslavement, robbery, murder," without "the poverty of the great majority that, despite all its labour, has up to now nothing to sell but itself, and the wealth of the few that increases constantly although they have long since ceased to work."[17] No longer would the machine, the marketplace, and impersonal economic calculation dominate human beings, treating them like things, "commodities," and fostering in them a hatred of productive work, each other, and themselves. For Marx, as for Freud, "work" and "love," productive self-fulfillment and the bonds of family and community, were the substance of life and purpose. By his "species nature," as Marx put it, man was both a productive and a social being, and most of the evils in the capitalist-commodity-competitive society were results of the multiple violations of those natural traits and needs.

Once capitalism gave way to socialism, society would be what its name implies, a cooperative community instead of a cruel and frantic battlefield. Work would again be a creative joy rather than an alienating burden. Relations between human beings in the family, community, society, and world as a whole would reflect authentic human values rather than impersonal, instrumentalist economic calculations. And, finally, "nations would learn war no more": national wars were caused mainly by capitalist profit motives, and socialism, lacking such motivations, would allow natural human sociability and sympathy to break down national boundaries and promote universal brotherhood.

Marxism, thus, helped fill the social conscience gap left by Renaissance rationalism and "humanism," which, for all their grand achievements in science, scholarship, technology, commerce, and organization were remarkably indifferent to the lives of the "masses." While Marxists enthusiastically welcome the achievements of science and technology, the identifying core of their program is their insistent return to the prophetic ideals of social justice.

But if reformist and apocalyptic Marxist movements are united by their prophetic ends, they could hardly be more divided when it comes to the means. Radically opposed though they are on this crucial issue, however, both can legitimately claim Marx as their teacher and guide; for Marx and his theories were as ambivalent about the route to the good society as they were committed to its realization. To begin with the apocalyptic Marxists, they can justly argue that Marx repeatedly and unequivocally insisted on the inevitability of violent revolution. The "abolition of the bourgeois relations of productions," he declared in his *Communist Manifesto*, "can be effected only by a revolution." Therefore, he went on, "the Communists everywhere support every revolutionary movement against the existing social and political order of things. . . . They openly declare that their ends can be attained only by the forcible overthrow of all existing social conditions."[18] Throughout the *Manifesto*, accordingly, one finds a host of words and phrases that could only reflect a firmly apocalyptic perspective. Those in search of evidence of the revolutionary Marx can find an abundance of similarly violent pronouncements in many other works, from his *Address of the Central Committee of the Communist League* (1850) to the *Civil War in France* (1871) and his 1880s letters to the Russian Populists, in which he defended their revolutionary strategy against the more patient perspective of his own early Russian supporters.

But Marx's revolutionary side is expressed in more than his rhetoric: it is an integral part of his essential theories, at least as Marx himself most often interpreted them. The pivotal Erfurt Programme of 1891 was entirely consistent with Marx's own reading of his predictions when it stressed the revolutionary consequences that would result from a constant intensification of working-class "insecurity, misery, oppression, enslavement, debasement, [and] exploitation."[19] That was the whole point of Marx's analysis of the inevitable breakdown of capitalism: the basic dynamics of the system necessarily caused successive economic depressions, each more prolonged and more painful than the last and each followed by a greater (and politically more powerful) concentration of workers in the big companies that survived the crises and swallowed up the little ones that did not. In the End, in the Last Days, when the workers could no longer endure their misery, there would be the final, violent, Gog-Magog class Armageddon in which they would rise up to expropriate the expropriators and inherit the earth. And it was all inevitable, absolutely assured by the dialectical laws of History that were as objectively true and ineluctable as were all other firmly established scientific laws.

One may poke holes in the theories, pull the foundations out from under them, marshal volumes of contrary evidence, and mock any number of embarrassing contradictions. None of that matters. It is the myth, as Sorel saw, and its inspirational powers that count. And apocalyptic Marxism is the perfect myth. Everything fits together so precisely, so "scientifically." It is all so simple and so easily grasped from a few pamphlets. Heaven is right around the corner for the righteous sufferers, and hell awaits the heartless sinners. The poor and pure cannot lose. To have History on one's side is even better than having God as an ally: a personal God can change his mind; impersonal History is driven along by laws that are as constant as the laws of planetary motion.

> We, indeed, know our way and are seated in that historical train which at full speed takes us to our goal. . . . [The historical process is] going to its logical conclusion with the unswerving character of astronomical phenomena. (Plekhanov)[20]

The tendencies of social development are such that the social system we consider as our ideal is inevitably coming: it will be the ineluctable result of the immanent, lawful historical process. . . . Thus, [our] ideal receives an objectively logical, scientific sanction that allows us to look bravely ahead. (Berdyaev)[21]

Historical inevitability and its dialectical contradictions thus served the "wretched of the earth" and their self-proclaimed revolutionary saviors as divine grace had served the first Christians—it offered hope to the hopeless, a crutch for the powerless. As a segment of ancient Jewry had given up faith in their own capacities to repair the world and surrendered the task to divine miracle, so did apocalyptic Marxists bow to the grace of the even stranger god of History. Marx had participated in a series of mid-century failed revolutions, and the central purpose of his Herculean economic, social, and historical research thereafter was to prove that History would do for the revolutionaries what they had been unable to do by themselves.

The dynamics involved the same dialectic of despair that had motivated the initial Judeo-Christian Apocalypse. The way down was again the way up. The terrible suffering experienced by helpless people would, itself, miraculously bring liberation. As Hellenistic Jewish-Christians had turned martyrdom into victory, so did Marxist revolutionaries adopt Hegel's dialectic to prove that each step downward into deeper misery simultaneously and inevitably hastened the coming of paradise. "Imperialist" wars and "capitalist" depressions became, for the apocalyptic Marxists, what the "fortunate fall" and "signs of the End" are for Christians, the same gratifying dialectic that Bakunin had in mind when he announced that "the passion for destruction is a creative passion."

The worse things got, the better. For a later generation of Marxist dialecticians, the Nazis would be preferable to the moderate Social Democrats ("social fascists," as the Communist Party called them), since the Nazis were so monstrously evil that they obviously must be the darkness—the Last Days—preceding the great dawn. Crucifixion remained the way to resurrection. The dialectic, in short, is the apocalyptic Marxists' sign of the cross, the symbol and promise of redemptive despair, with the proletariat as the suffering servant whose liberation will bring the millennial end of all classes, class struggle, war, injustice, and the multiple alienations that burden existence. Consequently, the world for apocalyptic Marxists was divided into the same Two Cities that Augustine had bequeathed Christianity, with the proletariat inhabiting the City of God and the bourgeoisie occupying the City of the Earth and Devil. No compromise could bridge the gap between them. Nothing but the complete annihilation of the dark forces—sinner or bourgeoisie—could assure the triumph of the light.

In apocalyptic Marxism, therefore, the Marxism of Lenin and Stalin, we see again the original Apocalypse in full array. The old and evil world will be completely and violently destroyed. It will be entirely replaced by a new, good world. Objective forces make the transmutation inevitable. Those chosen to guide the suffering pure into the new world are the Leader and his disciples, to whom the intentions and direction of those forces have been revealed. Since the inevitably violent destruction is the will and result of those higher forces, it cannot be blamed on the saviors. Included among those damned to weep and gnash their teeth are not only the sinners, but also those who were neither "hot nor cold," the Pharisees, the compromisers, the liberals.

Later in this chapter we will see more of this apocalyptic side of the Marxist heritage, as it took shape in Russia. But first we must turn to the other side of that heritage, the nonrevolutionary side of Marxism that fostered attitudes and actions as radically opposed to those of the apocalyptic Marxists as the original Biblical gradualist vision was opposed to its apocalyptic successors.

The "revisionist," nonrevolutionary Marxism that flourished in the West rests on the rejection of the two main pillars supporting the "orthodox," apocalyptic Marxism that took power in the East—historical inevitability and revolutionary dialectics. They were no longer needed: West European working-class movements were no longer helpless. With trade unions, political parties, and the other benefits provided by the bourgeois superstructure, such as education and civil rights (all of which Marx recognized and praised), the workers and their leaders were able to improve working and living conditions on their own. Able to fight for themselves, they could discard the crutch of the powerless, the hope in salvation from history and its dialectical cunning (transmuting misery into a guarantee of Paradise).

The "revisionists," no less than their apocalyptic rivals, could claim themselves to be good, indeed, the better, Marxists. While not denying the fact of Marx's revolutionary statements and crises theories, they argued that Marx's predictions had proven gravely flawed and, more important, that his own basic and most original theories should have led him to the right predictions, those consistent with the actual nonrevolutionary evolution of the West European working-class movements. However accurately the Erfurt Programme echoed Marx's expectations, working and living conditions for the workers had not steadily worsened into an ever-deepening misery that must inevitably end in revolution. Not only had those conditions steadily improved, but they had done so precisely because of the class struggle that was supposed to spark the revolution.

As the revisionists interpreted Marxism, Marx should have foreseen that evolution, since it was clearly the most logical outcome of his own description and analysis of capitalism and the road from it to socialism. Socialism, he had argued, was to come only *after* capitalism had fully matured; but a mature capitalism, as Marx himself described it, was characterized by a variety of progressive social and political institutions that strongly favored gradual reform over violent revolution—workers organized into trade unions and political parties that together could win steady improvements; a variety of civil and political rights associated with "bourgeois" constitutional-parliamentary government; and extensive public education that prepared the workers both to struggle successfully for their share of power and to use that power effectively. He should have assumed that the workers would take advantage of those opportunities to achieve reforms whenever they could rather than go on suffering passively their deepening "pauperization" while waiting for that promised distant moment of total liberation when History would deliver them dialectically from nothing to everything. And why had Marx not also guessed that the capitalists would be sensible enough to make concessions along the way in order to avoid the accumulation of revolutionary rage and zeal? It was as if Marx simply had to see the sinners punished, the expropriators violently expropriated, even though his own basic, "scientific socialist" theories pointed to a much more likely nonviolent, gradual transition from capitalism to socialism.

It took only a few more steps along this revisionist line of thought to convince the moderate Marxists that the gradualist evolution built into the "bourgeois" capitalist system could carry it all the way to socialism—from higher pay, shorter work weeks, and better working conditions, through government regulation and welfare legislation, to more and more extensive government ownership (through stock purchases, not seizures) by the "people's" parliamentary representatives, that is, democratic socialism. Not only was this scenario entirely consistent with what was actually going on and likely to continue in Western society, but it was also solidly good Marxism: if the economic substructure determined the social-political-cultural superstructure as Marx said it did, then it should be a continuing process, with each change at the bottom soon altering the character of the dependent structures above. A few quotations from Russian revisionist Marxist Peter Struve will illustrate this reasoning.

> In actual society there exists neither absolute opposition between the legal system and economics nor absolute harmony between them, but persistent, partial collisions and adjustments . . . by which the social reformation is accomplished.

> As a theoretical concept, the concept of social revolution is not only worthless and purposeless, but clearly inaccurate. For the modern mind, the "social revolution" . . . is nothing other than the protracted process of social transformation. . . . The social revolution is simply another name for social evolution and its results, and not a different concept.

> The argument of a complete difference between socialism and capitalism and of the impossibility of achieving socialism within the framework of capitalism and utilizing the means provided by the latter is an argument against historical determinism and against the possibility of socialism itself.[22]

As the left Hegelians had argued that Hegel's reconciliation and nondialectical quietism were fundamentally inconsistent with Hegel's own basic theories, so the Marxist "revisionists" maintained that Marx's revolutionary proclivities and proclamations were basically inconsistent with his "scientific" social and historical analyses. To bolster their position, they could also refer to Marx's own participation in the two activities that formed the core of the revisionists' gradualist outlook: trade unionism and labor party politics. Marx himself was fully aware of the possibilities opened to the working class by votes and strikes. His leadership of the workers' International and his perennial battles with Bakuninists and others in the International over the value of elections and the aims of trade unionism show this clearly.

Even in the early and explicitly revolutionary *Communist Manifesto* we find approving references to trade unions that "join together in order to keep up the rate of wages" and to the workers' "political party" that, in spite of setbacks, "continually reemerges stronger, firmer, mightier" and "compels legislative recognition of particular interests of the workers. . . . Thus the ten-hours' bill in England was carried."[23] Similarly, only a year after another revolutionary publication in response to the Paris Commune, Marx acknowledged his belief in the possibility of a peaceful transition to socialism. He considered it absurd and naively self-defeating to insist, as the Bakunin maximalists in the International did, that the workers focus exclusively on revolutionary actions to overthrow capitalism at the earliest opportunity and not waste their time trying to improve their conditions within capitalist societies.

> If, in the political struggle against the bourgeois State, the workers only succeed in forcing concessions, they are compromising, acting contrary to eternal principles. One must oppose any peaceful movements since they are the bad habit of the English or American workers. The workers should not struggle to get a general reduction in the length of the work day, since that would be tantamount to compromising with the owners, who would then be able to exploit them only ten or twelve hours a day instead of fourteen. Nor should they try any more to gain legal prohibition against children under ten in factories, since such methods would not end the exploitation of children over ten and would only commit another compromise prejudicial to the purity of the eternal principles. . . . In a word, the workers must cross their arms and not waste time with economic and political movements. Such movements can bring them only partial results. Being deeply religious, the workers must disdain such ordinary needs and declare as an act of faith: "Let our class be crucified, let our race perish, but let the eternal principles remain immacu-

late." Like pious Christians, they must believe in the words of the priest, despise the goods of this world in order to attain paradise.[24]

While this mockery of the Bakuninists (and its significant re-formist-apocalyptic analogy) came late in Marx's life, he had ex-pressed the same disdain for such doctrinaire and futile extremism as far back as the "revolutionary" *Manifesto,* when he criticized Ger-man revolutionary maximalists in terms that could as easily be ap-plied to the later Bakuninists and even more to the still later Lenin-ists. The German maximalists, Marx argued here, naively thought that a socialist revolution could take place at the beginning of the bourgeois stage, before the bourgeois society had developed within itself the necessary conditions for socialism. They had thought it enough to adopt French socialist ideas, ignoring the fact that, when those ideas "immigrated from France into Germany, French social conditions had not immigrated along with them." In attacking, as the German extremists did, "liberalism, representative government, bourgeois competition, bourgeois freedom of the press, bourgeois legislation, bourgeois liberty and equality . . . German socialism for-got, in the nick of time, that the French criticism, whose silly echo it was, presupposed the existence of modern bourgeois society with its corresponding economic conditions of existence and the political con-stitution adapted thereto."

In effect, the policies of these self-styled German "socialists" were "reactionary," not revolutionary: Germany "was on the eve of a bourgeois revolution," not a socialist revolution, and by prema-turely attacking the bourgeois political and economic achievements that the forthcoming German bourgeois revolution would provide, the German socialists were not only helping the reactionary German landed class defeat the more oppressive German bourgeoisie and forestall the introduction of those obviously progressive and desir-able bourgeois institutions, but they were also thereby depriving a genuine future socialist movement of the economic, political, and social prerequisites without which *democratic* socialism—as Marx un-derstood socialism—was inconceivable.[25]

As a further consequence of this nonrevolutionary Marxism, the movement was spared the elitist domination that always accompa-nied apocalyptic theory and practice. Waiting until the bourgeois society had fully matured and participating meanwhile in the progressive bourgeois institutions (public education, elections, trade unionism, civil rights, etc.) prepared the workers for active involvement and leadership in their own liberation from bourgeois capitalism and in the management of the democratic socialism that would replace it. Beneficiaries of the progressive bourgeois achievements, which Marx emphatically praised, the working class had no need of a "vanguard" whom God, Reason, History, or Nature had chosen to lead them into the new world.

Finally, and another step in their return to the prophetic vision, the revisionist Marxists acknowledged that Marxism was principally an ethical, idealistic program of ends and not at all the objective "science" that Marx had made it appear to be with his "laws" and pseudoempiricism. Echoing the idealism of an earlier moderate socialist, Ferdinand Lassalle, Eduard Bernstein considered socialism not a system that must inevitably come into existence as a result of objective laws, but as "something that ought to be, or a movement toward something that ought to be."[26] More confident now that conditions were indeed improving—Marx's gloomy and catastrophic "scientific" predictions notwithstanding—the revisionists felt strong enough to dispense entirely with the guarantees of historical inevitability. "Not only do the workers grow in numbers, but their economic, ethical, and political level rises as well, and thus grows their ability to be one of the governing factors in state and national economy."[27]

Rather than revise Marxism, the "revisionists" had brought out the nonrevolutionary core of Marxism by moving in two seemingly opposite directions. On the one hand, they called upon Marxists to pay attention to what was actually going on in society and not be blinded by the speculative historical and dialectical "laws" that Marx had derived from Hegel's abstract philosophy of history. In this sense, they wanted Marxists to be more genuinely empirical than Marx had been, to be really "scientific" in studying social existence rather than pseudoscientific, as Marx himself had been in his zeal to prove inevitability for his ideals. The revisionists believed they were saving the better Marx from the worse, as Marx believed he had done for Hegel: As Marx had discarded the "mystical shell" surrounding the "rational kernel" of Hegel's thought and set upright a worldview that was "standing on its head," so the revisionists wanted to save the rational kernel in Marx's mystical Hegelian intuitions and thereby bring socialism "out of the clouds of fantasy to the firm soil of the actualities of social existence."[28]

On the other hand, while putting Marx back on his feet, on the terra firma of empirical reality, the revisionists, following Lassalle and neo-Kantian Herman Cohn, simultaneously affirmed that Marxism was essentially not a science at all but rather a set of ethical ideals and a program for their realization. Socialists should, of course, make full use of empirical knowledge in pursuing their goals, but they should not assume that science could either set or justify those goals, much less prove their inevitable realization. Ideals could not be proven, and socialist ideals were no exception: they were chosen and defended on faith alone. The contrast between those views and the theories of the apocalyptic dialectitians soon to win power in Russia could not be greater.

Although the "Marxists" who triumphed in Russia under Lenin represented apocalyptic "Marxism," the Marxism that first emerged there and prevailed for the first three decades or so, was decidedly revisionist. Peter Struve's analysis, quoted earlier, of a gradual transition to socialism through the continuing interaction of the economic substructure with the political superstructure is one example. Since the present writes the history of the past and since the Leninists won the Russian present, until recently little attention has been given to those revisionist origins of Russian Marxism. Yet for several decades before the Bolshevik revolution, revisionism was the norm and Leninism very much the exception. In fact, the first Russian Marxists, those who became active in the early 1880s, were initially drawn to Marxism precisely because they opposed currents in Russian Populism that were later to reappear as Leninism.

By the end of the 1870s, most Russian Populists had lost hope in the peasantry as an effective or even active political force and had concluded that, whereas everything should indeed be done for the people, nothing much could be expected from them or by them: the "people's" revolution would have to be carried out not by the people, but by an elite revolutionary minority from the educated middle and upper classes. It was from the ranks of those Populists who rejected such elitist conclusions and who still believed in a popular mass movement that the first Russian Marxists emerged. They, too, after a while, had lost faith in the political potential of the peasantry, but instead of opting for the minority, conspiratorial, terrorist solution, as did their former confederates, they transferred their hopes from the peasantry to a new and more promising working class—the proletariat.

When, in the early 1880s, George Plekhanov, Vera Zasulich, Paul Axelrod, and other pioneer Russian Marxists began their work, the proletariat in Western Europe had already experienced two remarkably successful decades of organized economic and political action, both in their individual countries and internationally, through the Marxist-led International. What made Marxism particularly attractive to these erstwhile Populists was the fact that besides being the ideology for this politically active mass labor movement, Marxism was also a "science" of historical "laws" demonstrating the inevitable development in Russia of that same proletariat. The objective laws of history would save Russia as they were saving Western Europe: feudalism and its passive peasantry would inevitably be replaced by capitalism and the active proletariat who, in turn, would just as inevitably lead the way to Russian socialism.

It was only by heeding that lawful sequence of stages, Plekhanov insisted in his first Marxist publications of the early 1880s, that Russia, too, would progress into socialism. To do otherwise, to depend on the will and talents of an elite—at that time Populist—was to court disaster. "Not relying on the wisdom of the people," Plekhanov wrote, anticipating in these attacks on Populist elitism his Menshevik arguments against Lenin some twenty years later, "it [the organization] will retain the power it has seized in its own hands and on its own initiative undertake the organization of socialist production." Moreover, because they would lack all the economic, political, social, and cultural prerequisites for achieving a genuine democratic socialism—conditions that a mature capitalism would have provided them—the revolutionaries would have no choice but to "seek salvation in the ideals of a 'patriarchal authoritarian communism.'" Nor would that be the end of the tragedy.

> [T]here is no doubt that not only would the people fail to be educated for socialism, but they would lose completely all capacity for further progress. If they did preserve this capacity, they would do so only at the cost of reinstituting the same economic inequalities that the revolution had above all tried to eliminate.

Such would be the results of the policies advocated by those "who put their own will in the place of historical development, replace the initiative of a class by the initiative of a committee, and . . . transform the task of the entire laboring population of the country into the task of a secret organization." The people, the workers, wanted a real liberation, not just a change of masters; they wanted to "enter the arena of history as independent actors and not eternally pass from one tutelage to another. . . . The dictatorship of a class is as far from the dictatorship of a group as heaven is from earth." Finally, once the disaster had occurred, "only a new revolution can tear dictatorship from the hands of the dictator."

Having so prophetically foreseen much of later Leninism, Plekhanov no less insightfully provided the revisionist alternative—the "full voting rights for all adult men and women" that, he wrote, the English workers were demanding and that they regarded as the best way for them to win power and change the system. Together with that revisionist strategy went the correspondingly gradualist awareness that it would take time.

> They [the workers], of course, will not suddenly achieve this dominant position. Only gradually do they become a threatening power, excluding from the minds of their opponents any thoughts of opposition. For a long time, they will obtain only concessions [and] will demand merely those reforms that would give them not dominance, but only the possibility of growing and maturing toward future dominance; reforms that would satisfy only their most essential, most immediate needs and, if only slightly, extend the sphere of their influence in the social life of the country.

In sum, "the so-called revolution is only the last act in a long drama."[29]

Given the stage of Russian development at the time, the practical meaning of that strategy was support for an emerging Russian bourgeois capitalism, the next stage after the existing Russian feudalism. When we recall Marx's enthusiastic praise for bourgeois achievements, compared to the preceding feudal world, it is not surprising that young, Westernized Russian radicals considered that an added—or even, for some, the central—appeal of Marxism. Populism had placed Russian intellectuals in a depressing set of dilemmas. As educated Westerners, they were attracted to Western political and civil rights, material abundance, urban civilization, and general cultural diversity. But, as "conscience-stricken" intellectuals, they were convinced that all their attention had to be given to the needs of the masses, that political and cultural development would only further enrich the already privileged lives of the upper classes to which they belonged, and that economic modernization, however desirable, could only be achieved in Russia as it had been in the West, by ruthlessly exploiting the people.[30]

Marxism completely changed all that. As Marxists, middle- and upper-class radical intellectuals could sincerely believe that what they wanted—the political freedoms, the modern, Western economy and culture—was also best for the people: not only would the people gain from the representative government, trade unionism, and education that accompanied bourgeois capitalism, but they would also have been given, thereby, the instruments for their future socialist liberation. "One must not forget," the revisionist Struve wrote,

> that socialism for Marx signified an unrestricted cultural flowering. He demanded for his socialism all the cultural achievements of the bourgeoisie. . . . If the collapse of capitalism is unavoidable for the socialist reconstruction, and if the latter really implies general cultural progress, then [should there be a premature revolution] the social architect will be lacking a class sufficiently prepared for its historical task.

> The old Russian socialism [populism] seemed provincial and narrow-minded in comparison. The fact that Marxism took root among the Russian intelligentsia was evidence of a further Europeanization of Russia and of her readiness to share to the end the destiny of Europe. I myself felt very anti-nationalistic and was never tempted to assert Russia against the West.

If "our Easterners, thundering *ex oriente lux* at us . . . Westerners," begin by opposing European economic forms, revisionist Bulgakov warned, they will have to go on to reject "all the benefits of European culture which alone give beauty to our lives." And among such benefits, few were more appealing than the constitutional, representative system that, for all its shortcomings, seemed a marvel of freedom for subjects of Tsarist autocracy. There is little doubt that many became Marxists less because of Marx's historical law that made socialism the inevitable next stage *after* capitalism, than because of Marx's sociological law, which made constitutional, representative government and its accompanying civil rights the inevitable political system *during* bourgeois capitalism.

> I was . . . a constitutionalist and a political Liberal before the problem of Socialism arose before my mind. . . . I was interested in Socialism chiefly as an ideological force, which, according to the adoption of this or that sociological conception of Russia's development, could be turned either for or against the conquest of civil and political liberties. . . . What economic processes, what social relations and forces will determine the downfall of absolutism, the conquest of civil and political liberties, the establishment of a constitutional regime? We fully accepted the idea which Marx had once applied to Germany, namely that we were suffering not from the development of capitalism, but from its insufficient development.[31]

No less significant than this liberalism among Marxist intellectuals was a corresponding revisionism among Marxists active in the nascent Russian labor movement. Opposing what they called "impatient Marxism, negative Marxism, primitive Marxism (which entertains too schematic an impression of the class division of society)," they supported instead the same gradualist tactics—"the path of least resistance"—that defined revisionist policies in the West.

> The economic struggle, the struggle against capital on the grounds of day-to-day basic interests, strikes as the instruments of this struggle—this is the motto of the labor movement. . . . Let the workers conduct this struggle, knowing that they are fighting not for some future generation but for themselves and their children; let them understand that each victory, every inch seized from the enemy, is one more step climbed on the stairway leading to their own welfare.[32]

The high point in Russian Marxist revisionism came when these gradualist Marxists drew the same moral conclusions from their rejection of apocalyptic Marxism that their Western counterparts were drawing: ethics judged history and society; historical and social "laws" did not judge ethics. Just because something existed, to recall Hegel's rational reality, did not make it morally right or acceptable. Russian revisionists repeatedly stressed this fundamental moral autonomy and priority, as Belinsky had a half-century earlier when he rebelled against Hegel's comparable subordination of human beings and their ethical values to the will and whims of an amoral Absolute Reason.

> One need not believe in a mechanical necessity realizing [the aims of] progress in order to acknowledge the obligatory force of the tasks of progress. . . . The absolute character of the imperative "desire the good for its own sake" is not linked to any chance conditions fostering the realization of the good in history. . . . Merely because a particular [process] is actually occurring, does it follow that I should be attracted to it as something morally desirable? (Bulgakov)

> It does not follow from my having considered something as ethically desirable that this something will necessarily come into being. But, similarly, because something exists or will necessarily come about through the laws of nature, it in no way follows that I should regard it as ethically desirable. (Struve)

> The paths to the future are many and diverse, and there cannot be here any exact sociological prediction, since there are no historical laws according to which the ideal of a better future will be realized by some fatalistic necessity. (Berdyaev)

"Progress," Bulgakov wrote, "is not a law of historical development, but a moral task. Marxism represents the clearest version of the theory or the religion of progress. . . . Its strength, therefore, is derived not from its scientific, but from its utopian elements; not from its science, but from its faith."[33]

So often are Marxism and Leninism associated that they are usually fused into a single rubric, Marxism-Leninism. Yet they are in many ways sharply opposed. In part, Leninism represents a revival of revolutionary Populism, against which Russian Marxism first defined its theory and practice. Marxism, first of all, assumes a sequence of historical stages and, especially, the full maturity of capitalism before conditions are right for the establishment of democratic socialism. Leninism totally disregards all that and, like Populism, is prepared voluntaristically, "opportunistically," to seize power anytime.

> Suppose a historical situation has arisen (a war, an agrarian crisis, etc.) in which the proletariat, constituting a minority of the population, has an opportunity to rally around itself the vast majority of the laboring masses [the peasants]: why should it not take power then?[34]

As a second point of difference, Marxism argues that "existence" determines "consciousness," that, in particular, one's political views reflect one's economic class: socialism is the ideology of the proletariat, whose working conditions and lack of significant private property nurture a sense of social justice and cooperation; while "robber baron" individualism and immense private ownership make capitalism the ideology of the bourgeoisie. Lenin, on the contrary, argued that

> this [Social-Democratic] consciousness could only be brought to them [the workers] from without. The history of all countries shows that the working class exclusively by its own efforts, is able to develop only trade-union consciousness. . . . The theory of Socialism, however, grew out of the philosophic, historical and economic theories that were elaborated by the educated representatives of the propertied classes, the intellectuals.[35]

Socialism, in other words, is the ideology of an alienated segment of the bourgeoisie who must teach it to a proletariat incapable of arriving at such insights by themselves. The authoritarian implications are obvious.

Third, Marxism depends on the proletariat as its revolutionary class and has little interest in the peasantry or with anything else connected with "the idiocy of the countryside," to quote Marx. Lenin, because he was willing to take power while the Russian population was still overwhelmingly rural, had no choice but to depend principally on the peasantry, or, more accurately, on a peasant army mobilized for World War I.

Finally, Marxism considers socialism a dialectical "synthesis" uniting the virtues of socialist equality and communality with the achievements of capitalism that Marx so warmly praised—the advanced technology, high productivity, international economy, trade unionism, constitutional-representative government, civil rights and freedoms, public education, and so forth. Lenin, by assuming power before any of those "bourgeois" achievements had come to Russia (although they all were clearly beginning to emerge at the turn of the century), paved the way both for Stalin's forced economic development ("primitive socialist accumulation," Stalin called it, echoing Marx's description of "primitive capitalist accumulation") and Stalin's dictatorial domination (the political counterpart of that "primitive socialist accumulation" and the consequence of seizing power before a developed Russian bourgeois economy had provided Russia with the correspondingly bourgeois liberal political and cultural institutions).

Although Lenin persistently ignored Marx's theories in coming to power, he just as persistently justified his actions by appeals to those theories and vigorously opposed any philosophies that raised doubts about the possibility of attaining objective, scientific truths about social and historical laws. Why abandon guarantees of victory? Nothing inspires confidence, grounds legitimation, and promotes zealous adherence more than the conviction that history is on your side, and nothing more effectively justifies violence done for the good of the cause than the belief that the violence is objectively unavoidable, the inevitable consequence of ineluctable social and historical laws. Revisionists, humanists, and liberals all doubt. They know that they cannot know absolutely, and they are similarly aware of the darker side of their own natures that makes both ends and means as morally suspect as they are intellectually doubtful. The Crusader, Jacobin, and Leninist know only certainty and purity.

The result was once again a union of the worst of two worlds, in this case, Marxist and Populist. To be a Marxist meant to wait until capitalism had fully developed, until conditions matured to the point where violent revolution and its familiar postrevolutionary party dictatorship were highly unlikely. In that context, "scientific" certitude founded on objective, historical "laws" was not only less dangerous, but actually encouraged a nonrevolutionary patience, a willingness to wait for the maturation of conditions that were similarly nonrevolutionary. To be a Populist, on the contrary, meant to be ready at any time to take power as a conspiratorial elite. However, Populist theory lacked entirely a theory of scientific, historical "laws" that assured victory and sanctioned any and all violence.

Drawing on the negative features of both worldviews while ignoring their moderating sides, Lenin was a Populist in his elitism and readiness to come to power at any time, which, under Russian conditions, was a virtual guarantee of perpetual domination; and he was a Marxist in his conviction that objective, dialectical, amoral, historical laws justified all violence and domination. (Paradoxically, the absolute faith in objective historical "law"—Marxist—inspired the courage and will—Populist—to break that law and take power at the first opportunity.) Lenin was a Marxist and not a Populist in two other ways as well, both of which only exacerbated the harm done by this initial Populist-Marxist merger: he was dedicated to rapid economic development, and he took for granted the Marxists' two-cities division of the world into communist and capitalist countries and its corresponding messianic vision of an ineluctable communist global triumph. None of that was present in Populism.

Lenin may well have been fully aware (as his *State and Revolution* suggests) that he was using Marxist theories of historical and social laws and their millennial eschatology less because he believed them than because of their power to inspire. There were other available theories of history and society, such as those argued by Lenin's one-time ally, Bogdanov, that corresponded as closely to Lenin's voluntaristic practice as Marxist theories ran counter to it. But Lenin quite sensibly rejected them, preferring the more inspirationally powerful Marxist "science." (This was not a new phenomenon in Russian intellectual and political life. In the 1860s and 1870s, "materialists," "nihilists," and "positivists" talked endlessly about "science" and deeply felt that they, too, were entirely objective and scientific in the way they diagnosed the ills of society and prescribed remedies. But at no time did they let reality overwhelm theory: they simply turned to it for selected illustrations of their intuited truths. For the militants of the 1860s and 1870s as for their Bolshevik successors, to be "scientific" meant little more than to *feel* "scientific," "objective," "realistic," tough enough to accept the harsh facts of life and revolution, i.e., to bear—and cause—great suffering.)

In using Marxist "laws" not to analyze reality empirically, but to change it idealistically (consciousness, will, idea, and messianic revolutionary fervor), Lenin fused the two phases of Marx's own personal career. Marx had begun his political life as a "left" Hegelian with an idealist's faith in the will of the "critical" intelligentsia. The failures of the 1848–49 insurrections turned his hopes and focus away from the talents of a revolutionary elite toward slowly evolving social and historical processes that must inevitably succeed where the revolutionary intellectuals had failed. In his stress on the "consciousness" and will of an elite vanguard, Lenin returned idealism and revolutionary voluntarism (by way of Russian Populism) to "left Hegelians" and used, perhaps cynically, Marx's "laws" to bolster the confidence of that revolutionary will. It is no fault of Lenin that he is usually mistaken for a Marxist, that his basically Populist politics are so often missed or ignored. He not only was explicit about his non-Marxist voluntarism, but emphasized it repeatedly, in his stress on "consciousness," his disdain for trade union "spontaneity," and his insistence on the importance of theory in determining the course of revolution.

> Ideas become a power when they grip the people. And precisely at the present time, the Bolsheviks, i.e., the representatives of revolutionary proletarian internationalism, have embodied in their policy the idea that is motivating countless working people all over the world.
>
> But it is essential that leaders of the revolutionary parties, too, should advance their aims more comprehensively and boldly at such a time, so that their slogans shall always be in advance of the revolutionary initiative of the masses, serve as a beacon, reveal to them our democratic and socialist ideal in all its magnitude and splendor. . . .

It would be stupid to deny the role of fantasy, even in the strict-est science: cf. Pisarev on useful dreaming. . . . "Divergence be-tween dreams and reality causes no harm if only the person dreaming believes seriously in his dream . . . and if, generally speaking, he works conscientiously for the achievement of his fantasies."[36]

"Tailism," "spontaneity," remaining too close to "concrete" real-ity, and other comparable sins that so infuriated Lenin are all syno-nyms of Revisionism and its respect for historical stages and for the workers' own "consciousness," the consciousness that their "exis-tence" (not their intelligentsia leaders) had given them. Lenin de-spised a gradualist, moderate, trade union strategy for the workers, partly because it reflected a readiness to accept a bourgeois stage in Russian history.

The spontaneous development of the labor movement leads to its becoming subordinated to bourgeois ideology. . . . Hence our task, the task of Social Democracy, is to combat spontaneity, to divert the labor movement from its spontaneous, trade union-ist striving to go under the wing of the bourgeoisie, and to bring it under the wing of revolutionary Social Democ-racy. . . . Subservience to the spontaneous character of the labor movement, belittlement of the role of the conscious element, means, whether one likes it or not, the influence of bourgeois ideology among the workers. . . . Since there cannot be any talk of an independent ideology being developed by the masses of the workers in the process of their development—the only alter-natives are bourgeois or socialist ideology.[37]

Lenin could not bear the thought of reconciliation with a bour-geois Russia. He had come to hate the bourgeoisie and everything about them long before he had any serious interest in politics, ever since the time that his family's Westernized, "liberal" community had ostracized his mother after the execution of his brother for participat-ing in an assassination conspiracy against Tsar Alexander III. "From the age of seventeen, I began to despise the liberals . . . not a single liberal 'canaille' in Simbirsk came forward with the slightest word of sympathy for my mother after my brother's execution. In order not to run into her, they would cross to the other side of the street."[38] He began his "Marxist" career by disputing with Plekhanov the relationships between the proletariat party and the bourgeois constitutional liberals, whether or not, more specifically, it was necessary, as Plekhanov argued, to wait until Russia went through a bourgeois stage.

The foundations of Leninism can be found here, in this personal revulsion Lenin felt toward the bourgeoisie and in his essentially Populist conviction (also that of his martyred Populist brother) that a revolutionary elite armed with a firm will and the right ideas could mobilize the "people" (still, mainly, the Populists' peasantry) and establish socialism in Russia notwithstanding the complete absence of all Marx's economic, social, and political prerequisites. One could hardly imagine a more Hegelian and Populist and less Marxist concept of revolution. In effect, Lenin put Hegel back on his head: will, ideas, "consciousness," and an elitist, intellectual organization determined the course of history, not economic conditions. Lenin's idealism displaced Marx's materialism as Marx's materialism had earlier displaced Hegel's idealism.

The contrast between Leninism and Marxism is most apparent in their consequences. If Western European Marxism and its bourgeois milieu favored revisionism and, therefore, democratic socialism, Russian Leninism and its underdeveloped, third world milieu just as strongly favored the emergence of Stalinism. Since Lenin's premature, Populist revolution occurred before a Russian bourgeois evolution had gone far enough to produce a large and politically mature proletariat, Lenin did just what Plekhanov had warned Russian Populists not to do—he replaced the will of the working class by the will of a revolutionary party.

> We must train people who will dedicate to the revolution not a free evening but the whole of their lives; we must prepare an organization so strong that we can enforce a firm division of labor in the various aspects of our work.

> It is precisely because the crowd may overwhelm and crush the permanent troops that we must without fail "manage" to keep up with the spontaneous rise of the masses in our work of establishing an extremely systematic organization among the perma-

nent troops, for the more we "manage" to establish such an organization, the more probable will it be that the permanent troops will not be overwhelmed by the crowd, but will take their place at the head of the crowd.[39]

The next step in this political logic involved the vehicle through which this party of militant professionals would lead the backward masses.

All our Party recognizes now . . . that the Party nature of the trade unions must be attained exclusively by the work of Social Democrats within the unions, and that Social Democrats must form solid cells in the unions.[40]

To complete this proto-Stalinist strategy (as well as the model for the entire Soviet system of Party rule), Lenin had to make sure that the professionals charged with directing the workers through the "cells" were themselves "orthodox" and constantly under the control of Lenin and his central committee disciples. Lenin's solution for that problem was as simple as it was effective and enduring: a newspaper (*Iskra*) would guarantee that the party "line," as Lenin candidly called it, was communicated to all the professional members of the party, and a strictly centralized and rigidly disciplined party organization would assure obedience to that "orthodox" line.[41]

Bureaucratism versus democratism, i.e., precisely centralism versus autonomy, such is the organization principle of revolutionary social democracy as against that of the opportunists. The latter principle [autonomy] strives to go from below upward, and therefore defends as far as possible and wherever possible autonomy and democracy. . . . But the organization principle of revolutionary social democracy strives to go from the top downwards, and defends the enlargement of the rights and plenary powers of the central body against the parts. . . . Either recognition of the Organization Committee and subjection to it, or war.[42]

Plekhanov and his fellow democratic Marxists were aghast at this unabashed authoritarianism, and quite accurately and insightfully traced its source to Lenin's elitist distrust of workers' consciousness and corresponding disregard of basic Marxist theories.

> The debated question is precisely this: Does there exist an economic necessity which calls forth in the proletariat a "demand for socialism," makes it "instinctively socialist," and drives it—even when left to "its own resources"—along the road to socialist revolution, notwithstanding the stubborn and continual efforts of the bourgeoisie to subject it to their own ideological influence? Lenin denies this, in the face of the clearly expressed opinions of all the theorists of scientific socialism. And in that consists his great mistake, his theoretical fall into sin. . . . In the view of Lenin we see not Marxism but . . . a new edition of the theory of the hero and the crowd [Populism]. . . . Since he declares himself to be the only active element in history, he considers the masses as only . . . strong but obedient tools. (Plekhanov)

> Socialism is the first movement in history to base its entire course on the organization and independent action of the masses. The ultracentralism advocated by Lenin is not something born of a positive creative spirit but of the negative sterile spirit of the watchman. (Rosa Luxembourg)[43]

Trotsky perceptively saw the ultimate consequences (although he did nothing during the years he shared power to forestall them).

> The organization of the Party takes the place of the Party itself; the Central Committee takes the place of the organization; and finally the dictator takes the place of the Central Committee.[44]

In this, at least, Trotsky was right. Everything about the roots and nature of Leninism drove it from Lenin's voluntarist Populist strategy, through his resulting premature, apocalyptic revolution, into his authoritarian, postrevolutionary regime that, finally, formed the basis for Stalin's totalitarianism. The means once again determined the end. The dialectic that was to have made the last first, apocalyptically transmute Russia from Europe's most backward and repressive nation into its most advanced, most just, and freest society, became the

Bolsheviks' all-purpose justification for permanent violence—first the "left" Hegelian, Leninist violence to overthrow the old despotism, then the "right" Hegelian, Leninist-Stalinist violence to preserve and strengthen the new despotism. In and out of power, the dialectic served as the measure and model for all judgment and policy. Conflict and contradiction were honored as the only natural, acceptable, and expected process of change. Compromise was out of the question, other than as a delaying or deceptive tactic. There was no place for ordinary sympathy, empathy for the opponents' point of view, or even a wearied willingness just to live and let live.

If the Apocalypse of History as embodied principally in the theory and practice of Leninism-Stalinism has been even more brutal than the earlier Apocalypse of Faith and Apocalypse of Reason, it is, perhaps, because it incorporated their justifications for violence as well as adding its own. From the rationalists (via sixteenth- and seventeenth-century scientific theory and eighteenth-century Jacobin practice) came the rejection of all "subjective" feeling and judgment when considering "objective" social and historical processes. There was no place for anthropomorphic sentimentalism where natural, social, and historical "laws" were concerned. Hegel's real-rational demiurgic dialectic aggravated the danger: whereas the earlier rationalists were merely indifferent to distinctions between good and evil (having learned to observe human affairs as a branch of Descartes's "universal mathematics," as one would "lines, planes, and solids" and, with Hume, to treat the distinction between good and evil as one did that between hot and cold), Hegel's dialectic positively encouraged the violence of the "negation" and justified any evil considered "necessary" in the progress of the Absolute Spirit.

> Of course the path through life for the contemporary man is far from strewn with roses, and to the lot of his supporters there falls many thorny vines. . . . Necessity throws some overboard; while to others, it promises victory. Only the latter feel themselves free; the former have a sense of terrible dependency on forces beyond their control. (Berdyaev)[45]

Behind that rationalist contribution (Jacobin and Hegelian) to Bolshevik violence lay a much older rationalist tradition: Platonic idealism. First of all, it inspired a conviction that speculatively intuited ideas about "reality" were superior to conclusions reached by empirical observation. If there was a conflict between the ideas in the head of the intellectual and the actual facts outside, then the facts had to be reinterpreted accordingly. Second, and further exacerbating the danger of this solipsism, the Platonist's claim to superiority for the idea was based on the idea's all-encompassing perfection. Consequently, when the intellectual set out to change the "irrational," "contingent," "transitory," and "impure" facts to match the rational, necessary, eternal, and perfect idea-ideal, he could not stop until everything fit: nothing could be left out. Besides being necessarily authoritarian in his drive to make facts mirror his idea, the Platonist revolutionary must be totalitarian as well, leaving no part of society out of the perfect plan, no individual caprice free to disturb the order. Platonism, finally, must be radically elitist, since only the philosopher king and those toeing his "party line" had the genius to grasp the higher truths.

Finally, in this summary of earlier contributions to Lenin's Apocalypse of History, there is the heritage of the original Apocalypse. Even had Lenin not on occasion (as in *State and Revolution*) made his millennial vision quite explicit, it would be apparent enough in his life and works. His apocalyptic version of Marxist history is in no essential way different from the religious apocalyptic vision of a messianic transmutation. In both cases, the corrupt old world will be swiftly and violently destroyed; a new world will take its place; the savior and his party of disciples will lead the righteous wretched into the millennial kingdom; the rich will weep and gnash their teeth; and among the first to suffer for their sins are the Pharisaic moderates. What difference does it make whether the inspiration and justification are called Spirit or Science, God or History? Above all, what difference does it make to the victims if they are murdered in the name of God or because of the ineluctable laws of dialectic progress?

Lenin's fury against the enemy is the fury of the Taborites and Munster saints. For all of them, the world was sharply split between sinner and saved. For all of them there was a war to the death between the Two Cities, and changing the names of the inhabitants of the cities from saved and sinner to proletariat and bourgeoisie changed nothing.

We are no longer waging war against separate individuals, we are exterminating the bourgeoisie as a class. Do not seek in the dossier of the accused for proofs as to whether or not he opposed the Soviet government by word or deed. The first question that should be put is to what class he belongs, of what extraction, what education and profession. These questions should decide the fate of the accused. Herein lie the meaning and the essence of the Red Terror. (Latsis)[46]

At the end of chapter 2, we saw a variety of statements by Bolsheviks and other "secular" revolutionaries clearly expressing not simply religious sentiments and concepts but precisely those of the Apocalypse. Although this is not the place for a survey of Russian culture at the turn of the century, it is a commonplace for students of the era that it was a period of general apocalyptic fervor and expectation, that apocalyptic attitudes and themes flooded the arts, inspired important segments of the intelligentsia, and played a decisive part in the politics of extremist parties and factions. To understand the roots and character of Bolshevism, one must see through the "rationalistic" facade of Leninism and place it in the context of that general apocalyptic mood, the result, once again, of profound social crises. Famine, epidemics, prolonged economic depression, two disastrous and humiliating wars (1904 and 1914), successive political upheavals, rapid modernization with its customary dislocations and uncertainties, the influx of new ways of life and thought coming too quickly to be assimilated without severe culture shock—in other words, the usual setting for the confusion, fear, and anger that, from the Hellenistic era onward, have repeatedly sparked apocalyptic panic.

Lenin himself was generally circumspect in his choice of metaphors. At times, however, he, too, surrendered to apocalyptic rhetoric.

Revolutions are festivals of the oppressed and the exploited. At no other time are the mass of the people in a position to come forward so actively as creators of a new social order, as at a time of revolution. At such times the people are capable of performing miracles, if judged by the limited, philistine yardstick of gradualist progress.[47]

According to Trotsky, Lenin was millennially optimistic enough to believe, in 1918—and, Trotsky writes, to announce this belief repeatedly—that socialism would be fully achieved in just a few months. "These words," Trotsky recalls,

> seem quite incomprehensible now. Had there not been a slip of the pen? Did he not mean some years or even decades? No, there was no slip of the pen; other declarations of Lenin to the same effect may be found. I remember quite clearly how, in the earliest period, Lenin often repeated to the Council of People's Commissars that we would establish socialism in six months and be the mightiest country in the world.[48]

The early Bolshevik philosopher, Deborin, reflects the same heady apocalyptic expectation, and, once again, with reference to Lenin.

> For how could Lenin, this ever-forward urging, all-destroying revolutionary, recognize a finished and petrified world? Had he not to burn this world in the fires of revolution in order to create a new and better place?[49]

Thus, the Judeo-Christian Apocalypse, Platonism, Science and Reason, History, Dialectics, Economic Determinism—all joined to justify Lenin's apocalyptic violence.

> There can be no middle course. . . . Ruthless war must be waged on the kulaks! Death to them! Hatred and contempt for the parties which support them—the Right-Socialist Revolutionaries, the Mensheviks, and now the Left-Socialist Revolutionaries.

> The current policy of all bourgeois governments prepares daily new imperialist wars . . . and these wars result with objective inevitability from their whole policy. To lament under these conditions . . . the civil war against the exploiters and to condemn it, or to fear it, means in reality to become a reactionary. It means that one fears the victory of the workers which may cost tens of thousands of victims, and that one renders possible a new massacre by the imperialists, a massacre which cost millions of victims yesterday and will cost similar numbers tomorrow.[50]

Lenin had learned his Jacobin lessons well.

The bourgeois spinelessness of the minority [Mensheviks] and the whole incompatibility of their outlook with what revolutionary Marxism demands are best shown by their cries about "conspiracy," "Blanquism," "Jacobinism." This panic fear of Jacobinism is common to all the ... Girondins, opportunists, and revisionists in Social Democracy today.... Take the history of the French Revolution and you'll see what Jacobinism is. It is a struggle to achieve the end in view, with no shying away from drastic plebeian measures, a struggle without kid gloves, without tenderness, without fear of resorting to the guillotine.... Rejection of the Jacobin method of struggle leads quite logically to rejection of the dictatorship of the proletariat, that is, of the coercion which is necessary and obligatory, which is indispensable for the smashing and annihilation of the enemies of the proletariat and for securing the victory of the socialist revolution. A proper bourgeois revolution cannot be carried out without a Jacobin purge—to say nothing of a socialist revolution. It requires a dictatorship of the proletariat, and the dictatorship of the proletariat requires a Jacobin mentality in the people who set it up.[51]

Stalin's Gulag was the last stop for Plekhanov's ineluctable "historical train." As for the victims en route: "those who lie on the rails to stop the train of history must expect to get their legs cut off."[52] For a more concrete account of these objectively necessary historical amputations, we may turn to two witnesses, one from the Eastern branch of the faith, another from the early Soviet.

At first we lifted his legs off the ground showering his knees and ankles with blows from our steel pipes. Then, having disabled him, we pounded the counter-revolutionary element's cranium with a sledge hammer. The instrument made a knocking sound. We thus put a revolutionary end to a counter-revolutionary's life. Our unit then encircled the bloodied corpse and spat upon its counter-revolutionary form.[53]

The place had formerly been a garage, and then the provincial Cheka's man slaughter-house. And the whole of it was coated with blood—blood ankle deep, coagulated with the heat of the atmosphere, and horribly mixed with human brains, chips of skull-bone, wisps of hair, and the like. . . . The horrible den contained 127 corpses, but the victims of the previous massacre had been hurriedly buried in the adjacent garden. What struck us most about the corpses was the shattering of their skulls, or the complete flattening out of those skulls, as though the victims had been brained with some such instrument as a heavy block. And there were corpses the heads of which were altogether missing. But in these cases the missing heads cannot possibly have been cut off. They must have been *wrenched* off. . . . In this grave we found corpses with, variously, entrails ripped out, no limbs remaining (as though the bodies had literally been chopped up), eyes gouged out, and heads and necks and faces and trunks all studded with stab wounds. . . . And placed together in one corner of the grave we found a medley of detached arms and legs, as well as, near the garden fence, some corpses which bore no sign at all of death by violence. It was only a few days later that, on these unmarked bodies being subjected to postmortem examination, our doctor discovered their mouths and throats and lungs to be choked with earth. Clearly the unfortunate wretches had been buried alive, and drawn the earth into their respiratory organs through their desperate attempts to breathe.[54]

"Stop going against the wheel of History. Stop refusing orders," to quote a Cambodian victim who got in the way of the Wheel that propelled the dialectical demiurge inexorably forward.

The words induced us to think of a huge roller with unimaginable weight behind us all the time, and ready to crush any one of us into powder should we happen to slow down for any reason.[55]

As in all such sacred cruelty, the executioners view themselves as the purest of the pure, selfless martyrs bearing the heaviest of burdens for the salvation of others. "Do not let us forget," Bukharin once wrote in their honor (just a few years before they killed him), "how many of those [of the secret police] who remain are nervous wrecks and sometimes hopelessly ill. For their work was such a torture, it demanded such gigantic concentration, it was such hellish work that a truly iron character was required."[56]

As a duty of a new agent assigned to the Agitation Section, I had to fulfill the function of an "active Chekist." Thus, in my case, I had to be present at the carrying out of sentences of execution, that is be present for the shooting. . . . "Today you are assigned to the 'night operation' detail. . . . Get ready!" No matter how hard it was for me to watch people being killed, I did not have the right to refuse, and at 1 A.M. I was already in the commandant's office, waiting for the truck with the condemned to leave the Cheka building.

That whole terrible scene of human destruction with the shouts of the executioners, the moans and sobs of the condemned, lasted no less than three hours. I understand why those who fulfilled this duty drugged themselves with cocaine or alcohol. The nerves of a normal man could not stand it![57]

And none was judged purer, braver, or more devoted than Lenin's own Grand Inquisitor, Felix Dzerzhinsky.

Dzerzhinsky lived only for the Cheka, only for the terror; there was no other life for him. By his own proud admission, Dzerzhinsky, in the years of the Revolution, "did not once attend the theater or the movies excepting only a review of a film about Ilyich's [Lenin's] funeral. . . ." In this "monastic" life, so it seems, the sole entertainment which Dzerzhinsky allowed himself was the interrogation of prominent persons who had been arrested.[58]

Who doesn't remember Lyubyanka No. 11? In that building, in the smallest and most modest room . . . Comrade Dzerzhinsky spent his life in the first years of the Revolution. In that room he worked, there he slept, and there he received visitors. A simple American writing desk and an old screen, and behind that screen a narrow iron bed—that's how Comrade Dzerzhinsky's personal life was. He was at home with his family only on important holidays. He often worked around the clock interrogating prisoners. Almost completely exhausted, dressed in great hunting boots and an old shabby field-shirt, he ate at the same table where all the Chekist workers ate.[59]

Perhaps the most powerful, and surely among the most bizarre, testimonies to the depth of faith in History that motivated this systematic destruction of others and sacrifice of oneself, is that given by defeated Bolsheviks who participated in their own punishment once they were persuaded that their fate was the will of objective History. During the late 1920s, before the Stalinist terror apparatus began forcing "confessions" by physical and psychological torment in earnest, successive leaders of the Revolution submitted to Stalin's will, largely because their entire worldview, the faith to which they had given their lives and for which they had taken the lives of others, demanded it. In the name of that objective History, which always gave victory to the right cause, on the Hegelian ground that the Real was the Rational, these defeated leaders had approved the deaths of innumerable earlier losers doomed to Trotsky's "ash heap of History." Could they now deny the judgment of History simply because their turn had come? To do so would have meant not only to deny the meaning of their lives as revolutionaries, but to reduce a sublimely pure revolutionary war for peace, justice, love, and freedom into just another case of mass murder and to identify themselves as the murderers. It was better to surrender submissively, first to political defeat, and, later, to prison and death.

It is in this context that we can best understand Trotsky's declaration at the thirteenth Party Congress in 1924.

> None of us desires or is able to dispute the will of the Party. Clearly, the Party is always right. . . . We can only be right with and by the Party, for history has provided no other way of being in the right. The English have a saying, "My country, right or wrong," whether it is in the right or in the wrong, it is my country. We have much better historical justification in saying whether it is right or wrong in certain individual concrete cases, it is my party. . . . And if the Party adopts a decision which one or another of us thinks unjust, he will say, just or unjust, it is my party, and I shall support the consequences of the decision to the end.[60]

At the fifteenth Party Congress, in 1928, Kamenev made the following statement.

The battle in the Party . . . for the last two years has attained such a state of bitterness as to place before all of us a choice between two roads. One of these roads is that of a second party. That road under the conditions of the dictatorship of the proletariat would be fatal for the revolution. . . . That road is closed to us, forbidden and excluded by the whole system of our ideas, by all the teachings of Lenin on the dictatorship of the proletariat. . . . There remains consequently the second road. . . . This road . . . means that we submit entirely and completely to the Party. We choose that road, for we are deeply convinced that a correct, Leninist policy can be victorious only inside the Party, and only through it, and not outside the Party and against it. To take that road means that we submit to all the decisions of the Congress. . . . Harsh as the demands on us by the Congress may be, we are obligated to bow our will and our views to the will and views of the Party . . . the sole supreme judge of what is useful or harmful to the victorious surge forward of the revolution.[61]

Bukharin echoed these statements in his speech in 1929.

We consider it our duty to say that in this dispute the Party and its Central Committee were right. Our views, developed in well-known documents, showed themselves to be mistaken. Recognizing our mistakes, we on our side will apply all our strength, together with the whole Party, to conduct a determined battle against all deviations from the general line of the Party and, above all, against the right deviation [Bukharin's own faction] and conciliation with it, in order to overcome all difficulties and to guarantee the most complete and speedy triumph of socialist construction.[62]

It was a small step from this surrender in the name of history to the eerie confessions of these and other erstwhile leaders during the purge trials of the mid-1930s. There, Stalin's victims were depicted as vicious criminals not because they had actually committed the crimes of which they were accused, but because the things they had thought and said were "objectively" equivalent to those crimes, since such crimes would inevitably have been the results of their words and deeds. What the Party—custodian of history's laws—defined as the inevitable future consequences of past and present thoughts and deeds was already so objectively, tangibly factual that they might just as well have already occurred. In the logic of historical inevitability, to oppose Stalin, for example, meant to weaken Russia, which meant to help the Nazis, which was the same as being a Nazi agent, which, ergo, the accused "objectively" were, and which they themselves confessed to being once they fully understood these objective relationships.[63]

When, in that brief and precious "thaw" following Stalin's death, the survivors lashed out against the nightmare, they showed how aware they had been of its ideological sources, particularly the deification of "objective" historical "Laws." Restating the arguments Belinsky had used in his rebellion against Hegel and that revisionist Russian Marxists had used against Leninism, the Polish Marxist philosopher, Leszek Kolakowski wrote:

What right do I have in the name of that speculative dialectic of the future to renounce at present the highest values of human existence? . . . I will not support any form of historical existence solely because someone persuades me that it is unavoidable— even if I believe in its unavoidability, for which at present there is no evidence. If crime is the law of history, is the realization of this law reason for me to become a criminal?[64]

Hungarian writer Gyorgy Paloczi-Horvath similarly found the roots of the Leninist-Stalinist behemoth in the Bolshevik religion of history, in "the myth of historical necessity as revealed to those who wield power."

They fell in love so deeply with the generation of tomorrow, with the mankind to come, that there was hardly any love left for those who happened to live in today's world. They were brought up in a manner which only filled their hearts with cold and abstract feelings, and they thought that the generation of the day after tomorrow could be happy even if it was conceived in suspicion and fear.[65]

Especially significant were the audacious revisionist theories proposed by some of the bolder Soviet historians, supposedly the principal defenders of the faith. Since the Party ruled because it knew the laws of history, Leninism-Stalinism regarded the historian as "a fighter who sees his goal in placing the history of the past at the service of the struggle for communism" and who promotes in his works "a firm conviction of the inevitability of the triumph of communism." To achieve this task, the historian must foster "a scholarly understanding of the laws of development of society, implant . . . the conviction that the doom of capitalism and the victory of communism are inevitable."[66]

A number of daring "thaw" historians saw their role quite differently. For A. I. Gulyga, "each historical event possesses individual attributes characteristic of it alone, and to disclose these and preserve them for posterity is just as much the responsibility of the historians as is the generalization of materials studied by him." Clearly, this responsibility could not be met by "skimming over the surface, describing facts from the point of view of already prepared, well-known conclusions." As for the all-important "laws," A. I. Gurevich minimized their significance by arguing that "a scholar is necessarily concerned with a geographically limited and relatively brief phase of the historical process during which a general law may be only partly expressed by merely a few of its aspects or even a single one or it may not appear at all." "It is obvious," he went on in the same vein, "that History requires concrete explanations of occurrences, and mere references to sociological laws do not solve the problem." Having gone that far, Gurevich took a still more daring step away from orthodoxy by undermining the fundamental significance of "economic determinism," the core of social and historical analysis for the Marxist: "the concrete historical actions of people depend on the most diverse causes, among which, besides production, one must find a place for natural environment, national characteristics, psychology, ideology, external influences, all sorts of traditions, the level of cultural development, biological and demographic factors, and many others." Moreover, what place was there for historical prediction when "every historical event is the result of a convergence of many contributing conditions. A different convergence might result in a different event which, influenced by all the remaining factors, would in turn lead to consequences different from those that in fact occurred and, thus, there would begin an entire chain of events and phenomena—a different variant of development. . . ." But why should history be expected to predict, Gulyga asked, since "its view is retrospective: its attention is centered on results already achieved."

Rebelling against the political role they had been forced to play, that of secular priests providing the theological grounds—the historical "laws"—that justified Bolshevik domination, these Soviet historians now insisted that their concern was with specific facts, not general laws. "It is necessary to elevate the responsibility of the historians for the facts they use, for their authenticity," one military historian argued at a conference on historiography. "The value, the authority of historical investigation lies in its objectivity, in the truthfulness of the description of events and phenomena." Another participant at the conference took the same position, but more explicitly contrasted it with Stalinist "methodology": "Can one really limit oneself to statements from the classics of Marxism that were relevant to concrete situations, and that were, moreover, based on a study of sources and literature accessible to them at that time, before the appearance of a great deal of new factual data?" Gulyga was especially emphatic on this point: "The fact in historical science is not supplanted by the generalization; it is an end itself." For the historian, he wrote elsewhere, "the fact is not only material for generalization, not simply an example illustrating the action of a general law which can be left out or replaced by other."

But it was not only the individual fact that should be the focus of attention rather than the generalization: it was, especially, individual human beings, who were "endowed with consciousness and will, set for themselves specific aims, and strove to realize them." In attempting to grasp and portray these unique human experiences accurately, the historian "reconstructs the past in all its full-blooded, many-colored, living clarity." A leading Soviet medievalist, L. V. Cherepnin, supported his case for this personalized interpretation by recalling that the writer Gogol, during his short career as a historian, had been concerned with "all the shifts and shades of feeling, excitement, suffering and joy."

With this, the way was open to the most personal level of individual experience, the psychological. The historian, Gurevich wrote, "must consider in each concrete case how the social life he studies is reflected in the minds of people, articulated into concepts, images and feelings and how, after undergoing an appropriate subjective transformation, these factors determine peoples' actions, moving separate individuals as well as social groups and masses to one or another activity."

Most audacious of all was the conclusion that history was not only a science, it was also an art. "The proximity of history to art has long been known. In antiquity this idea found symbolic expression in the image of Clio, the muse of history. Voltaire, Schiller, and Pushkin embodied in their creative works a vital union between these two spheres of human culture.... History is dualistic by nature; there coexist here the abstract and the sensitively concrete, the conceptual and the visual picture of the past." Finally, since history was as much an art as a science and therefore studied individual experience "intuitively," what was needed was a more sensitive awareness of "the aesthetics of history," and, toward that end, the formation of a new "phenomenology of the spirit."

Simultaneously with this revisionist assault on historical materialism *(Histomat)*, a similar attack was launched against dialectical materialism *(Diamat)*, the philosophy of science and its laws. Recalling the relationship between sixteenth-century scientific rationalism and eighteenth-century Enlightenment rationalism, we see that this is more than a coincidental parallel. The astronomers and physicists of the sixteenth and seventeenth centuries concluded that the only way to know objective reality was to eliminate all subjective human values, aims, feelings, and so forth. Having done that, they arrived at a "clear and distinct" knowledge of an external reality of matter and motion that existed entirely apart from, and independent of, the mind, yet existed in exactly the way the rational, mathematical mind described it. Then came the "social scientists" of the Enlightenment, with historians leading the way, to claim the same objectivity and certainty for their knowledge of social reality. Hegel further strengthened and sanctified that claim to an objective knowledge of historical laws by making transcendent Reason, Idea, and Spirit the driving forces behind those laws, and Marx, following Feuerbach, set Hegel on his feet by putting productive forces and relationships in place of Reason, Idea, and Spirit. Lenin managed to have it both ways, following Hegel in practice, by giving priority to idea and will, while expounding "orthodox" Marxist materialism in his theories.

Unfortunately for Lenin's orthodox Marxist materialism, however, its claims to "objective" and "certain" social and historical laws were being made just when the conceptual model of the natural sciences that had long served as the foundation for such claims was coming under shattering attack. The basic assumptions of the natural sciences inherited from the sixteenth and seventeenth centuries and providing the ground for all the "social scientists" thereafter—eighteenth-century rationalists, nineteenth-century positivists, twentieth-century Marxists—were facing a vigorous challenge from radically new conceptions both of reality and of the mind's ability to know it "objectively." Physical reality no longer appeared to the natural scientists so hard and firm in its "matter" nor nearly so predictable in its "motion." Still worse, "clear and distinct" knowledge undefiled by subjective corruptions seemed increasingly unattainable. Step by step, as reality moved toward the immaterial "energy" and the line between the known and the knower faded, objectivity, certainty, and determinism were giving way to a humbler subjectivity, uncertainty, and indeterminacy. And again, at the close of the Newtonian-Cartesian era as at its beginning, what happened in the study of nature profoundly influenced what happened in the study of man and his society. Subjectivism, relativity, and "every-man-his-own-historian" (in a later formulation of the change) became hallmarks of the new state of the art for historians of human society, as they had for students of the natural universe.

This was a harsh blow for all historians who cherish their status as objective scholars and who did all they could to counter the assault and its implications, mainly by choosing subjects that allowed them to measure and count with the help of machines that are happily spared the curse of feelings, needs, values, and desires. But, unfortunate as all this was (and remains) for Western historians aspiring to be "scientists," the situation was far worse for their Leninist-Stalinist colleagues charged with disclosing the objective laws that legitimized Party rule. It was crucially important for Soviet philosophers of science, therefore, to keep Soviet historiography from suffering the fate that befell its Western counterpart and, toward that end, to guard the old materialist view of the world, with its firm materiality, impersonal objectivity, and assured predictability.

But they could not do so. They had to let science take its Western course: "Many of us still vividly remember," the physicist Kapitsa recalled, "how some of our philosophers, dogmatically applying the methods of dialectics, were proving the unsoundness of the theory of relativity. . . . And so the physicists went ahead and brought about nuclear reactions, verifying Einstein's law not in terms of single atoms, but on the scale of atomic bombs. . . . Think of the position in which they [the materialist philosophers] would have placed our country had they not been ready to apply practically the achievements of nuclear physics!" Similarly, with respect to another field of science that orthodox Soviet philosophers had long tried to shackle, "we may safely say that our conquest of space, of which we are so justly proud and for which the whole world respects us, could never have been made a reality, since it is wholly impossible to steer cosmic vehicles without having recourse to cybernetics."[67]

If historical materialism was severely undermined by the retreat of the dialectical materialists, it was even more radically challenged by the claims of its victims, those the Party so ruthlessly sacrificed for the "inevitable" future Kingdom. "I am sick of being a bridge between the old and the new world," one of the victims announced.

> I no longer want to go around with a sore and bloody back. Let me rest. . . . I am tired of struggling . . . struggling in science . . . struggling for bread . . . struggling for atomic energy . . . struggling for the development of the virgin land. Even for a quiet rest it is necessary to struggle. That's enough for me! Give me a chance to live as a human being![68]

> The Party is a mighty rock.
> Am I then one grain of dust
> damned to inaction?
> The Party is the mind of our class.
> Am I then to have nothing
> under my scalp?

> The Party is the ultimate voice.
> Am I only a trembling
> mute membrane?
> The Party is ultimate authority.
> Must I, a shoemaker,
> ask the Central Committee
> how to make shoes?

Must I, a gardener,
ask how to tend apple and cherry trees?
Must I, a musician,
explain the dancing notes in my head?
The Party is right.
Is he who stands at the top of the hierarchy
always right?
The Party is a monolith.
Am I a renegade
every time I doubt?[69]

"Man must not be played on like a flute," playwright Kozintsev wrote, drawing his inspiration from Hamlet and Kant, for each human being bears within himself "his own categorical imperative" and knows

> no dogmas, doctrines, preconstructed systems of thought; he is endlessly discontent and searching, with no group, camp or party behind him, no preacher, teacher or mentor beside him, bearing a catechism or manual of regulations in one hand and pointing a finger upwards in the other. . . . Never will he let himself be turned into a will-less 'flute' from which others can sound wrong notes. . . . Hamlet is educated and well read, but still more important is his freedom of thought, his boldly critical mind. Constant reflection, a painfully severe sobriety of mind, which rejects the futile solace of sweet illusion, and a refusal to make idols of other people, even those of wealth and power—here is the thread that ties Hamlet to Rousseau, Swift, Shchedrin, and Heine, and one could extend endlessly this list of names so dear to us.

Individual conscience, not objective historical laws and their self-chosen guardians, must decide questions of good and evil.

> "Conscience? What is conscience? I make it myself. Then why do I torment myself? From habit. The universal, seven-thousand-year-old human habit. Then we will get out of the habit and we will be gods." (The words of Ivan Karamazov.) Hamlet defends the universal human habit. He does not allow Claudius and Gertrude the stature of gods. This is his activity, aim, and revenge.[70]

With this reappearance of the individual and his personal emotions and concerns, Russian literature after Stalin came alive again, for a short time. The small events and intimate feelings that fill the lives of real people, however trivial they might seem to the laws of history, returned to a literature that, for decades, had been mobilized to fulfill the "task of the ideological reformation and education of the toilers in the spirit of socialism." Ambivalence, doubt, sorrow, personal conflict, and the darker aspects of Soviet life long excluded from Soviet literature came back. No more "varnishing," the writers vowed, no more lies.

> What can literature do against the pitiless onslaught of naked violence? Let us not forget that violence does not and cannot flourish by itself: it is inevitably intertwined with LYING. . . . The simple act of an ordinary courageous man is not to take part, not to support lies! . . . Writers and artists can do more: they can VANQUISH LIES! In the struggle against lies, art has always won and always will. Conspicuously, incontestably for everyone. Lies can stand up against much in the world, but not against art.
>
> Once lies have been dispelled, the repulsive nakedness of violence will be exposed—and hollow violence will collapse. (Solzhenitsyn)

> True, twenty years on earth is not so long, but I reviewed, reweighed the life I'd led: the things I'd said when saying them was wrong, the things I didn't say but should have said. (Evtushenko)

> For me, the lessons of Stendhal lie primarily in his exceptional truthfulness. Indeed, that is the most important thing for us— not only for writers, but for all people in the middle of the twentieth century. The more ardent one's attractions and repulsions, the more insistently the conscience and the mind demand truth. (Ehrenburg)[71]

Through it all, of course, the orthodox stalwarts did all they could to dam this flood of humanism. And they succeeded. Slowly, the Stalinists regained enough confidence, strength, and cohesion to drive Soviet culture back into its familiar deep freeze. Once more, the apocalyptic saviors had bequeathed a church powerful enough to guarantee that those to be saved would remain safely and purely frozen until the great fire of the final redemption.

NOTES

1. F. W. J. Schelling, *Philosophical Letters upon Dogmatism and Christianity*, in Ananda K. Coomaraswamy, *Buddha and the Gospel of Buddhism* (New York: Harper and Row, 1964), 197.

2. Johann Gottlieb Fichte, "The Way towards the Blessed Life," *The Popular Works of Johann Gottlieb Fichte*, vol. 2, trans. William Smith (London: Trubner, 1889), 295–97, 305–6, 308–9, 316, 341, 344–45, 357.

3. Arthur P. Mendel, *Michael Bakunin: Roots of Apocalypse* (New York: Praeger, 1981), 37–38.

4. Ibid., 108–9.

5. Hegel, quoted in K. R. Popper, *The Open Society and Its Enemies* (London: Routledge and Kegan Paul, 1949), 2:72.

6. Hegel, quoted in Popper, *Open Society*, 64.

7. Richard Schacht, *Alienation* (Garden City, N.Y.: Doubleday, 1970), 26; Nicholas Lobkowicz, *Theory and Practice* (Notre Dame, Ind.: University of Notre Dame Press, 1967), 144, 160.

8. Lobkowicz, *Theory*, 235.

9. August von Cieszkowski, *Prolegomena zur Historiosophie* (Berlin, 1838), 124, 128ff.

10. David McLellan, *The Young Hegelians and Karl Marx* (New York: Praeger, 1969), 83, 83–84.

11. Ibid., 66.

12. Herbert Bowman, *Vissarion Belinski* (Cambridge, Mass.: Harvard University Press, 1954), 113–14, 114; Mendel, *Bakunin*, 120–21.

13. Bowman, *Belinski*, 138–39, 138.

14. Mendel, *Bakunin*, 89–90.

15. Ibid., 24–25, 44–45.

16. Ibid., 169.

17. The quotations from Marx's *Communist Manifesto* are from the translation in Arthur P. Mendel, *Essential Works of Marxism* (New York: Bantam Press, 1961).

18. Ibid., 39–40, 43.

19. George Lichtheim, *Marxism: An Historical and Critical Study* (New York: Praeger, 1962), 289.

20. Arthur P. Mendel, *Dilemmas of Progress in Tsarist Russia* (Cambridge, Mass.: Harvard University Press, 1961), 112.

21. Ibid., 198.

22. Ibid., 173, 178, 180, 181.

23. Mendel, *Essential Works of Marxism*, 21–22.

24. Maurice Moissonnier, *La Première Internationale et la commune à Lyon* (Paris: Editions Sociales, 1972), 97–98 n. 3.

25. Mendel, *Essential Works of Marxism*, 36–38.

26. Peter Gay, *The Dilemma of Democratic Socialism* (New York: Columbia University Press, 1952), 149.

27. Ibid., 138.

28. Ibid., 131, 137.

29. Mendel, *Dilemmas*, 107–10.

30. Ibid., chap. 2.

31. Ibid., 140, 142–43, 178.

32. Leopold Haimson, *The Russian Marxists and the Origins of Bolshevism* (Cambridge, Mass.: Harvard University Press, 1955), 79, 86.

33. Mendel, *Dilemmas*, 188, 194, 204–6, 211, 221.

34. Stalin, quoted in Mendel, *Essential Works of Marxism*, 218–19.

35. V. I. Lenin, *What Is to Be Done?* (New York: International Publishers, 1929), 32–33.

36. V. I. Lenin, *Collected Works* (Moscow: Progress Publishers, 1964), 26:130, 9:113; Lenin, *What Is to Be Done*, 158–59.

37. Lenin, *What Is to Be Done*, 40–41.

38. Lenin, quoted in Haimson, *Russian Marxists*, 102.

39. Ibid., 119; Lenin, *What Is to Be Done*, 161.

40. Thomas T. Hammond, "Leninist Authoritarianism Before the Revolution," in *Continuity and Change in Russian and Soviet Thought*, ed. Ernest J. Simmons (Cambridge, Mass.: Harvard University Press, 1955), 154.

41. Lenin, *What Is to Be Done*, 152, 154–55.

42. Bertram D. Wolfe, *Three Who Made a Revolution* (New York: Dial Press, 1948), 259, 228.

43. Hammond, "Leninist Authoritarianism," 146–47; Wolfe, *Three*, 256–57.

44. Wolfe, *Three*, 253.

45. Mendel, *Dilemmas*, 199–200.

46. Merle Fainsod, *How Russia Is Ruled* (Cambridge, Mass.: Harvard University Press, 1958), 359.

47. Lenin, *Works*, 9:113.

48. Rene Füllop-Miller, *The Mind and Face of Bolshevism*, trans. F. S. Flint and D. F. Tait (New York: Putnam, 1927), 46–47.

49. Ibid., 63.

50. Lenin, *Works*, 8:130; *Polnoe sobraniie sochinenii*, 5th ed. (Moscow, 1959–65), 40:57–58, trans. in James F. McDaniel, "The Emergence of Terror in Bolshevik Russia," typescript, 51 and in "Political Assassination and Mass Execution" (Ph.D. diss., University of Michigan), 317.

51. Nikolay Valentinov, *Encounters with Lenin*, trans. Paula Rosta and Brian Pearce (London: Oxford University Press, 1968), 128.

52. *Rude Pravo*, quoted in *Time*, January 24, 1977, 39.

53. *Zenshin (Progress)*, quoted in *Mainichi Daily News*, trans. in C. Helman, "Students against Students" (University of Michigan History Honors Thesis, 1980).

54. Sergei Petrovich Melgunov, *The Red Terror in Russia* (London: J. M. Dent, 1925), trans. in McDaniel, "Political Assassination," 285–86.

55. John Barron and Anthony Paul, *Murder of a Gentle Land* (New York: Crowell, 1977).

56. *Pravda*, December 18, 1927, trans. in McDaniel, "Political Assassination," 299.

57. E. V. Dumbadze, *Na sluzhbe Cheka i Kominterna* (Paris, 1930), trans. in McDaniel, "Political Assassination," 298.

58. Roman Gul, *Dzerzhinskii, Menshinskii, Peters, Latsis, i Iagoda* (Paris, 1936), trans. in McDaniel, "Political Assassination," 295; McDaniel, "Emergence of Terror," 36–37.

59. Gul, *Dzerzhinskii*, trans. in McDaniel, "Political Assassination," 244–45.

60. Boris Souvarine, *Stalin* (New York: Longmans, Green, 1939), 362–63.

61. *15 Siezd VKP (b)*, 245–46.

62. *Itogi noiabrskogo plenuma TSK VKP (b)* (Leningrad, 1929), 284.

63. M. Merleau-Ponty, *Humanism and Terror* (Boston: Beacon Press, 1969).

64. Leszek Kolakowski, "Responsibility and History," in *Bitter Harvest*, ed. Edmund Stillman (New York: Praeger, 1959), 94–95.

65. Gyorgy Paloczi-Horvath, "A Meeting of Two Young Men," in *Bitter Harvest*, ed. Stillman, 92.

66. These and subsequent quotations from Soviet Historians, together with their sources, are in, Arthur P. Mendel, "Current Soviet Theory of History: New Trends or Old?" *American Historical Review* 72, no. 1 (October, 1966): 50–73.

67. Arthur P. Mendel, "The Rise and Fall of 'Scientific Socialism,'" *Foreign Affairs* October, 1966, 108.

68. Merle Fainsod, *How The Soviet Union is Ruled* (Cambridge, Massachusetts, 1953).

69. *Poprostu* (Warsaw), May 5, 1956.

70. Arthur P. Mendel, "Hamlet and Soviet Humanism," *Slavic Review* 30, no. 4 (December, 1971): 737, 742–43.

71. Alexander Solzhenitsyn, *Nobel Lecture* (New York: Farrar, Straus and Giroux, 1972), 33; Hugh McLean and Walter N. Vikery, eds., *The Year of Protest* (New York: Vintage Books, 1961), 122; Ehrenburg, in *Bitter Harvest*, ed. Stillman, 225–26.

5

Apocalypse and Nature

In fascism, the Apocalypse found a philosophy that let it act forthrightly and stop pretending that violence and hatred were really peace and love. All earlier millennial-apocalyptic movements were self-deceptively ambivalent about violence: it was a regrettable but necessary means to God's, Reason's, or History's ultimate kingdom of peace. Fascism, on the contrary, boldly glorified violence as a noble end in itself. As fascists, those who wanted to hurt and to kill could do so openly. Might was Right not because it served the cause of love or otherwise played some dialectical role in a perennial drama of redemptive suffering, but simply because that was the way nature worked and the way Providence wanted it to work. Since nature's primary, if not exclusive, concern was survival and growth, it was entirely appropriate that those strong enough to prevail in the endless struggle for the scarce prerequisites of life should dominate and guide the species into the future. Only unrestrained and unabated conflict could assure the dominance of the healthiest, the strongest, and, therefore, the best among each species, humans included. Correspondingly, it was right that the weak die before they harmed the species as a whole by multiplying and thereby perpetuating and spreading their weakness. What could be more "logical," "rational," or "scientific"?

Besides being spared the discomfort of pretence, the fascists also escaped the absurdity that mocked eighteenth-century rationalists when they turned to Nature to confirm their Enlightenment values and vision. The Philosophes, to recall the earlier argument, had called "natural" the Reason and Virtue that did not actually—"naturally"—exist and dismissed as "unnatural" the evils that did, in fact, exist. Fascism, on the contrary, could self-confidently acknowledge the identity of "is" and "ought": warfare, inequality, master-slave domination, and all other forms of violence existed because they should exist, because they reflected nature's admirably rational and effective way of assuring the survival of the fittest.

We had the moral right, we had the obligation toward our people, to kill this people which wanted to kill us. . . . Either we obtain the good blood which we can make use of, and integrate it with our nation, or, gentlemen—you may call it cruel, but nature is cruel—we destroy that blood. (Himmler)[1]

Fellow Germans, my measures will not be crippled by any judicial thinking. My measures will not be crippled by any bureaucracy. Here I don't have to worry about Justice, my mission is only to destroy and exterminate, nothing more. (Goering)[2]

Man has become great through struggle. . . . Whatever goal man has reached is due to his originality plus his brutality. . . . All life is bound up in three theses: Struggle is the father of all things, virtue lies in blood, leadership is primary and decisive. . . . The whole work of Nature is a mighty struggle between strength and weakness—an eternal victory of the strong over the weak. There would be nothing but decay in the whole of Nature if this were not so. States which offend against this elementary law fall into decay. . . . Through all the centuries force and power are the determining factors. . . . Only force rules. Force is the first law. . . . Always before God and the world, the stronger has the right to carry through what he wills. . . . The idea of struggle is as old as life itself, for life is only preserved, because other living things perish through struggle. . . . In this struggle, the stronger, the more able win, while the less able, the weak lose. . . . It is not by the principles of humanity that man lives or is able to preserve himself above the animal world, but solely by means of the most brutal struggle. . . . Man alone, of all living creatures, attempts to transgress the laws of nature. . . . One creature drinks the blood of another. The death of the one nourishes the other. One should not drivel about humane feelings. . . . Have no pity. Brutal attitude. Eighty million people must get what is their right. Their existence must be secured. Might is right. Greatest severity. . . . The Marxists taught—If you will not be my brother, I will bash your skull in. Our motto should be—If you will not be a

German, I will bash your skull in. . . . We want to make a selection from the new dominating caste which is not moved, as you are, by any ethic of pity, but is quite clear in its own mind that it has the right to dominate others because it represents a better race. (Hitler)[3]

There is no reason to doubt that these theories of struggle and domination were believed by fascist zealots as sincerely and fervently as the executioners of the Crusades and Inquisition, the tyrants of Munster, the Jacobin terrorists, and the Leninist-Stalinist Party believed the doctrines that justified their respective violence. Hitler was engaging in more than cynical propaganda when he obsessively used images and analogies from nature as evidence for his arguments about racial purity and violent struggle. He surely believed that, as he wrote, Aryan and Jew should no more mate than do animals of different species, that one race should be no more merciful to other, weaker races than are foxes to geese and cats to mice. After all, he asked, is the tiger to blame for eating his prey or should apes be condemned for trampling to death the antisocial apes in their herd? In light of these and countless other examples that Hitler drew from animal nature, what could be more "natural" than to strive to make the Aryan the "most voracious beast of prey the world has ever seen."[4]

Since violent struggle was the "elementary law" of nature expressing the very "instinct of nature," it followed that it was also a "divine law of existence"; for who, if not God, had created nature? Here again, Hitler was probably as sincere as were the other would-be saviors surveyed in the preceding chapters when he considered his disciples "apostles of a new spiritual doctrine," called his vision "prophecy" and his cause "sacred," denounced the Judaic ethic as a "sin against the Eternal Creator," and judged his great battles to be tests to determine whether he and his Germany were to be divinely ordained victors or another "sacrificial lamb."[5]

Nor was his logic any worse than that of his predecessors. If God had created the world and called it good, then the struggle and violence that had always and everywhere been so prominent in that world must also be good. And, from the fascist perspective, it worked splendidly: struggle brought strength, and the goal of mankind, as it was the goal of all other of God's natural creatures, was precisely to get stronger and stronger. The only difference between humans and other animals was that humans had the intellectual equipment to organize and direct the battles and the breeding rationally. It was more than coincidence that Hitler's Reichsführer of the SS and Chief of the German Police, Heinrich Himmler, had once been an agriculturalist and poultry farm manager. Himmler passionately believed in what he took to be Darwinist theories of struggle and survival and drew from them the appropriate conclusions for a national and, prospectively, global policy of rational eugenics.

> We know that these clashes with Asia and Jewry are necessary for evolution. . . . They are the necessary condition for our race and for our blood to create for itself and put under cultivation in the years of peace . . . that settlement area in which new blood can breed as in a botanical garden. . . . We have only one task, to stand firm and carry on the racial struggle without mercy.

> If the peace is a final one, we shall be able to tackle our great work of the future. We shall colonize. We shall indoctrinate our boys with the laws of the SS. . . . It must be a matter of course that the most copious breeding should be from this racial elite of the Germanic people. In twenty to thirty years we must really be able to present the whole of Europe with its leading class. If the SS, together with the farmers, then run the colony in the East on a grand scale without any restraint, without any question about tradition but with nerve and revolutionary impetus, we shall in twenty years push the frontiers of our Folk Community five hundred kilometres eastwards.

> What happens to a Russian and a Czech does not interest me in the slightest. What the nations can offer in the way of good blood of our type we will take, if necessary, by kidnapping their children and raising them here with us. Whether nations live in prosperity or starve to death interests me only insofar as we need them as slaves for our *Kultur:* otherwise it is of no interest to me. Whether ten thousand Russian females fall down from exhaustion while digging an anti-tank ditch interests me only insofar as the anti-tank ditch for Germany is finished.[6]

Since this credo was accepted by believers as entirely rational, natural, and divine, they had no more reason to feel morally guilty about the acts and consequences of their mission than the Crusaders, Inquisitors, Taborites, or Munster theocrats had felt about similarly fulfilling the will of God, the Jacobin Twelve had felt about letting the guillotine carry out the dictates of Reason, or the Cheka, OGPU, NKVD, KGB, and other gulag agencies felt and continue to feel about being the instruments for enforcing the objective Laws of History. In their own eyes and in the context of their cause and vision, they are all honorable heroes.

> Most of *you* know what it means when a hundred corpses are lying side by side, or five hundred or one thousand. To have stuck it out, and at the same time—apart from exceptions caused by human weakness—to have remained decent fellows, that is what has made us hard. This is a page of glory in our history which has never been written and is never to be written.[7]

While the fascists were the most recent celebrants of this tooth and claw rhetoric, they were hardly the first to propagate it. That jungle morality had hovered menacingly over and within European culture for a century before World War I and its aftermath added the final conditions needed for turning theory into practice. Hegel's dialectics and his might-is-right (the Real is the Rational) philosophy of history; natural and social Darwinism; the passions and power of nationalism, imperialism, and "robber baron" capitalism—all had contributed their portions to this witch's brew. But none of them added as much or as decisively as did an early and particularly robust offspring of Romanticism—the "life force" philosophy. *Lebensphilosophie* or *Lebensgefühle* and its cult of feeling, *Erlebnis* ("experience"), and *Sehnsucht* ("yearning") had become a constant in modern European thought and sentiment at least as far back as Goethe's Faustian Sturm und Drang heroics.

Let Us Hurl Ourselves Into Time's Dynamic Sweep.

I have long been disgusted with all knowledge.
In the depths of natural sensuality
Let us appease burning passions . . .

All mankind's portion I want to feel within myself,
seize with my soul the highest and the lowest, its
joy and woe . . .

World soul, come penetrate us! . . .
The eternal moves onward through all:
For all must decay into nothing
If it seeks the static stage of being.

When I cease moving, I am a slave.[8]

In this Dionysian underside of Romanticism, all that mattered
was raw life itself, life lived as fully and as passionately as possible.
Live intensely, never mind whether the aim or stimulation came from
the "highest" or the "lowest." Joy and torment were not only equivalent, but as often as not companions in an eternal "association of
voluptuousness, religion, and cruelty," as the romantic-mystic Novalis put it. Schopenhauer's "will to power," Bergson's *élan vital*,
Wagner's "headlong blind impulse" were all variations of Faust's
chthonic *Erdgeist*, the all-embracing, indomitable, formless, spontaneous, cosmic, instinctual, and chaotic vitalism. According to Wagner,
"I pour young Life through all your veins; Life is law unto itself."[9]

Am I to squeeze my body into stays, and straighten up my will
in law? What might have risen to an eagle's flight has been
reduced to a snail's pace by law. Never yet has law made a great
man; 'tis liberty that hatches our colossi and extremes . . . Oh!
that the spirit of Arminius still glowed in the ashes! Set me at the
head of an army of fellows like myself, and out of Germany shall
spring a republic besides which Rome and Sparta were but nun-
neries. . . . I am disgusted with this age of puny scribblers when
I read of great men in my Plutarch. . . . The fire of Prometheus is
burned out, and now they substitute the flash of sulphur; a stage
fire, which will not so much as light a pipe. The present generation is like rats crawling around the club of Hercules. (Schiller)[10]

For romantics who cherished the "life force" both as a law unto
itself and as an end in itself, nothing fueled the flames more than
distant goals, nothing was more distant than the unattainable, and

nothing was more unattainable than the indefinable—hence, the romantics' "nameless longing," "ceaseless longing" for the beyond, *dahin, au dela,* the other shore, the infinite and unknowable, Novalis's ineffable "blue flame" and Wagner's holy grail. But while all that may have been enough for impassioned poetry and piety, a dynamic "blond beast" vitalism needed still more exhilarating ingredients, and, it turned out, the best of all stimulants for the life force was the destruction of life itself.

"Germany needs a war of her own in order to feel her power," school teacher, gymnast, convict, nationalist Friedrich Ludwig Jahn said in 1815. The year before, he had explained why: "What medicine does not heal is healed by iron; what iron does not heal is healed by fire." Thus, as well, did Fichte believe that the "Volk ... has the moral right to fulfill its destiny by every means of cunning and force," since "between states, there is neither law nor right save the law of the strongest."[11] Fichte did not have to wait for Darwin to make this discovery, for the philosopher's Volk-State destiny was but his own romantic ego writ large.[12] And so it continued through the rest of this century of mounting fury, from the "blood and iron" German nationalism of the middle years to the orgy of savage pronouncements that swamped its final decades, the kind, for example, that Nietzsche gave the world.

> That new party of life which undertakes the greatest of all tasks, the improvement of mankind, including the ruthless destruction of all that is degenerate and parasitical, will make possible again that excess of life on earth from which the Dionysian condition must once more grow. . . . The weak and the failures shall be destroyed: first lesson of *our* love for our fellow man. And we must help them on their way.

> If his strength rank still higher in the hierarchy . . . , it is not sufficient for him to be capable of cruelty merely at the *sight* of much suffering, perishing, and destruction: such a man must be capable of himself creating pain and suffering and experiencing pleasure in so doing, he must be cruel in hand and deed.[13]

Popularizing a phrase that symbolized the essence of *Lebensphilosophie,* Nietzsche sanctified the "beast of prey, the magnificent, roaming blond beast lusting for booty and victory," and went on to define the ideal state for breeding the "beast": "the maintenance of the military state is the ultimate means of resuming or preserving the great tradition of the supreme human type, the strong type." Only when the "strong type" once more received the honor due him would man again "feel himself in every way to be a deified form and the justification of nature." As a first step, humanity must rid itself of the disastrous "herd mentality" that it had revered for nearly two thousand years under the influence of Christianity; for "Christianity aims at mastering beasts of prey; its modus operandi is to make them ill—to make feeble is the Christian recipe for taming, for 'civilizing.'"[14]

Not that Christianity itself was primarily to blame: the real and original culprit for Nietzsche was the Judaic morality that Christianity had foolishly inherited.

> It was the Jew who, with frightening consistency, dared to invert the aristocratic value equations good/noble/powerful/beautiful/ happy/favored-of-the-gods and maintain, with the furious hatred of the underprivileged and impotent, that "only the poor, the powerless, are good; only the suffering, sick, and ugly, truly blessed. But you noble and mighty ones of the earth will be, to all eternity, the evil, the cruel, the avaricious, the godless, and thus the cursed and damned!" . . . But what is all this talk about nobler values? Let us face facts: the people have triumphed—or the slaves, the mob, the herd, whatever you wish to call them— and if the Jews brought it about, then no nation ever had a more universal mission on this earth. The lords are a thing of the past, and the ethics of the common man is completely triumphant. I don't deny that this triumph might be looked upon as a kind of blood poisoning, since it has resulted in a mingling of the races, but there can be no doubt that the intoxication has succeeded. The "redemption" of the human race (from the lords, that is) is well under way; everything is rapidly becoming Judaized, or Christianized, or mob-ized—the word makes no difference.[15]

Much has been written to exonerate Nietzsche from association with later Nazism, even though the Nazis themselves, including Hitler, sang his praises. Nietzsche's relatives and admirers did, indeed, distort some of his works after he died. It is also true that he specifically denounced antisemitism and fanatic German nationalism, and, at times, defined his "superman" not as someone who could master and dominate others, but who had mastery over himself. However, it is no less true that he wrote the statements quoted above and very much else in the same vein and that, together, that message provided a rich store of encouragement and justification for the monstrosities that were to come. Nor is his responsibility abrogated by saying, as he does in introducing his *Will to Power*, that the book was "for *thinking*, nothing else: it belongs to those to whom thinking is a delight, nothing else."[16] Even were this remark not deleted, as it was by Nietzsche's sister, it would hardly have been enough to block the conclusions later drawn by those whose speciality and delight were in tormenting and killing rather than thinking.

Oswald Spengler's admirers claim a different ground for exonerating their hero: he learned his lesson and changed his mind about the "blond beast" when he saw the consequences. But his harm, too, had already been done and would go on being done as long as his works were read, as long as those so inclined could find legitimation for sadism in his praise of the "proud blood of the beast of prey," his assurance that "the great beasts of prey are noble creatures of the most perfect type and without the lies of human morality due to weakness," that "war is the prime fact of Life, is Life itself," and "that the beast of prey is the highest form of mobile life."[17]

> I call upon all those who have marrow in their bones and blood in their veins . . . Become men! We do not want any more chatter about culture and world citizenship and Germany's spiritual mission. We need hardness, a bold skepticism, a class of socialist mastermen.

> The cowardly security of the end of the last century is ended. The dangerous life, the stuff of which history is made, comes into its own once more. The time is coming—no, it is already here!—which has no place for tender souls and weak ideals. Primitive barbarism, which for centuries lay hidden and fettered beneath the strict forms of culture, is breaking out once more now that culture is complete, and civilization has turned to a healthy warlike joy in one's own strength, which despises the past of rationalist thought.[18]

Echoes of such pronouncements resound everywhere through these decades immediately before and after World War I, often in places where one would least expect to find them. In Thomas Mann, for instance, before he, too, learned his lesson.

> We had not believed in the war, our political insight had not sufficed to recognize the necessity of the European catastrophe. But as moral beings—yes, as such we had seen the trial coming—and still more, in some way we longed for it, felt in the depth of our hearts that the world, our world, could not go on like this any more . . . that world of peace, that *can-can* culture. . . . Horrible world, which now no longer is, or no longer will be, after the great storm passed by. Did it not crawl with spiritual vermin as with worms? Did it not ferment and stink of the decaying matter of civilization? (Thomas Mann)[19]

> We must recognise everything which resembles Western European ideas or which is even distantly related to commercialism as something much inferior to us. . . . Militarism is the supreme manifestation of the heroic spirit. It is the highest form of the union of Potsdam and Weimar. It is Faust and Zarathustra and the Beethoven scores in the trenches. (Werner Sombart)[20]

> The front has an irresistible attraction, because it is, in one way, the *extreme boundary* between what one is already aware of, and what is still in process of formation. Not only do you see there things that you see nowhere else, but you see emerge from within you an underlying stream of clarity, energy and freedom that is to be found hardly anywhere else in ordinary life. . . . I assure you that I'd a thousand times rather be throwing grenades or handling a machine-gun than be a supernumerary as I am now.

> Fascism opens its arms to the future. Its ambition is to embrace vast wholes in its empire. And, in the solid organization it dreams of, more care is given than you find anywhere else to maintaining and making good use of the elite (by which I mean an elite of mind and of personal quality). Within the field it seeks to cover, what it sets up, accordingly, satisfies more fully per-

haps than any other system the conditions we have recognized as fundamental for the city of the future. The only regrettable thing—and it is a very important one—is that the field it is concerned with is ridiculously restricted. . . . Fascism quite possibly represents a pretty successful blueprint for the world of tomorrow. It may even be a necessary phase during which men have to learn their business as men, on the reduced scale of the training ground. (Teilhard de Chardin)[21]

So widespread was this martial rhetoric that it comes as familiar echoes when we find it in recognizably protofascist writers such as Lagarde and Moeller.

Fighting is magnificent and more worthy of man than self-indulgence in smug comfort. . . . Eternal peace would be insupportable—it would be boredom, a yawning that would give us merely the philistine.

Does one want to make a pestilent heap out of humanity? . . . War has always been the national expression of the struggle for survival. (Moeller)

Only the Germanizing of the countries along our eastern border is a deed of the nation, which now vegetates passively, and which by reading and smoking comforts itself about its nullity. . . . They want to fight a war for a concrete ideal, they want danger, risk, sacrifice, and death, and do not want to regurgitate the platitudes that their grandfathers had already chewed on. (Lagarde)[22]

Young Adolf was, thus, a true son of his place and time when he welcomed World War I as

the redemption from the annoying moods of my youth. Therefore I am not ashamed today to say that, overwhelmed by impassionate enthusiasm, I had fallen on my knees and thanked Heaven out of my overflowing heart that it had granted me the good fortune of being allowed to live in these times.[23]

He was only expressing that "new and deeper longing," as the German historian Meinecke put it, that "sought to penetrate from life's civilized surface to its now terrifying, now tempting depths."[24] A tempting terror in the depths of raw and violent nature—here was indeed the essence of the apocalypse of nature and its rebellion against "life's civilized surface." Speaking from within the depths themselves, Lagarde summoned his readers to a violent "extirpation" of the "poisonous weed swimming on the surface," so that "the ancient gods will emerge from the depths."[25] It was while immersed in these same depths and honoring these same ancient gods that Novalis had earlier fashioned his cult of "voluptuousness, religion, and cruelty"; that Meinecke's fellow historian Ernst Troeltsch worshiped his "mixture of mysticism and brutality" and disdained civilization's "arid rationalism" and "leveling atomism," its merger of "platitude and pharisaism"; that Wagner discovered his "headlong blind impulse" and his mission to "deny our intellect" and "burst the chain of hindering consciousness"; and—the sum and outcome of it all— that Propaganda Minister Goebbels proclaimed his Nazi Party's plan "to cause outbreaks of fury, to set masses of men on the march, to organize hate and suspicion with ice-cold calculation, to unchain volcanic passions."[26]

Never before in the history of Western civilization had there been so radical a denial of all that had gone before. The earlier apocalypses of Religion, Reason, and History had all felt constrained at least to acknowledge the prophetic goals of peace, justice, and the other ideals of the Biblical heritage and "civilized surface," even though they betrayed those ideals by their violent means. For the fascist apocalypse of Nature, on the contrary, the means were also the ends: the violence and the vision were one and the same. Rather than hope and strive for justice and equality within each society and for peace between them, the "ancient gods" and their oracles from the "depths" denounced all such aims and concerns both as fundamentally contrary to the elemental laws of Nature and as evidence of a vulgar, cowardly, trivial, and soulless "pharisaism."

For these true believers in the depths, every step away from vital and violent nature in the direction of "civilization" had not been progress, but degeneration and corruption. Instead of liberating mankind, Western civilization had only crushed genuine freedom by stifling passion and spontaneity, repressing all emotions that were inconsistent with banal economic relations and routine familial and social patterns, and, as means toward those ends, imprisoning vital youth in schools that "crippled, tortured, and miseducated" them with dead facts and frigid rationalism. Pedants, shopkeepers, and clerks might well flourish in such a stultifying atmosphere, but not the authentic, strong, free, vital human beings who yearned to break loose and live heroic lives, in defiance of "static legalism."[27]

The cure was as obvious as the illness, since it was its exact opposite. All one need do to escape oppressive and degenerate civilization was "to lead men back to natural spontaneity and simplicity, away from the artificial. . . . Simplicity is the panacea for the evils of the present." In short, back to Nature. "Better to split wood than to continue this contemplative life of civilization and education; we must return to the sources, on lonely mountain peaks, where we are ancestors, not heirs."[28] If the life force vitalists and naturalists were sure of anything it was that science and its midwife, reason, were utterly blind to genuine truth and reality, particularly those at the depths and heights. We must look to the artist, not to the scientist as our teacher and guide, for the artist was the genius who knew the goal and the way, as Langbehn argued in his widely influential eulogy to *Rembrandt als Erzieher*. Both Rembrandt and his work, in Langbehn's version, summarized and encompassed virtually all the ideals through which the new vitalist "culture" intended to displace the decadent "civilization" of the Philistines: childlike simplicity, natural spontaneity, an Olympian will to dare and risk, an unerring intuition into the hidden and transcendent, a sense of awe and mystery, an abundance of unrestrained passions, and an exhilarating torrent of energy. These were the attributes that all true individuals should emulate and all healthy, natural societies foster, not those nurtured by civilization's cold, detached, and desiccated rationalists and shopkeepers.

The opposing sides were as distant from each other and as starkly irreconcilable as were the combatants in all the preceding Two-City apocalyptic dramas. "Civilization" versus "Culture," was the way the life force intelligentsia defined the struggle: "Culture is of the spirit and civilization of the stomach."[29] Fortunately for the cause of heroic "culture," it had on its side two immensely powerful forces that had been relatively uncontaminated by "civilization"— Youth and Volk (the "people"). Both remained close to nature, simplicity, and spontaneity, possessed the strength for heroic will and audacity, retained a capacity for faith and awe, boasted a disdain for reason and intellect, and enjoyed nothing so much as the rush of passions.

Much of the Nazis' vitalist "idealism" intentionally and emphatically catered to the experiences, tastes, and wishes of the young—physical strength, heroic courage, stoic endurance, nationalistic and martial bravado, comradery *(Bunderlebnis)*, a hard and simple life in the "great outdoors," disdain for "bourgeois" materialism, caution, and moderation, and a total rejection of "bookish" education with its mountains of tedious facts, mechanistic rote instruction, narrow and dehumanized specialization, dry rationalism, and stifling discipline. "The new intellectual life of the Germans is not a matter for professors," Langbehn wrote, "but for the German youth, especially the uncorrupted, uninhibited youth who have not yet been miseducated."[30] Throughout *Mein Kampf*, Hitler repeatedly returned to this theme, giving top priority in his educational schemes to physical education, particularly boxing, in order to harden the young. To educate meant to strengthen body and will, to teach the young how to act in the face of danger and how to suffer and sacrifice for the good of the Fatherland and the Race. If such bookish courses as history had to be taught, then care must be taken not to burden students with too many facts; instead, the goal should be to use the lessons of the past to inspire loyalty and patriotism in the present. "The decisive thing," in Hitler's words, "is not whether the youngster knows the battle plans of Salamis and Cannae, or whether he is able to recite all the lovely sentences of Homer, but whether he grasps the heroic spirit and whether the significance of Salamis comes alive again."[31] So dramatic were the Nazi victories at the student government elections of 1929 that they were described as a "National Socialist storm of the universities." The next year, the student body of one university after another fell to Nazi leaders—at Breslau, Giessen, Rostock, Jena, Königsberg, and Berlin. Similarly, whereas in 1931, members of the rival Social Democratic Party between the ages of eighteen and thirty accounted for 19.3 percent of that party, those in that age bracket made up 37.6 percent of the National Socialist Party that year and 42.2 percent the year after.[32]

As was true of most parts of the Nazi worldview, this cult of dynamic youth and its naturalist underpinnings were familiar phenomena in German cultural and political history. Over a century before Hitler, Friedrich Ludwig Jahn had gathered some of his students into a society of gymnasts who idolized physical strength and, even more, the nationalist struggles it would serve (by such enterprises as roaming the streets as vigilantes harrassing anyone whose dress or manner suggested insufficient nationalist identification). By 1817, Jahn had won a following of over a thousand young disciples in Berlin alone. Inspired by "Father John's" praise of war as the midwife of power and iron and fire as the best medicine for healing German fragmentation and forging a united Germany, his militant young gymnasts flocked behind him as volunteers in the war against Napoleon.[33] From such early nineteenth-century beginnings, through a variety of bellicose student fraternities, dueling societies, and veterans clubs to the immensely popular back-to-nature "Wandervogel" hiking and camping movement on the eve of Nazism, a rich soil was forming for the Nazi version of this perennial primitivism.

Karl Fischer, the "Führer"—as such leaders were called—of one such Berlin youth group formed at the close of the century for "roughing it" weekends, was already being greeted with a robust "Heil."[34] In fact, much of early Nazi ritual, song, uniform, and general esprit was directly and consciously inherited from the youth movement.

> The Youth Movement which we all know, the movement to which we all belonged in our time as senior schoolboys, was the first start of the revolutionary dynamism.... The youthful restlessness of the original movement may have turned into a revolutionary restlessness of a very brutal sort, but there is no doubt that beneath the "hiking" for its own sake, or the urge to get on the move in order to still the inner revolutionary unrest, and today's random revolutionary dynamism with its rage for marching, there are deep common elements. (Hermann Rauschning)[35]

One can see this association most clearly and ominously in the formation, in 1921, of a "Gymnastic and Sports Division" within the Nazi Party "to serve as a means for bringing our youthful members together in a powerful organization for the purpose of utilizing their strength as an offensive force at the disposal of the movement." Two months later, the name of the organization was changed to *Sturmabteilung* (storm section). By the following year, these "stormtroopers" were already marching in defiance of police bans and engaging in fierce street battles with the Nazis' political rivals.[36]

Important as the youth were, however, they took second place to the Volk as exemplar and conveyor of the Nazis' "uncorrupted, uninhibited" life force. Most directly in touch with "nature" and correspondingly farthest away from the enfeebling decadence of "civilization," the folk had long been the ideal embodiment of all good things for alienated upper- and middle-class intellectuals, who were in every way the exact opposite of their folk idol. In its modern European phase, this bizarre romance between the intellectual and the "people" extends from Rousseau's rustic idyll of the late eighteenth century and the early nineteenth-century adoration of the Volk's lore, song, costume, and "organically natural" way of life, through the impassioned nationalism of the mid-nineteenth century, to the racist doctrines at its end. Through it all, successive generations of European intellectuals produced an endless stream of books and articles eulogizing anything and everything about the people *Volk, peuple, narod,* who, no doubt, remained completely ignorant of how marvelous they were and what purity, power, and glory they possessed, until called upon in World War I to die in the millions for those myths.

From the perspective of the Apocalypse of Nature, what most concerns us in this adoration of the youth and Volk is the legitimation of extreme violence that was its corollary. As it was the violence of nature that made nature the foundation of Nazi ideology, so was it the presumably instinctual and authoritarian natures of the youth and the Volk that made them as well so centrally important to the cause. Both lived in or near the "now terrifying, now tempting" depths, along with the "ancient gods" that fascism worshiped.

> ... instinct is supreme and from instinct comes faith. ... While the healthy common folk instinctively close their ranks to form a community of the people, the intellectuals run this way and that, like hens in a poultry-yard. ... The psyche of the broad masses is accessible only to what is strong and uncompromising. ... The masses of the people prefer the ruler to the suppliant and are filled with a stronger sense of mental security by a teach-

ing that brooks no rival than by a teaching which offers them a liberal choice. . . . I also came to understand that physical intimidation has its significance for the mass as well as the individual.[37]

Once again, "Father John" had helped point the way, extolling "folkic thinking and feeling, loving and hating, intuition and faith,"[38] and for the same violent reasons that he had cherished such traits in his cohort of young thugs. Similarly, it was the Volk who, Wagner declared, "must burst the chain of hindering consciousness." "You err," he wrote in this same passage, "when you seek the revolutionary force in consciousness and would fain operate through the intellect. Not you will bring the new to pass, but the Volk which deals unconsciously and, for that very reason, from a Nature-instinct."[39] Rephrasing his earlier thoughts about the relationship between philistine professors and heroic youth to make them fit the Volk, Langbehn predicted that "in the end, the peasant may yet kill the professor; what is robustly original in the nature of the German may yet predominate over the artificial element of that nature."[40] "The main plank in the National Socialist programme," as Hitler stated it in 1937, "is to abolish the liberalistic concept of the individual and the Marxist concept of humanity and to substitute for them the *Volk* community, rooted in the soil and bound together by the bond of its common blood."[41]

Although the prophets of the life force thus found powerful allies in a youth "uncorrupted and uninhibited" and a Volk whose "volcanic passions" could "burst the chain of hindering reason," it is doubtful that youth and Volk would have been enough to spark and carry through the Nazis' apocalypse of nature. For that, the cult of Volk had to become the cult of Race. One might justify a Bismarkian realpolitik with the Fichtean claims that the Volk had "the moral right to fulfill its destiny by *every* means of cunning and force," and that "between states, there is neither law nor right save the law of the strongest."[42] But it is unlikely that such arguments could have borne the weight of genocide. And that "final solution" was the essence of Nazism as an Apocalypse of Nature: to annihilate the racial *untermenschen* or to enslave them to the master Aryan race and thereby fulfill our human species' providential destiny was both the means and the ends of Nazism, the ultimate and sacred mission of the Third Reich. All else was secondary and auxiliary.

In all that Hitler wrote and said—*Mein Kampf*, his speeches, the records of his private conversations—he obsessively returned again and again to racial ends and means. It is often said that the Third Reich in practice was a disordered maze of inconsistencies rather than the efficiently run state and war machine of the usual portrait. That may well have been the case. But the design of the whole was remarkably consistent. Everything fit. The progress of the human species and, thereby, the fulfillment of God's will, depended on conquest and domination by the superior Aryan race. In its domestic policies, consequently, the essential concern of the state must be to preserve Aryan purity by prohibiting any racial blood mixtures through marriages with non-Aryans and by a host of familial, social, and educational programs to mold young German men and women into a disciplined, militant, obedient Aryan Volk community unquestionably dedicated to the Führer and ready, at all times, to sacrifice their lives for the sacred Aryan mission. Only those who met all requirements of blood, character, and indoctrination would be considered healthy enough to breed the future master race. Germans who were physically or mentally defective faced euthenasia. As for the inferior races, they must either be exterminated as lethal vermin or enslaved to Aryan overlords. After the conquest, the racially inferior countries would be turned into colonies to provide space and resources for the Aryans. This, in essence, was the Third Reich's millennium, and, until its completion, the Aryans must go on fighting to conquer new lands, to crush those who stood in the way, and to temper further the body and will of the "blond beasts."

That pseudo-Darwinian naturalism of the Nazi apocalypse was the Führer's principal gospel. It not only inspired and formed Hitler's central philosophy, but selected as well most of its imagery. Thus, countries were seen as bodies, living organisms.[43]

> Could anyone believe that Germany alone was not subject to exactly the same laws as all other human organisms?

> From a dead mechanism [the state] there must be formed a living organism.

> An attempt to restore the border of 1914 would lead to a further bleeding of our national body . . . so that there would be no worthwhile blood left.

[The] task . . . was . . . to build up the entire administration [of the state] . . . until it became a close organic whole, pulsing with life.

So much blood has been drawn off . . . into German economic life abroad . . . that the circulation has been stopped.

The Polish Corridor . . . is like a strip of flesh cut from our body . . . , a national wound that bleeds continuously, and will continue to bleed until the land is returned to us.

Because of grave internal and external threats, mainly from world Jewry, the German-Aryan "organism" was in danger of decomposition or disintegration.

The Jew becomes a "ferment of decomposition" among people and races, and in the broader sense a dissolver of human culture.

The Jew is . . . himself no element of organization, but a ferment of decomposition.

The bourgeois parties . . . bore the ferments of decay in their own bodies.

Today the army carries with it the talisman of political immunity against any attempt at disintegration.

There has been effected an . . . immunization of the German Reich against all the disintegrating tendencies.

The "disintegrating" agents are experienced as germs, diseases, infections, and parasites attacking the body.

The discovery of the Jewish virus is one of the greatest revolutions that has ever taken place. The fight we are carrying on is of the same nature as that waged by Pasteur and Koch during the last century. How many diseases have their origin in the Jewish virus! . . . We shall only regain our health when we eliminate the Jew.

[The Jew] is and remains the typical parasite, a sponger who like a noxious bacillus keeps spreading as soon as a favorable medium invites him.

Against the infection of materialism, against the Jewish pestilence, we must hold aloft a flaming ideal.

I gave the order to burn out, down to the raw flesh, the ulcers of this poisoning of the wells.

The Austrian state['s] weakness in combating even malignant tumors was glaring.

The starting point of this plague in our country lies in large part in the parliamentary institution.

What had to be reckoned heavily against the Jews in my eyes was their activity in the press, art, literature, and the theater. . . . This was pestilence, spiritual pestilence, worse than the Black Death of olden times, and the people was being infected with it! . . . bear in mind that for one Goethe, Nature easily can foist on the world ten-thousand of these scribblers who poison men's souls like germ-carriers of the worse sort.

Succumbing to the disease meant a loss of "purity."

Men do not perish as a result of lost wars, but by the loss of that force of resistance which is contained only in pure blood.

There is only one holiest human right, and this right is at the same time the holiest obligation: to see to it that the blood is preserved pure.

The impotence of nations, their own death from old age, arises from the abandonment of their blood purity.

Blood mixture and the resultant drop in the racial level is the whole cause of the dying out of old cultures.

Sexual relations between the races was the enemies' most effective strategy for contaminating Aryan purity.

> The ice-cold calculation of the Jew is to begin bastardizing the European continent . . . and to deprive the white race of the foundations for a sovereign existence through infection with lower humanity.

> With satanic joy in his face, the black-haired Jewish youth lurks in wait for the unsuspecting girl whom he defiles with his blood, thus stealing her from her people. With every means he tries to destroy the racial foundations of the people he has set out to subjugate. Just as he himself systematically ruins women and girls, he does not shrink back from pulling down the blood barriers for others, even on a large scale. It was and it is Jews who bring Negroes into the Rhineland, always with the same secret thought and clear aim of ruining the hated white race by the necessarily resulting bastardization, throwing it down from its cultural and political height, and himself rising to be its master. . . . For a racially pure people which is conscious of its blood can never be enslaved by the Jew.

> Systematically these black parasites of the nation defile our inexperienced young blond girls and thereby destroy something which can no longer be replaced in this world. Both, yes, both Christian denominations look on indifferently at this desecration and destruction of a noble and unique living creature, given to the earth by God's grace.

Defense against such infections restored the endangered body to health—rebirth, resurrection.

> Thus there came the mighty miracle of the German resurrection.

> Today Germany has in truth risen again.

> As you leave this gathering . . . you will take with you the feeling that a people has arisen again: A Reich has been renewed.

> It is like a miracle that in so few years we should be able to experience a new German resurrection.

Since violent struggle was "the divine law of existence," mankind's "most sacred duty" was "to take care that the blood is kept pure, thus preserving the best part of humanity."[44] Not to do so, to allow pure Aryan blood to mix with the blood of inferior races, was to permit the procreation of "monstrosities halfway between man and ape" rather than "beget images of the Lord."[45] To corrupt the divine image in this way was "a sin against the will of the Eternal Creator": "our Churches, too, sin against the Lord's image" by perpetuating the Jewish heresy of helping the weak, the poor, and the infirm, thereby allowing the human species to "degenerate" into a "physically botched and hence spiritually tattered pack of ragamuffins." As the "apostle of a new spiritual doctrine," Hitler saw himself chosen to lead mankind back to the natural course Providence had intended man to follow. "In the last years I have experienced many examples of intuition. Even in the present development I see the prophecy. . . . However weak the individual may be when compared with the omnipotence and will of Providence, yet at the moment when he acts as Providence would have him act he becomes immeasurably strong." "A protective Providence places you over the new forces of our Nation," Hitler said in his address as the new chancellor, referring to President Field Marshal Hindenberg. In appropriately millennial form, he considered his mission of establishing a "thousand year Reich" as one of "the last, greatest decisions on the globe."[46]

Although with limited success, Nazi propagandists did what they could to portray Hitler not only as a national and racial saviour but as the new Christian saviour, representing a "positive" Christianity, strong and vital, in place of the sickly, weak, and negative religion that Christianity had taken over from the Jews. "Perhaps now will come that other Christianity of anger and will, which would be the true Christianity of our humanity,"[47] Moeller had written in the early years of German fascism. Similarly, in the words of official Nazi clerics:

> This is our faith: after two thousand years the Eternal has summoned the Germans to fulfill the mission that he laid in the cradle of the race. (Leffler)

We believe on this earth solely in Adolf Hitler. We believe that
National Socialism is the sole faith and salvation of our people.
We believe that God has sent us Adolf Hitler. (Ley)

As Christ in his twelve disciples raised a stock fortified unto
martyrdom, so in Germany today we are experiencing the same
thing . . . Adolf Hitler is the true Holy Ghost. (Kerrl)[48]

In sum, "Choose between Israel and Germany," Pastor Leffler wrote
in his *Christ and the Third Reich*. Only one of them could be the true
"chosen people" representing the "God of History."[49]

Either the heritage of Israel or fascism, with its "ancient gods"
revived from the "depths." "Wotan, as the eternal mirror of the pri-
meval soul-forces of the nordic man, is living today as five thousand
years ago."[50] For almost two thousand years, the Jew had been the
universal alien in the Christian world and, therefore, the universal
scapegoat, always there to bear the blame for whatever went wrong.
And very much indeed had gone wrong for Christian Germany in the
decades leading to Hitler—a shattered national pride in 1918 after a
glorious span of stunning national victories, a series of crushing economic disasters, and a wide variety of related dislocations and deprivations, social and psychological. The Jews were blamed for all of it.
For the more "socialist" among the National Socialists, international
Jewish capitalists brought on the depression and the massive unem-
ployment. For the more "nationalist," Jewish Bolsheviks were using
the crisis to stir up class conflict and destroy Germany. For all of
them, Jewish international power had manipulated the hands that
struck the infamous "stab in the back" and were the principal support
for and personification of the urban-commercial-scientific modernity
and its rationalistic "civilization" that so disgusted and enraged
Aryan "culture." If modernity alienated man from his community
and replaced the "organic," familial village community by a frag-
mented urban society internally rent by conflicting interests, it was
the fault of the cosmopolitan Jews with their markets, divisive political parties, parliamentary squabbles, and destructively analytic and
critical intellectualism. If modern man was alienated from nature, it
was because of the Jew, that inveterate city dweller and leading representative of such unnatural ways of life. If man was alienated from
himself by the bookish rationalism that repressed spontaneous and

healthy emotions and crippled physical vigor, it was ultimately due to the Jewish Talmudic obsession with the mind at the expense of everything else in life. In brief, everything that fascist writers denounced as sick and degenerate—and that included liberalism, "rationalism," parliamentary politics and elections, trade unionism, compassion for the weak, tolerance, and civil rights—was identified with the Jews and their heritage.

Wotan, the God of power and violence, the life-force God beyond good and evil who loved only the strong, the heroic, and the "noble," could not live in the same world with the God of the Jews and their constraints, their "herd" moral code, their ideals of peace and social justice, their concern for the weak, and their insistence on free will. Conventionally understood, the basis of antisemitism through the centuries and the soil in which Nazism flourished (and without which its genocidal doctrines could never have gained broad support) was the claim that the Jews had killed the God of the Christians. Yet, it may be, and the Nazi horror suggests as much, that the millennia-long persecution leading to the Holocaust occurred not because Jews killed the God of the Christians, but because, as Nietzsche lamented, Jews gave the world the God of thou-shalt-not. To return man to a tooth and claw, "spontaneous" nature and permit him to live the life of the "uncorrupted, uninhibited" "blond beast," one had first to rid the world of the Jew and his thou-shalt-nots. Put another way, when mankind descended to the lowest depths of dehumanized barbarism that it had ever reached, it lashed out with instinctual precision against those who had reached humanity's highest moral peaks, high enough, in any case, to have given our civilization its moral purpose and, thereby, its dignity.

Yet, considering the boundless evil of Nazism, is it right to include it among the heirs of the apocalyptic tradition? The principal signs of that pattern and heritage are indeed there—the total and violent destruction of the present world and creation of a radically new order under the leadership of a saviour and his disciples in the name of a higher law and Providence. But does not the Nazis' praise of violence as a glorious end in itself make the differences more decisive than the similarities? Not if one considers the actual deeds and effects of earlier apocalyptic movements. Crusaders, Inquisitors, the tyrants of the New Jerusalem of Munster, Taborites, Jacobins, Leninists, and Stalinists all assured the world that the violent means would lead to a peaceful end, but their living practice and the only ends they actually achieved never got beyond the violence and domination. Since the victims were just as victimized, what difference did the sanctimonious rhetoric make? One might take this argument a step further: it may be that the only "ends" achieved were the violent "means," because those "means" best reflected the genuine desires and motivations of the leaders. Individuals join, act, and, especially, rise to leadership in movements that specialize in domination and mass murder, because at some level they want to dominate and murder. For apocalyptic religious zealots, Jacobin rationalists, and Leninist-Stalinist historical determinists, there is a rhetoric of peace and love to disguise (from themselves, perhaps, as well as others) and to sanctify the brutality. Thanks to their pseudo-Darwinism, the fascists could be more honest with themselves and others.

NOTES

1. Ernst Nolte, *Three Faces of Fascism* (New American Library, 1969), 499, 503.

2. Alan Bullock, *Hitler: A Study in Tyranny* (London: Odhams Press, 1952), 239.

3. Ibid., 31, 79, 362–63, 483; Nolte, *Three Faces*, 525, 528, 529.

4. Nolte, *Three Faces*, 526.

5. Bullock, *Hitler*, 49, 352, 365, 521; Nolte, *Three Faces*, 525–26, 528–29.

6. Bullock, *Hitler*, 638–39.

7. Ibid., 639.

8. Goethe, quoted in Peter Viereck, *Metapolitics: The Roots of the Nazi Mind* (New York: Capricorn Books, 1961), 23, 36, 44, 45.

9. Ibid., 41, 104, 123–24.

10. Martin E. Malia, "Schiller and the Early Russian Left," in *Russian Thought and Politics*, ed. Hugh McLean, Martin E. Malia, and George Fischer (Cambridge, Mass.: Harvard University Press, 1957), 175.

11. Viereck, *Metapolitics*, 73, 84, 194.

12. "I lift my head bravely to the ominous rocky heights and to the raging flood and the roaring storm clouds swirling in the seas of fire, and I say: 'I am eternal, and I defy your power! Break all upon me, and you earth and you heaven, commingle in wild tumult, and all you elements, spume forth and roar and smash in wild strife the last atom of the body I call mine—my will alone with its resolute purpose must yet soar, brave and indifferent, above the ruins of the world, for I have grasped hold of my vocation, and it is more enduring than you. It is eternal and, like it, I too am eternal' " (Johann Gottlieb Fichte, "Einige Vorlesungen über die Bestimmung des Gelehrten," *Johann Gottliebe Fichte's Sammtliche Werke* [Berlin, 1845], 4:322–23).

13. Nietzsche, quoted in Nolte, *Three Faces*, 555–57.

14. Ibid., 556; Viereck, *Metapolitics*, 295.

15. Friedrich Nietzsche, *The Birth of Tragedy and The Geneology of Morals* (Garden City, N.Y.: Doubleday, 1956), 167–70.

16. Nietzsche, quoted in Viereck, *Metapolitics*, xxi.

17. Spengler, quoted in Viereck, *Metapolitics*, 182, 189, 296.

18. Spengler, in *Free Life* (Streatham, England: Carisbrooke Press, n.d.), vol. 3, no. 4: 20.

19. Mann, quoted in Fritz Stern, *The Politics of Cultural Despair* (Garden City, N.Y.: Doubleday, 1965), 257.

20. Werner Sombart, in *Free Life*, 20.

21. Teilhard de Chardin, quoted in Emile Rideau, *Teilhard de Chardin: A Guide to his Thought*, trans. Rene Hague (London: Collins, 1967), 289–91, 478.

22. Stern, *Cultural Despair*, 58, 101, 237, 244, 251–52.

23. Ibid., 257n.

24. Ibid., 211n.

25. Ibid., 55n.

26. Viereck, *Metapolitics*, 7, 41, 104, 124.

27. Ibid., 110; Stern, *Cultural Despair*, 44, 102–9, 110–13, 136, 137, 164–67.

28. Stern, *Cultural Despair*, 58, 153, 168.

29. Ibid., 246.

30. Ibid., 169.

31. Ibid., 167n.

32. Peter Lowenberg, "The Psychohistorical Origins of the Nazi Youth Cohort," *American Historical Review*, (December 1971), 1469–70.

33. Viereck, *Metapolitics*, 63–89.

34. Stern, *Cultural Despair*, 223–24.

35. Ibid., 225.

36. Bullock, *Hitler*, 66–67.

37. Ibid., 39, 341.

38. Viereck, *Metapolitics*, 69.

39. Ibid., 105.

40. Stern, *Cultural Despair*, 189.

41. Bullock, *Hitler*, 369.

42. Viereck, *Metapolitics*, 194.

43. The subsequent excerpts from Hitler's works are drawn from Richard A. Koenigsberg, *Hitler's Ideology* (New York: Library of Social Science, 1975). The selections used here are only a few samples from pages of similar statements that, taken together, show unmistakably how obsessed Hitler was with this sociobiological thought and imagery.

44. Nolte, *Three Faces*, 528; Adolph Hitler, *Mein Kampf* (New York: Reynal and Hitchcock, 1939), 389.

45. Hitler, *Mein Kampf*, 389.

46. Ibid., 389, 390, 413, 416, 521; Bullock, *Hitler*, 49, 243, 352.

47. Stern, *Cultural Despair*, 249.
48. Viereck, *Metapolitics*, 287–89.
49. Ibid., 288.
50. Alfred Rosenberg, quoted in Viereck, *Metapolitics*, 292.

6

Paradise Now: The Counterculture

In midcentury, two decades after the defeat of fascism, throngs of Western youth flocked to a new credo that was, for opposite reasons, even more radically alien to Western civilization than fascism had been. Fascism, notwithstanding its many primitive and medieval features, still reflected, albeit in an insanely extreme form, the instrumentalist obsession with power that had generated Western "progress" since the Renaissance. And that obsession was the "culture" the new credo "countered." To those young men and women of the 1960s and early 1970s who chose, in Timothy Leary's words, to "turn on, tune in, and drop out," not only had the civilization of power and progress failed them wretchedly, but so had all the millennial visions that promised to do better. As for the bright hopes of reason, science, and technology, they had been vaporized at Hiroshima, gutted in ecological disasters, and stifled under the weight of ever-more dehumanizing organization. Nor did the hopes of the reformers and their liberal democracy fare better in the judgment of this generation raised on the ruins of all the grand illusions. Those hopes had been mocked too often by, at best, a pathetic inability to solve the real problems; at worst, a cynical connivance with the causes of those problems; and, in any case, a seemingly inseparable attachment to a culture of competition, commercialism, and materialism that systematically betrayed all the ideals that this same culture sanctimoniously preached.

And so they dropped out—the endlessly publicized "hippies" and the countless unsung heroes of this movement who secretly withdrew to attend quietly to their souls, wasting time as wantonly as time had wasted their achieving parents. Why, they asked, invest the one and only life given them in some grimly alienating function? Why not devour time luxuriously, profligately, voluptuously, if that meant nurturing the many joys open to body, mind, and spirit? Why not whimsically go from this to that, indulge one's sensitivities and intellect in a profusion of celebrations of all that is rich and fine and beautiful? Why exchange the bounteous, delightful present for fictional futures that never come? Why sacrifice one's life to the impersonal and oppressive institutions that comprised the achievement society or succumb to the psychosis that built and sustained it—the enslavement to time, work, success, "delayed gratification," efficiency, prudence, and the rest of the code. For the counterculture, it was all a vast and cruel hoax, a grotesque deception that had compressed their elders into dehumanized parcels of roles, functions, and skills, which, sociology notwithstanding, the young refused to accept as man's fate. They wanted here and now to make that leap into the realm of freedom. Or, as Parisian graffiti everywhere proclaimed in 1968—"Enjoy without Restraint!" "Accept your desires as Reality!" "Don't Change your Job, Change your Life!" "Be Realistic, Demand the Impossible!" "Change, remove barriers, push and shove the universe, and love, and don't make up your mind, and try everything."[1]

> Listen to the songs in the sky, and in the wind, and in the breezes and trees and anything that's growin'. Listen to the sun get up in the morning and go down at night. . . . The solution is only in your own heart. You've got to believe that you yourself are going to make it through all the things that Want You, all the advertisements that Grab You, all the languages that Limit You, to make it through all the American scene, all the world scene. That's what kids are trying to do—make it through. One way to make it through is to go around. (Arlo Guthrie)[2]

"The first commandment," Charles A. Reich told his readers in *The Greening of America*, one of the most popular works of this latest millennial upsurge, "is—thou shalt not do violence to thyself. It is a crime to allow oneself to become an instrumental being, a projectile designed to accomplish some extrinsic end, a part of an organization or a machine. It is a crime to be alienated from oneself, to be a divided or schizophrenic being, to defer meaning to the future. . . . The commandment is: be true to oneself."[3] Similarly, anarchist theorist Murray Bookchin made the following statement.

> The means now exist for the development of the rounded man, the total man, freed of guilt, the workings of authoritarian modes

of training, and given over to Desire, to the sensuous apprehension of the marvelous. . . . A qualitatively new order of possibility faces our generation—the possibility of a free, nonrepressive, stateless and decentralized society based on face-to-face democracy, community, spontaneity, and a new, meaningful sense of human solidarity. . . . We believe that technology has now advanced to a point where the burden of toil and material necessity could be removed from the shoulders of humanity, opening an era of unprecedented freedom in every aspect of life, a nonrepressive civilization and human condition in which man could fulfill all his potentialities as a rounded, universal being. . . . Revolution cannot end with the traditional goal of the "seizure of power"; it must culminate in the here and now with the dissolution of power as such—the power of the state over society, of centralized political entities over community, of the older generation over the younger, of bureaucracy over the individual, of parental authoritarianism over youthful spontaneity, of bourgeois routine over daily creativity, of sexual, racial, cultural, and national privilege over the unfettered development of human personality.[4]

The message was the same in the far more influential pronouncements of the Hegelian-Marxist philosopher, Herbert Marcuse. Everything in the prevailing "one-dimensional" rationalist society must give way to "a universe where the sensuous, the playful, the calm, and the beautiful become forms of existence and thereby the Form of the society itself, . . . a society in which the non-aggressive, erotic, receptive faculties of man, in harmony with the consciousness of freedom, strive for the pacification of man and nature." Even "a socialist society can and ought to be light, pretty, playful."[5]

Recalling those days in an interview twenty years later, one Haight Ashbury veteran remembered the "blue skies, great drugs, free concerts in the park, everybody friendly, places to crash in abundance. Gurus, incense, tinkling bells. Everything was new and exciting." The drugs were a special focus in memory for the editor of one 1960s era counterculture monthly: "LSD was the catalyst for experiencing a deeper sense of our humanity than most of us had been taught or expected to exist. It was more than colors and lights. It was a sense we were all united together on a planet in a universe that was unified and could be experienced as a great, harmonious and ecstatic unity." A press release for "the first Human Be-In and Gathering of the Tribes" in Golden Gate Park proclaimed that "a new free vital soul is reconnecting the living centers of the American body. Berkeley political activists and the love generation of the Haight-Ashbury will join together to pow-wow, celebrate and prophesy the epoch of liberation, love, peace, compassion and the unity of mankind. Hang your fear at the door and join the future."[6] And through it all ran the exhilarating beat of acid rock, the mellow sounds of folk music, the songs of the Grateful Dead, Jefferson Airplane, the Who, Jimi Hendrix, Janis Joplin, Joan Baez, the Beatles, the Mamas and the Papas, Peter, Paul and Mary, Simon and Garfunkel . . .

Here was a reversal of values and attitudes at least as radical as those that accompanied the transitions from the Greco-Roman civilization into the medieval world and from the medieval into the Renaissance culture that has structured and guided the last five centuries of life in the West. In some ways, the movement represented a return to a medieval worldview and, as such, a shift in the cultural pendulum away from the apocalyptic pole of instant and total transmutation of the fallen world and back to the pole of instant and total detachment from it. By comparison, the Marxist and Freudian "revolutions" were timidly restrained. Marx may have been enraged by a political economy that displaced a sensible and humane "use value" by a cruel and demeaning "exchange value," alienated the worker from his product and production through capitalist ownership, promoted the worst kind of antagonistic relationships between individuals rather than foster a sane mutuality, and favored the owner over the producer in the distribution of status, education, power, and cultural opportunity. However, Marx had nothing at all against work, discipline, efficiency, and a steady increase in productivity through "rational" organization and technological progress. The same was true of Freud: for all his insights into the nature of "civilization and its discontents," he regarded most personal and social constraints and deprivations, particularly those associated with family and work, as both inevitable and noble.

The counterculture spurned all such pessimistic analyses and assumptions. The multiple alienations that oppressed modern man and stifled his potentials—alienation from others, from nature, and from himself—were as unnecessary as they were cruel. Moreover, rather than depend on these sources of discontent for continued productivity and progress, civilization was now in imminent danger of ending in nuclear or ecological holocaust unless such dangers were removed. Nor was the remedy difficult or distant, at least in principle. All society had to do was alter its aims and motivations. Small, not big, was beautiful. Less was more, since the adoration of more, bigger, faster, and the like had devastated the individual and society to the point of moral, physical, psychological, and social ruin. The result was a sick society in which individuals furiously fought each other and sacrificed themselves in order to pile up material objects that meant less and less to them the higher the pile. In its Reformation beginnings, this "Protestant Ethic" at least had a semblance of rationality—total sacrifice in this life was payment for total bliss in the next. But to go on with that lifelong self-destruction in our era of essential disbelief was nothing less than "institutional psychosis," as Norman O. Brown put it in *Life Against Death*, one of the most widely read works of the movement.

To make matters worse, this psychosis of "economic man" was continually spreading like some lethal malignancy, "rationalizing" one area of personal and social existence after another until virtually everything in life was experienced and judged in terms of efficiency, achievement, and productivity.

> In Europe my professional life was an appendix of my personal life. Here I find that the opposite is true, my private life has become an appendix. . . . American society wanted all of you and did not tolerate any subordination to private affairs of your socially required and assigned activities. American society appeared a more serious society—one which meant business and would not tolerate any foolish or eccentric indulgences even in your private time. (Franz Alexander)[7]

Everything that had once been the substance and meaning of the "good life," the life of authentic self-fulfillment and community, the classical, medieval, and aristocratic ideals of leisure and service, had been so effectively and thoroughly displaced that they were no longer even memories. The only "reasonable" and even conceivable existence was that of a productive human machine, efficiently fulfilling the tasks assigned by the masters—society and organization. To justify such totally alienating "work" by arguing a need to earn money to buy desirable "goods" was, for the counterculture, a transparently feeble self-deception: the hardworking consumers convinced themselves that they wanted or needed those "goods" mainly in order to give at least an appearance of sanity to the obsessive self-sacrifice. One did not work to buy products; one bought products in order to make compulsive work seem sane.

At an early stage of this evolution, the Frankenstein story was a popular metaphor for the submission of human beings to the control of artificial creatures they themselves had made. For the counterculture, however, that image was no longer adequate. The problem was now far worse than the domination of individuals by their own machines; for individual human beings had transformed themselves into veritable machines, defining and evaluating themselves almost exclusively in terms of their products and the efficiency of their production. Although "time" comes in many forms—the variable subjective time of shifting moods, the cyclical time of seasons, the sacred time that is timeless—machine man honors only one time, the tick-tock time of equal segments moving only forward, the machine time that measures productivity. Few ever leave that demiurgic treadmill long enough to discover that there is a present to be lived as well as a future to be built.

As with all other machines, the human machine, according to this counterculture portrait, remains indifferent to the specific content of his or her job, efficiently fulfilling whatever tasks are assigned, however meaningless. To learn this art of doing efficiently and precisely tasks that personally mean nothing is the primary aim of public education. Incessantly pressured by too many assignments, deadlines, examinations, and grades, students soon learn to repress any concern about the relevance or value of what they are doing and quickly become efficient computers, ever more skillfully storing and retrieving great quantities of information and mastering designated techniques. The tasks are zealously or bitterly fulfilled, never questioned, and whatever pleasure may be derived from the exercises comes not from new insights gained, a sense of personal growth, or the joy of the experience, but from the stamp of official approval from the taskmasters for a job—any job—well done.

The faculty tell him what courses to take (in my department, English, even electives have to be approved by a faculty member); they tell him what to read, what to write, and frequently, where to set the margins on his typewriter. They tell him what's true and what isn't. . . . When a teacher says "jump," students jump. . . . They've learned one thing and perhaps only one thing during those twelve years. They've forgotten their algebra. They're hopelessly vague about chemistry and physics. They've grown to fear and resent literature. They write like they've been lobotomized. But, Jesus, can they follow orders! . . . What school amounts to, then, for white and black kids alike, is a twelve-year course in how to be slaves. What else could explain what I see in a freshman class? They've got that slave mentality: obliging and ingratiating on the surface, but hostile and resistant underneath. . . . And what makes this particularly grim is that the student has less chance than the black man of getting out of his bag. Because the student doesn't even know he's in it. . . . Students don't get emancipated when they graduate. As a matter of fact, we don't let them graduate until they've demonstrated their willingness—over sixteen years—to remain slaves. And for important jobs, like teaching, we make them go through more years, just to make sure. (Jerry Farber)[8]

It is in this context that the counterculture offered an answer to one of the strangest enigmas in popular education—the insistence that all students, at all levels, study mathematics far beyond the simple arithmetic that most of them would later find useful: nothing competes with mathematics for teaching future machine men and women how to concentrate intensely on the most precise achievement of personally meaningless tasks. With nothing but abstract symbols—numbers, letters, lines—entirely empty of anything substantive with which healthy personal emotions could empathize, yet at the same time requiring absolute precision, mathematics is behavioristically the ideal subject for training youngsters to do assiduously and meticulously work that means nothing to them.

It is in vain that I tell Emberlin that counting is the easiest thing in the world to do, that when I am utterly exhausted, my brain, for lack of ability to perform any other work, just counts and reckons, like a machine, like an Elberfeld horse. It all falls on deaf ears. . . . Emberlin can never enter a tiled bathroom now without counting how many courses of tiles there are from floor to ceiling. He regards it as an interesting fact that there are twenty-six rows of tiles in his bathroom and thirty-two in mine, while all the public lavatories in Holborn have the same number. He knows now how many paces it is from any one point in London to any other. . . . He likes giving us statistics about the speed of light or the rate of growth in fingernails. He loves to speculate on the nature of odd and even numbers. . . . He will have lost all traces of his reason, but he will be able to extract cube roots in his head. It occurs to me that the reason why Eupompus killed himself was not that he was mad; on the contrary, it was because he was, temporarily, sane. He had been mad for years, and then suddenly the idiot's self-complacency was lit up by a flash of sanity. By its momentary light he saw into what gulfs of imbecility he had plunged. He saw and understood, and the full horror, the lamentable absurdity of the situation made him desperate. (Aldous Huxley)[9]

With sociobiologists comparing human communities to those of ants and termites; computer visionaries arguing comparable similarities between human and artificial "intelligence"; organization and information theorists extolling systems that discount and discard just those attributes and potentials that distinguish the human being from the ant and termite; and Skinnerian behaviorists providing the cyborgs their appropriate mind and emotions; the dangers for humanity seemed unmistakable to this next generation of recruits for the organizations. After dominating for so long, human beings were rapidly being supplanted by a new form of "life"—the organization. The organization meets all the requirements of a living "organism." Its principal concern is to sustain its own "existence"; it consumes resources that keep it alive, and it releases wastes; it struggles with competitors for territory and scarce supplies; if successful in this struggle, it grows, merges with other organizations, and has offspring (who usually leave home, but keep in touch—unless they kick up their heels and go off on their own); if the organization fails to adjust appropriately—cybernetically—to changing environments, it weakens and dies; and it has subordinate parts or organs whose function is to serve the organization and keep it healthy and prospering.

Human beings are among those parts (although not among the most important). They are shaped and trained to fulfill their roles efficiently. When they can no longer do so, they are replaced. Then, they generally die, since they were never taught how to live apart from the systems, live for their own personal ends and delights, and any natural capacities for such genuine life were either drilled out of them or left to atrophy.

> He's made a lot of money, and at the age of sixty he's finally found out that, as far as he's concerned, his life is nothing. Because he sees that in five years or ten years he's going to die and he sees that he's got all his "goal," and he's still nowhere. Life itself was just a vehicle for him to attain these exterior goals. So now what is he going to do? How does he handle life? Because he has no goals to preoccupy his mind, what's to preoccupy his mind now is *life,* and he can't handle that. This cat at sixty is where I am at twenty. When I'm sixty, I don't want to be where he's at. Being desperate at twenty you still feel you can know yourself, but at sixty—where do you go from there?[10]

The counterculture promised liberation now. There was no need to put off redemption to some distant future, reconcile oneself to an intolerably slow reformist change, or depend on the caprice of divine grace and miracle. Freedom and Paradise could be attained here and now by the thoughts and actions of ordinary mortals. Nor, finally, was there any need for the violence and dialectical martyrdom so dear to the hearts of earlier millennial revolutionaries; for the revolution this time was to occur not primarily in the world outside, but in the world within; not through either apocalyptic transmutation or gradual transformation, but through intellectual and spiritual transcendence and transfiguration. The price of Paradise was nothing more miraculous nor violent than a new understanding, a new and higher consciousness, a new set of eyes with which to see the redeemed reality.

> Every perception is a creation—"when we see physical objects we are makers or poets." Or gods; the world is our creation.

When a man sees all in all, then a man stands beyond mere understanding. Everything is symbolic, everything is holy.... Every book a bible; and books in the running brooks.... "Hence all things, from the heavenly bodies to the smallest flowers, could be looked upon as gods."... Hierophantes everywhere: the presence is not real until it is present everywhere. In the bread and wine of every meal.... Bread and wine; or air.... Our breath is not an image of a more divine thing: it is the divine thing, the breath of life, the creator spirit, which defies us. (N. O. Brown)

They are emancipated beings. For them the world is not what it seems to us. They see with other eyes. We say of them that they have died to the world. They live in the moment, fully, and the radiance which emanates from them is a perpetual song of joy. (Karl Schapiro)

If the doors of perception were cleansed everything would appear to man as it is, infinite. (Blake)[11]

We must learn to see reality as did Blake—with "eyes of flesh; eyes of fire"—and, above all, abandon the Newtonian, rationalist, one-dimensional prism.

Now I a fourfold vision see,
And threefold in soft Beulah's night
And twofold Always. May God us keep
From Single vision and Newton's sleep!

To see a World in a Grain of Sand
And a Heaven in a Wild Flower
Hold Infinity in the palm of your hand
And Eternity in an hour.

Western civilization since the Renaissance has been so obsessed with the future and so insistent on changing things, that it has had no time or interest—no eyes—for the present. That, to the counter-culture, is its original sin, error, and tragedy. The way out must therefore be a radical reversal of this focus: the present rather than the future; wonder and joy rather than ambition and achievement; grateful acceptance rather than anxious change. In other words, *Be, Here, Now*, to quote the title and message of one of the movement's classics.

To learn to see properly, and thereby attain Paradise now, the counterculture generation—of all ages—undertook an intensive self-reeducation, a kind of reprogramming of its own values, needs, aims, feelings, and attitudes. They found some help in earlier phases of their own Western culture, among the romantic and metaphysical poets, late medieval religious mystics, German philosophical idealists, and back-to-nature authors of the Rousseau, Tolstoy, or Thoreau tradition. But the opposing weight of rationalism, pragmatism, instrumentalism, empiricism, theories of progress, and especially the cult of achievement and efficiency was too much for those few voices. So, for reinforcements in its gargantuan effort to lift itself by its own bootstraps, the counterculture turned to the East (at the same time and with the same zeal that rebels in the East were turning Westward in an even more arduous effort to achieve the "modern" world that the counterculture was struggling to leave). In Buddhism, Taoism, and Hinduism, the counterculture found just what it needed for refashioning and refocusing its vision, and year after year it devoutly immersed itself in the new lessons, in the hope of acquiring Eastern eyes and, through them, Eastern "awareness."

The first lesson to learn was how to abandon the future and, with it, all thought of changing things.

> The "right here" and the "right now" of this instant is the totality of your universe, as it "is." This *is* it, no more and no less. Accept it and find peace; wish it were different, and create your own suffering. (R. McDougal)

> As long as we have some definite idea about or some hope in the future, we cannot really be serious with the moment that exists right now. (Suzuki Roshi)

> Enlightenment is being *awake* in the nowness. (Chogyam Trungpa)[12]

234 / Vision and Violence

We must accept what is. "Let it Be." No striving to change or acquire. Our actions should not be tied to goals: "wu wai."

> (As I) sit quietly, doing nothing,
> Spring comes and grass grows of itself.
>
> No drives, no compulsions,
> No needs, no attractions:
> Then your affairs
> Are under control.
> You are a free man. . . .
>
> Emptiness, stillness, tranquility, tastelessness,
> Silence, non-action: this is the level of heaven and earth.
> This is perfect Tao. Wise men find here
> Their resting place.
> Resting, they are empty. . . .
>
> (Chung Tzu)

The secret is to cease trying to master and control: "abandonment to the nature of things"; "caught up into the life of the Universe"; "wise passiveness."[13]

> Things are arranged for one, if one only trusts. . . . It is more like things happen, one no longer carries plans around in one's head, no designs, no purposes, no goals, just the NOW. Joy is like a river, it flows ceaselessly. It seems to me that this is the message which the clown is trying to convey to us, that we should participate through ceaseless flow and movement, that we should not stop to reflect, compare, analyze, possess, but flow on and through, endlessly, like music. This is the gift of surrender and the clown makes it symbolically. It is for us to make it real.[14]

> When water is still, it is like a mirror, reflecting the beard and the eyebrows. It gives the accuracy of the water-level, and the philosopher makes it his model. And if water thus derives lucidity from stillness, how much more the faculties of the mind? The mind of the Sage being in repose becomes the mirror of the universe, the speculum of all creation.[15]

But what about all the evil in the world, the poverty, wars, disease, famines, oppression? Alas, we now learn from the East that the struggle against evil and the commitment to world repair that were bequeathed to the West by the ancient Hebrews and that have motivated much of modern Western civilization were radically misguided, the results of a fundamental misunderstanding of reality, another example of warped vision, unawareness, lack of genuine enlightenment. Evil is not only inevitable in life, but is the very stuff of life itself, as the Buddha taught.

> This, O monks, is the Ariyan Truth of Suffering: Birth is suffering, old age is suffering, sickness is suffering, death is suffering, to be united with the unloved is suffering, to be separated from the loved is suffering, not to obtain what one desires is suffering; in short, the fivefold clinging to the senses is suffering.

> This, O monks, is the Ariyan Truth of the Origin of Suffering: It is the will to life which leads from birth to birth, together with lust and desire, which finds gratification here and there; the thirst for pleasures, the thirst for being, the thirst for power.[16]

For the Taoist, it is as absurd to think of eliminating evil and striving to replace it with good as it would be to try to eliminate valleys while keeping the peaks, or to eliminate night and have only day, or down and have only up. This is similarly stated by the Hindu and Buddhist.

> The immortal man overcomes both the thoughts—"I did evil" and "I did good." Good and bad, done or not done, cause him no pain. (Upanishads)

> By a man without passions I mean one who does not permit good and evil to disturb his internal economy, but rather falls in with whatever happens, as a matter of course, and does not add to the sum of his mortality. (Chung Tzu)

> Growth, change, birth and death, yin and yang, good and bad, this and that, and on and on. Like a cosmic movie, it unfolds before you. It is you, and You are It.[17]

As Hindu sage Sri Ramakrishna taught, "when the divine sight is opened, all appear as equal and one, and there remains no distinction of good and bad, high and low."[18] In its most extreme form, this universal acceptance went beyond abandoning the struggle against evil: since evil was so inextricably part of the texture of Being, one must, when called upon, participate in it, as Krishna instructed Arjuna.

> One shall not absolve oneself from an obligation consequent on one's birth . . . even if it involves evil. For all undertakings are surrounded by evil as fire is surrounded by smoke.

> Even if thou wert the most sinful of sinners, yet thou shouldst pass over all guilt with the boat of knowledge alone.

> Even without thee, all the warriors who are standing in battle array will not remain (alive). . . . They are already beforehand slain by me: be thou merely the tool. (Bhagavad Gita)

Through such "enlightenment," Lord Krishna persuaded Arjuna to overcome his unenlightened reluctance to kill the relatives and friends who stood between him and royal power. Blake, a counterculture favorite, taught the same lesson.

> They take the Two Contraries which are call'd Qualities, with which Every Substance is clothed: they name them Good and Evil. From them they make an Abstract, which is a Negation Not only of the Substance from which it is derived, A murderer of its own Body, but also a murderer Of every Divine Member: it is the Reasoning Power, An Abstract objecting power that Negatives every thing. (Jerusalem)

> . . . the roaring of lions, the howling of wolves, the raging of the stormy sea, and the destructive sword, are portions of eternity too great for the eye of man. (The Marriage of Heaven and Hell)

Other western intellectuals who had drunk deeply from this well of "understanding" also brought this message to the counterculture.

Govinda, the seeker, found out finally who he was when he kissed Siddhartha's forehead. In a moment out of time he had a vision of the infinite variety of the transient forms of life and death, a new-born child, a dying carp, a murderer in the act of stabbing and, simultaneously being beheaded, men and women making love, corpses, animal heads, Krishna—all loving, hating, dying, and being reborn. (H. Hesse)

The righteousness of the living dead is an abominable nullity. They, the sheep of the meadow, they eat and eat to swell out their living nullity. They are so many, their power is immense, and the negative power of their nullity bleeds us of life as if they were vampires. Thank God for the tigers and the butchers that will free us from the abominable tyranny of these greedy, negative sheep. (D. H. Lawrence)

Line in nature is not found;
Unit and universe are round;
In vain produced, all rays return;
Evil will bless, and ice will burn.

(Emerson)[19]

In sum, what our Judeo-Christian culture calls "evil" is either the "wheel of suffering" that is life itself, or a pole of the yin-yang ground of Being, or the Karmic aftermath of actions in earlier incarnations, or an aspect of nonexistence, illusory "appearance"—Maya—that the unenlightened mistake for reality. There is, indeed, a sublime and sacred order that gives meaning and structure to reality, but it is as far removed as possible from the ethical order of good and evil and its dedication to a repair of the world. It is the pattern composed by the eternal balance between opposites that are always here and now, a harmonious dance around a sacred center, a Platonic Beauty, with contrasting darks and lights, foolishly called evil and good, a dramatic play to delight the gods, with villains as necessary to the drama as saints. If the concept of "the Good" enters at all, it is as a synonym for the Beauty of this harmonious order, dance, and balance, as it had been for Plato.

Find composure in the Center, while the galaxies swirl before your humbled eyes. Harmony lies amongst the chaos. There is nothing to achieve. . . . Things are simply "as they are." One has no standards to live up to. Live in that space beyond assertion and denial. Existence is a dance of patterns before the mind's eye, a living, pulsating mandala.[20]

Only by freeing oneself from attachment to external appearances and conventional social entanglements can one discover and enjoy this tranquil center and its sacred harmony.

Learned Audience, what are Dhyana and Samadhi? Dhyana means to be free from attachment to all outer objects, and Samadhi means to attain inner peace. If we are attached to outer objects, our inner mind will be perturbed. When we are free from attachment to all outer objects, the mind will be in peace. . . . To keep our mind free from defilement under all circumstances is called "Idealessness." Our mind should stand aloof from circumstances, and on no account should we allow them to influence the function of our mind. (Hui Neng)

Neurotic mind is a tendency to identify oneself with desires and conflicts related to a world outside. (Book of Great Decease)

This conflict is the result of our conditioning. Conditioning is attachment: attachment to work, to tradition, to property, to people, to ideas, and so on. (Krishnamurti)[21]

There were any number of cosmological scenarios offered by Eastern wisdom and its Western religious, mystical, and romantic counterparts to promote this radical detachment from conventional social goals and motivation. Most effective was the conviction that all such aims were illusory, figments of unenlightened minds, fleeting, shadowy appearances that crumble into the nothingness they are at the slightest probing of illuminated insight. Why let such trivial fictions push you around, tell you what to do, turn you into a slave, destroy your spirit and life? The most harmful illusion of all, the bête noire of Eastern wisdom and its counterculture adherents was the illusory "self"—the "ego." No sooner did one accept the existence of the ego than one was trapped into a struggle to preserve it and to acquire more and more material objects to enrich it, as well as honor and power to glorify it. Conversely, no sooner did one cease clinging to this illusion of a "self," than one lost as well the desire to acquire this and that to protect and enhance it. And with the death of that desire, all objects, society, and the future lost their claims on us. This was authentic freedom.

> We need only drop the effort to secure and solidify ourselves and the awakened state is present. . . . The effort to secure our happiness, to maintain ourselves in relation to something else, is the process of ego. But this effort is futile because there are continual gaps in our seemingly solid world, continual cycles of death and rebirth, constant change. The sense of continuity and solidity of self is an illusion. There is really no such thing as ego, soul, or *atman*. It is a succession of confusions that create ego. The process which is ego actually consists of a flicker of confusion, a flicker of aggression, a flicker of grasping—all of which exist only in the moment. Since we cannot hold on to the present moment, we cannot hold on to me and mine and make them solid things. (Chogyam Trungpa)[22]

It was because we so fear the death of this illusory ego that we devote our lives to building monuments—wealth, children, books, fame—that will remain after us and thereby keep our "selves" alive. We, thus, in effect, die twice: at the end of life and all during it, by devoting our lives to the vain hope of somehow avoiding death. As N. O. Brown wrote, "animals let death be a part of life, and use the death instinct to die: man aggressively builds immortal cultures and makes history in order to fight death."[23]

> When you do not realize that you are one with the river, or one with the universe, you have fear. Whether it is separated into drops or not, water is water. Our life and death are the same thing. When we realize this fact we have no fear of death anymore, and we have no actual difficulty in our life. (Suzuki Roshi)[24]

To give up "self" is to receive "Self." The enslaved, alienated, miserable "self" is but the persona molded by social conventions and institutions. By ending the clamor of desire and its principal agent, rational thought, one allows the emergence of the authentic Self within all beings, the Self that unites us to ultimate and eternal Being. In an elemental transfer of allegiance, the human being abandons the personality that was forged by society and history and that ruthlessly subordinates him to them and reclaims the authentic Being that he or she shares with the Universe and the Eternal. Once again, to find oneSelf, one must lose oneself.

> Therefore, when the world appears [to be real], the Self does not appear; and when the Self appears [shines] the world does not appear. (Ramana Maharshi)

> Only when the finite mind is annihilated, is blown out like the flame of a candle by the breath of Divine Wisdom, and *Nirvana* is realized, can there be true knowing of mind. (Tibetan Book of the Great Liberation)[25]

Dropping out of society and history and their obsessions with time, future, and achievement, leaving the external world and its ego-centered "wheel of suffering," and turning inward, the reborn soul finds and merges with authentic Being, the One, the All, the Ultimate, the Universal, the Eternal, Absolute Love and Truth. If one just stopped desiring this and that from the world outside and quieted analytic thinking, which was always trying to change or acquire one thing or another, then the vast and marvelous riches of the inner world would soon rise by themselves to flood the soul, reveal the true Self, and thereby bring the individual being back home again to the One Universal Self, Being, and Mind.

> So the mind must die to everything it has gathered—to all the habits, the imitated virtues, to all the things it has relied upon for its sense of security. Then it is no longer caught in the net of its own thinking. (Krishnamurti)

> Were you now to practice keeping your mind motionless at all times, whether walking, standing, sitting, or lying; concentrating entirely upon the goal of no thought-creation, no duality, no reliance on others and no attachments; just allowing all things

to take their course the whole day long, as though you were too ill to bother; unknown to the world; innocent of any urge to be known or unknown to others; with your minds like blocks of stone that mend no holes—then all the Dharmas would penetrate your understanding through and through. In a little while you would find yourselves firmly unattached. (Huang Po)[26]

The paths to counterculture liberation were many. For some, it was enough to stay immersed in the never-ending stream of literature that again and again repeated the new gospel—withdraw, turn inward, stop wanting things and change, and open oneself to the Universal, the One, the Eternal. For others, more disciplined spiritual exercises, "sadhana," were needed to transmute the dull, old, corrupt self into the bright, new, pure Self: yoga, meditation, mantras, mandalas. Still others needed to add physical to spiritual distance, and retreated into the "simple life" of nature, communes, and crafts. Going beyond their own immediate needs, some concentrated on new modes of education in the hope of sparing future generations the alienating dehumanization, repression, and regimentation that had guided their own crippling education.

To learn delight, not aggression; sharing, not eager acquisition; uniqueness, not narrow competition. To learn heightened awareness and control of emotional, sensory and bodily states and, through this, increase empathy for other people (a new kind of citizenship education). To learn how to enter and enjoy varying states of consciousness, in preparation for a life of change. To learn how to explore and enjoy the infinite possibilities in relations between people, perhaps the most common form of ecstasy.

The way to effect the most profound cultural transformation is not to expend one's energies in attacking institutions or industrial society as a whole (for that kind of negative conflict inevitably turns one into the enemy) but to surround the demoralized society with a new radiant envelopment of symbols, a new field of consciousness, a new mythology. . . . At a university the program of residence is instruction in the informational disciplines of the sciences and the humanities; at Lindisfarne the program of residence is instruction in the transformational disciplines of Yoga, Sufism, Buddhism, as well as the esoteric schools of our own Judaic and Christian traditions.[27]

For most, however, the transmutation could only come after profound disruptions, personal and social. Norman O. Brown, for example, declared all-out war against the "institutional psychosis" that dominated and drove the compulsive work and death culture. Dreading death, he argued, "civilized" Westerners responded as infants, clinging to surrogate mother organizations and willingly regressing to infantile helplessness and dependency: take care of us, feed us, protect us, oh Society, oh Institution, oh Corporation, and we will gladly give you our minds, our wills, our very souls! "The adult life remains fixated to this world of infantile fantasy until the adult ego is strong enough to undo the basic repression and enter the kingdom of enjoyment."[28]

No less responsible than the mother-image for this infantilizing repression was the role and symbol of the father, the Ur-authority on whose tyrannical model all kings and gods are formed, the source and agent of the castration-conscience that generates much of the self-flagellation inherent in the "work ethic." To be free, one must, above all, be free of him-Him: "a son without a father; the Oedipus complex transcended. Without descent, without genealogy; no more generations; the world of generation and death transcended. . . . The absence; a withdrawal, leaving vacant space, or void, to avoid the plenum of omnipresence. The god who, mercifully, does not exist."[29]

No longer the God in the Garden "calling Adam, where art thou? Let there be no answer."

Adam awakes from his sleep and there is no longer any separate Eve. . . . No longer any mother Eve. . . .

Archaic consciousness was strong enough to recognize a debt of guilt; Christian consciousness is strong enough to recognize that the debt is so great only God can redeem it; modern secular Faustian man is strong enough to live with irredeemable damnation; full psychoanalytic consciousness would be strong enough to cancel the debt by deriving it from infantile fantasy. (N. O. Brown)[30]

Once free of the mother and father who molded us for social self-destruction, we open to the discovery of new parents whom we can trust to bring us authentic life and joy.

> But who is my father; and who is my mother? Is it the Blessed Virgin, the Air we breathe, the world-mothering air.... "He who meditates on the Universal Self ... as identical with the self, eats food in all the world, in all beings, in all selves." (N. O. Brown)[31]

Our real parents live not in our houses, but in all the Nature around us.

> This needful, never spent
> And nursing element;
> My more than meat and drink,
> My meal at every wink. (N. O. Brown)[32]

Finally, there were the drugs—the quickest and most effective way to dislodge the old ego, experience union with the Universal, see the world through Blake's fourfold vision, replace the progress of Becoming with the eternity of Being, and be born anew and forever.

> I was entering into another dimension of existence. "I" was not. Everything was totally dissolved into a flow of matter continuously moving.... Awareness that I, the others, are only collections of clusters of molecules, which are all part of the same stream.... I felt as though my outer shell was disintegrating, and the "essence" of me was being liberated to join the "essence" of everything else about me. (Timothy Leary)

> We, and I felt this quite distinctly, were inviolable, we had arrived, we were unified with the ground of being, we were already transfigured, dead and at the same time so intensely alive as never before.... I had that wonderful relaxation of the barriers which I have known before—the wonderful relief, the laying down of psychological burdens which has come to be identified in my thinking with the relaxation of the ego.

Another conviction quickly arose: it was that each positive emotion and its negative antithesis indeed constitute one quality rather than two . . . in the same way the dark colors in a painting give beauty and contrast to the pastels, the negative emotions are equally necessary to give depth and meaning to the positive ones; that one could not truly appreciate love without first knowing hate, or beauty without having seen ugliness, or any positive emotion without awareness of its antithesis.

I sat there and knew again the oneness of all things by the sounds of the restless sea, the mournful clang of the buoy bell, the cry of the sea gull as it flew ahead of the storm, but no one of these was alone. They were each a part of the whole. So am I. Nothing exists anywhere which I am not a part of, and which is not a part of me.[33]

The counterculture, thus, found the way back home again, all the way back to the Garden, where the only time was the eternal present and the only life was play. How sadly wrong humanity had been, all this time, to make work and deprivation the highest form of sacred devotion rather than joy and playful celebration! The sages of all eras and places had always known this.

What is God after all? An eternal child playing an eternal game in an eternal garden. (Aurobindo)[34]

As God plays with the time of this outward world, so also should the inward divine man play with the outward in the revealed wonders of God in this world. (Boehme)[35]

To Conceiv aright and to Enjoy the World, is to Conceiv the Holy Ghost, and to see His Lov. . . . For when you are once acquainted with the World, you will find the Goodness and Wisdom of God, so manifest therein, that it was Impossible another, or Better should be made. Which being made to be Enjoyed, nothing can Pleas or serv Him more than the Soul that enjoys it. For that Soul doth accomplish the End of His Desire in Creating it. (Traherne)

Man only plays when in the full meaning of the word he is a man, and he is completely a man only when he plays. (Schiller)

As soon as a man apprehends himself as free and wishes to use his freedom . . . then his activity is play. (Sartre)

What we call the world-process and creation is nothing but a game . . . that the Spirit plays with itself, as sunlight "plays" upon whatever it illuminates and quickens. . . .

When the whole human race is rocking with laughter, laughing so hard that it hurts, I mean, everybody then has his foot on the path. . . . If you know what freedom means, absolute freedom and not a relative freedom, then you must recognize that this is the nearest to it you will ever get. (Henry Miller)[36]

This and this alone is true freedom. For the Hindu:

Sometimes naked, sometimes mad,
Now as a scholar, now as a fool,
Thus they appear on earth—
The free men!

For the Zen Buddhist:

Oh, this one rare occurrence,
For which would I not be glad to give ten thousand
    pieces of gold!
A hat on my head, a bundle around my loins;
And on my staff the refreshing breeze and the full moon
    I carry!

For the romantic poet:

The earth is all before me. With a heart
Joyous, nor scared at its own liberty,
I look about; and should the chosen guide
Be nothing better than a wandering cloud,
I cannot miss my way.

> Leave Books and
> Come hear the woodland linnet,
> How sweet his music! On my life,
> There's more wisdom in it. (Wordsworth)

And for the mystic naturalist:

> Rise free from care before the dawn, and seek adventures. Let the noon find thee by other lakes, and the night overtake there everywhere at home. There are no larger fields than these, no worthier games than may here be played. Grow wild according to thy nature, like these sedges and brakes, which will never become English hay. . . . Let not to get a living be thy trade, but thy sport. (Thoreau)[37]

In sum, "Except ye become as little children, ye can in no wise enter the kingdom of heaven."

> The world was beautiful when looked at in this way—without any seeking, so simple, so childlike. The moon and the stars were beautiful, the brook, the shore, the forest and rock, the goat and the golden beetle, the flower and butterfly were beautiful. It was beautiful and pleasant to go through this world like that, so childlike, so awakened, so concerned with the immediate, without any distrust. (Hesse)

> Grit in the Ey or the yellow Jandice will not let a Man see those objects truly that are before it. And therefore it is requisite that we should be as very Strangers to the Thoughts, Customs and Opinions of men in this World as if we were but children. . . . With much adoe I was corrupted; and made to learn the Dirty Devices of this World. Which now I unlearn, and becom as it were a little Child again, that I may enter the Kingdom of God. (Traherne)

> The wonder and mystery of life—which is throttled in us as we become responsible members of society! . . . I want to pass beyond the responsibility of fatherhood to the irresponsibility of the anarchic man who cannot be coerced nor wheedled nor ca-

joled nor bribed nor traduced. . . . Everything which the fathers
and mothers created I disown. . . . In retraversing the first bright
world which I knew as a child I wish not to rest there but to
muscle back to a still brighter world from which I must have
escaped. What this world is like I do not know, nor am I even
sure that I will find it, but it is my world and nothing else intrigues me. (H. Miller)[38]

It is easier to summarize the counterculture of the 1960s and
early 1970s than it is to judge it. For one thing, its impact and influence are still very much with us, in the many "networks" of "new
age" and "new dimension" attitudes and activities. In the lives of
those involved in such experiences, the 1960s themselves never
ended, even if media coverage of them did. But a more important
reason for making evaluation difficult is the ambivalence of the counterculture heritage. A case could be made in its defense as a positive
contribution, particularly through its criticism of our culture's excessive organization; obsession with the future, efficiency, and productivity; and all but exclusive attachment to rationalism and analytic
mastery, to the detriment of other human attributes, emotions, and
potentials. Moreover, there has indeed been something of a "greening" of America as a result of those years. Lives have been enriched,
broadened, and "liberated" in the directions that the counterculture
preached.

One might even argue that these "new dimensions" were introduced, or at least popularized, at just the right time. Not only had
the engines of our economy and technology by then provided the
means for this partial loosening and easing, but current ecological,
psychological, and political problems and dangers suggest that earth
and humanity have had about all they can take of the post-Renaissance, "achievement-oriented" mentality. On the cybernetic model,
if an organism does not learn from its changing environment and
make the necessary adjustments, it will die. As a consequence of
some five hundred years of "rational progress," the psychological
stress on "economic man," the pollution of the earth and depletion
of its resources, and the unthinkable dangers facing the world as a
result of the alliance of science and power represent precisely the
kind of altered environment that would favor a countercultural pacification adjustment.

More conservatively, one might consider some central aspects of the movement a reaffirmation of an earlier cultural mode that our own civilization used to cherish as the "good life," where one could "enjoy good friends and good wine, a choice library, tranquillity, and the contemplation of the cosmos, the world and its affairs. To be free of necessity and therefore free to do whatever one wants to do for itself alone—this . . . was the pursuit of happiness."

> Men like Washington, Jefferson, George Mason, and John Adams were more like the Greeks in holding that happiness lay in tranquillity, good company, and cultivating the mind, and not in political affairs. Jefferson would be so disturbed at having to leave Monticello for public matters that his enemies thought he was putting on an act. But there on his land he had "the blessing of being free to say and do what I please."[39]

Psychologist Franz Alexander nostalgically recalled remnants of that ideal, still lived in Europe at the time. Similarly, the illustrious nineteenth-century Russian aristocrat and writer, Alexander Herzen, urged his son not to concern himself with the future, but to remember that "each historical moment is complete and self-contained, like each year with its spring and summer, its winter and autumn, its storms and fine weather."

> . . . each period is new, fresh, full of its own hopes, carrying within itself its own joys and sorrows. The present belongs to it. But human beings are not satisfied with this. They want the future to be theirs as well. . . . Are we morally free beings, or wheels in a machine? I prefer to think of life, and therefore of history, as an end attained rather than as a means to something else.

To sacrifice the present for the future, Herzen believed, meant "to condemn all human beings alive today to the sad role of caryatids supporting a floor for others some day to dance on . . . or of wretched galley slaves, up to their knees in mud, dragging a barge filled with some mysterious treasure and with the humble words 'progress in the future' inscribed on its bows."[40] For the ancient Greeks, our "work ethic" world was a world for slaves obliged to suffer alienating labor in order that a favored few could truly live genuinely human lives, lives of leisure and "free" time for the "liberal (free) arts," that is, intellectual inquiries, aesthetic pleasures, and athletics enjoyed for their own sake rather than for some useful "purpose."

In this, at least, the medieval clerics agreed entirely with their pagan rivals, to judge, for example, from Josef Peiper's description of the clerics' world in his *Leisure the Basis of Culture*. In fundamental contrast to the world of work and mastery, the world of leisure, he writes, involves an inward calm, a receptivity, a contemplative awareness that steeps itself in the whole of creation, emanating an essential confidence that can let things just happen, without striving busily to master and order them, that is content just "listening to the essence of things." The mood is one of holy communion with all things of the world and of life, and it is a mood not gained through rigorous intellectual analysis—a work bias that Peiper blames on Kant—but through intuition, illumination, and vision. Nor, for Peiper, does moral duty require emotional deprivation and repression—another flaw in Kant's philosophy: the highest good, as Thomas Aquinas saw, springs from love, from Eros, and is not at war with it. As with poetry, philosophy, and love, the experience of leisure resides entirely in the world of ends, not means, and it is also as an end in itself, not as raw material for use or as an enemy to be mastered, that nature should be enjoyed. In sum, "man celebrates and gratefully accepts the reality of creation in leisure, and the inner vision that accompanies it." He learns to see anew, to wonder and marvel, to experience the joy of first encounter, to see with the eyes of the poet and the child, to sense life as simultaneously play and prayer.[41] In his now-classic description of Tolstoy's insights and sensibility, Sir Isaiah Berlin evokes the same mood and, in countercultural Eastern terms, "awareness."

> Wisdom is the ability to allow for the (at least by us) unalterable medium in which we act—as we allow for the pervasiveness, say, of time or space which characterize all our experience. . . . It is not scientific knowledge, but a special sensitiveness to the contours of the circumstances in which we happen to be placed; it is a capacity for living without falling foul of some permanent condition or factor which cannot be either altered, or even fully described or calculated; an ability to be guided by rules of

thumb—the "immemorial wisdom" said to reside in peasants and other "simple folk"—where rules of science do not, in principle, apply. This inexpressible sense of cosmic orientation is the "sense of reality," "the knowledge" of how to live. . . . We are immersed and submerged in a medium that precisely to the degree to which we inevitably take it for granted as part of ourselves, we do not and cannot observe it as if from the outside.[42]

Critics of the counterculture not only denied anything positive in it, but denounced it as a dangerous, protofascist explosion of irrationalism and violence. While "irrationalism" did prevail (although, along the lines argued previously, nothing may be more "rational" for Western civilization now than *that kind* of "irrationalism"), comparisons with fascism essentially miss the mark. Fascism denounced conventional bourgeois morality and society as too timid, constrained, peaceful, and weak. The counterculture denounced them for being too competitive, aggressive, and obsessed with power. Fascism idealized war; the counterculture, peace. For the fascists, the state was supreme; the counterculture was radically individualistic and anarchic, insisting on decentralized, direct, local "participatory democracy." Although the ideologists of both were "anti-intellectual" and had a lot to say in defense of "feelings" and against science and "rationalism," the "feelings" glorified by fascism involved spartan deprivation to temper the will and violent struggle to test it; whereas those honored by the counterculture urged tranquillity, gentleness, mutuality, and playful delight. For the fascists, master-race domination was the ideal; for the counterculture, the ideal was universal justice, equality, and brotherhood. Finally, fascism was, in part, the consequence of loss and insecurity; the counterculture was the child of affluence.

However, in another respect (besides, that is, the shared anti-intellectualism), the comparison is warranted. Ultimately, the counterculture, too, was a "politics of cultural despair," to recall Fritz Stern's phrase. On the surface, this hardly seems accurate. After all, most interpretations of the counterculture stress its roots in prosperity, in too-liberal and overindulgent child raising, in too many and too easy life options and opportunities. Things were too good; so good, in fact, that one could now jettison the rigorous work ethic and self-sacrifice that had gone into providing this fortunate generation with everything necessary to make the leap to freedom and live genuinely human lives.

Logically, that mood of security and ease should have prevailed, given the affluence and the opportunities. Yet it clearly did not. Beneath the facade of bliss, joy, and carnival celebration there were too many obvious currents of uncertainty, insecurity, confusion, and fear. And how could it be otherwise, considering the portrait of society and its probable future that the counterculture itself endlessly presented as justification for its withdrawal? Confronting, as the "drop outs" never tired of saying, the more-than-likely end of civilization and, perhaps as well, all mankind from nuclear or ecological disaster, the counterculture's rejection of a future-oriented worldview seemed only a reasonable conclusion from the assumption that there would be no future of any kind.

Against that background, all the "joy" seems little different from the whistling-in-the-dark euphoria that accompanied all earlier millennial illusions of an immediate liberation from a failed world. From this perspective, the counterculture of the 1960s and early 1970s, along with its many heirs that continued to thrive thereafter, are but the latest example of gnostic withdrawal, the most recent of a long series of "failures of nerve" that extend from the rise of Christianity (Judaism in a state of despair), through the successive late medieval and early modern religious millennial movements, down to nineteenth- and twentieth-century romanticism, philosophical idealism, and sundry occult, mystical, and religious-revivalist movements. The profusion of science fiction and our fascination with outer space and other worlds are telltale expressions of this gnostic escapism from a world judged hopelessly flawed and doomed.

The most revealing sign of the escapism that links the counterculture with earlier millennial movements is the explicitly regressive character of its vision. Norman O. Brown may be quite correct in his description of the infantile motivations behind our surrender to organizations in return for submissive security. But is his Paradise of "polymorphous perversity" in endless present delight any less infantile? Indeed, one could hardly design a vision that corresponded better to the "symbiotic couple" and "dual unity" (infant and mother) than the counterculture's "higher consciousness" surveyed earlier in this chapter. If Marcuse's universe of "the sensuous, the playful, the calm, and the beautiful" is just another Eden, it is also, by that very identity, one more dream of infancy and childhood regained, not, of course, as it was, but as later fantasy portrays it—where desire and reality are always one and the same. Virtually the entire counterculture reflects this regression. On the more obvious level, there is the wish to be totally free, to satisfy at once all desires, to play carefree, and, explicitly, to return again to childhood. Somewhat less apparent, but more important, are the expressions of infantile narcissism: the wish to surrender the ego and, in effect, return to the period before the self was formed, when one was still part of the maternal "dual unity"; the constant talk of merging again into some all-embracing Being who provides everything one needs and fills one's soul with joy; the frequent oral imagery used to describe that spiritual nourishment; the desire to quiet the constant din of thought, to return, that is, to an infantile state of elemental feeling; the frequent references to the entire experience as "return" and "rebirth."

Perhaps the portraits that describe the tranquil world within are so like one another, no matter how different their authors' cultures, simply because the underlying infant-mother duality recalled in those descriptions is so universal. And, thus, as well, do we find everywhere much the same Paradise, the idealized and projected image of the ever-present residue from that infantile Eden. Nor is it surprising that whole communities respond to prolonged cultural breakdown as individuals do, by regressing for solace to fantasies that reflect that earliest sanctuary. It may well be that all insecurities, individual or social, recall the basic insecurity of the deprived and anxious infant, and that all blessed Edens, whether divine kingdoms within or visions of millennial kingdoms in the world outside, resurrect our first miraculous provider and protectress.

This inner maternal refuge, loyally remaining within us throughout our lives, may be the source of our noblest utopian ideals of harmony, peace, love, and justice, the inspiration that draws us romantically to "mother nature," the model from which we define beauty in the world and create it in our culture, and that tranquil inner space that is always there for solace. One positive contribution of the counterculture was to call attention to our society's self-destructive neglect of that interior world. Its negative side, however, was its tendency to compensate for that neglect by vastly and dangerously exaggerating the role of that inner retreat, submitting far too much of personal and social existence to the control of infantile memories and desires.

In the East, the long reign of such escapist mythologies together with the resulting atrophy of will and capacity to confront reality reasonably and responsibly did much to cause the seemingly endless and boundless misery that is today the hallmark of this Third World. There are few more "vicious" circles: depressed circumstances promote the flight inward, which, in turn, only exacerbates the real problems by their neglect, thereby further encouraging escapism, and so forth. Getting the West started down that slippery slope has always been the gravest danger of the successive failures of nerve, from the Hellenistic Gnostics to the countercultural "drop-outs." At least since the Renaissance awakening from the medieval dream, that danger has been averted, and it was averted once more with respect to the countercultural challenge.

The causes of the counterculture's failure are many, among them our civilization's essential commitment to this world. That commitment, in fact, was doubly strong; in addition to the initial attachment to the world bequeathed by both our Judaic and our Greco-Roman heritage, there was now the force of the activist worldview that had dominated the West for some five hundred years since the demise of the medieval "kingdom of God within." Yearn as they repeatedly might for the tranquil life apart and within, Westerners, for the most part, are pulled back again and again by the world's call. For most it is the familiar call of wealth, honor, or power. Hegel once wrote about a double alienation: if devoting ourselves to the world involves alienation from our "true" inner selves, so does remaining apart from the world, since it is only through involvement in the world that we generally acquire the social approval, the channel for self-expression, and the sense of power—of somehow making our existence matter— that motivate so much of Western thought and action.

For a few, however, the call back to the world was the call of compassion. All the ingenious Eastern intellectual convolutions that transfigured evil out of existence could not silence the awareness that we are our brothers' keepers, that we cannot individually go home again or return to the garden until all of us do, and that those who try to do so will find the home empty and the garden rank.

I am still very unwell, and tormented between the longing for rest and lovely life, and the sense of this terrific call of human crime for resistance and of human misery for help, though it seems to me as the voice of a river of blood which can but sweep me down in the midst of its black clots, helpless. (John Ruskin)

Three passions, simple but overwhelmingly strong, have governed my life: the longing for love, the search for knowledge, and unbearable pity for the suffering of mankind. . . . Love and knowledge, so far as they were possible, led upward toward the heavens. But always pity brought me back to earth. Echoes of cries of pain reverberate in my heart. Children in famine, victims tortured by oppressors, helpless old people a hated burden to their sons, and the whole world of loneliness, poverty, and pain make a mockery of what human life should be. I long to alleviate the evil, but I cannot, and I too suffer. (Bertrand Russell)

What is it to me that I understand ideas, that to me there is opened a world of ideas in art, in religion, in history, when I cannot share this with all who should be my brothers. . . . Sorrow, heavy sorrow overcomes me at the sight of barefoot boys playing knucklebones in the street, of ragged beggars and a drunken coachman, of a soldier coming from a parade, of a bureaucrat hurrying by with a briefcase under his arm. . . . And after this does a man have the right to forget himself in art, in science! (Vissarion Belinsky)

Remember how things were: the educated minority, having long enjoyed its privileged position, its aristocratic, literary, artistic leanings, governmental ambience, at last felt a pang of conscience and remembered its forgotten brothers. . . . For it is they, none other, who are dying of hunger, of cold, it is they whose muttering we hear about us and below us, in garrets and in the cellars, while we sit at the *piano nobile*, "over pastry and champagne" talking of socialism. (Alexander Herzen)

There is a tale that a man inspired by God once went out from the creaturely realms into the vast waste. There he wandered till he came to the gates of mystery. He knocked. From within came the cry: "What do you want here?" He said: "I have proclaimed your praise in the ears of mortals, but they were deaf to me. So I come to you that you yourself may hear me and reply." "Turn back," came the cry from within. "Here is no ear for you. I have sunk my hearing in the deafness of mortals." (Martin Buber)[43]

Herbert Marcuse, the counterculture's leading social philosopher, displayed that agonizing ambivalence with poignant intensity and with some very disturbing consequences. How delightful it must have been for him to imagine that "universe where the sensuous, the playful, the calm, and the beautiful become forms of existence and thereby the Form of society itself," to summon society to the cause of "the miniskirts against the apparatchiks," and to hail the young rebels' "methodical disengagement from and refusal of the Establishment, aiming at a radical transvaluation of values . . . a break with the familiar, the routine ways of seeing, hearing, feeling."[44] Yet, when the dam of repressions actually broke and the Yippies and Hippies swept across the land, he was shocked by these "wild ones and the uncommitted, the escapists into all kinds of mysticism, the good fools and the bad fools, and those who don't care what happens." Suddenly, the marvelous affluence that was to allow us all to live lives of joy and celebration, became for him a "cruel affluence," an "affluent monster." And why? Because "this society is obscene in producing and indecently exposing a stifling abundance of wares *while depriving its victims abroad of the necessities of life.*"[45]

Marcuse was here publicly disclosing the truth that he must have known all the time: there were two radically opposed uses for the affluence—to finance the "leap to freedom" for the favored few or to do something to alleviate the misery that crushed the lives of the countless have-nots throughout the world (including those in the West). Much as he dearly wanted to lead others into that world of "the sensuous, the playful, the calm, and the beautiful," he had for too long been a dedicated socialist (and even longer a morally committed Jew) to ignore the world's pain. Consequently, we find him summoning his readers to the revolution that "subordinates the development of productive forces and higher standards of living to the requirements of creating solidarity for the human species, for abolishing poverty and misery beyond all national frontiers."[46] At times, his ambivalence forces him to shift directions in midstream: the revolution "would have the chance of turning quantitative technical progress into *qualitatively different ways of life* [counterculture]—precisely because it would be a revolution occurring at a high level of material and intellectual development, one which would enable man to *conquer scarcity and poverty*" [Old Left].[47]

It was in part to solve just this kind of dilemma that, as we have seen, the millennial ideal first entered the culture of the West. Neo-Platonism, Gnosticism, and the other occult voices prevalent in Alexandria and other Hellenistic centers pointed to a way out of the intolerable world. But Judaism insisted that it was, after all, God's world, and must therefore be honored as our proper home. Those among the Jews who found both sides equally compelling—the rejection of the existing world in favor of an ideal realm and the necessity of remaining in the world—quickly reached the logical compromise: stay in the world, but transmute it miraculously—and violently—into the Paradise that the Gnostics and other idealists imagined. And since humanity had proven itself so utterly incapable of making the world even a little better, much less a second Eden, one must trust this radical transmutation to divine grace and its agent, the Messiah.

Following a similar route through the ambivalence, Marcuse arrived at much the same conclusion. The only difference—minimal, as I have tried to show—was that, as a secular millennarian, Marcuse's Messiah was a revolutionary elite. Of course, it would be better if the oppressed masses themselves could achieve their own liberation, but they had been too effectively brainwashed by the "one-dimensional" establishment to realize that their true interests lay in taking over the system and using it for their own good (whatever that was: compassionate service to the Third World or countercultural liberation). So, the enlightened few (who, however, were just as uncertain as to which of those alternative goals to pursue) would have to take the lead and save the people from and for themselves.

> [The people] cannot reject the system of domination without rejecting themselves, their own repressive instinctual needs and values. We would have to conclude that liberation would mean subversion against the will and against the prevailing interests of the great majority of the people. . . .

In the last analysis, the question of what are true and false needs must be answered by the individuals themselves, but only in the last analysis; that is, if and when they are free to give their own answer. As long as they are kept incapable of being autonomous, as long as they are indoctrinated and manipulated (down to their very instincts) their answer to this question cannot be taken as their own.[48]

Marcuse's attempt to avoid somehow that dismal authoritarianism must be embarrassing to read for those who admire the man and his work.

True, such government, initially, would not have the endorsement of the majority "inherited" from the previous government—but once the chain of the past governments is broken, the majority would be in a state of flux, and released from past management, free to judge the new government in terms of the new common interest. To be sure, this has never been the course of a revolution, but it is equally true that never before has a revolution occurred which had at its disposal the present achievements of productivity and technical progress. Of course, they could be effectively used for imposing another set of repressive controls, but our entire discussion was based on the proposition that the revolution would be liberating only if it were carried by the non-repressive forces stirring in the existing society. The proposition is no more—and no less—than a hope.[49]

Elsewhere, however, he is much bolder—almost Jacobin and Leninist—in his willingness to do what must be done.

Tolerance cannot be indiscriminate and equal with respect to the contents of expression, neither in word nor in deed; it cannot protect false words and wrong deeds which demonstrate that they contradict and counteract the possibilities of liberation. . . . Society cannot be indiscriminate where the pacification of existence, where freedom and happiness themselves are at stake; here . . . certain policies cannot be proposed, certain behaviour cannot be permitted without making tolerance an instrument for the continuation of servitude.[50]

Becoming more authoritarian with each step in this elitist logic, Marcuse argued that the policy of "selective tolerance" will

> include the withdrawal of toleration of speech and assembly from groups and movements which promote aggressive policies, armament, chauvinism, discrimination on the grounds of race and religion, or which oppose the extension of public services, social security, medical care, etc. Moreover, the restoration of freedom of thought may necessitate new and rigid restrictions on teaching and practices in the educational institutions which, by their very methods and concepts, serve to enclose the mind within the established universe of discourse and behavior. . . . Since when is history made in accordance with ethical standards?[51]

Repeating the experience of his millennial predecessors, Marcuse, too, suffered the Dostoyevskian dialectic that turned the dream of total freedom into the reality of total domination. With the stars of "the sensuous, the calm, and the beautiful" in his eyes, he wants nothing to do with authoritarianism and violence. He praises the counterculture for avoiding them and for following the tautological dictum that the "end must indeed appear in the means to attain it," that there must be "an ingression of the future into the present":[52] if peace and freedom are the ends, then they can only be attained through peace and freedom, not violence and domination. In this genuinely countercultural mood, he was delighted to see in the "New Left" a humane, patient, "step-by-step" politics and a preference for "spontaneity." But then he became "realistic," and the stars went out.

> To be sure, within the repressive society, and against its ubiquitous apparatus, spontaneity by itself cannot possibly be a radical and revolutionary force. It can become such a force only as the result of enlightenment, education, political practice—in this sense, indeed, as a result of organization. The anarchic element is an essential factor in the struggle against domination: preserved but disciplined in the preparatory political action, it will be freed and *aufgehoben* [raised to a higher level] in the goals of the struggle. Released for the construction of the initial revolu-

tionary institutions, the anti-repressive sensibility, allergic to domination, would militate against the prolongation of the "first phase," that is the authoritarian bureaucratic development of the productive forces.[53]

Fortunately for those destined for this authoritarian anarchism, Marcuse's millennial revolution never left the drawing board. All those whom his wishful thinking had chosen to lead the revolution—workers, students, third world rebels—failed to live up to expectations. The third world Leninists—Mao, Che, Ho—did indeed play their violent parts, but their distant successes had little effect on the basic structure of the "one-dimensional" Western society. Norman O. Brown's bizarre fantasies of violent apocalyptic explosion and transmutation were even more distant from reality, although fascinating as echoes of their religious sources and, thereby, a summary of the basic theme of this study.

> On the other side of the veil is nothing; utopia; the kingdom not of this world. The utopia of nihilism, the negation of the negation; the world annihilated. . . . To bring this world to an end: the consummation devoutly to be wished, the final judgment. . . . Overcoming this world, abolishing it. . . . The revolution, the revelation, the apocalypse, is vision. . . . The sacrifice of Isaac was not actually carried out . . . the sacrifice is really carried out in Jesus, for the first and for the last time; now once and for all to bring the world to an end. . . . We must look to the end. The Christian prayer is for the end of the world: that it may come quickly. The aim is to bring this world to an end; the only question is how. . . . Go down and stay down, in the forbidden zone; a descent into hell . . . only by going deeper into the cave can we find our exit . . . and so our identification with those below. The revolution is from below, the lower classes, the underworld, the damned, the disreputable, the despised and rejected. . . . To seduce the world to madness . . . [we must], as Conrad said, immerse within the "destructive element" . . . there is no breakthrough without breakage. . . . It is not true unless it hurts; the evidence is martyrdom. . . . Extremism. Truth is not in safety or in the middle . . . the road of excess which leads to the palace of wisdom. . . . The body is made whole by being bro-

ken. . . . The real prayer is to see this world go up in flames . . . to bring this world to an end, in a final conflagration, or explosion, bursting the boundaries . . . the final conflagration; or apocalypse. The unity of life and death as fire . . . not catharsis but cruelty. . . . The fire next time. The revolution, or second coming. . . . Learn to love the fire. The alchemical fire of transmutation. . . . Violent eruption, vulcanism; the patient becomes violent, as he wakes up. The madness of the millennia breaks out: madness is, Dionysus is, violence. Love is violence . . . birth is bursting, the shell burst. The start is violent. The great heroic deed is to be born; to slay the dragon, to kill the mother, to conquer Tiamat. Every child, like Athena, is born fully armed; is a knife that opens the womb. . . . Not peace but a sword . . . destroy this temple, and in three days I will raise it up.[54]

There seemed no limit to Brown's flights of violent fancy and demonic posturing as he worked himself up, and, apparently, hoped to work his readers up, to a point of welcoming the "witches' brew . . . that horrible mixture of sensuality and cruelty," the "final convulsion and sinking down into a nothingness that often leads to the gravest disasters . . . the sexology of de Sade and the politics of Hitler."[55]

The counterculture did, at times, enact Brown's rhetorical madness—the Charles Manson horror, for example. But, media focus notwithstanding, such events were extraordinarily rare, considering the extremism of the millennial vision, the intensity of the passions, the explicit credo of emotional release, and the immense numbers of young people involved. What violence there was usually came from the side of those assigned to defend society against the largely nonviolent demonstrations, and the victims were, generally, the "rebels" themselves, whether through suicidal "mind-expanding" experiments, vulnerability to criminal assault, emotional breakdown, or, most often, wasted years and life.

It could be argued, in fact, that countercultural sentiments and ideas helped restrain the violence that might otherwise have been much greater in the concurrent movements protesting the Vietnam War, demanding student, minority, and women's rights, and campaigning for better environmental and social welfare legislation.

None of those movements in themselves reflected the countercultural vision surveyed here: there was nothing new in antiwar movements or in efforts by those deprived of their share of rights and power to win that share. All of that was clearly a continuation of the familiar "Old Left" social activism for "reform" and "progress," and while those who considered themselves part of the counterculture did sometimes participate in such demonstrations against the "system," it was, more often than not, less the goals of the demonstration than the heady experience of demonstrating that drew their involvement. For them, turn on, tune in, and drop out meant just that—escape into another world in the company of kindred spirits and let the hung-up society go right on strangling itself.

NOTES

1. Personal observations by the author.

2. Arlo Guthrie, *New York Times*, 11 January 1970.

3. Charles Reich, *The Greening of America* (New York: Random House, 1970), 225.

4. Murray Bookchin, *Post-Scarcity Anarchy* (New York: Anarchos, n.d.), 1, 9.

5. Herbert Marcuse, *An Essay on Liberation* (Boston: Beacon Press, 1969), 25–26, chap. 2.

6. Lisa Ryckman, "Summer of Love," *Ann Arbor News*, 30 June 1987.

7. Arthur P. Mendel, "On the Eve of Freedom," *Ingenor* (College of Engineering, University of Michigan), Spring, 1968, 22.

8. Jerry Farber, *In Loco Parentis* (New York: Anarchos, n.d.), 1–3, 5.

9. Aldous Huxley, "Eupompus Gave Splendor to Art by Numbers," in *Limbo* (London: Chatto and Windus, 1970), 208–10.

10. Arthur P. Mendel, "Eve of Freedom," 20.

11. Norman O. Brown, *Love's Body* (New York: Random House, 1966), 229–30, 239, 255; Karl Schapiro, quoted in R. A. Durr, *Poetic Vision and the Psychedelic Experience* (New York: Dell, 1970), 207.

12. These and subsequent quotations are from Russell McDougal, *Mirror of Mind* (Chickasha, Okla.: Open Window Books, 1976), ix, 6, 14, 98.

13. Wordsworth and Emerson, quoted in Durr, *Poetic Vision*, 68, 190.

14. Karl Schapiro, quoted in Durr, *Poetic Vision*, 206–7.

15. Chung-tzu, quoted in Allan Watts, *The Watercourse Way* (New York: Pantheon Books, 1975), 47.

16. Ananda K. Coomaraswamy, *Buddha and the Gospel of Buddhism* (New York: Harper and Row, 1964), 90–91.

17. Ibid., 178; McDougal, *Mirror*, ix; Albert Schweitzer, *Indian Thought and*

Its Development, trans. Mrs. Charles E. B. Russell (Boston: Beacon Press, 1957), 43.

18. Durr, *Poetic Vision,* 199.

19. Herman Hesse, D. H. Lawrence, and Ralph Waldo Emerson, quoted in Durr, *Poetic Vision,* 96, 178–79, 188.

20. McDougal, *Mirror,* ix.

21. Ibid., x, 92, 56; J. Krishnamurti, *Commentaries on Living,* 2d ser., ed. D. Rajagopal (Wheaton, Ill.: Theosophical Publishing House, 1958), 5.

22. Ibid., 44, 98.

23. Norman O. Brown, *Life Against Death* (Middletown, Conn.: Wesleyan University Press, 1959), 101.

24. McDougal, *Mirror,* 104.

25. Ibid., 88, 92.

26. Ibid., 70, 104.

27. George B. Leonard, *Education and Ecstasy* (New York: Delacorte Press, 1968), 132–33; William Irwin Thompson, *Passages About Earth* (New York: Harper and Row, 1973), 192–93.

28. Brown, *Life,* 270.

29. Brown, *Love's Body,* 54–55, 261.

30. Ibid., 54–55, 88–89; Brown, *Life,* 292.

31. Brown, *Love's Body,* 166.

32. Ibid.

33. Durr, *Poetic Vision,* 144, 145, 146, 171.

34. *Matagiri Book List* (1974–75), 15.

35. Brown, *Life,* 33.

36. Durr, *Poetic Vision,* 198, 200–201, 234; Brown, *Life,* 33.

37. Durr, *Poetic Vision,* 71–72, 202, 205–6.

38. Ibid., 41, 46, 116, 119–20.

39. Sebastian de Grazia, *Of Time, Work and Leisure* (New York: Twentieth Century Fund, 1962), 279–80.

40. Alexander Herzen, *From the Other Shore* and *The Russian People and Socialism* (New York: World Publishing, 1963), 35–37.

41. Josef Peiper, *Leisure: The Basis of Culture* (New York: Pantheon Books, 1952).

42. Isaiah Berlin, *The Hedgehog and the Fox* (New York: Mentor Books, 1975), 103, 104–5.

43. W. G. Collingwood, *The Life of John Ruskin* (London: Methuen, 1911), 153; Bertrand Russell, *The Autobiography of Bertrand Russell* (New York: Bantam Books, 1968), 3–4; Herbert E. Bowman, *Vissarion Belinski* (Cambridge, Mass.: Harvard University Press, 1954), 129, 143; Alexander Herzen, *Other Shore,* 67, 93.

44. Marcuse, *Liberation,* 6, 25–26.

45. Ibid., 6, 7, 60; italics added.

46. Ibid., ix–x.

47. Ibid., 18–19; italics added.

48. Ibid., 17; Herbert Marcuse, *One Dimensional Man* (Boston: Beacon Press, 1964), 6, 40–41.

49. Marcuse, *Liberation*, 70–71.

50. Herbert Marcuse, "Repressive Tolerance," in Robert P. Woolf, Barrington Moore, Jr., and Herbert Marcuse, *A Critique of Pure Tolerance* (Boston: Beacon Press, 1965), 88.

51. Ibid., 100–101, 103.

52. Marcuse, *Liberation*, 88–89.

53. Ibid., 89.

54. Brown, *Love's Body*, 161, 177, 178, 180, 185–87, 189, 219, 222, 227, 232, 233, 241–42, 261.

55. Ibid., 175–76.

7

Full Circle: Fundamentalism

The counterculture did much to mellow, ease, and "green" the anxious world of obsessive work and "one-dimensional" rationalism. But it obviously failed in its larger, Bodhisattvian mission of teaching humanity how to "turn on, tune in, and drop out." The pull of the world was too great.

In the decades since the counterculture 1960s and early 1970s, consequently, there have been a variety of compromises between countercultural withdrawal and conventional engagement. The yuppie style of the 1980s is the most prominent example. Who could be more involved in the world of success and achievement? Yet, the motivations behind the zeal were much the same as they had been for the insistent detachment that many of these same men and women had experienced in their earlier, counterculture days. It was still a decidedly "me" generation: the principal, if not exclusive, concern of these young adults remained what it had been—themselves. There was nothing even remotely similar to the character of the "Protestant-ethic" generations, who had preferred investment, sacrifice, and the future to consumption, pleasure, and the present, and who had put the needs of others—family, community, posterity—before their own. For all their enthusiastic involvement in the world, the yuppies were as devoted to the ideals of "Be, Here, Now" as many of them had been during the counterculture era.

This blend of "in" and "out" was apparent in the way the yuppie culture adopted counterculture ritual and style. With barely a pause to comment on it, the yuppies swept aside Freud's theories about "civilization and its discontents" by simultaneously enjoying both "one-dimensional" economic achievement and the sexual and other emotional liberations bequeathed by the counterculture. Similarly, the drugs, yoga, and meditation that were to have freed "economic man" from the chains of materialism and competition were deftly remodeled into tools for improving the appearance of the chains and even making them feel liberating. Transcendental Meditation and other comparable cult systems that had been employed by the East for centuries as methods of getting off "the wheel of suffering" were bought and sold on the promise of speeding advancement up the "ladder of success."

One mind-altering drug was lauded by "a thirty-nine-year-old career woman who sees people only by appointment in her corporate milieu," because it made "you feel very benevolent. You have benevolence towards everyone. You want to kiss and hug your friends. . . . It is just un-bee-leeeeeve-uh-bul. . . . I know it sounds hippy-dippy, but it strips away the layers of fear, and gives you this clarity of vision about yourself." It is the familiar counterculture litany, until, that is, we go on to learn that rather than help the user "let go," it makes "you really feel in control."

"The '80s are all about control, money and responsibility. This is the drug of the '80s." "Control, money and responsibility" notwithstanding, the drug still offered "the possible return to the state mythologically described in Genesis."[1] Singles bars, happy hours, body and fashion fetishes, delayed or avoided marriages, few or no children, and, above all, everything "cool" and uncommitted—such was the style and ethos of this "lite generation."

> "Light is a way of thinking that we've come to in the 80s. It's an umbrella phenomenon where lightness transforms itself into the cars we drive, the lightness in a room, our diet, as well as lightness in the relationships we have. . . ." They can undergo psychoanalysis in one sitting, because today's psychotherapy skips the formative years, namely childhood. For health care, busy executives can turn to a so-called Doc in a Box, a storefront medical clinic with extended hours, higher prices, and no appointment, no referral—no medical history necessary.

> There is light culture (books on tape), light shopping (buying clothes by video), light politics (candidates who run on image, not issues), light responsibility (the lowest voter participation of any democracy), and light music (Lite FM, where the heavy bass line has been removed so that the sound does not jar or stir listeners).[2]

The yuppie culture blended the worst of the two competing worldviews. It devoted itself strenuously to the work world, yet basically disdained that world, unbeguiled by the ethic of striving and service that had legitimized and even sanctified that world for earlier generations. Similarly, while it richly enjoyed the emotional release of the counterculture, it did so without the counterculture's conviction that such liberation represented a spiritual and even social revolution. The result was a bizarre combination of zealous enterprise, mindless thrills, and spiritual detachment, the ideal type for the organization, which took full advantage of it.

> Representatives of some of the nation's largest corporations, including IBM, AT&T, and General Motors, met in New Mexico in July to discuss how metaphysics, the occult and Hindu mysticism might help executives compete in the world marketplace. . . . "I think it's as much a political movement as a religious movement," he says, "and it's spreading into business management theory and a lot of other areas. If you look at it carefully you see it represents a complete rejection of Judeo-Christian and bedrock American values. . . ." The Ford Motor Company, Westinghouse and the Calvin Klein fashion house are among scores of major companies that have sent employees for training, according to "human potential" organizations such as Transformation Technologies, Lifespring and Actualizations. . . . Kevin Garvey, an author and researcher on New Age topics in Carlisle, Pa., cites an Army recruiting slogan, "Be all that you can be," as evidence of what he contends has been a significant influence of EST, Lifespring and other New Age programs in certain quarters of the military. . . . In the early 1980s, he said, officers at the Army War College at Carlisle, some of whom were graduates of EST and were former members of the radical Students for a Democratic Society, conducted a study aimed at creating a "New Age Army." The slogan, a derivative of the "you create your own reality" orthodoxy of New Age groups, grew out of this work.[3]

Ultimately, both the "counter" and the yuppie cultures are death cultures: to live mystically or frenetically "as though there were no tomorrow" is to confess a loss of faith in tomorrow, any tomorrow. Uncertainty and fear are the core of the euphoria as they generally

268 / Vision and Violence

are in obsessive self-absorption, whether the narcissistic hedonism is spiritual or material. The counterculture and the yuppie generation were both End Time cultures, displaying the same loss of hope in the future that had motivated and accompanied all such gnostic negations in the past. With little reason to hope for a future, given the likely fusion of nuclear weapons with primitive emotions, why not just "Be, Here, Now" in one way or another? Even had the secular gods of Reason, History, and Nature not died, what appeal could any of them have had for this first generation in human history that, in addition to fearing its own death, had to accept the very real possibility (if not clear probability) that it would have no heirs. By the time the yuppie generation entered society, forty years had passed since the introduction of the Bomb. Most people in the counterculture and everyone in the yuppie generation had passed their entire lives under the threat of total human annihilation, constant discussion of that threat, and a pathetic sequence of feeble defensive responses, each less reassuring than its predecessor.

We are once again, in other words, in a time of troubles, the favored soil for apocalyptic fear and fantasy.

> The seeds of collapse are sprouting everywhere. Those seeds are unemployment, inflation, economic uncertainty, the energy crisis, the uncertainty of oil supply, terrorism, violence in the streets and politicians who cannot cope, economists who cannot cope and diplomats who cannot cope. We are living in apocalyptical times. To me, we are facing quite possibly the thermonuclear gas chamber of the future—a kind of global Auschwitz.[4]

In part, that grim portrait is based on harsh realities; in part on a selective perception that focuses only on the dark side; and in part on the mood and mentality that generate this gloomy focus. Constantly and from all sides, the press, television, literature, and the arts have hammered away at us with their batteries of violence, suffering, catastrophes, and unprecedented dangers. Our most recent past seems one long nightmare of pain and loss. Great and small wars, economic breakdown, genocidal famines, political turmoil, hopeless poverty, ideological witch-hunts, mass murders, natural disasters, an epidemic of terror, new incurable diseases, family disintegration, the rampant spread of crime, drugs, and suicides. Nothing seems to hold, anywhere, on any level—physical or emotional, personal, familial, communal, national, or global. And the future promises only more of the same or worse, much worse. At such times of trouble, even sane warnings that urge rational and humane policies only seem to make matters worse by heightening the awareness of the danger.

If the Bomb does not get us, we are assured, ecocatastrophe will. By 1980, so *Life* predicted in 1970, city folk would have to wear gas masks to survive and, by 1985, the amount of sunlight reaching the earth would be reduced by half. State-of-the-art computers convinced the Club of Rome in 1972 that overpopulation, pollution, resource depletion, and continuing industrialization would bring on the "ultimate collapse" of the "world system." In only nine years (from 1972), there would be no more gold in the world; in fifteen years, no more silver, mercury, or tin; in twenty, no more oil. Combining these prophecies with those anticipating future violent "North-South" (rich-poor; developed-underdeveloped) conflict and viewing both through a Marxist lens, Willy Brandt clearly saw a "catastrophic global war" on the near horizon. Biologist Paul Ehrlich placed his holocaust bet on overpopulation. By 1983, he predicted, there would be a billion deaths from starvation; steak would be only a memory; food would be rationed (only children receiving "special low-mercury cod"); blacks and other poor would be rioting against population control laws legislated mainly against them; Japan, driven by starvation, would build nuclear bombs and join the Soviet Union against the United States, which, in turn, would respond with a preemptive strike.[5]

It is not surprising given the intensity and duration of the current troubles and dangers, that science fiction and other escapist fantasies have become so popular. From the *China Syndrome* warning of nuclear disaster to the *Close Encounters of the Third Kind* promise of other-worldly salvation is as short a step in our time as it was when desperate Hellenistic Jews and Gentiles flocked to the promise of a "new heaven and new earth." But science fiction fantasies, counterculture visions, and yuppie frenzy are all fly-by-night amateurs when it comes to meeting the needs of End Time fears and hopes. They are no match for the tried and tested experts in the field—the religious Fundamentalists. We have come full circle.

Armageddon—Not a Reason to Fear, but to Hope!

World events in fulfillment of prophecy show that we are deep into the "last days," in "critical times hard to deal with" (2 Timothy 3:1–5). This means that we are nearing the Biblical "Armageddon. . . ." However, the approach of Armageddon should not be a cause for fear, but for real hope! Why? Because Armageddon is God's war to cleanse the earth of all wickedness, paving the way for a bright, prosperous new order! The Bible explains that then the righteous "will possess the earth, and they will indeed find their exquisite delight in the abundance of peace" (Psalms 37:11). . . . With bad conditions forever gone, every day of life then will be a delight. Not even sickness or death will mar the happiness of people. God will "wipe out every tear from their eyes, and death will be no more, neither will mourning nor outcry nor pain be anymore" (Revelation 21:4). . . . After Armageddon—a marvelous new order of peace and security.[6]

It's Happening Now, Endtime Messenger, Late Great Planet Earth, Voice of Armageddon, Road to Armageddon, Doomsday, Ultimatus—the titles are enough to bring us the message of the approaching catastrophic End. Hal Lindsey, identified by the *New York Times* as the best-selling writer of the 1970s, assures his vast audience that there will be "earthquakes, freak weather, famine, plagues and a global war," and that he is offering humanity "a chance to escape the destruction by coming into a personal relationship with Jesus Christ: We will be with Jesus Christ while the earth is being judged for its rejection of the Savior."[7]

The 1967 edition of the Scofield Reference Bible similarly brought to the two million who bought it the promise of rising together with the resurrected dead into the clouds to join Jesus, while seven years of destruction annihilated those left below. Earthquakes, pestilence, plagues, fires, floods, and international wars would punish the world for its sins: the Chinese assault alone would kill half of those remaining after the other torments had done their work. But, in keeping with the St. John original, still more waves of horror would punish the unbelievers when Satan was later unleashed. That done, the true believers would henceforth live forever in bliss, the sinners burn forever in hell, and the present earth once and for all disappear in flames, to be replaced by the "new heaven and new earth."[8]

It is all providentially inevitable, all working out according to Biblical prophecy. One must not oppose, but understand in the light of revelation.

> [E]verything suddenly makes sense: wars and the horrors of war, earthquakes, terror, and persecution take on new meaning and become signs and signals that point to something. They are the agonies of a world coming to an end; they are the birth pangs of a new life surpassing human imagination. . . . Yet, despite its eeriness, the question of the disciples—"When will this [absolute] end come?"—is overshadowed by a peculiar peace. They tie the question about the fall of the temple and of the world to the question of the Lord's return. Thus, the triumph of God stands at the end of all endings. And therefore, the dissolution of everything that exists or counts in the world is not totally without a note of comfort. (Helmut Thielicke)[9]

Everything that makes this century the most brutal and destructive in human history becomes, for the believers, irrefutable proof that this is the very best of all centuries precisely because it is the last century, the eve of the Kingdom: "An April 25 letter writer said that he could not imagine Jesus shouting that we cannot afford to be No. 2 in defense. Little does this person realize that Jesus will be leading the front in the War of Armageddon."[10]

> We are not to weep as the people of the world weep when there are certain tragedies or breakups of the government or the systems of the world. We are not to wring our hands and say, "Isn't that awful?" That isn't awful at all. It's good. That is a token, an evident token of our salvation, of where God is going to take us. (Pat Robertson)[11]

> "You will hear of wars and rumors of wars. . . . Nation will rise against nation, and kingdom against kingdom." So Jesus replied to His disciples' question: "What will be the sign of your coming and of the end of the age?" (Matthew 24:3, 6, 7). Continuing His

answer to the apostle John a half century later, Jesus enlarged on how human warmongering would escalate into worldwide war incited by the "spirits of demons performing miraculous signs," driving blindly the heads of state "of the whole world, to gather them for the battle on the great day of God Almighty . . . to the place that in Hebrew is called Armageddon. . . ." WWI was fought in Western Europe. WWII enveloped three of the world's five continents and three of its five oceans. Armageddon will involve the nations "of the whole world," and as such will indeed be WWIII.

Mankind indisputably is headed for world war. "This is independent of man's will." Surely that has to be one of the most amazing statements in the annals of political atheism: that world war is "independent of man's will." It is precisely what Jesus assured John: that mankind would bottom out by falling into the hands of demonized rulers, who, with minds drugged and bewitched by Satan, would march him down the road to Armageddon. "It is too late to avoid the third World War," reckons Aleksandr Solzhenitsyn, as he witnesses the gladiatorial beating of war drums and immolational battle cries from Moscow to Washington, to Southeast Asia, to the Middle East, to Angola, to Rhodesia. (John Wesley White)[12]

It is foolish to resist. It is too late. The earth is doomed.

Pardon my pessimism, but when I think of China's nuclear development in the light of their past, I see no future for the known world beyond the year 2000. (Tim LaHaye)

But most scientists agreed that man is doomed and only the time and manner of his demise are in question. (Malcolm W. Browne)

That day is coming. The disasters of this life—pestilence, famine, wars, natural catastrophes—are only little judgments which come in the most part from man's own activities. When the day of God's wrath is revealed, these things will pale by comparison, and no one who is not united to Christ by faith will be able to stand against Him. (James Montgomery Boice)[13]

Considering the effect of the weapons ready and waiting to carry out the universal annihilation, the Gospel prophecies of destruction by fire seem right on the mark.

> . . . all history is pointing forward to a climactic event when everything now seen will be purified by fire. This is not fanciful imagination but the clear and repeated testimony of the Bible. Our Lord Himself said such would take place. . . . The Bible says: "But the day of the Lord will come as a thief in the night; in which the heavens shall pass away with a great noise, and the elements shall melt with fervent heat, the earth also, and the works that are therein shall be burned up." (Billy Graham)[14]

Since the many millions who find comfort in this vision vote for political leaders who will help decide whether or not those final fires rage, the danger of this sacred expectation would be immeasurably great even if it were confined to the "people." But that is not the case. The apocalyptic vision, with its dialectic of bliss through catastrophe, is also propagated to the best educated by illustrious theologians. Consider two of them, first, Jurgen Moltmann.

> But again and again, this inner light of freedom became the consuming flame of revolution and directed itself outward. . . . The new is proclaimed in judgement over the old. . . . God kills and brings life. . . . The new is preceded by the destruction of the old, that which has become guilty, and not by the development or evolution of the old. . . . God's new reality is always like a *novum ex nihilo*. . . . By "resurrection" the earliest Christians did not mean a return of the dead Christ into life or restoration of the fallen creation. They meant, rather, the entrance of something completely unexpected, the inbreaking of a qualitatively new future and the appearance of a life which is no longer "life toward death" but "life out of death."[15]

The far more influential Teilhard de Chardin, whose early penchant for exhilarating violence we have already seen, expressed his views in the following manner.

> The spirit cannot free itself except by some clean break, some escape of a completely different order from the slow elaboration

of matter that led up to the elaboration of the brain. . . . The end of the world: the overthrow of equilibrium, detaching the spirit fulfilled at last, from its material matrix. . . . Not a gradual darkening, but a sudden blaze of brilliance, an explosion in which thought, carried to the extreme, is volatized upon itself. . . . Before passing into the beyond, the world and its elements must attain what may be called their point of annihilation. . . . Evolution is reaching its climax in disintegration. . . . There is already a general realization that the universal turbulence, far from being an incoherent dream, disguises and paves the way to, a divine advent. . . . Let us not be frightened, therefore, of what at first sight might look like a final and universal discord. What we are suffering is only the price, the annunciation, the preliminary phase of our unanimity. . . . But the Scriptures teach us that at the same time it will be rent by a profound schism between those who wish to break out of themselves that they may still become masters of the world, and those who, accepting Christ's word, *passionately await the death of the world that they may be absorbed with it into God.*[16]

As the final and catalytic detail in this nightmare, we have occasional hints that those with the apocalyptic power to break the seals, sound the trumpets, and overturn the bowls share these expectations, divide the world into the Two Cities of all good and all evil, and feel themselves summoned to ignite the catastrophe.

It may seem melodramatic to treat the twin poles of human experience represented by the United States and the Soviet Union as the equivalent of Good and Evil, Light and Darkness, God and the Devil; yet, if we allow ourselves to think of them that way, even hypothetically, it can help clarify our perspective on the world struggle.[17]

On at least four occasions, or so President Nixon said in an interview after he left office, he had considered using nuclear weapons—once during the Vietnam War and three times against the Soviet Union (when the Russians seemed poised to attack Israel near the end of the 1973 Arab-Israeli Yom Kippur War and Nixon wanted to let them know that "the U.S. would resist them conventionally and [by] nuclear means," and twice when there was a danger of a Russian attack on China: "What would we do? There was no question what we would have done").[18]

Addressing a body of clerics, President Reagan reminded his audience that "there is sin and evil in the world, and we are enjoined by Scripture and the Lord Jesus to oppose it with all our might," that the Soviet Union is "the focus of evil in the modern world," and that there was "profound truth" in the sentiments of one father who said, "I would rather see my little girls die now, still believing in God, than have them grow up under Communism and one day die no longer believing in God." According to one report, "Reagan is known to have read and discussed with fundamentalist friends like Falwell and Pat Boone such pulp versions of Biblical prophecy as Hal Lindsey's *The Late Great Planet Earth,* which strongly hints of nuclear Armageddon." "In 1980," the report continues, President Reagan "mused on television that 'we may be the generation that sees Armageddon.'" The following year, he said to Jerry Falwell, "Jerry, I sometimes believe we're heading very fast for Armageddon right now." In 1983 he said much the same to Thomas Dine, director of AIPAC (American Israel Public Affairs Committee): "I turn back to your ancient prophets in the Old Testament and the signs foretelling Armageddon, and I find myself wondering if we're the generation that's going to see that come about."[19]

In the recollections of James Mills, former president pro tem of the California state senate, Reagan had been pondering the Apocalypse for a long time. Recalling a conversation in 1971, Reagan's first year as governor of California, Mills recounts Reagan's remarks about Ezekiel 38–39.

"In the thirty-eighth chapter of Ezekiel, it says that the land of Israel will come under attack by the armies of the ungodly nations, and it says that Libya will be among them. Do you understand the significance of that? Libya has now gone communist, and that's a sign that the day of Armageddon isn't far off."

"It also says that Ethiopia will be among the evil powers, Governor," Mills replied. "I can't see Haile Selassie, the Lion of Judah, teaming up with a bunch of commies to make war on God's chosen people."

"No, I agree that everything hasn't fallen in place yet," Reagan continued. "But there is only that one thing left that has to happen. The Reds have to take over Ethiopia."

"I don't think that's very probable," Mills said myopically.

"I do," Reagan said. "I think it's inevitable. It's necessary to fulfill the prophecy that Ethiopia will be one of the ungodly nations. . . . All of the prophecies that had to be fulfilled before Armageddon have come to pass. In the thirty-eighth chapter of Ezekiel it says God will take the children of Israel from among the heathen, where they'd been scattered, and will gather them again in the promised land. That has finally come about after two thousand years. For the first time ever, everything is in place for the battle of Armegeddon and the second coming of Christ. . . . Everything is falling in place. It can't be much longer now. Ezekiel says fire and brimstone will be rained upon the enemies of God's people. That must mean that they'll be destroyed by nuclear weapons. They exist now, and they never did in the past. . . . Ezekiel tells us that Gog, the nation that will lead all of the other powers of darkness against Israel, will come out of the north. Biblical scholars have been saying for generations that Gog must be Russia. What other powerful nation is to the north of Israel? None. But it didn't seem to make sense before the Russian revolution, when Russia was a Christian country. Now it does, now that Russia has become communistic and atheistic, now that Russia has set itself against God. Now it fits the description of Gog perfectly."[20]

In the opening chapters of this book, we reviewed the two phases of early apocalyptic Christianity, the initial passive era, extending from the Gospels through much of the Middle Ages, and the late medieval era of violent messianism. While aspects of both are present in the current reborn fundamentalism, it is explicitly and forthrightly the intention of U.S. fundamentalist leaders to be intensely active, at least to the extent of galvanizing the true believers into a powerful political force influential enough to determine policy in all branches of the U.S. government—executive, legislative, and judicial—and at all levels, from federal to local. No political action organization is more efficiently run. None have more complete computer lists of supporters and donors. Having thoroughly merged politics and pulpit and mobilized an immense media empire for their message, fundamentalist organizations have pressed their cause with the familiar zeal of millennial crusaders. Their success has been phenomenal, not surprisingly considering the fact that, according to a 1984 Gallup poll, some 40 percent of the U.S. electorate identify themselves as "born-again evangelicals."[21] Liberal members of Congress have fallen one after another before the organization's propaganda assault. Those still in office are admittedly afraid of being next on the hit list. Whereas candidates for public office, especially the highest, only recently vowed an absolute separation between their private beliefs and their official responsibilities, they now enthusiastically parade their godliness in the hope of winning the support, or at lest neutralizing the opposition, of fundamentalist preachers and publicists.

In the mid-1980s, evangelist Pat Robertson emerged as the most likely fundamentalist leader to activate this enormous political force. A practitioner of faith healing, speaker in tongues, and self-proclaimed "Prophet of God," Robertson preaches to a television audience estimated at 27 to 28 million monthly. Nor does he doubt, as he made clear in his 1984 book, *Answers to 200 of Life's Most Probing Questions*, that the End is near, that all the prophecies are swiftly being fulfilled.

> This tells me that we are getting very close to the time when God is going to say that the human race has gone far enough. He may be ready to step in to terminate this phase of human activity and to start another one. . . . That is why I firmly expect to be alive when Jesus Christ comes back to earth. . . . He will resurrect those who have been born again. They will then be joined with the spiritual bodies that have been prepared for their spirits, . . . [These bodies will have] incredible powers, such as being able to move through physical objects like walls and doors and travel great distances instantaneously. . . . Those who have done evil will be sent to hell. Forever. But those who have lived in accordance with the righteous teachings of the Lord will live forever with God. . . . Everyone must be born again before he or she can enter heaven. Anyone who has not been transformed in

his spirit would be a source of spiritual contagion, contamination, or rebellion in heaven. A little tendency to sin today could grow into a hideously dangerous nature in, say, a million years. Therefore, the seeds of rebellion will never be allowed to enter heaven.[22]

"The Christians have won...! What a breakthrough for the Kingdom!" Robertson wrote to his supporters in Michigan after they had succeeded in winning most of the Republican precinct delegate seats and, thereby, the power to choose Republican candidates for state offices (including the State Supreme Court and the Michigan State School Board) and delegates to the 1988 national convention.

We know it can happen elsewhere. We saw the hand of God going before us in Michigan, affirming our every step. We went to city after city, and everywhere I found thousands of believers jumping to their feet, ready to work, ready to pray, ready to give—thrilled that their time had finally come.[23]

Direct physical violence has not been a part of this mainline fundamentalist activism. But it is there on the fringes. From 1982 through 1984, thirty cases of bombing or fires at abortion clinics and offices were reported in this country. It is all "for the glory of God," in the words of one bomber. Another confessed that his four-month campaign of violence was undertaken on order from God and the Archangel Michael. A third was only fulfilling his duty as a member of "the Army of God." One set off his bombs as a "gift to Jesus for his birthday." As for the legitimation: "The spiritual underpinning for the group's militarism," according to a leader of The Covenant, Sword and Arm of the Lord, "is contained in Matthew 10:34: 'Think not that I am come to send peace on earth; I come not to send peace, but a sword.'"[24]

There are also a number of paramilitary, neo-Nazi, racist, and anti-Jewish groups, identifying themselves as part of the general "Christian Identity" movement or other similarly militant Christian organizations. The Aryan Nations, Posse Comitatus, the Order, The Covenant, Sword and Arm of the Lord (CSA), the National States Rights Party, National Alliance, Farmers' Liberation Army, and the Christian-Patriots Defense League, are examples. The CSA made the headlines in the spring of 1985 when the FBI and other law enforcement agencies raided its Ozark compound and found, along with piles of conventional neo-Nazi hate literature, an arsenal of weapons, including bombs, plastic explosives, hand grenades, land mines, machine guns, and antitank and antiaircraft weapons. For target practice, there was a human form dressed as a police officer with a star over its heart—the Star of David. Among the sixty men and women belonging to the 240-acre collective were some twenty-four wanted by the police on such charges as murder, robbery, burning of Jewish establishments, and blowing up pipelines.

The Covenant, Sword and Arm of the Lord, and its associates in the Order and the Aryan Nation Church of Jesus Christ Christian, regard themselves as "footsoldiers of Armaggedon," defending Christianity against Jews, whites against blacks, and Americans against an enemy alliance of Jews, blacks, and Communists. Their basic doctrine claims the displacement of the Jews by the Aryan white race as God's chosen people, praises as divine the mission of Adolf Hitler, alleges a master plan by Jews to drive blacks into the Civil Rights movement in the hope of weakening white Christendom through racial corruption, and warns against the accompanying efforts by Jews to dominate the U.S. government from Tel Aviv through their conspiratorial organization, ZOG (Zionist Occupation Government).

So awesome and immediate is this Jewish threat in their eyes that the CSA felt obliged to issue "A Declaration of War" (12 November 1984) against the presumably Jewish-controlled U.S. government. Although their short-run tactical solution is to establish an Aryan "Promised Land" in the Pacific Northwest, "where we can move and protect our lands and seed line," they are convinced that only the overthrow of this Zionist-dominated U.S. government can save the white race from the racial suicide that the present government, under Jewish influence, is promoting. According to Gary Noble, second in CSA command, the "Declaration" and the war for survival, which the CSA would lead, would fulfill the will of God by following the example of medieval Christian Crusaders. As part of his service for the Hayden Lake, Idaho, community (Aryan Nations' headquarters), Reverend Richard Butler blessed a sword over the altar, vowing to "fight rather than turn them [their children] over to Satan and the government. And we will die if we have to."

Members of the Order were convicted of killing a Jewish talk show host and charged with planning the "assassination of federal officials, politicians and members of the Jewish faith; bombings; the polluting of municipal water supplies; and the training of certain individuals in urban and guerilla warfare"—all toward their principal goal: "to overthrow the government of the United States by force and violence and to form a separate Aryan Nation within the United States." A man and woman threatened to blow up a school room, holding 150 children, unless the couple received the million dollars that they needed to finance their white supremist revolution. Twenty-seven-year-old David Rice stabbed to death a Seattle lawyer, his wife, and two children as a blow against communism and because he believed, according to an acquaintance, that "America was controlled by a Jewish elite who were subverting our national principles." Michael Ryan and his son were charged with "lurid acts of torture" and murder in the name of God. Louis Ray Brown, Jr., "ambassador at large" of the Aryan Nations, worked out a system of points to be awarded to "Aryan warriors" for "killing blacks, Jews, Federal officials, journalists, and informers."[25] Robert Miles, leading participant in the Aryan Nations Church of Jesus Christ, founder of the Mountain Church of Jesus Christ the Savior, and a highly regarded intellectual of the Order provided a theoretical ground for its racist ideology in his belief that "whites were brought to Earth as travelers from another planet to conquer it."

In a class by itself, as evidence of the violence inherent in the fundamentalist revival, is the tragic case of Reverend Jim Jones and his disciples. Reverend Jones began his ministry, after his 1964 ordination into the Christian Church (Disciples of Christ), by "teaching a brand of Christian goodness as pure as that preached by Jesus himself in the Sermon on the Mount."[26] As another follower recalled, "he spoke beautifully; he seemed so benevolent; he talked about equality for all people."

During this first period of his evangelical career, Reverend Jones became increasingly convinced that only a Marxist, socialist community could solve basic individual and social problems, and it was with the aim of establishing such a community that he led a large contingent of his congregation to Guyana in 1974. The result, to quote one member, was "a noble and beautiful experiment in revolutionary Christian socialism," a veritable "Shangri-la."

On 18 November 1978, almost all the members of the colony, over 900 men, women, and children, followed the last commandment of their leader and committed suicide (some willingly and some under brutal duress) or were murdered. For weeks thereafter, the press and public were deluged with accounts of the Reverend and his Shangri-la. "At various times, Reverend Jones claimed that he was the reincarnation of either Lenin, Jesus Christ, or one of a variety of other religious or political leaders. He claimed that he had divine powers and healed the sick. He said that he had extrasensory perception and could tell what everyone was thinking." "It was like he wanted to believe he was God." Everything was under his absolute and relentless control. Even "romantic entanglements" required the approval of his "relationships committee." Equality was, indeed, achieved, but it was the equality of deprivation and grueling labor. Those assigned to the fields and orchards labored eleven hours a day, six days a week, while guards patrolled the settlement to make sure no one left. Constant work proved devotion: "dark circles under one's eyes or extreme loss of weight were considered signs of loyalty." "They ate rice for breakfast, rice water soup for lunch, and rice and beans for dinner. They had vegetables three times a week, and an egg and cookies on Sunday."

To stir flagging spirits and remind the colonists of their spiritual purpose, the Reverend—"Father" or "Dad" as he wanted them to call him—"would broadcast for hours on end while we worked in the fields or tried to sleep." His authoritarianism, however, was evident long before the Guyana "concentration camp," as some of the survivors referred to it. In the mid-1960s, the Reverend had set up an "interrogation committee" to harass members of his San Francisco congregation who disagreed with him, and when he moved to Guyana he left behind an "administrative department" with which he communicated in code nightly to instruct his lieutenants on the treatment of "traitors." Once the colony was established, violent "punishment" became routine.

It was nothing bad what the guy did, but Jim Jones took the law into his own hands. They beat him up on a stage in the compound. The blood was running off of his face, and they sent him down the aisles. The people were asked to beat him some more. Jones said they could finish it off. So they hit him, and Jones said, "Kick him where he deserves it." And they did. He just swelled up, that poor guy. I couldn't believe it. Nobody ever told me this stuff was going on.

Jones wanted the parishioners to call him "Dad." To him they were "my children." He began treating them as such, ordering them paddled with a four-foot-long "board of education" for such minor sins as smoking or leaving a stove burning. "He began to delight in the beatings," said Al Mertle. Victims were expected to say, "thank you, Father," after their punishment. Jones then would embrace them and say: "Father loves you. You're a stronger person now. I can trust you." Miscreants were told to box with opponents whom Jones had selected to pummel them. Nurses stood by to attend injuries.

Deborah Blakey, a defector, said misbehaving children were taken to a well "to see Bigfoot," then lowered head first into the blackness until they screamed, "I'm sorry, Father, I'm sorry," contritely enough for Jones's satisfaction.

They kept him drugged and confined him in a narrow room, with half a dozen others. He would complain from inside that the bugs were biting him, that he had a high fever. But they wouldn't let him out. When he finally came out, sick, they fed him tranquilizers in his food.

Last June, one former member . . . said in a deposition in a Guyana custody case involving a child in the Jonestown commune: "The Reverend Jones labeled any person who left the commune a 'traitor' and 'fair game.' He steadfastly and convincingly maintained that the punishment for defection was death."

But, Mr. Stoen said, Mr. Jones maintained discipline by keeping the members so tired that they had little time to complain, and by what he called "catharsis sessions," in which dissidents were ridiculed and beaten with paddles.

We were threatened with murder if we left and with the murder of our children. We were trapped. We just couldn't leave, and we didn't.

As though this terror were not enough to force vigilant submission, the Reverend fostered acute paranoia. Once a week he showed movies describing the Nazi treatment of the Jews and said that the U.S. government was going to treat the blacks the same way. "He said the CIA was out to get us; he didn't like the United States. He told us to believe in Marxism. He hated everybody, the president, but he liked Hitler and Lenin." "There was constant talk of death. In Jonestown the concept of mass suicide for socialism arose. Because our lives were so wretched anyway, and because we were so afraid to contradict Reverend Jones, the concept was not challenged." At weekly emergency drills, during which "we were informed that our situation was hopeless and that the only course of action open to us was mass suicide for the glory of socialism. . . . We were told everyone would be tortured by the mercenaries [hired by the CIA] if we were taken alive." "I can say without hesitation," the Reverend is quoted as having told one member, "that we are devoted to a decision that it is better even to die than to be constantly harassed from one continent to the next." "If they ever put me in jail," Jones instructed one follower, "or if I'm killed, we're all to commit suicide, killing the children first, then ourselves." To prepare them, he had "mass suicide drills, where he tells all the people, hundreds of people, to drink a certain drink," and he said, "that's fatal, you're going to die in forty-five minutes, I want to see how you feel about dying for socialism." "Everyone, including the children were told to line up," another survivor recalled in her account of one of those "white nights." "As we passed through the line we were given a small glass of red liquid to drink. We were told the liquid contained poison, and we would die within forty-five minutes. We all did as we were told." "There is great dignity in dying. It is a great protest, a great demonstration for everyone to die." Thus, everything was well thought through and well rehearsed when the Reverend told his followers that "the time has come for us to meet in another place. . . . To die in revolutionary suicide is to live forever."

Masochistic self-punishment and sadistic domination are so intertwined in all of this that it is difficult to distinguish between them. Everything the Reverend told his followers emphasized passive martyrdom as the way to escape the pain of life and the imminent threat of still greater suffering. Yet the brutal sadism of his own domination is obvious, and he himself ordered the murder of Congressman Ryan and his party, as they were preparing to return to the United States after investigating Jonestown.

Many of his followers shared the Reverend's sadomasochism. They submitted to his domination and humiliations and, in the end, obeyed his orders to kill their own children and themselves. Yet it was not the Reverend himself, but his cult members who guarded the compound, beat and otherwise brutalized other members, killed Congressman Ryan and four others in his party, signed pledges vowing to kill the sect's enemies, accepted their appointment by the Reverend as avenging "angels" to get back at his enemies after his death, sliced the throats of one of the Reverend's closest aides (Sharon Amos) and her three children, and forced those who resisted the poison to drink it and take their place in the mass suicide. ("She struggled pretty hard, she didn't want to die," but the victim was finally injected with the poison; another woman "balked at taking the poison and Jones' followers shouted abuses at her calling her a traitor"; "I saw a girl named Julie Reynolds being forced to take the poison"—she kept spitting it out, but the Reverend's "nurses" kept forcing her to take it.) Members' letters found in the compound after the tragedy poignantly reveal the psychological disorders that permitted it.

Generally, I found people in leadership too lax and trusting of those who might become traitors, too many loopholes, many ways for people to get out . . . I think a great deal about being tortured. It is one thing to get up and say, "I will endure torture" but it is another to actually face having your leg slowly sawed off or your nails pulled out. I wonder if I will be able to hold out until I am unconscious . . . I will endure until I am dead. I even think of the worse thing I could endure and that would be to jump into a pit full of snakes. It is the most horrible way I can think of dying but I would do it. I would have to, not want to, but have to. I will never be a traitor to Communism whether you be dead or alive. I will endure and not let you down, nor shall I let down Chego Vara [Che Guevara] or Patric Lumumbo or Allende or the defendants in the Haymarket affair or Malcolm X or Martin Luther King or Harriet Tubman. I shall not let this movement down. I shall not beg for mercy either in that last moment. I shall proudly die for proud reason. You can count on me even if all desert you. I shall be by your side whether it be tangible or in spirit. If, suddenly, a U.S. vessel or plane will come to get us all to take us back with promises of all the luxury and benefits if we would sell you out, I would not get on board because I am attracted to your goodness as magnets attract one another.

I also think I'm a traitor, not a revolutionary because I'm afraid of fighting because I'm sure I will just get shot and not die, captured then tortured. That's what I'm afraid of.

I couldn't stand to see the children tortured. I still think of mine first. I couldn't watch my baby dropped from a window. I'd probably fall apart. I can't be trusted. That's why I always vote for revolutionary suicide . . .

I know you are the Truth and the way. I am so grateful for the day I met you and Mother. I feel so guilty for the time I let you down in Brazil. I just had no sense. I hope I die before I ever betray you. You are the only Friend I have. . . . I am hoping to become a True Communist since I know what it means.

If the capitalists came over the hill I just drink the potion as fast as I can do it. I wouldn't let the capitalists get me but if they did I would not say a word. I'd take the pain and when I couldn't stand it anymore I'd pass out.

Echoing the era of Christianity's birth, the current Christian fundamentalist revival is closely tied to the fate of the Jewish people. In the original, however, the influence was direct: early Judeo-Christianity was primarily the response of some Hellenistic Jews to their prolonged suffering and hopelessness. In our own era, the impact is indirect: a principal response of Jews themselves to the Holocaust was Zionism and founding the State of Israel, and it was the extraordinary success of that movement of hope, return, and reconstruction that, in turn, powerfully encouraged Christian fundamentalists. For them, triumphant Zionism proved their central prophecies. Everything, as President Reagan said, was falling neatly into place, especially in the Holy Land, where the sacred drama had begun and where it was destined soon to end with the return of Jesus and the establishment of his thousand-year Kingdom. This had long been the core of the fundamentalist vision.

> Israel's return to the Holy Land is an event which is occurring today—and it is an outstanding sign that the second coming of Christ is near. (A. J. Huffer)

> We must look beyond the passions of man in this struggle for the Holy Land and see the restoration of Israel as a fulfillment of this great plan. It is one of the greatest "signs of the times" signaling the nearness of the second coming of Jesus Christ our Lord. *(Pentecostal Evangel)*

> The return of the Jews to Palestine is one of the greatest modern fulfillments of Bible prophecy, ranking along with the fulfillment of Daniel 12:4. The events in Palestine today are in many ways a key to the understanding of the continuing fulfillment of prophecy leading up to the battle of Armageddon and the second advent of Christ. *(Palestine, Jews, and Bible Prophecy)*

> One may feel a great dislike for the Jews as a people and may believe that they have been unfair to the Arabs, but whether one likes or dislikes the Jews does not change the Bible prophecies. *(Palestine, Jews, and Bible Prophecy)*

> It [the 1948 Arab-Israeli War] looked as if the tiny unprepared State of Israel would be crushed—but Bible prophecy was being fulfilled. *(Palestine, Jews, and Bible Prophecy)*

> The present regathering being witnessed by our generation is the largest movement of the people of Israel since the days of Moses, and may be understood to be the beginning of that which will be completed subsequent to the second coming of Christ and the establishment of his kingdom on earth. (J. Walvoord)[27]

But there was much pain and devastation yet to be suffered before that glorious End. First, there would be seven years of "tribulation." Israel would face a combined assault of Russia in the North,

China and India in the East, and—a recent addition—Islam. For help, Israel would ally itself with the prophesied ten nations in the West (the European Common Market). The war would be devastating. Israel's enemies would be destroyed, including some 83 percent of Soviet soldiers (according to Reverend Falwell).[28] But Israel, too, would suffer terribly. Besides the immense losses in the war itself, Israel would discover that the leader of the ten-nation alliance was really the Anti-Christ out to dominate Israel. It is just then that Christ would return to lead the armies of God against the Anti-Christ in the fields of the valley of Armageddon (Mount Meggido). With that, the remaining Jews, grateful for salvation and at last convinced that Jesus was their Lord, would accept the true faith, and peace and joy would reign for a thousand years thereafter. Those who had already been saved in Christ before all this happened would, of course, be spared, rising in "rapture" into the clouds to reside with Jesus until his thousand-year reign began below. As for the Jews who continued to deny the Truth,

> Zechariah tells us that two parts or two-thirds of the Jews shall be cut off. One-third perished under Hitler, two-thirds shall perish under the Anti-Christ (Zech. 13:8–9). . . . The recent suffering in Germany involved the mass murdering of some five times as many Jews as in the fall of Jerusalem; one-third of all Jews on earth perished under Hitler, two-thirds if prophecy is to be fulfilled, if the words of Jesus are to be held trustworthy. (C. H. Stevens)

> The final blow upon this unfortunate and stubborn people will come during the Tribulation period; and it will be this awful time of suffering that shall break their will and turn the remnant to acceptance of the once hated Nazarene, the Lord Jesus Christ. (H. Armstrong)

> [Reverend William L.] Hull told the correspondent of a Toronto newspaper that the six million Jewish victims of the Nazis were doomed to perish in Hell, and would not enter paradise, because they had not accepted the belief in Christ. Moreover, he said, Eichmann's sins were not as great as those of the average man who denied Jesus as the redeemer. (Y. Malachy)

The sad condition of being scattered to the ends of the earth has persisted until the twentieth century, and with it has come untold sufferings to the people of Israel. . . . But, according to the prophets, the end is not yet and ahead of Israel is a terrible time of suffering before the day of restoration. . . . Heart-rending as it may be to contemplate, the people of Israel who are returning to their ancient land, are placing themselves within the vortex of this future whirlwind which will destroy the majority of those living in the land of Palestine. (J. Walvoord)[29]

Because of the key role that Israel plays in the fundamentalist vision, and notwithstanding the disastrous fate predicted for the Israelis themselves in that vision, mainstream Christian fundamentalists enthusiastically celebrate Israel's successes and achievements through gala banquets and prayer breakfasts, a steady stream of radio and television broadcasts, and an equally steady flow of fundamentalist delegations and tour groups to the Holy Land. Organizations established in Israel promote this support and direct it into practical channels. For example, a "Jerusalem Temple Foundation" (established by the Jewish founder of the Faithful of the Temple Mount) had five U.S. fundamentalists on its board of six. They included the director of the Stanford Research Institute, whose publications include "restoration" tracts (concerning the restoration of the Temple Mount to the Jews as a prerequisite for the return of Jesus); an oil magnate, friend of President Reagan, chairman of the 1985 "national prayer breakfast in honor of Israel," and self-styled "Nehemiah" (the ancient restorer of the Temple and herald of the Messiah); a devoted "Christian Zionist," who, among his other projects, promoted the Jewish acquisition of Moslem buildings in the "old city" and provided financial aid to the Yeshiva Ateret Cohanim (dedicated to the rebuilding and management of the Third Temple to be constructed on the Temple Mount after the assumed disappearance of the present Islamic mosques); and the head of a theological school in San Diego, who dealt with Israel's Chief Rabbis and with the government's advisor on Christian affairs.[30]

Jewish officials, both in the Israeli government and in diaspora organizations, publicly welcomed this support, as Prime Minister Menachem Begin did when he bestowed the Jabotinsky medal on Reverend Jerry Falwell. After all, the much-needed support is here and now, while the prophesied suffering and conversion are in the future and, in any case, part of a tradition that Jews reject.

Even more reminiscent of conditions surrounding the birth of Christianity than the indirect impact of Zionism on Christian fundamentalism is the emergence in Israel of a radical *Jewish* fundamentalism that once again, as in Hellenistic times, parallels the Christian vision and zeal. If the return to Zion, the establishment of the Jewish state, and the extraordinary series of military victories against what seemed overwhelming odds convinced Christians that their prophecies would soon be fulfilled and their Messiah returned to them, one can imagine the effect those "miracles" must have had on many Orthodox Jews. For almost two thousand years, Jews had prayed for the return to Zion and waited for the Messiah who would lead them back. At first, through the early Zionist settlement decades, the Orthodox were adamant in insisting that the Messiah must appear before the return and national rebirth. While there is still an influential non- or even anti-Zionist contingent among the ultraorthodox, many of the ultras have come to believe that, since all those marvelous victories clearly revealed the hand of God, these must surely be "Messianic times," the End of Days, the eve of the Kingdom of God in the form of a Third Temple Torah state. "My actions are not calculated to speed up the Messianic redemption," Rabbi Waldman, a leader of this Jewish messianism, argued; "rather, it is the messianic redemption which makes me speed up my actions."[31]

> We are witnessing the realization of the prophecies concerning the return of the people of Israel to its land and the renewal of Israeli rule. This is the supreme and wondrous revelation of the beginning of the redemption. (Isaiah Bernstein)[32]

In Yeshiva courses, lecture series, and political debate, this triumphalist Jewish Messianism became, in the 1980s, one of the most popular public themes in Israel. Several institutions in Jerusalem were zealously at work preparing for the time when the Third Temple would be rebuilt, animal sacrifices revived, and Israel once again ruled by a Sanhedrin of Torah sages. Even Third Temple clothing styles were displayed and seriously discussed: "The renewed use of tekhelet-dyed cords for tzitzit fringes on the corners of Third Temple era shirts is an exciting prospect," one such enthusiast announced, then went on to describe how the Israel Fibre Institute, where he worked, was experimenting with dyes in order to reproduce the exact color required by ancient tradition. When Rabbi Peretz, Minister of the Interior under the Peres-Shamir "unity government" of the mid-1980s, proclaimed that "the Torah is our platform," he was stating the aim of many Israeli Orthodox religious communities and parties dedicated to achieving the Torah State by steadily increasing their already considerable influence in public education, the legal system, and the media.

The Jewish fundamentalists, no less than their Christian counterparts, are eager to use the full power of the state, in part through their "swing" vote block of parliament seats, to enforce their revealed truths and norms, even though many of them reject the pre-Messianic Zionist state in principle. Toward that sacred end, the liberal ideals of tolerance, freedom of expression, and democratic process are easily dismissed: how can such purely man-made conventions compete with the Word of God? "We will not accept the norms that are generally accepted by the public at large. These norms do not involve us, since Israel is a chosen people and should be above these norms." The "Kach" movement, under the leadership of Rabbi Meir Kahane, brought the issue to a head by forthrightly stating a basic assumption that had long been quietly accepted by many of the Orthodox: political democracy, cultural pluralism, and religious toleration must all give way to divine commandment, as stated in the texts of the faith and interpreted by Orthodox Rabbis. That is the meaning of Torah State.

Since that is, as yet, only an ideal and since the present state remains essentially secular, many militant, "ultra" Orthodox, the "Haredim" (the God fearing), feel they are justified in using what power they have to enforce God's will. One strategy is to give their parliamentary votes to whichever major party supports their single-issue religious platform. Another strategy is organized harassment, especially against those living in or near the "ultra" communities (or communities they hope to control)—destroying "immoral" advertisements; bombing newsstands that sell secular papers; assaulting "offensive" businesses (e.g., restaurants or theaters); slashing tires; making threatening phone calls; stoning Sabbath-violating vehicles; leaving garbage, dung, and dead animals on doorsteps. Repeated accounts of such attacks are printed in the press, as well as statements by those who admit being too fearful of reprisals to complain.

For these "ultras," a live-and-let-live policy might be acceptable while in exile, since the Diaspora was only a temporary residence and since, in any case, Jews lacked the power to have it any other way. But in the Holy Land! The very fact that Jews had returned home was proof enough that these were Messianic times and that Israelis must now move forward to prepare the way for the complete Messianic redemption by turning the secular state into a holy Torah State. Secular Jews were holding back the Redemption by their nonobservance of religious laws, and God would continue to punish them for this. The Israeli military casualties in Lebanon were so high, for example, because young women are drafted into the army and, therefore, into a life of immorality; children on a school bus from the town of Petach Tikva were killed in a collision, because God wanted to punish the townspeople for allowing a theater to remain open on the Sabbath. The rabbis who made those statements were both members of the Israeli Parliament at the time, and one was the Minister of the Interior.

But it is especially with regard to the boundaries of the Holy Land itself, the Land of Israel, that the Jewish fundamentalists zealously demonstrate their messianic commitment. The land—all of it— is holy because God promised it to the Jews and because only there can Jews fulfill all the 613 commandments. To regain all the Land of Israel, to hold it, and to make it a Torah State are all simultaneously preparations for the coming of the Messiah, guarantees of his coming, and signs that this is indeed the Messianic time in which he will come. The divine directive must be obeyed: "every place whereon the soles of your feet shall tread . . . from the wilderness and Lebanon, from the river Euphrates, even unto the uttermost sea shall your coast be." Once won, that promised land must be kept: it would be sacrilege to surrender any of it. "Any concession or annulment of Israeli control on even the smallest part of our homeland and its transfer to a Gentile authority is absolutely prohibited by the Torah," in the judgment of the late Rabbi Zvi Yehuda Kook, generally regarded as the spiritual inspiration and leader of this territorial Messianism. For further support, the fundamentalists refer to the sage Nahmanides, who interpreted Numbers 33:53–54 ("And you shall take possession of the land and settle in it, for I have given the land to you to possess it") to mean that, "We are commanded to take possession of the land . . . we should not leave it in the hands of any other people or allow it to lie waste . . . we are commanded to enter the land, to conquer its cities, and to settle our tribes there . . . for this is the commandment of conquest." It was on these passages from Numbers and Nahmanides that the Council of the Chief Rabbinate based its prohibition against surrendering any part of the Holy Land once it was acquired.

Every thought, prayer, and action that participates in this sacred redemption helps purify the Holy Land and its holy people. In the words of a sermon published after the Yom Kippur War,

> We have to see the greatness of this hour in its biblical dimension, and it can be seen only through the messianic perspective . . . only in the light of the Messiah. . . . Why did the war of Gog and Magog come? . . . After the establishment of the Kingdom of Israel, the war can have only one significance: the purification, refining, and cleansing of Israel.

For the mystics among these "ultras," the redemption of all the Land of Israel holds an added and awesome spiritual meaning: recovering all of the Holy Land is a victory over the dark, other, evil side of cosmic Being and, thus, an immense stride toward the reunion of God with his Shekhina, his feminine hypostasis, alienated from him at the time of creation. Signs are studied and alphabetical letters endlessly rearranged according to the numerical equivalents (Gematria) that will reveal the hidden course of events and disclose the where, when, and how of prophecy.

Rapture and radiance, through the purification of suffering. It is the same "mystical realism" that we have seen so many times before, first in its religious and then in its secular modes, the same fusion of the symbolic and the real, transcendent and temporal, metaphysical and physical, spiritual and material, fantasy and fact. Once again, as at the birth of Christianity, zealous Jews, too Jewish to follow the gnostic route of forthright mystical withdrawal from the corrupt world—the Holocaust world—into a divine kingdom within, are pressing the time to make that corrupt world into a divine Now.

And once again, as it always seems to be in such millennial

enterprises, the means adopted swiftly move from hope and prayer to sacred violence, in this case against both Jews, who must be forced by the would-be theocrats to obey the commandments and, even more insistently, today's "Amelikites," who threaten the chosen people from outside and defile the Holy Land from within: "there is an educational stream in Israel which sees in Israel's enemies the image of Amalek in the Book of Joshua." For the fundamentalist ultraorthodox, the Word of God had long ago established the strategy and tactics: "Howbeit for the cities of these people that the Lord thy God giveth thee for an inheritance, thou shalt save alive nothing that breatheth and shall utterly destroy them: the Hittite, and the Amorite, the Canaanite, and the Perizzite, the Hivite, and the Jebusite. . . ." In its March 1979 session, the Council of the Chief Rabbinate also found justification for such treatment of the enemy in Deuteronomy 7:2, in which the people were told, "Thou shalt make no covenant with them, nor show mercy unto them." Other passages, from the Talmud and Maimonides, were used by the council to sanction its judgment that "You shall not give them a place of settlement on the soil." One soldier from a Yeshiva asked his Rabbi about a Talmudic commandment to "smite him first who rises to smite thee." The rabbi answered that "in wartime this is the reasonable inference regarding the non-Jew: He must always be considered to be intending to kill you unless it is clear that he has no such evil intentions." The soldier responded: "I have understood the following from your letter: in wartime, I am permitted, nay commanded, to kill every Arab man and woman who crosses my path if there is any suspicion that they are aiding the war against us, either directly or indirectly."

It is difficult to guess the extent of such extreme sentiments and attitudes. According to one authority, this "messianic trend" is found "among large sections of the religious Zionist youth movements, in public schools, yeshiva high schools, student bodies, yeshiva military units, settlers in the territories [Judea and Samaria], and members and supporters of the Greater Land of Israel movement and the Tehiya party."

Given this background, there should have been little surprise when, in the summer of 1984, twenty-five young Orthodox men were arrested, charged, and later convicted of such terrorist acts as an assault on Hebron Islamic University in which three Arab students were killed and a dozen wounded, the bombing of a schoolyard in Hebron in which two students were seriously injured, the car-bomb crippling of several Arab officials, and preparations to blow up five Arab civilian buses as well as the Dome of the Rock and Al-Aksa Mosques. Nor, keeping this same background in mind, should there have been the surprise there was when large segments of the population expressed sympathy for the young men. Rabbi Yitzhak Peretz, soon to become Minister of the Interior, called them "precious souls full of love for their people," and felt that "they should not be judged by ordinary standards." Rabbi Levenger was particularly graphic in his praise: had the twenty-five not "risen and cut off their legs [the Arab officials], who knows where we would be today." Earlier he had provided the appropriate Biblical justification for retaliation against the Arab murderers of Jews in Hebron: "Have you killed and also taken possession." He felt, in fact, that the twenty-five had not gone far enough in their bombing of the Arab officials: for "their legs were cut off but not their tongues," and they could, therefore, still go on propagandizing and organizing against Israel.

Statement after statement quoted in the press expressed this support, if not always for the terrorist deeds, at least for the doers, the "pure Jews whose lives are dedicated to the Zionist achievement," "the pride of Israel," "heroes of Israel," the "best among us." According to one poll, over half the population felt that way. (Although one wonders if many of them would have gone along with Knesset member Meir Cohen-Avidov: "we should gouge out the eyes and rip out the gut" of Arab murderers, or with the author of an article in a Russian emigre publication: "We hope that the members of the underground did indeed rip off the legs of the mayors and kill a few young snakes at the Hebron College. Thank God we have boys like these.")

Conventional nationalism, fury at Arab terrorist strikes against Jewish civilians, and fear of more in the future all contribute to the complex motivations for committing and defending such actions. And a distinction should be made between reasonable security concerns and messianic zeal. There is no doubt, however, that for many of those involved in the terrorist Orthodox underground, as well as many of the rabbis who inspired them, messianism and other religious assumptions and commitments were a decisive influence. In a "Dear Brothers" letter, several underground leaders wrote to the rest of the group (after discussing studying Torah together while in prison) that their aim was "to found a popular movement for redemption": "We aim for the complete redemption and our purpose is to struggle for it." Similarly, the title one underground activist gave to an eight-page confession was, "For the Redemption of the Nation."

With the exceptions of the Jonestown massacre and the violent acts of organizations like the Order and the CSA in the United States and the Jewish "ultra's" underground in Israel, the violence in Christian and Jewish fundamentalism has been effectively bridled thus far. The same cannot be said for the third religion currently experiencing the spread of fundamentalist extremism—Islam. In Khomeini's Iran, the "ultra" priests have won complete power and built a violently repressive "holy land" that Christian and Jewish extremists can only dream about.

The core and foundation of Khomeini's vision is the absolute unity of religion and politics. They had been virtually identical in the reign of the Prophet Mohammed. Since the Koran is divinely perfect, and since the Prophet brought the word, will, and guidance of God to earth and humanity, it follows that the laws of his Koran should define and direct all human behavior and relations in society and that the priests, who best understand those laws, should rule. The Prophet had said: "I have bequeathed to you that which will always be a guide to you, if you will take hold of it; the Book of God and the practices of my life." Sunni Moslems interpret that as meaning the Koran and the "sunna" (what Mohammed said and did during his lifetime). Shi'ites add a phrase: "the Book of God, and the practices of my life *and of my family,*" meaning by that added phrase, the family of 'Ali, (who had married the Prophet's daughter Fatima) and the religious leaders (the Imams) after him. That Shi'ite addition, in turn, determines the meaning of the Koran verse, "O you have faith, obey God, obey the Prophet of God, and obey the issuer of orders": for the Shi'ites, in keeping with the additional phrase quoted above, that "issuer" was the clergy, especially those who had attained the highest religious rank, the Ayatollas.[33]

Describing the Shi'ite view of politics, Shi'ite political theorist Ali Shariati contrasted the concept of *siyasat*, 'taming a wild horse,' with the western democratic understanding of politics. In the West, he wrote, the aim is to provide the greatest happiness for the greatest number, whereas, for the Shi'ites, the aim is to "tame" the people by educating them to live according to the Koran. Strong leadership and, at times, repressive force is needed to achieve that end. In the words of another Shi'ite scholar, Allama Tabatabai:

Just as children, orphans and the insane need guardians, so society needs a supervisor. If there is only law and no head, society falls apart. . . . [Islam] is neither democratic nor communist. The lawmaker is God, and changes are not made by majority opinion. . . . What people want is the result of what they are taught. They can be taught to want what God wants. . . . The ill done our part of the world by democracy is only a social form of what was done individually earlier by Alexander and Genghiz Khan. . . . Now it is done more subtly by technology and psychology, so people do not even realize what is happening and are not aroused to revenge.[34]

Or, as preacher Shaykh Mohammad Taqi Falsafi put it:

Does man naturally turn towards justice? No. Man is first an animal and then a person. . . . The verse I cited ("We send our Prophets with signs and miracles, a book and scales of justice") is followed by "and we created iron," that is, the sword. Justice without the sword is impossible. Justice and freedom must be forced on people.[35]

Together with this absolute right of religious leaders to dominate and mold society, the Koran provides the program and policies the guardians are to enforce. For decades before Khomeini's revolution, the clerics had given the closest study, in their madrasa, to the future reformation of society on the model of the Koran and to the laws toward that end covering all aspects of individual and social existence—government, economics, taxation, family relations, education, styles of dress, eating habits, reading materials, anything and everything relating to sexual relations, and so on.

Since it is the word and will of God that the Ayatollas, "God's shadow on earth," are enforcing in their puritanical code, all means are acceptable, especially in the *takhliya* phase of the transformation, the period when the corrupt ideas and practices of the old society are being purged. Accordingly, over 500 people were executed during the first six months of Khomeini's power, among them those killed for "sexual deviance, pornography, [and] prostitution."[36] By 1985, over 6,000 had been executed, according to Amnesty International. The opposition Mujahideen put the total executed at 50,000 and those imprisoned on political charges at 140,000. Long lists of torture victims complete the account. "We must purify. We must renew,"[37] in the words of Revolutionary Committee member Ayatollah Moham-mad Reza Mahdain-Khani, echoing Stalin, Lenin, Hitler, Robes-pierre, Muntzer, and all other saviors, great and small, licensed to kill by God, History, Reason, or Nature.

The enemy, once again, is sin, in this case all forms of Western cultural influence. There is no need to review this portrait of Western corruption, "savagery" posing as "civilization," in Khomeini's words.[38] Not only is this fundamentalist litany of modern sin all too familiar, but it is everywhere much the same, the one truly ecumenical sermon uniting Moslem, Christian, and Jewish "ultras." At its center and focus is the eternal temptress, Eve, and everything that entices man's submission to her wiles—"immodest" dress, seductive movies, alcohol, mixed social gatherings, and so forth.

> Open display of female beauty leads men to mental illness through desiring more than they are allowed or able to have, and through the ill effects of masturbation, aggravated by the availability of explicit films, books, and magazines. . . . The intoxication of love leads to the overpowering of the rational soul *('aql)* by baser nature *(nafs)*; the ensuing madness can lead to sins of incest, murder, suicide, and the enslavement of the self to another rather than only to God (Islam). . . . Women are not . . . equal to men. They are after all biologically different: they bear children, they menstruate, they are more emotional. If they are more emotional, then society is better off if government, war and justice are left to men. . . . And, to quote the famous sermon of the first Imam, 'Ali: "[Women] are deficient in faith, deficient in shares, and deficient in intelligence. As regards the deficiency in their faith, it is their abstention from prayers and fasting during their menstrual period. As regards deficiency in their intelligence, it is because the evidence of two women is equal to that of one man. As for the deficiency of their shares, that is because of their share in inheritance being half of men. So beware of the

evils of women. Be on your guard even from those of them who are reportedly good. Do not obey them even in good things so that they may not attract you to evils."[39]

The targets attacked by Khomeini's revolutionary guards were selected as symbols and channels of Western corruption—liquor stores, cinemas, banks, tourist hotels, restaurants, airline offices, and the westerners' businesses, living quarters, official embassies, and libraries. There is no middle ground in this war against the West and, especially, the "Great Satan," the United States. "Either all the mullahs should join with me or they are no better than revisionists. Unless they speak out, it shows that they have chosen to side with Satan."[40]

The root of Shi'ite authoritarian fundamentalism is the same as the root of all other fundamentalist movements—the dialectic of suffering. The Shi'ite gospel is mainly a story of defeat, persecution, and martyrdom. The central issue around which the plot unfolds involves the contests for succession to the Prophet Mohammad's dual political-religious empire. The Shi'ites bear the long tradition of the losing side. They are the "Party of 'Ali" (Shi'iat 'Ali), the supporters of the claims of 'Ali, husband of Mohammad's daughter Fatima, and his heirs. As the losers, they led in successive opposition movements against the successful caliphs and what to them was the caliphates' immorality, corruption, and class oppression. Consequently, they became identified both with the cause of religious purity and with the grievances of the people. Also, as in the suffering of the early Christians and the millennia-long Calvary of the Jewish people, constant defeats and persecution generated a cult of martyrdom. Shi'ite martyrology begins when 'Ali, after being twice deprived of succession to the Caliphate, was cynically deceived out of his position as fourth caliph and assassinated. The victor, Ibn Mu'awiya, then poisoned one of 'Ali's sons, Hasan, and broke a pledge to return the caliphate to 'Ali's family by making his own son, Yazid, his successor rather than 'Ali's second son, Husayn. In an ensuing battle between Yazid and Husayn, Husayn was first betrayed by those who he thought were his allies; then, in the key and sacred battle of Karbala, he was killed along with all but two of his followers. Not satisfied with Husayn's death, Yazid desecrated the body (trampling it "into a formless mass of blood, mud and bone") and killed three of Husayn's sons. Along the way, a number of less important kin and supporters met similarly grim fates.[41]

Gathered into a single, composite drama of repeated martyrdom, those events together form the focus of the "Shi'iat Ali." In major and minor religious ceremonies, in sermons throughout the year, in studies at the religious schools, and in processions commemorating the martyrdom, this gospel of purity and pain is retold and relived again and again. The sinless souls of the true heirs of the Prophet suffer every manner of pain and indignity at the hands of the blasphemous tyrants. And how better demonstrate one's devotion both to the martyrs and to their truth than to suffer vicariously their sacred agony. Through the first ten days of the month of Muharram, leading up to 'Ashura (the tenth day of Muharram, on which the battle of Karbala was fought) processions move slowly through the streets illustrating the events in the drama. Among the displays in one such procession, for example, was a float with a man in white "holding the head of Husayn and alternately polishing it with a rag and clapping his hand to his thigh and mouth in a gesture of disbelieving grief" and another representing "Husayn's bloodied corpse, with live pigeons feeding on him. . . ." Interspersed among the floats were "double columns of black-shirted young men chanting . . . or beating their chests with both palms and occasionally slashing their foreheads with knives. . . . From all 'seventeen' neighborhoods, they parade through a tent decorated with printed cloth from Isfahan, keeping up a steady rhythm of flagellation and chanting."

In one story recounting the tragedy, we hear 'Ali telling Fatima what awaits their family.

> Two necks will be pierced by arrows: 'Ali's neck is only so threatened by 'Umar; Husayn's neck will be pierced. Two heads will droop in chains; 'Ali is dragged before Abu Bakr by 'Umar: Zayn-al 'Abidin is dragged to Damascus before Yazid. Two sides will be hurt: Fatima, when 'Umar forces the door against her, falls down; Husayn, when his side is pierced by a dagger, will roll in agony from side to side. Two arms will be broken by flogging: Fatima's by 'Umar's whip: Say-nab's by Shimr. Two hands will be cut: both belonging to 'Abbas. Two marriages will be funerals: Fatima's wedding at which seventy-two camels were slain; Qasim's at which seventy-two people were slain.[42]

Through constant retelling and ritual celebration, the Karbala drama is always present as a mirror and metaphor for interpreting all later events. Thus, "every day is Ashura the tenth of Muharram, when Husayn was killed in the battle of Karbala and every place is Karbala." "This annual ritual drama in fact lasts the entire year. The Shi'ite calendar invests the entire year with meaning in terms of Karbala-related stories." "Wherever the Muslim is, is a field of struggle where the forces of justice and legitimacy are confronted by the forces of tyranny. Every day of his life is a day of battle in which he should seek either triumph or martyrdom."[43]

To die in this struggle is to be blessed, as 'Ali and his family of martyrs were blessed, and to ascend directly to Paradise. "Death is a welcome escape from a world of tribulation." The model, once again, is 'Ali. Unlike Caliph 'Umar, whose only thought when struck by an assassin was vengeance against the assassin, 'Ali cried out when struck down, "O God, most fortunate am I!"[44] So central is this reverence for Karbala martyrdom in the faith of the Shi'ites that the prophecy of its coming is set even as far back as Adam.

When the Prophet Adam, may peace be with him, descended upon the earth, he was looking for Eve around the world until he traversed to the Desert of Karbala. When he entered the Desert, waves of sorrow and sadness approached him. When he reached the death place of the Martyr Imam Husayn, may peace be with him, his foot caught a rock and blood started to flow from it. Then he raised his head to Heaven and said: "O Creator, I travelled in all the lands and I experienced no sadness and misery which has come to me here. Have I done any sin that you are punishing me for it?" Then God replied, "O Adam you have done no sin, but a son of yours shall die here from injustice and oppression. I wanted your blood to flow on this land the way his blood shall flow here." Adam asked, "O Creator, is Husayn a Prophet?" God answered "[Husayn] is not a Prophet, but he is the son of my Prophet Muhammad." Adam asked, "Who is the murderer?" God replied, "His murderer is Yazid whom the people of Heaven and Earth curse." Then Adam asked Gabriel, may peace be with him, "What should I do?" Gabriel said, "Curse Yazid." The Prophet Adam cursed the Damned One [Yazid] four times.[45]

Through centuries of defeat, Shi'ites drew comfort and hope from this tradition of helpless martyrdom for the same reason that Christians saw guarantees of salvation in their crucified Jesus, and Jews saw the promise of returning to Zion in their oppressive exile. It is the dialectic of despair, the core of the Apocalypse, through which the helpless suffering itself miraculously becomes the instrument and assurance of redemption: Crucifixion as the alchemy for Resurrection. God is a good and all-powerful parent, and since He created and controls the world, He will surely rescue us, reward us for our guiltless suffering, and punish the sinners who tormented us.

As both Jews and Christians trace the lineage of their promised liberator back to the powerful empire builder, David, so the Shi'ites trace their messiah back to the still more successful political leader, Mohammed. In the words of the Prophet himself: "If there were to remain in the life of the world but one day, God would prolong that day until He sends in it a man from my community and my household. His name will be the same as my name. He will fill the earth with equity and justice as it was filled with oppression and tyranny."[46] From the reign of 'Ali to the death, in 872, of Hasan Ali 'Askari, there were eleven "Imams," the supreme spiritual leaders to and through whom the Prophet had bequeathed the true faith. The son of the eleventh Imam was to be the promised savior, the Mahdi, the "Imam of the Period," the "Lord of the Age." While the boy's father, Hasan, lived, the boy was kept in hiding, since the caliph, aware of the belief that the boy was the expected messiah and anxious to crush these rivals once and for all, had sent out agents to kill him. "After the martyrdom of his father, he became Imam and by Divine Command went into occultation. Thereafter, he appeared only to his deputies and even then only in exceptional circumstances." But this twelfth Imam and Mahdi did not entirely abandon his people: he selected a deputy to answer questions and guide the Shi'ites in his name. Four such deputies succeeded each other down to the death of the last in 939. With that began the "major occultation," which would continue until God willed the time right for the reappearance of the Mahdi, who, to recall again the words of the Prophet, would "fill the earth with equity and justice as it was filled with oppression and tyranny."[47]

The Shi'ite millennial scenario was, thus, ready and waiting: a downtrodden community of true believers persecuted through the centuries because of their loyalty to the true faith and waiting for their savior, the Mahdi, to return, destroy the evil kingdom of the caliphate and other Yazid incarnations, reestablish the unity of true faith and power as it was under the Prophet, and thereby "fill the earth with equity and justice." Meanwhile, to keep hope alive and ease the pain, there was the hagiography and theology of martyrdom and a strategy of passive submission and sanctified dissimulation (taquiya).[48]

Long-suffering passivity, an emphasis on the inner world of the spirit, absorption in prayer, study, and ritual, and complete dependency on the guidance of religious leaders may seem radically inconsistent with Khomeini's violent words and deeds. Yet martyrdom of oneself and persecution of others have gone together so often in religious history that the alliance should by now be taken for granted. From St. John's Apocalypse through all later religious and secular apocalyptic-revolutionary movements, helpless suffering generally has been avenged through visions of violent punishment for the sinners, Papists, royalists, bourgeoisie, Jews, or other scapegoat demons, depending on the particular Apocalypse. The dialectic of despair has two faces, masochistic and sadistic.

The kinship and interaction of the two sides in this dialectic of despair is apparent in the continuing role that martyrdom plays in Khomeini's violent regime. It remains the principal liberating and sanctifying experience, except that the martyr now dies heroically in battle as a saintly warrior rather than submissively as a powerless victim. The thousands upon thousands of youngsters who flung themselves, wave upon wave, against Iraqi guns as well as the suicidal terrorist bombers and assassins are sanctified as holy martyrs and share with the first glorious martyr 'Ali, the blessed reward of immediate heavenly salvation ("Karbala 5" was the code name the Iranians gave to their major offensive against Iraq in early 1987).[49] The young Shi'ite zealot who blows himself up in a car-bomb assault against the minions of the "Great Satan" is committing both suicide and murder. "A number of the students swarming in to take our embassy in Teheran had looks of rapture on their faces, reflecting the hope that our Marines would shoot to kill and thus gain these students instant access to a better life."[50]

The circumstances that sparked the shift from passive to active martyrdom among the Shi'ites are much the same as those that ig-

nited comparable explosions earlier and elsewhere. The basic ingredients are all there: a severe intensification of popular discontent, in
part caused by rapid social and cultural dislocations; a weakening
power at the top through division among the ruling elites, including,
particularly, the military; and a revolutionary leadership capable of
taking advantage of those conditions and skillfully manipulating the
appropriate apocalyptic-revolutionary ideology and rhetoric, in this
case the Karbala tradition.

If, in that tradition, the caliph had generally been condemned
as the source of corruption and heresy, the westernizing Shah was
the reincarnation of Yazid himself, the villain of Karbala who had
killed and desecrated the saintly Husayn. And if the Shah was the
Yazid of the day, then Khomeini must be the long-awaited liberator.
"For years in rawdas the Shah had been identified with the archtyrant
Yazid, whereas Khomeini was seen to uphold the ideals of Husayn.
In 1978, during Muharram, the religious leadership called for
marches instead of the traditional mourning processions. As the passion of the year increased, more and more people called Khomeini
'Imam Khomeini'; and the religious dates of the year became staging
times for major demonstrations."[51] On his return from exile to direct
the revolution, Khomeini was greeted accordingly.

> If the Hidden Imam had in truth reappeared after eleven hun-
> dred years, the fervour could hardly have been greater. People
> were shouting "The soul of Hussein is coming back!" "The doors
> of Paradise have been opened again!" "Now is the hour of mar-
> tyrdom!" and similar cries of ecstasy.[52]

"I take this opportunity," Khomeini said on his arrival, "to declare the end of *taquiya*," the passive dissumulation forced upon the
Shi'ites through centuries of oppression. With the end of *taquiya* and
the corresponding replacement of the customary mourning and self-
flagellation processions by militant and defiant marches, the shift of
martyrdom from passive to active accelerated, with explicit echoes
of Karbala all along the way. "Without doubt," Mohamed Heikal
wrote in his survey of the revolution, "it was the willingness of almost the entire population of the principal cities to face martyrdom,
indeed to welcome it—the Karbala complex—which ensured that the
Revolution would triumph."[53] Not that the arrival of Khomeini in-

spired this return to Karbala: echoes of Karbala had been accompanying the resistance from the beginning. When, for example, the army raided the Madrasa Faydiyya in 1975, banners urged the religious students to martyrdom: "Death is better," recalling the remark by Husayn at Karbala that "Death is better than life under oppression."[54]

The Karbala martyrdom tradition was particularly important in Khomeini's "Gandhian" policies toward the Shah's army: "Do not attack the army in its breast, but in its heart. You must appeal to the soldiers' hearts even if they fire on you and kill you. Let them kill five thousand, ten thousand, then twenty thousand—they are our brothers and we will welcome them. We will prove that blood is more powerful than the sword." "You have opened fire," Khomeini wrote in one of his messages after the army had intervened to quell a riot. "Very well—fire again. It is your own brothers and sisters who will receive your bullets, but they will be praying forgiveness for you." When troops were sent to restore order on another occasion, "the crowds in the streets greeted the soldiers with flowers."[55]

In one of the most comprehensive and influential studies of fascist psychology, this combination of masochism and sadism was identified as the basic character of the "authoritarian personality."[56] Listing a few attributes of that portrait of the authoritarian personality should be enough to show its relevance here: a fervent and inflexible adherence to traditional values; a submissive, uncritical attitude toward idealized moral authorities; a tendency to be on the lookout for, and to condemn and punish, those who violate traditional values; an intense interest in the sexual lives of others and a rigid defense of what is judged to be proper sexual standards; a belief in mystical determinants of the individual's fate; and a tendency to believe that wild and dangerous things are going on in the world.

The significance of this sadomasochistic pattern is not limited to recent fascism and current fundamentalist extremism: the pattern is readily applicable to all the apocalyptic movements reviewed in the preceding chapters. The fusion of masochism and sadism is apparent on virtually every page of St. John's Revelation; it characterizes the thought and behavior of those engaged in the frenzied medieval "pursuit of the millennium"; and it helps explain the combination of martyrdom and mass murder that has accompanied all modern apocalyptic revolutions, from Robespierre's to Lenin's and beyond.

If sadomasochism is the psychology of the Apocalypse, it is because that malaise is the voice of the pain, fear, and rage that wells up when circumstance and character combine to make people feel helpless and desperate in the face of prolonged suffering. Sometimes the desperation is quiet and depressed, sometimes it is explosively aggressive; but in all cases it confesses radical loss of faith in the world as it is, a declaration that one can no longer tolerate either the pain or the conventional remedies for easing it. All existing reality is denounced as irremediably evil, and the helpless turn in absolute faith to a promised salvation and savior. In return for an assured entry into the new heaven and new earth (or new society or new order), and a no less reliable guarantee that those judged responsible for the suffering will "weep and gnash their teeth," the victims gratefully surrender their will and lives to the savior and his disciples and zealously join sadomasochistic crusades against the sinners.

Those familiar conditions and reactions are once again increasingly apparent: the extraordinary popularity of the irrational—the occult, astrology, mysticism, shamanism, and so forth; the continuing appeal of science fiction and comparable other-world fantasies; the cults (Unification Church, Divine Light Mission, Hare Krishna, Universal Church of God, People's Temple, Children of God, etc.); the growing fundamentalist, Pentacostal, and charismatic movements in Christianity, Judaism, and Islam; the burgeoning pseudoreligious organizations (EST, Synanon, Scientology, etc.)—all achieved their extraordinary success by responding to the pain, fear, and confusion experienced by badly injured refugees from a deprivational reality. Lost, they crave guidance. Confused, they crave Truth. Frightened, they crave protection and reassurance. Angry, they crave revenge. Guilty, since, as monotheists (Christians, Jews, and Moslems) who cannot blame God for their suffering, they accept or even intensify that suffering as a just and purifying punishment that will bring forgiveness and salvation. The liberators and redeemers (once considered cranks or worse, but now, adored and followed) provide it all. In return, the true-believing remnant joyfully give the same obedience and reverence that they had given in their earliest childhood. That is the way back to and into the infantile Paradise, where bliss is restored to the reborn Adam in return for a surrender of the moral free will and individual judgment that had accompanied the initial "expulsion" from the maternal Eden.

NOTES

1. *Detroit Free Press*, 1 July 1985; italics added.

2. *New York Times*, 13 August 1986.

3. Ibid., 29 September 1986.

4. Samuel Pisar, quoted in Furio Colombo, *God in America: Religion and Politics in the United States*, trans. Kristin Jarratt (New York: Columbia University Press, 1984), 89–90, 120.

5. Charles Krauthammer, "The End of the World," *New Republic*, 28 March 1983, 12–15.

6. "Are We nearing Armageddon," *The Watchtower*, Kingdom News No. 31.

7. Terry Zintl, "Signs of the End Obvious," *Detroit Free Press*.

8. William Martin, "Waiting for the End," *Atlantic*, June 1982, 31–37.

9. Helmut Thielicke, "Twilight of the Day, the Life the World," in *Endtime*, ed. William Griffin (New York: Collier Books, 1979), 42.

10. *Detroit Free Press*, 6 May 1983, Letters to the Editor.

11. Martin, "Waiting," 34.

12. John Wesley White, "Apocalyptic Signs," in *Endtime*, ed. Griffin, 102.

13. Tim LaHaye, "Anticipating the End"; Malcom W. Browne, "When and How Will the End Come"; James Montgomery Boice, "Day of the Lord, Day of Christ"; in *Endtime*, ed. Griffin, 67, 68, 96.

14. Billy Graham, "Biblical Climax," in *Endtime*, ed. Griffin, 67.

15. Jurgen Moltmann, *Religion, Revolution, and the Future*, trans. M. Douglas (New York: Scribner, 1969), xii, 9, 17, 33.

16. The quotations from Teilhard de Chardin are taken from Emile Rideau, *Teilhard de Chardin: A Guide to His Thought*, trans. Rene Hague (London: Collins, 1967): "The Future of Man," 55–56, 195, 306–7; "Making of a Mind," 165; "The Phenomenon of Man," 287–88; "L'energie humaine," 78; "Vision of the Past," 233.

17. Richard Nixon, quoted in John E. Mack, "But What About the Russians?" *Harvard Magazine*, March-April 1982, 24, 53.

18. *Detroit Free Press*, 23 July 1985.

19. *Jerusalem Post*, 2 November 1984; *Newsweek*, 5 November 1985, 57; *New York Times*, 9 March 1983.

20. James Ridgeway, "Apocalypse Now: Reagan's Reflections on Armageddon," *Santa Barbara News and Review*, 5 December 1985.

21. *Detroit Free Press*, 10 August 1986.

22. *New York Times*, 24 June 1986; *Detroit Free Press*, 14 September 1986.

23. *Detroit Free Press*, 17 July 1986.

24. *New York Times*, 28 April 1985.

25. For the sources of the quotations in the text and similar material concerning this movement, see *International Herald Tribune*, 7 January 1985; *New York Times*, 27 December 1984, 6 January, 15 February, 24 April, 4 April 1987; *Village Voice*, 12 November 1985; *Los Angeles Times*, 21 January 1985; *Washing-*

ton Post, 12 December, 18 December, 26 December 1984; *Detroit Free Press*, 14 July, 14 September 1986, 26 April 1987.

26. The information on Reverend Jones and the Jonestown tragedy is from the *New York Times*, 2, 21, 26, 29 November and 4 December 1978; *Detroit Free Press*, 25, 26, 27 November and 3, 13 December 1978; *Ann Arbor News*, 26 November 1978.

27. Yona Malachy, *American Fundamentalism and Israel* (Jerusalem: Institute of Contemporary Jewry, 1978), 41, 43, 97, 102–4, 107, 133, 151, 153, 157, 171.

28. *Newsweek*, 5 November 1984.

29. Malachy, *American Fundamentalism*, 99, 105, 132–33, 152, 153.

30. "Slouching Towards Armageddon," *Jerusalem Post* (International Edition), 17–24 June 1984; "Fundamentally Flawed," *Jerusalem Post Magazine*, 14 September 1984; "Conservative Chic," *Jerusalem Post Magazine*, 2 November 1984.

31. *Jerusalem Post*, 9 August 1984. Unless otherwise stated, the information and quotations relating to the Jewish religious extremist movements in Israel are drawn from the *Jerusalem Post*, daily and international editions, and *In Jerusalem*, a *Jerusalem Post* local supplement. The period covered is approximately one year beginning in May 1984. The arrest of twenty-five Orthodox young men as "underground terrorists" responsible for a series of bombings and conspiring to carry out further such assaults stimulated a torrent of articles, official statements, letters, and debates appearing daily throughout that year.

32. Michael Shasher, "The State of Israel and the Land of Israel," *Jerusalem Quarterly*, Fall, 1980, 60.

33. Mohamed Heikal, *The Return of the Ayatollah* (London: Deutsch, 1981), 80–81; Michael M. J. Fischer, *Iran From Religious Dispute to Revolution* (Cambridge, Mass.: Harvard University Press, 1980), 151.

34. Fischer, *Iran*, 154–56.

35. Ibid., 156.

36. Ibid., 219.

37. Ibid., 218–19.

38. Ibid., 132.

39. Ibid., 161–62.

40. Ibid., 202, 208; Heikal, *Return*, 88, 138.

41. Fischer, *Iran*, 260–62.

42. Ibid., 21, 170–71, 175, 262.

43. Hamid Algar, *The Islamic Revolution in Iran* (London: The Muslim Institute, 1981).

44. Fischer, *Iran*, 16, 175.

45. Ibid., 26.

46. Allamah Sayyid Muhammad Husayn Tabataba'i, *Shi'ite Islam*, trans. S. H. Nasr (Albany, N.Y.: State University of New York Press, 1975), 211.

47. Ibid., 210–11.

48. Fischer, *Iran*, 68.

49. *New York Times*, 10 January 1987.

50. Robin B. Wright, *Sacred Rage: The Crusade of Modern Islam* (New York: Simon and Schuster, 1985).

51. Fischer, *Iran*, 183.

52. Heikal, *Return*, 177.

53. Ibid., 176.

54. Fischer, *Iran*, 125, 127.

55. Heikal, *Return*, 145–46, 156.

56. T. W. Adorno, E. Frenkel-Brunswick, D. Levinson, and R. N. Sanford, *The Authoritarian Personality* (New York: Harper and Row, 1950).

8

The Middle Ground

The argument leads to disturbing conclusions and expectations. Because of our culture's particular religious roots and history, the model of the Apocalypse is always on hand and in mind to motivate and guide us in times of social turmoil. And we are now, again, in such a time. The worldwide and rapid spread of religious fundamentalism, the corresponding decline in tolerance and pluralism, and the popularity of "moral crusades" clearly reflect the malaise. Extremists from all the relevant faiths—Christianity, Judaism, Islam, Bolshevism, and Rationalism—seem to be setting the stage for the self-fulfillment of their shared Apocalypse.

In a worst case scenario, U.S. fundamentalism could grow powerful enough to become a decisive influence in the Congress and Presidency. Evangelist Pat Robertson hoped to do just that by winning the 1988 presidential election. Convinced that Reagan's 1980 election was "a direct answer to prayers to God," that "in my lifetime, I will see the fall of the evil empire," Robertson, or someone sharing his worldview, could be the white-horse savior who pushes the Armageddon button.[1] In the Middle East, a likely flash point for sparking a first and last global nuclear exchange, we already have a rapidly expanding Shi'ite fundamentalism craving martyrdom and the smaller but growing influence of a Jewish fundamentalism apparently determined to build a Torah State on the entire Land of Israel whatever the costs. A dramatic increase in Islamic fundamentalism, beginning in the late 1970s, among the Sunni Arabs in Israel itself adds still more fuel to the flames. Inspired by Khomeini's victories and successively disappointed in their own nationalist aspirations by the failures of the Arab League (Egypt and Syria), the PLO, and the United Nations to establish a Palestinian state either alongside or, preferably for them, in place of Israel, Arabs both in Israel and in

Judea/Samaria (the West Bank) are turning to fundamentalist religious leaders for guidance.

> First you have to build belief. Once that is strong enough, the gun can be carried and no power on earth can stop you. Empty people will always turn their backs to the gun. Full people will face it with their chests because they know that if they die, they go to paradise and if they live they will have victory—but either way they win. . . . So now young people have turned to something that the Israelis can never break. Islam cannot be broken. The Israelis can uproot my trees or burn my house, but they can't take Islam away from me. I am right. They are wrong. God is on our side. . . . You will not be here. We will fight until you leave the land which you defiled. Then we will cleanse the Temple Mount with rose water, just as we did after the Crusades.[2]

A common apocalyptic vision drives each of these movements toward self- and world destruction. For apocalyptic Christian fundamentalists, global devastation is inevitable and welcomed as the harbinger of the Savior and their own "rapture" and redemption. For the orthodox Bolshevik, dialectical conflict remains the only "orthodox" way to the inevitable triumph of communism and the burial of capitalist imperialism. For the Islamic zealot, nothing is more sacred or desirable than martyrdom in the struggle for the true faith. For the militant, ultraorthodox Jew, this is the Messianic Age and God will protect his chosen people no matter what they do, what risks they take, as long as it is directed toward establishing the Third Temple Torah State on the whole Land of Israel. Finally, behind and through it all is the rationalists' endless (in both senses of the word) "progress" in science and technology, providing all these crusaders with the instruments for their mutual annihilation.

It is a possible scenario. But is it likely or probable? If probability rests on past experience, then the answer should be no. All earlier apocalyptic panics were transitory, and, however powerful their impact, none of them, after all, destroyed the world. Yet, is that past relevant now that apocalyptic leaders own nuclear weapons? Imagine the war between Hitler and Stalin with some 50,000 nuclear warheads between them! Our time is indeed the first time that could be the last time. Denial is beneficial in some illnesses: it keeps the spirits up and by that alone promotes healing. But if it inspires a Pollyannish disregard for both the dangers and the available remedies, it is insanely self-destructive.

Are there such remedies? It is most unlikely that anything will be done about the scientific-technological-weaponry factor in this morbid equation. The deed is done, and humanity will henceforth remain capable of destroying itself. Mankind has now come fully of age and attained absolute responsibility for itself. Until now, at least a little bit of Eden remained: whatever damage we did to ourselves, the nature of things was such (or the good parental God made sure) that we could not annihilate ourselves as a species. We are now free to make that choice, too. All protective limits are gone. Throughout the history of the Jewish people in Christendom, every Jewish parent was an Abraham and every Jewish child an Isaac. Simply giving birth to Jewish children placed them on a special altar for possible annihilation. In this grim sense, every child in the world today is a Jew. Since we are not likely to move backward in knowledge and technology, our best strategy for survival is to alter the worldviews that threaten to use those weapons of mutual self-destruction. However, considering that the horrendous danger present in those weapons helps foster the regressive self-destructive ideologies favoring their use, the prospects do not seem very promising here either.

Such, in any case, is the view through apocalyptic dark glasses. Dismal pessimism is always both a sign of an apocalyptic era and one of its most effective promoters. In fact, the prospects for cooling apocalyptic emotions and attaining a maturity of thought and action corresponding to the maturity of power we now possess are not at all so bad. But to see things that way, we must restore our Biblical trust and vision. No matter what happened to the "people of the Book" through their long Calvary in Christendom, no matter how devastating or relentless the blows or how hopelessly bleak the future might seem, their basic trust, hope, and effort continued. The world remained, for them, good because their parental God who created it had called it good, very good. They could not simply run away from it through inner or transcendent spiritual voyages. And since they had been created in God's image and assigned an active and responsible partnership in the completion of creation through the "repair of the world," neither could they betray their charge and surrender to illusions of sudden, miraculous, and total transmutations. Even the genocidal Holocaust inspired, for the most part, neither mystical withdrawal nor apocalyptic delusions, but rather a rededication to creative, rational, patient, and arduous labors to repair the ruins once again and, in the process, reestablish their ancient homeland.

"Discreetly, drop by drop, the process of renewal comes about," as one early Kibbutz settler expressed the Biblical *tikun ha'olam* ('repair of the world'). Nor was he alone.

> Not in revolution, not in war lies the crown of existence, but in growth. . . . A revolution cannot be accomplished in one stroke. A good farmer wouldn't act that way. He would proceed gradually. . . . They used to warn us against an exaggerated faith in man and society. So we arrived at a belief in man that was free of cheap enthusiasm, but rich in love for the man who strives for the sublime but with an understanding of his weakness. . . . I can see in my imagination how we shall build the foundation of a national life. Stone by stone we are rebuilding the land laid waste thousands of years ago. I am happy that I am one of the builders. . . . We could start our enterprise the "easy way," and it might be that we would give evidence thereby of greater heroism and devotion; however, it is not our wish to take pride in our moral splendor, but to accomplish something real . . . we must feel our way cautiously; we must be as accurate and attentive as possible.[3]

"My dreams were opulent, my demands modest," Chaim Weizman recalled. "Build under any circumstances," he said elsewhere, "a brick at a time, if necessary; but never stop building." Writer Joseph Chaim Brenner, for all his uncompromising ardor and usual pessimism, summed up the balance perfectly when he wrote in a letter that one must "forgo mysticism and imagination; It is necessary to increase realism and holiness in the world." Holiness as the vision; realism as the means to its realization. Perhaps the finest expressions of this gradualist merger of idealism and realism, the sacred and the secular, to come from the early settlement era in Israel were those of the philosopher-prophet of the kibbutz movement, A. D. Gordon.

"And behold a ladder set up on the earth, and the top of it reached to the heavens" (Genesis 23:12). And what are we looking for—is it not a place for a ladder? . . . People simply work. . . . Sometimes the work is difficult, clogged with pettiness; together with all this, it may happen that into your soul there is born a feeling like that of cosmic exaltation. . . . The day will yet dawn when your sons and daughters will dream a dream, and the dream will be great, a profound dream, reminding you of what you are shown here. Your sons and daughters will come to seek the interpretation of their dream in the land of their fathers. They will seek it with all the power of their hands, with all the strength of their hearts. They will dig it out of hidden places; they will carry on every kind of work in the field and in the vineyard in seeking for it. They will renew the earth and their lives in their search.[4]

Not the top of the ladder. Not even the first rung up. Simply a foothold for it. And dreams, wonderful dreams, but to be realized not through violent struggle, but by "every kind of work in the field and in the vineyard." Do you want "cosmic exaltation"? Then "simply work." The choice, thus, is not between all or nothing: there is also *something*. Ideals and visions, indeed, have often inspired apocalyptic violence, both religious and secular-revolutionary. But the response to that sad fact should not be to blame and abandon the ideals and the visions; it should be to blame and abandon the apocalyptic violence and specific theories and interpretations, religious or secular, that justify it.

The attitudes and feelings expressed in these quotations are hardly novel in Judaism. They are but a restatement of its main themes, as they first took shape in the Hebrew Bible and later became, through the humanist credo of commitment to this world and its gradual improvement, the core of Western civilization after the medieval hiatus. Repeatedly, throughout the modern era, that heritage has been challenged, usually at times of social disruption and fear. Each time, the challenge was defeated. There is good reason to expect the same outcome again.

Consider, for example, the fate of the gloom-doom prophets of the 1960s and 1970s, those predicting one or another demise of our civilization from nuclear, ecological, or economic disaster. A conference of "futurists," meeting in 1983 (when everything should already have ended, according to the earlier Jeremiads), seemed to have all but forgotten those dire predictions. For these latter-day prophets, the future was immensely long and still wide open to across-the-board progress. Less and less time would be given to "work" and more to lifelong education. Some 90 percent of the world's population would live in "supercities" and live very well indeed. Surprisingly, "there is no evidence that population growth has a negative effect on economic development." In fact, "the poor are not getting poorer; the poor are getting richer . . . getting better off at a rate at least as fast as the rich."[5] The point is not whether any of this is valid or not; the point is the optimism and "basic trust" in the future and in mankind's ability to guide and mold it progressively, sanely, and morally. That is the gradualists' vision, hope, and commitment.

A corresponding return to basic trust and optimism similarly characterized a remarkable trend among Western youth in the late 1980s. As though awakened from a bad dream (with a yuppie ending), they seemed to have rediscovered value and moral purpose. Movements for nonviolent social progress not only regained respectability, but they were led for a time by that very segment of society that had earlier glorified the counterculture's "cop out" exit from the world—the rock groups and their heirs: from Woodstock to Live Aid, Farm Aid, "We are the World," Sun City, "Hands Across America," and a revival of social-conscience/protest songs. Both alternatives to gradualist involvement and reform had been tried and discredited. A half-century of secular apocalyptic politics had piled up too many grotesque betrayals, too much cruelty and bloodshed for comparable fantasies to draw significant support even among the customarily zealous and rebellious youth. And, at the opposite pole, the three or so decade flirtation with Gnostic-Eastern detachment and withdrawal and an equally solipsistic yuppie consumerism had proven too lonely, too vacuous, too bereft of honor and dignity, too dull, and, in general, too radically inconsistent with the deepest and most insistent values of Western culture. One may at least hope that this return of the prodigals to patient commitment will continue, broaden in scope, and prove to be as richly beneficial for society as were the contributions of earlier progressive generations.

Paradoxically, one can also find grounds for hope in the very source that generates the current apocalyptic dangers—the religious world of Christianity, Judaism, and Islam. The apocalyptic malaise, in the form of fundamentalist extremism, has activated powerful reactions from within these religious communities. Among Christians, a return to and concern with this world had gone on far too long for them to be beguiled or frightened into escapist apocalyptic fantasy. Pentacostal and charismatic evangelism, for all its media prominence, is still disdained as "holy roller" fanaticism by most Christians. In 1986, at the very time when so much was being written and said about the rapid spread of fundamentalism in the United States, the voters dealt harsh defeats to fundamentalist candidates. The fundamentalist movement as a whole suffered further shattering blows the following year as a result of disclosures of sexual scandals and financial deception involving several of the most prominent and popular television evangelists. "National credibility for the cause of Christ," to quote Jerry Falwell, "is at an all-time low." (Nor is it likely to have been improved by evangelist Oral Roberts's announcement that he had been gifted with divine powers: "I won't tell you how many of the dead have been raised under my ministry. I had to stop and go back in the crowd and raise the dead person so I could go on with my service." He had also been told by God that he "will be coming back with my son to reign" together with Jesus.)[6] In fact, the attitudes and actions of Christian leaders and congregations seem to be shifting in just the opposite direction—toward a revival of the nineteenth-century "social gospel." The popular "liberation theology" and its dedication to a variety of progressive social causes, and, even more dramatically, the successive conferences of clerics in support of nuclear disarmament, world peace, ecumenical cooperation, and social welfare programs are as far removed as possible from the End Time schadenfreude that finds gratifying apocalyptic confirmation in the woes of the world. Christian statements such as the following by Thomas Merton are surely more characteristic of contemporary Christian thought and sentiment than are the apocalyptic pronouncements quoted in the preceding chapter.

> When [sic] the Christians began to look at Christ as Prometheus. . . . You see what I mean? Then they justified war, then they justified the crusades, then they justified pogroms, then they justified Auschwitz, then they justified the bomb, then they justified the Last Judgement. . . . "All right," they say, "if

we can't make it to the wedding feast (and they are the ones who refused), we can blow up the joint and say it is the Last Judgement. . . ." The example of Taoism in China in the chaotic period of the third to the first centuries B.C. is there to show how an otherworldly spiritualism in public life can end in the worst kind of arbitrary tyranny. The intellectual and spiritual man cannot, therefore, justify themselves in abandoning society to the rule of an irrational will to power.[7]

A similar argument can be made with reference to fundamentalist extremism among Orthodox Jews. Militant, ultraorthodox messianism is indeed real and growing. Yet here, too, as in the case of U.S. radical fundamentalism, the danger must be seen in the proper context and perspective. Israeli President Chaim Herzog undoubtedly spoke for the vast majority of Israelis, religious and secular, when he said (with reference to the terrorist acts of the religious "underground") that "only a sick and distorted mind could believe that any good would come of a horrible crime like blowing up a passenger bus, carrying men, women, and children, Jews, Arabs, and foreign tourists, or the murder of students in their schoolyard." Several rabbis of communities settled in Judea and Samaria (the West Bank), where many of the underground activists lived and where they have their most solid support, were admittedly "shocked" by such actions and denounced them as "perversions" and a betrayal of Judaism. New groups within the Orthodox religious community had even earlier organized to combat the "perversions," and adopted for themselves such names as Strength and Peace (Oz veShalom) and Paths of Peace (Netivot Shalom). Leaders of the National Religious party, once the leading religious party and, in part, to blame for the nationalistic excesses of its religious youth movement, attacked the extremism as "an evil spirit that has gripped the religious public, leading to hatred and fanaticism. . . . An evil genie has been let loose among us and the Third Commonwealth is in danger."[8]

If opposition from within the Israeli religious community to religious fanaticism has been significant, one can imagine the attitudes of the secular community, which includes most of the government and the majority of the Israeli citizenry. New laws protecting Israeli democracy against the extremists have been passed, and a variety of educational and media programs have been launched to enhance public commitment (especially among the youth) to toleration and democratic processes. Nor is this simply a matter of "left" and "right": it was a "right" government that arrested and imprisoned the religious underground. The relationship between secular and sacred in Israel is immensely complex, given the traditional Jewish *religious* commitment to society and politics, in general, and the implications of power in the Holy Land in particular. Still, the clear dominance of the secular community over the religious, both in Israeli society and in its parliament, the strong disapproval of violence and intolerance even among most of the religious, the weight of normative Judaism and earlier Jewish history, Israel's continuing close association with Western cultural and political ideals and institutions—such influences make it most unlikely that the apocalyptic zealots will ever be in a position to play their part in the kind of "worst case" scenario outlined earlier.

There is also, finally, cause for optimism with respect to Islamic religious extremism. Not only does the history and religious worldview of the predominant Sunni Moslems ill dispose them to apocalyptic Khomeiniism, but, even among the Shi'ites, such radical violence (however potential in the Karbala paradigm) is highly irregular and unusual. Concerning suicide attacks, for example:

> The Prophet Mohammed himself disapproved of suicide and is said to have refused to say the traditional prayers of mourning for those who died by suicide. According to Islamic teaching, a person who commits suicide, no matter what the circumstances, is not allowed to enter paradise. To the contrary . . . his punishment in hell is to be the endless repetition of the act by which he killed himself.[9]

In effect, there is something of an unwitting alliance joining the moderates of all three religions against the fanatics in each of them. But, of course, the alliance is much broader than that, since it encompasses as well much of the Western secular world, intensely jealous as it is of hard-won gains of free conscience, tolerance, civil liberties, and democratic process.

Extremism of a different sort has similarly encouraged another and even more promising alliance. As religious extremism has dialectically promoted a hopeful alliance of religious moderates, so has the extremism of nuclear terror fostered a de facto alliance between the great powers and a reassuring constraint within each of them. In Marxist-Leninist theory and practice, the dialectic has generally served to foster violence between the class enemies. Now, nuclear bombs have dialectically transformed the dialectics! They have so heightened the "quantity" of destruction, that they have "qualitatively" changed the relationship between the national "class" enemies, away from violent confrontation toward more reasoned negotiation and even occasional cooperation. The extraordinary meeting at Reykjavík in 1986 and the subsequent negotiations toward eliminating nuclear missiles in Europe and sharply reducing the number of intercontinental missiles is encouraging evidence of this shift back toward détente. Here, even more clearly than in the doomsday predictions of economists and ecologists, we have witnessed a clear reduction in apocalyptic expectation. Far fewer today than, say, two or three decades ago, would feel or say the things felt and said in these excerpts from the Henry Miller–Lawrence Durell correspondence.

> [T]his coming month will see some sort of diabolical conjunction, very similar to the set-up in August 1914 and September 1939. . . . By the time we get back to Europe it will be about as interesting as the deserts of Texas. I think a very short war—say six months—could account for all the major cities of Europe [March 1948]. . . . I've resigned my post here and propose to reach London by Christmas—probably an atomic Christmas [September-October 1948]. . . . If World War III doesn't break out in a few weeks (as I firmly expect) [August 1953].[10]

Rather than win wars for one or another side, current military technology has averted wars: the existence of that universally destructive technology has checked and even reversed the kind of reciprocal challenge and response that earlier had quickly escalated into full-scale war.

There may be a most encouraging principle here. We have seen repeatedly in this study that, through the dialectic of despair, having too little inspires the fantasy of getting everything, at once and violently. What we are witnessing now is the opposite: having too much also breeds its own negation. Too much destructive power cripples all destructive power. Too much progress craves simplicity. Less is more. Small is beautiful.

From this perspective, the entire experience of western culture and society seems to have followed a bizarrely dialectical road that took us in exactly the opposite direction from the one we thought we were following. We assumed, and were constantly assured, that "progress" was liberating us from medieval insecurity, ignorance, fear, self-disdain, and dehumanizing dependency; that stage by stage, we were gaining more freedom, more security, more power over our own fate, and greater individual pride and dignity. Yet, what in fact happened? Where have we arrived? Economic, technological, political, and organizational progress steadily reduced us in practice to obedient cogs and functionaries. The social sciences and depth psychology provided the theories to explain and justify that submission by telling us that we are the determined products of socialization, unconscious impulses, or biological forces that are beyond our individual control. "High tech" computer and robotic theory and practice are redefining our glorious Reason—once the substance of that Great Chain of Being that placed us second only to God's Angels—into a set of information strategies and programs that any good computer can perform far more deftly. Science and technology have arrayed against us a battery of nuclear, ecological, and other dangers that constantly threaten our survival. And, finally, secular rationalism has left us entirely alone with our woefully limited and uncertain intellectual and moral resources to meet these challenges.

In short, the unprecedented, post-Renaissance hubris fostered an unprecedented contemporary doubt in ourselves. At no other time in human history have we had less grounds for pride in ourselves and our "powers." Yet, in this may lie our best reason for hope. When certainty gives way to doubt, the Apocalypse gives way to the gradualist vision and life. To coerce, repress, or kill those who oppose our cause, religious or secular-revolutionary, we must believe absolutely that the cause is True. The essential service of God, Reason, History and Nature for the apocalyptic-authoritarian personality and movement is to provide that bedrock, objective, necessary, absolute Truth. In its name, one can—indeed, one must—do anything, however abhorrent it might seem, and yet remain pure and good. In apocalyptic upheavals, one appeals to God, Reason, History, and Nature as the "Higher" Truth or Good not in order to fulfill ethical commitments, but rather to violate them. Conventional ethics can stand alone. No deified, transcendent, all-mighty, irresistible, ineluctable God, Reason, History or Nature is needed to tell us that it is better to help than to hurt, that being kind is morally better than being cruel. But they seem to be needed, or at least have been used repeatedly, to persuade us that the reverse is true. While those higher truths have often encouraged and strengthened conscience, they have at least as often been called upon to stifle it. It has long been a commonplace for religious philosophers that "ethics" and "religion" represent two quite different and often sharply contradictory authorities, and that genuine faith must give priority to the latter. "Thou shalt not kill" has seldom been the standard for zealous true believers. It is another commonplace that much of the violence and other evil in history has been done in the name of sanctified "higher" Truths and Ends.

But doubt and awareness of limits do not imply or justify inaction and detachment. If apocalyptic maximalism errs at one extreme, Platonist, gnostic, Eastern, and other mystical escapism inward and upward err at the other. At times, the two are polar ends of a single syndrome: loss, fear, and desperation first drive the victim out of the world into interior Edens of purity and perfection; then, loneliness, vengeful anger, a craving for honor and power, and/or a projection of purification rituals (from self-punishment to world punishment) drive him back into the world in order to purify it into a mirror image of the interior Eden.

Neither all nor nothing, but something. We can only freely choose with doubt and work with hope. There are no guarantees either that the purpose is the right one or that it must inevitably triumph. Still, we alone are responsible for achieving our civilization's goals, those that were first announced to the world by the ancient Hebrews. The "repair of the world" still means the establishment of peace and social justice, the attainment and preservation of individual freedom, since, in that tradition, all are equally created in the image of God and most exhibit a reverent concern for the welfare of this planet assigned to our common care.

Humanity has only begun to realize those ideals. Once again, in fact, as often before, important ground has been lost and old battles must be fought again, in defense of reason, conscience, and freedom against authoritarian regimes and the new fundamentalism, and in defense of social justice and elemental compassion, against the new conservatism. Moreover, we must also set to work, as the counterculture has shown us, to repair the immense damage done to our earth and, no less, to ourselves, by centuries of reckless material progress. Although undoubtedly rooted in an admirable return to the world and commitment to its improvement, our misguided, excessive, too swift, and often destructive progress has led to new problems whose solution must join the attainment of peace, social justice, and personal freedom as priority planks in the "repair" agenda.

Fortunately for those who would share in this repair enterprise, the gradualist outlook and prophecy is as self-fulfilling as the apocalyptic. The better social and personal conditions become as a result of the "repair," the more support there is likely to be for moderation. It has always been social breakdown and prolonged suffering that sends crowds of desperate victims rushing into the arms of the violent saviors, who are always around but, until such breakdowns, generally ignored. In the end, it comes down to a platitude, as familiar as it is fortunate: Good conditions help foster good people, and good people choose good ends and means. They ignore the apocalyptic extremists, and they realize, in the words of one Talmudic sage, that "it is not for us to finish the task, but neither can we desist from it."[11] Something: not all or nothing. For more recent guidance, those in search of models and methods could look to the direct descendents of those who first called us to the "repair of the world," as, back again in their homeland, they inch their way toward overcoming seemingly insurmountable difficulties. However slow the going, most of them remain satisfied with the hope that, to quote former Israeli President Yitzhak Navon, "maybe we can make little breakthroughs,"[12] knowing, as Jerusalem Mayor Teddy Kollek once said, that "some problems are not to be solved, but to be lived with . . . and when the chance comes one just nibbles away at them, then stops and waits for the next opportunity to nibble away a little more."[13]

NOTES

1. *New York Times,* 18 September 1986; *Detroit Free Press,* 14 September 1986.

2. *New York Times,* 29 April 1987.

3. Arthur Mendel, Abraham Yassour, and Joseph Blasi, eds., *Hagshama: Diary of the Kibbutz*, forthcoming.

4. A. D. Gordon, *Selected Essays*, trans. Frances Burnce (New York: League for Labor Palestine, 1938), 120–21, 135, 138–39.

5. *Detroit Free Press*, 5 October 1985.

6. *New York Times*, 2 May 1987; *Detroit Free Press*, 27 June 1987.

7. Thomas Merton, *Seeds of Destruction* (New York: Farrar, Straus, and Giroux, 1964), 112–13, 273–74.

8. *Jerusalem Post*, 3–10 June 1984, 24 June–1 July 1984, 31 August 1984.

9. *New York Times*, 16 February 1986.

10. *Lawrence Durrell and Henry Miller: A Private Correspondence*, ed. George Wickes (New York: Dutton, 1963), 246, 250, 252, 296.

11. Rabbi Tarfon, *Avot*, chap. 2, Mishna 76; *Talmud, Nezikin* 8.

12. *Jerusalem Post*, 11 September 1984.

13. Lecture by Teddy Kollek to students of Hebrew University, Mt. Scopus Campus, Jerusalem, 30 August 1984.

Bibliography of Recent Books
on the Millennium

Abanes, Richard. *End-Time Visions: The Road to Armaggedon?* New York: Four Walls Eight Windows Press, 1998.

Alexander, Paul. *The Byzantine Apocalyptic Tradition,* ed. Dorothy deF. Abrahamse. Berkeley: University of California Press, 1985.

Andrews, Valerie, Robert Bosnak, and Karen Walter Goodwin, eds. *Facing Apocalypse.* Dallas: Spring Books, 1987.

Baumgarten, Albert I., *The Flourishing of Jewish Sects in the Macccabean Era: An Interpretation.* Leiden: Brill, 1997.

Blake, Jack. *Comes the Millennium.* New York: Thomas Dunne Books, 1996.

Bloom, Harold. *Omens of the Millennium: The Gnosis of Angels, Dreams, and Resurrection.* New York: Riverhead Books, 1996.

Boyer, Paul. *When Time Shall Be No More: Prophecy Belief in Modern American Culture.* Cambridge, MA: Harvard University Press, 1992.

Brasher, Brenda. *Give Me That Online Religion: Churches, Cults, and Community in an Information Age.* San Francisco: Jossey Bass, 1999.

Bull, Malcolm, ed. *Apocalypse Theory and the Ends of the World.* Oxford: Blackwell, 1995.

Campion, Nicholas. *The Great Year: Astrology, Millenarianism and History in the Western Tradition.* London: Penguin, 1994.

Clébert, Jean-Paul. *Histoire de la fin du monde.* Paris: Belfond, 1994.

Cohn, Norman. *Cosmos,Chaos and the World to Come: The Ancient Roots of Apocalyptic Faith.* New Haven: Yale University Press, 1993.

Cook, Stephen L. *Prophecy and Apocalypticism: The Postexilic Social Setting.* Minneapolis: Fortress, 1995.

Cook, Stephen L., ed. *Countdown to 2000: Essays on Apocalypticism. Union Seminary Quarterly Review* 49 (1995).

Couch, Mal, ed. *Dictionary of Premillennial Theology.* Grand Rapids: Kregel Publications, 1996.

Daniels, Ted. *A Doomsday Reader: Prophets, Predictors, and Hucksters of Salvation.* New York: New York University Press, 1999.

Daniels, Ted. *Millennialism: An International Bibliography.* New York: Garland Press, 1992.

Delhoysie, Yves, and Georges Lapierre. *L'incendie millénariste*. Paris: Cahors, 1987.

Delumeau, Jean. *Mille ans de bonheur: Une histoire du paradis*. 2 vols. Paris: Fayard, 1992–95.

Emmerson, Richard K., and Bernard McGinn, eds. *The Apocalypse in the Middle Ages*. Ithaca: Cornell University Press, 1992.

Gould, Stephen Jay. *Questioning the Millennium: A Rationalist's Guide to a Precisely Arbitrary Countdown*. New York: Harmony Books, 1997.

Grosso, Michael. *Millennium Myth: Love and Death at the End of Time*. Wheaton, IL: Quest Books, 1995.

Hamm, Mark S. *Apocalypse in Oklahoma: Waco and Ruby Ridge Revenged*. Boston: Northeastern University Press, 1997.

Heard, Alex. *Apocalypse Pretty Soon: Travels in End-time America*. New York: W.W. Norton and Co., 1999.

Hill, Christopher. *The English Bible and the Seventeenth-Century Revolution*. London: Penguin, 1994.

Hill, Michael Ortiz. *Dreaming the End of the World: Apocalypse as a Rite of Passage*. Dallas: Spring Publications, 1994.

Idel, Moshe. *Messianic Mystics*. New Haven: Yale University Press, 1998.

Johnson, Paul E., and Sean Wilentz. *The Kingdom of Matthias: A Story of Sex and Salvation in 19th Century America*. New York: Oxford University Press, 1994.

Katz, David S., and Richard H. Popkin. *Messianic Revolution: Radical Religious Politics to the End of the Second Millennium*. New York: Hill and Wang, 1999.

Keller, Catherine. *Apocalypse Now and Then: A Feminist Guide to the End of the World*. Boston: Beacon Press, 1996.

Kennedy, Teresa. *Welcome to the End of the World: Prophecy, Rage, and the New Age*. New York: M. Evans and Co., 1997.

Kreuziger, Frederick. *Apocalypse and Science Fiction: A Dialectic of Religious and Secular Soteriologies*. AAR Academy Series, 40. Chico, CA: Scholars Press, 1982.

Kumar, Krishnan, and Stephen Bann, eds. *Utopias and the Millennium*. London: Reaction Books, 1993.

Lamy, Phil. *Millennium Rage: Survivalists, White Supremacists, and the Doomsday Prophecy*. New York: Plenum Publishing, 1996.

Landes, Richard. *Relics, Apocalypse, and the Deceits of History: Ademar of Chabannes, 989–1034*. Cambridge, MA: Harvard University Press, 1995.

Levine, Robert M. *Vale of Tears: Revisiting the Canudos Massacre in Northeastern Brazil, 1893–1987*. Berkeley: University of California, 1992.

Lieb, Michael. *Children of Ezekiel: Aliens, UFOs, the Crisis of Race, and the Advent of the Endtime*. Durham, NC: Duke University Press, 1998.

Lifton, Robert Jay. *Destroying the World to Save It: Aum Shinrikyo, Apocalyptic Violence, and the New Global Terrorism*. New York: Henry Holt and Co., 1999.

McGinn, Bernard. *Antichrist: Two Thousand Years of the Human Fascination with Evil*. San Francisco: HarperCollins, 1994.

McGinn, Bernard, and Martin Marty, eds. *Encyclopedia of Apocalypticism*. 3 vols. Chicago: University of Chicago Press, 1998.

McIver, Tom. *The End of the World: An Annotated Bibliography.* Jefferson, NC: McFarland, 1999.

Noble, David. *The Religion of Technology: The Divinity of Man and the Spirit of Invention.* New York: Alfred A. Knopf, 1998.

O'Brien, Conner Cruise. *On the Eve of the Millennium: The Future of Democracy through an Age of Unreason.* New York: Free Press, 1994.

O'Leary, Stephen D. *Arguing the Apocalypse: A Theory of Millennial Rhetoric.* Cambridge, MA: Harvard University Press, 1994.

Ossio, Juan M. *Ideologia Mesiánica del Mundo Andino.* Ignacio Pardo Pastor, 1973.

Parfrey, Adam, ed. *Apocalypse Culture.* Venice, CA: Feral House, 1990.

Patrides, C. A., and Joseph Wittreich, eds. *The Apocalypse in English Renaissance Thought and Literature.* Ithaca: Cornell University Press, 1985.

Peterson, Rodney. *Preaching in the Last Days: The Theme of the "Two Witnesses" in the Sixteenth and Seventeenth Centuries.* New York: Oxford University Press, 1993.

Quinby, Lee. *Millennial Seduction: A Skeptic Confronts Apocalyptic Culture.* Ithaca: Cornell University Press, 1999.

Ravitzky, Aviezer. *Messianism, Zionism, and Jewish Religious Radicalism.* Chicago: Chicago University Press, 1995.

Robbins, Thomas, and Susan J. Palmer, eds. *Millennium, Messiahs, and Mayhem: Contemporary Apocalyptic Movements.* New York: Routledge, 1997.

Rollin, Henri. *L'Apocalypse de notre temps: Les dessous de la documentation allemande d'après des documents inédits.* Paris: Editions Allia, 1991.

Schwartz, Hillel. *Century's End: An Orientation Manual toward the Year 2000.* New York: Doubleday, 1990, 1996.

Shaw, Eva. *Eve of Destruction: Prophecies, Theories and Preparations for the End of the World.* Chicago: Contemporary Books, 1995.

Singer, Daniel. *Whose Millennium? Theirs or Ours?* New York: Monthly Review Press, 1999.

Spence, Jonathan. *God's Chinese Son: The Taiping Heavenly Kingdom of Hong Xiuquan.* New York: W.W. Norton and Co., 1996.

Stearns, Peter. *Millennium III, Century XXI: A Retrospective on the Future.* Boulder, CO: Westview Press, 1996.

Strozier, Charles. *Apocalypse: On the Psychology of Fundamentalism in America.* Boston: Beacon Press, 1994.

Strozier, Charles B., and Michael Flynn, eds. *The Year 2000: Essays on the End.* New York: New York University Press, 1997.

Sugden, John. *Tecumseh, A Life.* New York: Henry Holt Publishing, 1997.

Tabor, James, and Eugene Gallagher. *Why Waco: Cults and the Battle for Religious Freedom in America.* Berkeley: University of California, 1995.

Thompson, Damian. *The End of the World: Faith and Fear in the Shadow of the Millennium.* London: Sinclair Stevenson, 1996.

Verbeke, W., D. Verhelst, and A. Welkenhuysen, eds. *The Use and Abuse of Eschatology in the Middle Ages.* Louvain: Catholic University Press, 1988.

Weber, Eugen. *Apocalypses: Prophecies, Cults and Millennial Beliefs through the Ages.* Cambridge, MA: Harvard University Press, 1999.

Wessinger, Catherine. *How the Millennium Comes Violently: From Waco to Heaven's Gate*. New York: Seven Bridges Press, 1999.

Wessinger, Catherine, ed. *Millennialism, Persecution, and Violence: Historical Cases*. Syracuse: Syracuse University Press, in Press.

Wojcik, Daniel. *The End of the World as We Know It: Faith, Fatalism, and Apocalypse in America*. New York: New York University Press, 1997.

Index

Ann Arbor Paperbacks

Waddell, *The Desert Fathers*
Erasmus, *The Praise of Folly*
Donne, *Devotions*
Malthus, *Population: The First Essay*
Berdyaev, *The Origin of Russian Communism*
Einhard, *The Life of Charlemagne*
Edwards, *The Nature of True Virtue*
Gilson, *Héloïse and Abélard*
Aristotle, *Metaphysics*
Kant, *Education*
Boulding, *The Image*
Duckett, *The Gateway to the Middle Ages* (3 vols.): *Italy; France and Britain; Monasticism*
Bowditch and Ramsland, *Voices of the Industrial Revolution*
Luxemburg, *The Russian Revolution* and *Leninism or Marxism?*
Rexroth, *Poems from the Greek Anthology*
Zoshchenko, *Scenes from the Bathhouse*
Thrupp, *The Merchant Class of Medieval London*
Procopius, *Secret History*
Adcock, *Roman Political Ideas and Practice*
Swanson, *The Birth of the Gods*
Xenophon, *The March Up Country*
Trotsky, *The New Course*
Buchanan and Tullock, *The Calculus of Consent*
Hobson, *Imperialism*
Pobedonostsev, *Reflections of a Russian Statesman*
Kinietz, *The Indians of the Western Great Lakes 1615–1760*
Bromage, *Writing for Business*
Lurie, *Mountain Wolf Woman, Sister of Crashing Thunder*
Leonard, *Baroque Times in Old Mexico*
Meier, *Negro Thought in America, 1880–1915*
Burke, *The Philosophy of Edmund Burke*
Michelet, *Joan of Arc*
Conze, *Buddhist Thought in India*
Arberry, *Aspects of Islamic Civilization*
Chesnutt, *The Wife of His Youth and Other Stories*
Gross, *Sound and Form in Modern Poetry*
Zola, *The Masterpiece*
Chesnutt, *The Marrow of Tradition*
Aristophanes, *Four Comedies*
Aristophanes, *Three Comedies*
Chesnutt, *The Conjure Woman*
Duckett, *Carolingian Portraits*
Rapoport and Chammah, *Prisoner's Dilemma*
Aristotle, *Poetics*
Peattie, *The View from the Barrio*
Duckett, *Death and Life in the Tenth Century*
Langford, *Galileo, Science and the Church*

McNaughton, *The Taoist Vision*
Anderson, *Matthew Arnold and the Classical Tradition*
Milio, *9226 Kercheval*
Weisheipl, *The Development of Physical Theory in the Middle Ages*
Breton, *Manifestoes of Surrealism*
Gershman, *The Surrealist Revolution in France*
Burt, *Mammals of the Great Lakes Region*
Scholz, *Carolingian Chronicles*
Wik, *Henry Ford and Grass-roots America*
Sahlins and Service, *Evolution and Culture*
Wickham, *Early Medieval Italy*
Waddell, *The Wandering Scholars*
Rosenberg, *Bolshevik Visions* (2 parts in 2 vols.)
Mannoni, *Prospero and Caliban*
Aron, *Democracy and Totalitarianism*
Shy, *A People Numerous and Armed*
Taylor, *Roman Voting Assemblies*
Goodfield, *An Imagined World*
Hesiod, *The Works and Days; Theogony; The Shield of Herakles*
Raverat, *Period Piece*
Lamming, *In the Castle of My Skin*
Fisher, *The Conjure-Man Dies*
Strayer, *The Albigensian Crusades*
Lamming, *The Pleasures of Exile*
Lamming, *Natives of My Person*
Glaspell, *Lifted Masks and Other Works*
Grand, *The Heavenly Twins*
Cornford, *The Origin of Attic Comedy*
Allen, *Wolves of Minong*
Brathwaite, *Roots*
Fisher, *The Walls of Jericho*
Lamming, *The Emigrants*
Loudon, *The Mummy!*
Kemble and Butler Leigh, *Principles and Privilege*
Thomas, *Out of Time*
Flanagan, *You Alone Are Dancing*
Kotre and Hall, *Seasons of Life*
Shen, *Almost a Revolution*
Meckel, *Save the Babies*
Laver and Schofield, *Multiparty Government*
Rutt, *The Bamboo Grove*
Endelman, *The Jews of Georgian England, 1714–1830*
Lamming, *Season of Adventure*
Radin, *Crashing Thunder*
Mirel, *The Rise and Fall of an Urban School System*
Brainard, *When the Rainbow Goddess Wept*
Brook, *Documents on the Rape of Nanking*
Mendel, *Vision and Violence*
Hymes, *Reinventing Anthropology*
Mulroy, *Early Greek Lyric Poetry*